U0165681

國際環境法專論

吳嘉生 著

五南圖書出版公司 印行

自 序

　　「環境保護」從上個世紀中葉以來，開始受到各國逐漸地重視，也均設置有專責主管機關掌理相關事宜，我國自然也不例外。然而，各國國情不同，經濟發展的程度也不盡相同。因此，各國對於經濟保護的標準，也就自然地有所差異。

　　在這樣的背景之下，聯合國的主導各種國際會議及國際公約的簽訂成了國際環境保護的「共識」；國際社會中的主要國家紛紛加以參照而加以「內國法化」。作者思考這類國際關係保護的議題及國際標準有必要加以引進與採納，在這樣的動機之下，才有本書之問世。

　　最後，也要感謝五南圖書公司的幾位老朋友的熱心相助，藉此聊表謝意！

吳嘉生

台北大學法律研究室

2012.10.13

作者介紹

吳嘉生　教授

現職：國立臺北大學法律學系專任教授

最高學歷：美國聖路易大學法律博士

主要經歷：

1. 教育部數位學習認證審查委員
2. 教育部智慧財產權保護訪視委員
3. 教育部國防通識教育暨校園安全訪視委員
4. 經濟部創新研發計畫專案審查委員
5. 國家考試出題命題閱卷及典試委員
6. 高等教育評鑑中心評鑑委員
7. 國防大學軍法官班及軍法預備軍官班特聘講座教授
8. 法務部司法官訓練所講座教授
9. 國家文官學院特聘講座教授

學術成就及榮譽：

1. 中華民國證券櫃檯買賣中心，法律專家審議代表
2. 桃園縣環保科技園區發展委員會委員
3. 國防部「人才培訓」方案規畫委員
4. 中山科學研究院專利申請評選委員
5. 教育部大專校院智慧財產保護方案推動委員
6. 國立高雄第一科技大學「科技法律評析」編輯
7. 傑賽普國際模擬法庭辯論賽台灣區法官

行政經歷：

1. 國立臺北大學學務長

2. 國立臺北大學通識教育中心主任
3. 國立臺北大學財經法學系主任
4. 中興大學法商學院（臺北大學前身）進修推廣中心教務主任
5. 中興大學法商學院（臺北大學前身）課務組組長
6. 中興大學法商學院（臺北大學前身）研教組組長

專業領域：

1. 國際法相關領域：如國際環境法、國際公法、國際私法、國際經濟法。
2. 知識產權法相關領域：如專利、商標、著作權、網路資訊法…。
3. 英美法與比較法相關課程

A.教師專業表現與服務目錄

國立臺北大學管考績優教師表揚狀

傑賽普國際法庭模擬辯論賽台灣區評審法官（初賽／複賽／決賽）（多任）

新北市政府新北市勞資爭議主任仲裁委員（100.5.1至103.4.30）

桃園縣政府聘書—環保科技園區發展委員會委員（99.4.1至101.3.31）

桃園縣政府聘書—環保科技園區設置計畫發展審議委員會委員（96年至98年）

桃園縣政府聘書—環保科技園區入區廠商／研究機構之興建、營運績效評定委員（98年至100年）

新竹市政府市政顧問（100.8.3至103.12.24）

台東縣政府縣政顧問（98.04.01至98.12.19）

中正大學專家顧問聘書—100年擔任台灣法律資訊中心專家顧問

中興大學法商學院（臺北大學前身）教務分處課務組組（84年至86年）

中興大學法商學院（臺北大學前身）教務主任

高等教育評鑑中心基金會99年度大學校院系所評鑑委員

高等教育評鑑中心基金會96年度大學校院系所評鑑委員

致理學院財經法律系演講感謝狀（100.10.3）

南台科技大學99年12月14日「2010企業及財經法律學術研討會」與談人

靜宜大學法律系98學年度「民事損害賠償制度——特別法上之規範與實踐學術研討會」主持人（99.06.04）

高雄第一科技大學科技法律研究所99年度「科技法律評析」編輯委員會委員

臺北大學95年碩士學位論文口試委員

臺北大學100年碩士學位論文口試委員

臺北大學97年博士學位論文口試委員

中正大學99年博士學位考試委員

臺北大學98年擔任教育部「培育優質人力促進就業計畫——大學畢業生至企業職場實習方案」實習委員會委員

司法院司法人員研習所94年第2期培訓高等行政法院法官研習課程之從著作權利法到電子商務法之問題與研究課程講座

司法官訓練所94年司法官班46期第二階段「英美法學名著選讀」課程

臺北市政府「2006生技獎」審查委員

考試院92年公務人員特種考試第二次警察人員考試典試委員

考試院93年交通事業郵政人員升資考試增聘命題兼閱卷委員

考試院93年公務人員特種考試外交領事人員考試及93年公務人員特種考試國際經濟商務人員考試典試委員

考試院94年公務人員特種考試司法人員考試口試委員

考試院94年公務人員特種考試司法人員考試閱卷委員

考試院95年公務人員特種考試外交領事人員考試及95年公務人員特種考試法務部調查局調查人員考試口試委員

考試院95年公務人員特種考試外交領事人員考試及95年公務人員特種考試法務部調查人員考試命題兼閱卷委員

考試院95年公務人員特種考試民航人員考試及95年公務人員特種國際經濟商務人員考試典試委員

考試院95年公務人員特種考試司法人員考試及95年軍法官考試閱卷委員

考試院98年公務人員特種考試外交領事人員及國際新聞人員考試、98年公務人員特種考試法務部調查局調查人員考試、98年公務人員特種考試國家安全局國家安全情報人員考試、98年公務人員特種考試原住民考試命題兼閱卷委員

考試院公務特考：警察人員／關務人員／海關人員／退伍軍人轉任公務員典試委員

考選部專利師考試審議委員

行政院農委會農業生技園區入園甄審委員

財團法人中華民國證券櫃檯買賣中心上櫃審查部審議委員

中央印製廠採購評鑑委員會委員

開南法學編輯委員會第2期委員（多任）

清華大學科技法律研究所「國際商務仲裁」兼任教授（多任）

致理技術學院多媒體設計系「科技與法律」兼任教授（多任）

真理大學財經法學期刊編輯顧問

行政院第8次全國科技會議課程提綱委員。

台灣電力公司「98年度北一區抄表工作委外服務招標案」審查委員

行政院金融監督管理委員會銀行局「97年度英譯委外服務招標案」採購評選委員會委員

高雄第一科技大學科技法律研究所96年度「科技法律評析」編輯委員會委員

高雄第一科技大學97年度科技大學自我評鑑專業類科法律研究所自評委員

稻江科技暨管理學院財經法律學系96年度上半年大學評鑑系所再評鑑自評委員

臺北市內湖區麗山國民小學溫水游泳池97年委託民間營運管理案之甄選委員

全國農業金庫股份有限公司「農貸帳務管理系統建置計畫之主系統開發」評選委員

國立台灣大學醫學院附設醫院復健部義肢室醫療合作案甄審委員會委員

宜蘭縣政府「宜蘭利澤工業區外防風林地民間促參方式進行風力發電園區」甄審委員

教育部97年數位學習課程與教材認證國貿組審查會議審查委員

教育部98年大專院校校園保護智慧財產權行動方案訪視計畫訪視委員

B.專書著作

年度	書目
1998	國際法與國內法關係之研析，五南圖書出版公司。
1999	智慧財產權之理論與應用，五南圖書出版公司。
	國家之權力國際責任，五南圖書出版公司。
2000	國際法學原理－本質與功能之研究，五南圖書出版公司。
2001	美國貿易法三〇一條款評析：智慧財產權保護之帝王條款，元照出版社。
2003	電子商務法導論，學林文化有限公司。
2004	國際貿易法析論，翰蘆出版社。
2006	資訊倫理與法律，國立空中大學。
	銀行法釋論，新學林出版社。
2008	當代國際法上，五南圖書出版有限公司。
	當代國際法下，五南圖書出版有限公司。
	國際經濟法析論，文笙書局。
2009	智慧財產法通論，一品文化出版社，7月出版。
2010	法學英文精練，一品文化出版社。
	英美法導論，一品文化出版社。
2012	法律倫理專論，台北：一品文化出版社。
	國際環境法專論，台北：五南圖書出版有限公司。

C.期刊論文

年度	編號	期刊論文（TSSCI等同於SSCI）
1994	1	對三〇一條款應有之認識，軍法專刊，第40卷第7期，1994，第18～24頁。
	2	評析歐洲競爭法之起源，中興法學，第37期，1994，第189～217頁。（TSSCI）（英文版）
	3	從高華德案論國際條約終止之美國模式，中興法學，第38期，1994，第45～75頁。（TSSCI）（英文版）
	4	特別三〇一條款評析，朝陽大學法律評論，第60卷第11-12期，1994，第13～20頁。
1995	5	論三〇一條款之產生，法學叢刊，第40卷第1期，1995，第73～86頁。
	6	超級三〇一析論，朝陽大學法律評論，第61卷第1-2期，1995，第2～12頁。
	7	著作權法與圖書館－以公平使用為原則為中心，台北市立圖書館館訊，第12卷第3期，1995
	8	從美日貿易衝突論超級三〇一，中興法學，第39期，1995，第157～176頁。（TSSCI）
	9	研究美國保護智慧財權之貿易立法，軍法專刊，第41卷第3期，1995，第5～13頁。
1996	10	著作權法中公平使用原則之探討——兼論圖書館之著作權問題，書苑，第27期，1996，第31～38頁。
	11	探討著作權法中之公平使用原則，軍法專刊，第43卷第5期，1996，第1～7頁。
	12	從中、美智慧財產問題論特別三〇一，中興法學，第41期，1996，第245～259頁。（TSSCI）
	13	國際法之過去、現在與未來，中興法學，第41期，1996，第51～149頁。（TSSCI）
	14	中華人民共和國著作權法評析，中興法學，第40期，1996，第155～215頁。（TSSCI）（英文版）
1997	15	論污染者付費原則之國際法規範，軍法專刊，第43卷第5期，1997，第9～16頁。

年度	編號	期刊論文（TSSCI等同於SSCI）
1997	16	對國際法產生之探討，中興法學，第43期，1997，第31～126頁。（TSSCI）
	17	美國一般三〇一、特別三〇一與超級三〇一之比較研究，朝陽大學法律評論，第63卷第10-12期，1997，第2～19頁。
	18	研析國際法產生之淵源，軍法專刊，第43卷第9期，1997，第8～22頁。
	19	中國大陸與美國商務仲裁之比較研究，中興法學，第42期，1997，第18～24頁。（TSSCI）（英文版）
1998	20	環保糾紛解決之研究，中興法學，第44期，1998，第1～49頁。（TSSCI）
	21	研析國際條約之保留，軍法專刊，第44卷第6期，1998，第15～27頁
1999	22	個人在國際法上地位之研析，軍法專刊，第45卷第2期，1999，第4～18頁。
2000	23	研析智慧財產權之立法保護——以美國為例，中興法學，第45期，2000，第205～260頁。（TSSCI）
2001	24	人權之憲法保障，憲政時代，第27卷第1期，2001，第3～38頁。
2006	25	全球治理下之世界貿易組織，曾華松大法官古稀祝壽論文集——論權利保護之理論與實踐。
2008	26	Choice of Law and Intellectual Property，法學理論與文化，李岱教授祝壽論文集。
2009	27	Innovation Analysis of Market Competition，ChihLee Law Review，頁147-190。（英文版）
2012	28	Economic Diplomacy，ChihLee Law Review。（英文版）

D.研討會論文

年代	論文內容
2005	評論人，區域經濟統合下，美國、日本及我國有關「自然人移動」規範之比較，國際投資法學術研討會，輔仁大學財經法律系。
2006	主持人及發表人，Calculating Damages of Patent Infringement-Revisited，國際專利法制研討會，臺北大學財經法律學系主辦。
	主持人，國際智慧財產權研討會，世新大學，智慧財產法律研究所。
2007	主持人，被忽略的（立法）事實——實證科學在規範論證中的可能角色，2007年第二屆全國法學實證研究研討會（報告人：邱文聰），主辦單位：交通大學、政治大學；承辦單位：政治大學
2008	主持人，從學術共享精神檢討政府資助大學研究成果之專利政策，第12屆全國科技法律研討會，交通大學科技法律研究所
2009	發表人，網路侵權問題研究，幹部研討會，德明財經科技大學主辦。
	發表人，網路法律問題面面觀，教學卓越發表會，屏東科技大學主辦。
	發表人，防制人口販賣研究，教學卓越發表會，德明財經科技大學主辦。
	發表人，防制人口販賣觀念宣導，北二區人權教育研習營，德明財經大學。
	主持人，國際移民行為對防法人口老化的政策思考，台北大學通識教育中心。
	與談人，法律選擇：國家利益與個人利益之協調（報告人：李光波），第五屆海峽兩岸國際私法學術研討會，主辦單位：台灣國際私法研究會、中國國際私法學會；承辦單位：玄奘大學、武漢大學國際法研究所。
2010	與談人，台灣競爭法律的專利權行使——兼論對中國大陸的借鑒（報告人：寧立志所長，武漢大學），2011科技法律國際學術研討會暨海峽兩岸智慧財產權法律研討會，高雄第一科技大學。

年代	論文內容
2010	與談人,從侵權行為法新體系再論智慧財產權之間接侵權,2010兩岸四地財產法學術研討會,中正大學。
	與談人,電視節目版式法律保護之研究,企業及財經法律學術研討會,南台科技大學。
2011	發表人,全球化下資訊之傳播與交流,台灣法律資訊中心,中正大學。
	與談人:「入世十年四問」(發表人,清華大學車丕照教援,第三屆兩岸國際法學論壇學術研討會,2011)國際法學會。
	主持人兼評論人:雲端運算與資訊保護之探討——以美國法為主,2011年科技法律學術研討會,高雄第一科技大學。
	發表人,法學英文之教與學,專業法律英文教與學工作坊,南台科技大學,財經法律研究所
2012	發表人,災害防救法評釋,台灣海洋大學2012學術研討會

E.政府委辦研究計畫

年度	補助單位	研究計畫名稱	時間
1996	行政院文化建設委員會	文化創新:智慧財產之開發與保護專題研究	1995年至1996年
2007	教育部	96年度法律專業科目教學改進計畫——智慧財產權理論與實務(計畫主持人)	2007.06.01至2008.07.31
2008	內政部警政署刑事警察局	「有關IP監察技術可行性評估與法制分析之研究(上)—第二類電信監察法制分析研究」(計畫主持人)	2008.07.31至2009.01.31

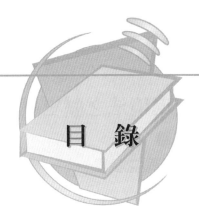

目　錄

表目錄

第一章　緒　論

壹、國際環境問題之出現

　　國際環境法這個領域之出現，就如同人權法之情形一樣，主要的發展乃是二十世紀中葉起透過大量的雙邊條約以及多邊條約的簽訂完成，才有今天的面貌之呈現。但是難以否認的是它也是經由幾個關鍵的不具拘束力的國際文件及存在於習慣法中的重要法則和環境法的基本原理，才能夠在國際社會受到重視。而這些文件或法則之存在或發展乃是要在人類所存活的「資源活動」（Resource Activities）的領域下，去尋求及解決源起於「岩漿圈」（Lithosphere）、「水圈」（Hydrosphere）及「大氣層」（Atmosphere）等所發生的問題及進一步的保護作法。

　　無可諱言的是許多與環境有關的問題，像「氣候變遷」（Climate Change）、「酸雨」（Acid Rain）、「臭氧破裂」（Ozone Depletion）、「水源共享」（Shared Water）以及「核子意外事件」（Nuclear Accident）等現象或事件成為具有「全球性性質」（Global Nature）的國際社會共同關切的課題。如此一來，以傳統「主權」（Sovereignty）觀念所構成的「國家疆界」（National Boundary）成為「不具真實的時代誤導」（Spurious Anachronism），在某種情形之下變成了「危險的幻象」（Dangerous Fiction）[1]。在這樣的情形之下，任何一件原本是一個單一國家的環境問題事件，就跨越了國界而成為一個國際環境保護相關的跨國事件或跨國議題。

　　就這樣，「國際環境法」（International Environmental Law）乃從國際公法的領域，「萌芽而生」了。而此一相對其他領域來得「年輕」而新

---

[1]　See Maurice F. Strong's Forward for International Environmental Law and World Order (St. Paul, M.N.: West Publishing Co., 1994). p. vii.

的科目，可以說大致上是建立在全球性的「環境現象」（Global Phenom-ena）的基礎之上以及「國際性的集體作法」（International Collective Mea-sures）上來針對那些環境改變的負面效應下，所提出之因應對策。而在後者的這一層面來看，很明顯的受到各國的經濟發展及人類環境學的重大影響。具體的來加以檢視，可以了解到人類社會追求無窮盡的物質享受帶動了科技的進步，進而促進了蓬勃的經濟發展。然而，人類為了滿足自我的需求，而大量的擷取地球上的生態資源；同時，又因為利用方式的不當或科技進步的有限性，造成了生態上難以恢復的改變。例如土壤、生物、大氣、河川、海洋、森林等，都因為人類的經濟發展而遭受到嚴重的破壞。

當然，經濟發展，對於每一個國際社會的成員，均是相當重要的。可以這麼說，從環境保護的角度來檢驗經濟角色的因素，是那麼樣的關鍵，它對環境的改變有那麼「微妙的」貢獻，它也可以引導潛在的力量來減低經濟發展對環境所造成的負面「後果」（Consequences）。而此一經濟因素對於環境所造成的「負面後果」則不是人類社會所能承擔得起的。在發展經濟的同時，絕對不能忽略了環境的角色；因為環境的角色對於國際社會中各國所追求的「永續發展」（Sustainable Development），才是真正的核心議題。如果忽略了或拿捏的分寸不夠精確，則對整個國際社會而言，均會是一場「大浩劫」。

就因此，國際社會對於環境問題所造成的對全人類的生存發展，開始注意到了，也開始認知到：任何人類的活動所造成的對於環境的威脅，將是全人類所必須面對的最大的生存挑戰。直截了當的說，那些威脅來自於所有人類活動或發展的各種層面；它可包括來自於各種源頭的未加區分的危險廢棄物、垃圾及意外事件之漏油所造成的污染，以及那些「去樹林化」（Deforestation）及「棄置化」（Desertification）所造成的植物之喪失與動物生命的流棄。所有這些情形更會因為各國沒有節制的發展及沒有前瞻性的「經濟發展政策」（Economic Development Policy）的交互影響而變得更加惡化下去。所幸，到當下來看，這些「威脅」是不會被侷限於某一個單一國家的疆界領域之內。對於環境的威脅已經跨越了各國的疆界而威脅到國際社會中所有的國家。

如此一來，國際社會中的幾個主要國家及各該國家的學者專家們很自然地開始對與環境議題有關的各種問題之探討，展開了各種研究與論述。國際法學者的努力自然也不例外。而國際法這個領域之研究也展現了一個新視野。在過去的百餘年來，國際法所側重的議題大約均是在有關於環境的保護以及對於自然資源的利用。國際法學者們在這樣的氛圍下，開始在他們自己所認知的環境議題上，去尋求發展出功能性的研究方法與科技作法來解決在相關環境議題上，所引起之各種問題。跟隨而來的是環境事件就一直以「爭端解決」（Dispute Settlement）的程序來處理。如果要特別指明的話，就是以國際法中的「國家責任」（State Responsibility）應用在所遭遇到的國際環境事件上。而對於國際社會中所遭遇到的新的環境議題或課題，例如有關防止跨國污染之防制責任及國家對於領域內自然資源的永久主權等，自然是國際環境法學者所不會忽略的課題。

貳、國際環境問題之範圍

近幾年來，關心環境保護的專家學者已經注意到了對於國際環境保護所面對的危險在程度上，加劇了不少；並且在環境問題的研究範圍上亦擴大了不少。僅就此二大項而言，至今已成了國際社會所顧慮的重要主題。這些種類延伸的範圍包括：「大氣污染」（Atmosphere Pollution）、「海洋污染」（Marine Pollution）、「全球暖化」（Global Warming）以及「臭氧層破裂」（Ozone Depletion）、核爆之危險及其他「特別危險性物質」（Extra-Hazardous Substance）之危險和野生物種滅絕之威脅，均是當下國際環境保護所要共同面對的重要議題。

以上所提及的那些種類，均具有「國際面相」（International Dimension）。在以下二方面特別明顯[2]：第一，污染源起於某一特定的國家之

---

[2]　Malcolm N. Shaw, International Law, 6th ed. (Cambridge, UK: Cambridge University Press, 2009), p. 845.

內，常常會對其他的國家造成「嚴重的影響」（Serious Impact）。最主要而明顯的例子是「酸雨」（Acid Rain），在一個國家境內的工廠所噴出的化學物質，彌漫到空氣中，再與水及陽光作出反應之後，就形成了「酸性物質」（Acid），這樣就被風所帶動，到最後所造成的雨則掉落到距離起初污染事件所在的幾千里外的其他國家境內；第二，就現在的狀況來審視，環境問題很明顯的沒有辦法以單一國家的力量，個別的行為來加以解決。就因為如此，污染國與被污染國之間的合作，就變成非常必要的。然而，問題在相關的一些案例上，就會變得更加的複雜了，那就是往往很難決定或是不太可能去「確認」（Identify）某一個特定形式的環境污染是源起於哪一個國家。一個最可以說明的例子就是「臭氧層破裂」（Ozone Depletion）。換句話說，污染的「國際性質」（International Nature）不論是在它的源起，抑或是它所造成的損害，從目前的情況來看是有必要的要有一個國際的「回應」（Response）而這個觀點在國際社會的學者專家之間，是大家所能接受的「共識」（Consensus）。

參、國際環境問題之法制化

國際社會在面對環境事件之處理上，長久以來由國際法學者及環境問題之專家來共同面對時，往往習以為常地適用國際社會的「爭端處理機制」（Dispute Settlement Mechanism）來因應。再就是環境問題演變成「跨越疆界」（Transboundary）的跨國問題是愈益明顯。對於環境問題的演變與發展之下，國際社會中的學者終於賦與了一個新的名稱——國際環境法（International Environmental Law）來加以「歸類」（Categorize），將其指示為一組國際法的規範，將其應用在環境問題的處理上。但是，事實上，許多學者僅願意局限於將國際法之研析與探討，擴大到應用在環境問題上面去而已。學者專家間對於國際法與環境問題的處理；大致上分成了兩大派的見解。其中的一派提出以一般國際法原理的作法來處理環境問題；他們認為國際環境法的概念，給予一般人士一個不正確地誤導的印

象，而將「國際環境法」獨立於一般國際法原理之外。這一派學者的代表人物是英國學者布朗利（Ian Brownlie）。根據他們的觀點，這樣的概念，僅僅是個擬制的假象；因為那只是將一般國際法的原理與法規應用在環境問題的背景之下而已。相反的，另一派學者則認定已形成了一個獨立的國際環境法領域。這一派學者的代表人物則是單自教授（Philippe Sands）。他們主張環境問題的處理，已經自成一格，它包含了許許多多的「實質性」（Substantive）「規範」（Norm），正因為這樣的原因，那是相當具有正當性的將「國際環境法」的那些「實質性規範」自成一組法學領域而獨立於一般國際法之外。

更進一步來加以審視，「自然資源」（Natural Resource）從定義上來看可以不用懷疑的已成為「環境」的一部分。或者可以這麼明白的指出：雖然對於環境的保護與自然資源之利用，是兩個領域之「相互連接」（Interlinked）的。但是事實上具有不同領域背景的獨立學派的不同專家學者，似乎也已經「合流」（Emerge）在一起——那就是那些考慮到環境問題的人士與那些著重於經濟發展與企業專家的律師們已經結合在一起了。更具體的研析其中的發展，可以了解到的是著重於環境問題的律師，很清楚的採取了保護環境的立場，而且幾乎把「利用」（Exploitation）的問題，加以「邊緣化」（Marginalized）。而在另一個專業的自然資源律師，則主要的是將重心放在「經濟發展」的理由上，而沒有充分注意到長期的環境問題的考量上。在這樣的意識下，國際環境法一直被認定是「綠色法律」（Green Law），特別著重於對於「自然」（Nature）的保護。而「自然資源法」（Law of Natural Resources）則被認為是「硬法」（Hard Law），而特別致力於有關於自然資源利用之經濟利益的保護。一直到最近這些年來，「永續發展」（Sustainable Development）概念的出現，以上兩種不同的認知之專家學者，開始融合為一，而有了交集。

肆、國際環境法之界定

　　一般而言，國際環境法是一個「國際公法」（Public International Law）的領域下，被那些在「環境背景」（Environmental Context）下，進化出來的原理或法則之適用，所特別註記而成的主題性領域。而那些原理或法則，例如「風險預防原理」（Precautionary Principle）與「無傷害原理」（No Harm Principle）等均是源起於或成為一部分的一般國際公法；它可以在本書中的相關章節，如國際公法之起源、「國家管轄權之行使」（Exercise of State Jurisdiction）及國家責任（State Responsibility）查見它的說明或描述。因此，從目前國際環境法中所論及之實體部分來加以審視，它是傳統一般國際公法的一部分，而並非全然地分開來的自我獨立的全新領域。在這樣的認知之下，它相當程度的可以類化或雷同於國際人權法、國際海洋法或國際經濟法。但是，就最近幾十年來的演進發展及內容本質的充實，它值得我們將它以一個獨立領域對待之。雖然，從組織結構的觀點來切入當下的國際環境法，它比上面所提及的國際法衍生出來的新興領域，要來得沒有那麼充分的發展；例如，它沒有如同國際海洋法或世界貿易組織的「全球環境機構」（Global Environmental Organization），不具有處理國際環境事件的「能力」（Competence）。它也沒有如同世界貿易組織的「爭端解決機制」，不能自行解決國際環境爭議事件。縱使如此，我們只能說，它仍然只是發展中的「軟法」（Soft Law）。它仍然有相當大的成長空間。

　　更進一步來審視，就環境問題的處理來切入，管制或規範各國的「國家行為」（State Conduct），就一般性的法則或特定的法則，在國際社會中確實有重大的成長；但是，難以否認的是就國家的國際義務來保護或「保存」（Preserve）「環境之本身」（Environment perse），仍然是欠缺一般之「習慣法」（Customary Law）或「條約法」（Treaty Law）來加以規範各國所應受到「拘束」之規範；至少以「國際現實」（International Reality）來檢視，是不足的；但可以確定的是：在「習慣國際法」（Customary International Law）中對國家可以課相關的「不作為義務」（Negative Obligation），所謂的「不傷害原理」（No Harm Principle）或是各國有義務在它的管轄領域之內，不得使用某些作法或採取某些措施，對其他國家造成環境的傷害，或是有害於全球環境的保護。這樣的規範在國際社會中業已獲得相當程度的共識；甚至於可以成為「習慣國際法」對各國所要求履行的國際義務。

伍、基本議題研究解析

在國際環境法的專業化與分工化現象的明顯與突出的表現之下，這樣的現象是否會成為國際社會愈來愈受到重視的原因，這可能仍然是各界關心人士值得辯論的一個題目。但是擺在眼前的一個不可否認的事實是——國際環境法這個領域在二十世紀末至二十一世紀初的今天，正在作「解釋性」的大量增加。這樣的解釋性研究國際環境法制規範的釐清，在當下至少涵蓋下列幾個「爭議」（Issue）問題的結構與程序問題的鑽研，而不是以它的內容作為研究的重心。簡單的說，就是要對國際環境的基本概念名詞定義，從架構上及問題解決程序去著手而成為研究重心之所在。其中重要的主題至少包括下列幾個單元：

一、法制設計（Legal Regime Design）

在什麼層級之下來行使「環境管理」（Environmental Governance）？是全球性的？區域性的？抑或只是國家性的？在可使用的「規範性工具」（Regulatory Instrument）之下的選擇時，什麼是主要的待解決之爭議問題？在正式的與非正式的規範差異範圍之下，何者較為重要？要如何去瞭解當下「全球環境管理」（Global Environmental Governance）機制之設計？以及國際環境法如何與國際法的其他領域有關聯性與它們之間的關係又是如何？

二、分析工具（Analytical Tool）

　　其他的專業訓練，例如國際關係、經濟學、倫理學等如何地去幫助我們進一步地更深入的了解國際法？而在其中法律又扮演什麼樣的角色去了解國際環境法中所碰到的各種專業領域？

三、標準化發展（Normative Development）

　　國際環境「規範」（Norm）是如何出現的？又是如何發展的？以及政策、原理、法規、習慣在國際環境保護規範之形成中，扮演什麼樣的角色？條約及非政府機關的機制又是如何地占有一席之地？

四、關鍵概念（Key Concept）

　　什麼或哪些是國際環境法深層的「概念結構」（Conceptual Structure）？什麼或哪些是重要的「關鍵定義」來強調更特定的環境保護法規、原理及程序要求？

五、環境行動者及機構（Environmental Actor and Organization）

　　國際環境保護程序的形成過程中，「誰」是主要的「行動者」（Actor）？在形成的過程中及執行的作業中，它們又扮演了什麼樣的角色？

六、履行與執行（Implementation and Enforcement）

　　國際環境法的有效性會達到什麼樣的範圍及程度？要如何讓國際環境保護規範受到最有效地遵守與提升？

　　雖然到目前為止，仍然有一些學者，例如布朗利（Ian Brownlie）等人主張國際環境法不過是將國際法應用在環境問題的處理上。但是，整體而言，國際環境法來到二十一世紀的今天，已經成長到一個完整而獨立的專業領域，它呈現出完完全全地具有本身的獨特性質，有它自己的立法、行政程序及基本概念。

第二章　分析工具理論及實務研究

壹、國際關係理論（International Relations Theory）

　　自從1990年代初期以來，有關於國際環境法制規範及國際組織之機制是加乘的「指數」（Exponential）來成長的。國際環境協定的簽訂數目及參加者的比率，也有顯著的增加。雖然如此，這樣並未能反映環境相關「法律制定」（Law-making）的活動對於各國及其他「國際行為者」（International Actors）的所作所為有「成比例的影響」（Proportional Impact）。環境問題在許多方面仍然是呈現了很敏銳緊張的現象，而且對於現行的既存機制的環境爭議問題如「生物多樣性」（Biodiversity）及「全球氣候變遷」（Global Climate Change）似乎是比以往任何時候都要顯得是束手無策。因此針對國際環境法問題的因應，乃有國際法與國際關係的「跨領域」（Interdisciplinary）研究的出現。在國際法領域之內進一步使用國際關係理論乃成了近十餘年來的顯學。對於這樣的研究方法，一般均加以定位為「國際關係理論」，簡稱「國關研究」。

　　既存的國關研究有四種理論取向，其中居於主流的現實與自由兩大主義著重於國家的權力與利益面相，視環境問題為原有「安全」或「制度合作」研究的一個新類型，是新酒裝舊瓶。非主流的建構主義與批判理論則轉向質疑理性主義的角度，去強調觀念、認知、話語、規範、社會結構等問題，試圖從反思的過程中跳脫以國家為本位之思考（參見表2-1）。

一、現實主義（Realism）

　　現實主義的主張者，他的觀點反映出了國際政治中傳統的「國際現實」的霸權主義心態。他們非常傳統的本能的認為[1]：因為國家總是捉住

---

[1]　蔡育岱與熊武合著，國際關係之理論與實際，台北，鼎茂圖書出版公司，2010年，第174頁。

表2-1　國關理論對國際環境問題之分析

理論	核心觀點	對環境問題的論述	對國際環境問題之解析
現實主義	權力取向、物質本位、安全至上、相對獲益與欺詐使得合作困難且短暫	環境問題的本質仍是「安全」、權力依舊是國家主要的考量、自利心不會因環境問題而有例外	大國或強權主導環境合作的態樣、模式與主要內容
自由（制度）主義	利益取向、物質本位、理性選擇、絕對獲益與效用最大化促使合作在無政府狀態下形成	環境問題可以透過國際制度／建制得到適當的處理、不同行為者間雖利益不盡一致，但合作依然可行	正式的國際組織或非正式的制度、規範將促進環境領域的合作，國家若理解環境惡化的成本將危及未來的經濟發展時，制度或規範便容易獲得遵守
建構主義	觀念取向、非物質本位、行為者與所處之結構相互影響、非單一或既定的無政府邏輯	個人或社群可以透過科學知識取得影響國家行為的機會、關於環境的科學知識可以制約權力	觀念與知識有助於環境保護的議程設定（但對談判和履約的影響則較小）
批判理論	反思與質疑人類社會中普遍存在之權力結構不對稱、物質決定論、資本階級宰制其他社會階層的失衡現象	環境問題是人類社會結構不均的反映、環境問題與南北國家的經濟發展和資源分配不均息息相關	不平等的權力關係讓環境領域的合作難以達到普遍的共識，資本優勢者決定了合作制度中的遊戲規則

※資料來源：參考蔡育岱與熊武合著，國際關係之理論與實際，第179頁表1製成。

機會不斷增加自己的權力，並用權力去界定自我利益，並不惜犧牲他國的權力或利益。因此國家彼此間不具信賴關係，或是僅有很少的信任。在國際政治中，國家不僅要追求本身權力的最大化，還必須防止體系中有任何其他行為者取得此種絕對優勢之地位，因此，國際關係便是國家間為了

獲得安全而無法歇息的一場競爭互動關係。從而，雖然國家間偶有合作的可能及事實，但基於國際政治中具有「主導性的安全競爭邏輯」（The Dominating Logic of Security Competition），合作的可能性十分微弱。

　　從無政府狀態、權力、利益等現實主義的觀點來看當代的環境問題，不確定性（Uncertainty）、相對獲益（Relative Gains）和利己主義（Egoism），使得環境相關議題的研究和理論發展受到局限，並與舊有的「安全」（Security）議題本質相似，而將重心置於下列兩點：（一）環境問題有無可能影響或衝擊國家間的權力分布？例如新聯盟的形成與對抗（窮國與富國間的南北衝突）？（二）既存的國際制度或安排是否有助於解決和管理當代的環境問題或危機（合作懷疑論）？基於這樣的思考，現實主義者認為，即便由環境面相來解讀國際政治，主權（Sovereignty）依舊是國家最核心的關切，無論南方或北方國家皆然。檯面上種類繁多的各式國際環境協定恐怕僅是表象，因為條約之中具有強制力和制裁效果者寥寥可數。國家偏好以模糊的用語、含混的目標來呈現這些環保文件，並有選擇性的去執行或接受對其較為有利的條文規定或是義務承擔。以此觀之1992年里約會議中，北方國家對於本國消費和資源使用方式的堅持，以及南方國家拒絕談判有關森林開發議題的表現自明。

　　惟現實主義者未全然否認國家有時會透過制度來解決一些國際性的環境問題，但其強調制度或任何形式的合作所以形成，以及此種關係中的規則，不過只是個別國家出於自利的思考；更確切的說，環境制度或環境合作中的規則反映出的是國際政治大國間權力分配的情形。強國多半是創建、形塑以及影響國際制度或合作成敗的幕後推手，他們藉由制度滿足對於世界權力的掌控，或是在現有的優勢地位上繼續加碼。

二、自由主義（Liberalism）

　　回顧自由主義的發展，大概可以簡單的說明如下[2]：

---

[2]　同前註，第176頁。

　　自由主義的思想起源至少可追溯至格羅秀斯（Hugo Grotius）有關國際法的論述，後經Kant的闡釋及國際聯盟（League of Nations）的實踐而漸臻成熟。二十世紀的50至60年代，歐洲地區的整合實踐將近／舊功能主義（Neo-functionalism/Functionalism）的研究成果帶入自由主義，並促成1970年代之後有關「相互依存」（Interdependence）現象的研究[3]。自由主義有關制度（institutions）的研究可以Keohane與Nye在1979年出版的《權力與相互依存》（*Power and Interdependence*）一書為濫觴。該書以國家間在國際制度之下的互動為研究重點，提出有關國家合作的相關理論及分析：Keohane個人在1984年所寫的另一本《霸權之後》（*After Hegemony*）書中，更進一步說明了國際政治中合作與衝突並存的現象。

　　自由主義開始關心環境問題並將研究焦點投注於「環境建制」（Environmental Regimes）的時間點約在1970年代末，它與現實主義相似處在於兩者同屬國家中心論和至少在某一程度上的結構形塑論。自由主義認為任何跨國性的議題，就是「集體行為」（Collective Actions）如何解釋的問題，以及與「公共財」（Public Goods）有關的問題[4]。在「互賴」的思考基礎上，自由（制度）主義相信生態問題同樣也具有相互依存的現象，基於當代環境問題所形成的威脅與損害，已遠遠超出任何單一國家的控制和解決能力範圍，使得各主權國家必須尋求某種程度的國際合作並參與某種建制，以作為因應環境問題對自身利益與安全造成的衝擊。而當某一國際性的環境建制形成之後，其原則、規範、規則和決策程序，必然會對參

---

[3] 主流國關理論中的自由主義流派眾多，此處所要探討為自由主義在制度（institutions）方面的作用，關於「制度」的用語在內涵上包括「建制」（regimes），有關制度與建制或國際組織（international organizations）的區分及異同，學界有認為國際法與國際建制和國際制度是相近的，因為它們都是國家彼此協商而達成的法律規則（rules）。Keohane將制度定義為「用以規定行為的角色、行動的限制，以及形塑預期的一組持續且相互關聯的規則」。依此觀點，則制度尚包含了官方與非官方的協定。或許因為如此，在20世紀70年代以前，一般係將國際制度（international institution）等同於國際組織（international organization），而所謂的國際制度法，實際上就是國際組織法。對國際組織的研究，以學者David Mitrany的「功能主義」（functionalism）為早期的代表。

[4] 同前揭註1。

與該建制之行為體的權力與行為具有某種「禁止」（Injunctions）性質的
法律拘束，使其行為受到限制。易言之，自由（制度）主義較現實主義樂
觀，認為透過制度所達成的國際環境領域合作，將能克服集體行為的缺陷
與裨益當前環境問題的改善。

三、建構主義

　　「建構主義」（Constructivism）有時被納入後實證主義（Post-posi-
tivism）中的一支，認為其立場上傾向批判國際關係主流理論的反思主義
（Reflectivism），是理性主義（Rationalism）之外的另一種研究取向。
建構主義強調行為者與結構間的相互構成（mutual constitution），即一
方面行為者具有修正或改變結構的能力；另一方面結構對行為者的選擇
自由產生制約，同時也對特定行為者產生「構成效果」（Constitutive Ef-
fects），例如賦予行為者「行動正當性」（Empowering Effect）、「形
塑」（Shape）行為者對自我角色的「認同」（Identity）[5]。

　　價值、認同，以及觀念在建構主義的認知中是會影響國家合作與否，
或亦戰亦和的變數。當一個新的安全觀念與新的安全實踐被推出後，其反
覆重塑或累積的效果將造成國際實踐上的改變，構成國家合作處理特定問
題的新模式。鑑此，建構主義認為，國際間既已存在的環境制度及其相關
措施，可代表環境安全治理的規範已然確立，而其反覆的實踐可以做為制
度強化或持續維繫的基礎。例如「聯合國政府間氣候變遷小組」（United
Nations Intergovernmental Panel on Climate Change, IPCC）持續的全球暖化
報告提出和政策建議，即是最佳佐證[6]。

　　建構主義一方面利用社會學的觀點，解釋國際制度所扮演的角色是建
構國家的認同與參與談判時的立場，而不是如同理性主義所認為的那種戰
略互動和工具理論的觀點；同時強調認知（Cognitive）的因素是釐清國際
合作中「動態性」（Dynamics）的關鍵，以「知識」（Knowledge）取向

---

[5]　同前揭註1，第177頁。
[6]　同前註。

為基礎,對代表國際合作的制度進行不同於自由(制度)主義的研究,其中最具代表性的學者Peter Haas的「知識社群論」(Epistemic Communities)或「國際政策學習與協調」(International policy learning and coordination)的相關研究[7]。簡言之,建構主義中將觀念或認知視為一種新知識的產生,並視為環境制度形成的幕後推手,因為它能使國家改變原本對利益的觀點[8]。

四、批判理論(Critical Theory)

「批判理論」(Critical Theory)致力於修正當前國際政治充滿物質權力鬥爭的本質,以增進國際間真摯的和平。針對現實主義強調國家是自利的行為者此一核心觀點提出挑戰,認為「觀念」(Ideas)或「話語」(Discourse)才是國家行為的根源。批判理論從根本上否定現實主義將國家行為視為一被給定的(the given)外在世界之結構下的函數,指出國家行為並非全然地受到客觀物質世界及其結構的影響;相對的,指出觀念形塑物質世界的作用力也不容小覷[9]。

自由(制度)主義中的「制度」觀是批判理論的另一個反思對象,它們希望透過修正以利益或工具論思維為主導的制度規則或話語,以一個「多元的安全共同體」(Pluralistic Security Community)作為代替[10]。認為國家在此共同體下,能依據共有和共享的「規範」(Norms)協手齊心維持國際秩序的穩定。就論述的內容來看,批判理論與現實主義或自由(制度)主義顯然是用不同的「本體論」(Ontology)與「知識論」(Episte-

---

[7] Peter M. Haas, "Introduction: Epistemic Communities and International Policy Coordination." *International Organization*, Vol. 46, No. 1 (Winter 1992): 1-35 (especially at 27).

[8] 學者Young提出「權力、利益、觀念」分類法:權力主要是在談霸權與制度形成或維持的關係;利益則和自由(制度)主義的論述相近;觀念(也就是「認知」)則視新知識的產生為環境制度形成的幕後主力,因為它使得國家改變原本對利益的觀點。

[9] 同前揭註1,第178頁。

[10] 在此共同體之下,個別國家的利益即是國際社會全體的利益(national interests are international interests)。

mology）來解讀與認知國際關係；前者在歷史脈絡的背景下，將主體與客體的關係視為相互作用與互為建構的一種現象。而後者認為有一客觀的知識與物質世界存在，並將研究的客體從中予以區隔。

在批判理論下，變動可能性受到極大的重視，亦即沒有什麼既存的教條或原則是不能被質疑與解構的。相對的，如何解釋客體與主體間的關係，適度的將不同的規範或是觀念引入兩者的互動中，促使現有的不平衡情況發生轉變或增加這種可能性，方是此理論著墨之所在。因此，批判理論致力於主流國關理論對於環境問題研究的典範轉移（Paradigm Struggles），認為如果不將國家中心的政治思考予以糾正，環境問題永遠無法改善[11]。

貳、綠色理論（Green Theory）

一、綠色理論之主題（Subject of Green Theory）

「綠色理論」（Green Theory）在國際關係領域的發展與第三次大辯論有一定程度的相關性[12]，研究者將重心聚焦傳統國關理論所忽視與邊緣化的個人或國家以外的社群，例如原住民、生態學家、消費者、綠色政黨、非政府組織等凡追求修正全球貿易、國際援助模式或貸款制度中的不公平，以促進各國平等發展與環境永續的參與者。綠色理論的焦點通常有兩個主題：（一）反省「以人類為中心的」（Anthropocentric）思考，抑制將非人類的自然世界作為人類生活之用的工具論主義[13]；（二）反省成長應否受有限制的問題。故而，綠色理論在某程度上可被歸為國際政治經濟學、規範理論或世界主義的範疇中，作為強調環境正義與環境治理民主

---

[11] 同前揭註1，第178頁。

[12] 由於綠色理論內容上具一定的批判性，並與傳統主流的理性主義國關理論本質相左，故在分類上亦有學者將之納入批判理論的範疇。

[13] 學者Eckersley認為綠色理論是一種生物中心主義（ecocentrism）。

性的研究取向。

二、綠色理論之主要派別

　　綠色理論是環境政治理論的代名詞，但不以關懷環境污染和生態破壞為限。不同的綠色理論流派對於人類社會的政治、經濟、文化結構，及在背後驅動國家政策的認知或意識型態提出批判，強調非物質的意識結構、重視人與自然和諧關係，認為科技並非萬能，經濟並非首要；環境倫理、性別文化及社會正義的價值皆具有決定環境與人類未來命運之重要性；主要派別有下列五種[14]：

（一）深層生態學（Deep Ecology）

　　或可稱「生態中心主義」（Ecocentrism），有以下三項基礎核心假設：1.地球上所有生物均有其與生俱來的價值和生存的權利，自然生態並非以作為人類可使用之資源或工具而存在；2.凡地球上的生物彼此間均有一種休戚與共的聯繫關係，沒有任何一種實體可以脫離於全體。生物與非生物，人類與非人類之間，沒有絕對的界限存在；3.基於地球的有限「承載力」（Carrying Capacity），世界的人口數必須有所控制，人類並非演化過程中的唯一主體，不應侵奪其他物種的生存權。

　　深層生態學目前已成為環境政治學領域中的主要流派，同時對現代環境運動產生很大影響。其主要目的在於修正以「人類為中心」的偏差環境認知，並將道德因素注入與延伸到自然時節與物種的保護，強調各生物體間的和諧平等共處，以及發展不應危害自然的觀念。

（二）生態後現代主義（Ecological Postmodernism）

　　現代主義（Modernism）的思想自法國大革命後長期支配著西方文化，其中科學的理性啟蒙思維讓人類走出過往的迷信和無知。然而，啟蒙

---

[14] 同前揭註1，第180頁至183頁。

思想所促成的後果，是讓人類過度的強調理性和自我意識，使得為了滿足自身需要可以肆無忌憚的「利用」自然，以致現今環境問題難以解決。生態後現代主義站在反絕對科學與環境本位的立場，指出文明與科技所解決或滿足的問題和它所製造出來的問題幾乎相差無幾，甚至反而更多。因此，追求進步而不知節制，環境惡化與崩潰將是必然的結局。此種反現代化的後現代主義同時強調「差異性」的重要，主張將自然的多樣性予以呈現。

　　另外，在現代主義的研究中，有關「自然」的論述並不多見，物質優先和人類本位的核心價值成為世界運作的必然邏輯（強權者的邏輯），環境與生態沒有獨立探討的必要和價值，因此自然地被排除於研究範疇之外。但事實上，人與自然的價值關係卻在當代生態危機中漸漸被突顯出來，因此，生態後現代主義從哲學的立場對人類主體意識予以否定，並主張生態倫理的重要性。

（三）社會生態學（Social Ecology）

　　反對透過國家機器作為解決環境問題的方法，是一種無政府主義在環境領域的應用。社會生態學以激進的態度對任何形式的宰制關係加以否定，倡導不需任何制度化或制度化極少的草根性環境民主運動，藉此避免代議政治在人民與其日常生活問題解決間的鴻溝發生。為了抑制宰制關係的形成，社會生態學思考的重心是人類社會中的階級制度、父權制傳統，指出此種不公允的權力結構是人類假借自然之名所建構出來的假象。唯有將階級概念和宰制關係衝破，人與自然才可能和諧共存。不過須注意的是，某些社會生態學家認為人類在演化過程中與其他生物相比，是有自我意識的個體。

（四）生態社會主義（Eco-socialism）

　　相較於前述三種綠色理論，生態社會主義排斥一切「反人類」觀點的說法，並將研究重心放在「人類的生產活動」上，認為此乃人與自然間關係最為重要的部分。此主義對於環境問題的界定較為廣泛，包括車輛污

染、都市中心人口老化、綠地面積縮減等，其中最為關切的是失業與貧窮問題。

生態社會主義者認為環境問題實際上是社會問題與政治問題的綜合，而其中的禍源便是資本主義制度，因為它無限追求利潤的生產方式必然對自然環境形成破壞，並隨著當今全球化的現象加速各式生態危機的轉移和擴散。北方國家利用貿易對南方國家進行資源的剝削，作為維繫既有的經濟規模與生活水準，但貿易背後的環境生態成本卻轉嫁給南方或發展中國家承擔。

生態社會主義與馬克思主義具有相似的本質，認為經濟理性會使勞動者變成機械，使人際關係變成金錢給付關係，而人與自然的關係變成工具利用關係。簡言之，資本主義下的生產模式與整個地球生態系統之間是相互衝突的，環境惡化是資本主義為人類社會帶來的宿命，唯一的辦法就是對資本主義提出質疑與批判，不再抱持生產力的提升是推動社會進步的觀點，因為毫無節制的生產不僅加劇了人與自然關係的衝突，更衍生出環境危機，同時更可能把原本用以刺激生產的科學技術變成統治人類的工具。

（五）生態女性主義（Eco-feminism）

作為女性解放運動的分支，生態女性主義係一種結合環境惡化與婦女地位不平等的性別論述，認為人類社會對於女性的壓迫和環境惡化與生態不安全之間存在著某種因果關係。其中「自由女性主義」（Liberal Feminism）主張由既存的政治體制進行修正，透過制度改革調和人與自然間的衝突關係；「文化女性主義」（Cultural Feminism）則是把環境問題歸責予父權體制中的分工宰製關係，強調環境惡化對於女性安全和繁衍人類後代的負面影響；「社會女性主義」（Social Feminism）和前述生態社會主義相近，但強調的是女性在生產與「再生產」（Reproduction）關係中的功能與角色，希望突顯自然與女性同為具有行動力的實體和永續發展的核心。

生態女性主義的分類或區分並不限於上述的態樣，但諸多論述彼此均有其共同的本質，即從女性的生理角色、照料子女和家庭的社會角色，發

展出一種「關懷的倫理」（Ethic of Care）思考，並將母親的角色與環境進行有機聯繫，從而利用倫理原則重新界定人類與自然的關係[15]。

表2-2 綠色理論各派別之主要論點

理論	論述核心
深層生態學	修正以「人類為中心」的偏差環境認知、強調生物體間的和諧
生態後現代主義	人類過度強調理性和自我意識，是造成環境惡化的主因、人類主體意識必須修正，環境倫理應予關注
社會生態學	反對透過國家機器作為解決環境問題的方法，倡導不需任何制度化或制度化極少的草根性民主環境運動
生態社會主義	環境惡化與人類的生產活動密切相關，資本主義是惡化環境的元兇、放棄生產力提升是推動社會進步的觀點
生態女性主義	人類社會對於女性的壓迫和環境的惡化與不安之間具有關聯性

※資料來源：參考蔡育岱與熊武合著，國際關係之理論與實際，第183頁改製。

參、經濟理論（Economic Theory）

國際法，特別是國際環境法的存在及其功能，主要的即是在「形成」及限制國際社會中的各個主體的「行為」。就本質而言，它告訴了各個主體，特別是國家，哪些是它們被允許去「從事」的行為，又有哪些是它們被禁止去做的，以及哪些行為是被要求去做的。就這個層面來看，國際法與「內國法」（Domestic Law）是沒有什麼差別的。然而，在其他的各方面來說，它們之間的差別就難以同日而語了。基本上，內國法的運作是「垂直的」（Vertical），有個有執行能力的中央政府，是上對下的上下隸屬關係。而在國際法的方面，就完全不是這回事。國際法的運作乃是在國際社會之中，它不存在有一個權力核心的中央政府，它的執行能力，要仰

---

[15] 同揭前註1，第183頁。

賴各主權國家彼此的相互尊重及同意去接受國際法的拘束；在國際社會當中，各國之間不具有上下隸屬關係。彼此之間所具有的是「平行關係」；換句話說，國際法的存在於國際社會之中，其落實與執行是所謂的「水平的」（Horizontal）體系之下。

　　從上述的國際法與內國法的執行層面之落差來看，國際環境法基本上所具有的屬性乃是屬於國際法的一環，可是國際環境法的特質卻與其他的國際法「家族」，如國際貿易法又有所不同。基本上，國際貿易法的形成有其歷史背景的因素，而國際環境法具有今天的面貌，大致上來說不同於國際貿易法。國際貿易法形成主要是各國家之間基於平等互惠的基礎，彼此同意，以某些規範來進行貿易；而國際環境法的有效履行則與國際貿易法大大地不同。它的形成在多數的情形，各國並非基於平等互利的基礎，明顯的例子就是過去幾十年來所存在的「南北對話」（North-South Dialogue）及「京都議定書」（Kyoto Protocol）等所發生的問題，在在顯示，每個主權國家基於本身的立場或經濟發展的需要，對於環境保護的標準自然會有不同的立場與需求。僅就此點而言，國際環境法與國際貿易法之間，就有相當大地差異，而且是可以理解的。

　　從前述所言，以相同的邏輯來推理，國際環境法的經濟理論就不難理解。這個問題的實質問題，就是在於解決為什麼各國願意去服膺國際環境法的規範。這個問題的核心即在於有什麼利益讓各主權國家願意去「遵守」國際環境法的規範？或是有什麼「誘因」（Incentive）或「利基」（Niche）來讓國際環境法可以在各主權國家管轄領域內加以落實？這就是本章所要研究的重心之所在。

　　一般而言，在執行一個指示性或相當高度規範性的體系或市場機制之下的運作，主要的是要檢視「執行誘因之運作層面」（Operative Aspects of Incentives for Performance）以及「不執行之障礙」（Disincentives of Nonperformance）。在國際環境法制協定或規範方面，能夠對已簽訂者

及潛在的新參加者提供誘因的例子有[16]：1987年蒙特婁議定書（Montreal Protocol on Substances That Deplete the Ozone Layer）、聯合國氣候變遷框架（架構）公約（United Nations Framework Convention on Climate Change; UNFCCC）以及聯合國生物多樣性公約（United Nations Convention on Biological Diversity）。它們這些所提供之「誘因」，大概都是以下列的方式提供：技術協助（Technical Assistance）、專案設計或專題計畫基金（Project or Program Fund）以及其他各種態樣之資源，來提供經濟上的誘因，用以執行或履行國際環境法規範或標準之確定。這也就滿足了所謂「遵照理論」（Compliance Theory）的要求。因為此處所謂的「遵守」（Compliance）乃是指特定的行為（Action）或不行為在一個國際條約或協定中所考量到的，需要由簽約者或參加者去履行或完成條約或協定的規定或要求。如此，則因為「遵守」的原因，自然就達成了「履行」（Implementation）的「效果」（Effectiveness）。

對於國際環境法規範下的「遵守」也同時滿足了國際條約或維也納條約法公約的要求——「條約必須遵守」（Pasta Sunt Servanda）之金科玉律。這在某種程度的意涵上，自然也就成了各國「遵照」國際環境法規範的「誘因」。這也就是國際環境法提供了「經濟理論」的基礎。再進一步分析下去，遵守的經濟理論，如果基於詳盡的「經濟分析」（Economic Analysis），從「運作的關聯性」（Operational Relevance）的目的來看，可以有下列五種類別，提供各種不同的「實體決策者」（Entity Decision-Maker）在作決策時作為參考[17]：

一、遵照之邊際成本（Marginal Cost of Compliance）

二、不遵照之邊際成本（Marginal Cost of Noncompliance）

三、遵照之邊際效益（Marginal Benefit of Compliance）

四、不遵照之邊際效益（Marginal Benefit of Noncompliance）

五、誘因與障礙之角色（Role of Incentives and Disincentives）

---

[16] David Hunter, James Salzman and Durwood Zaelke, International Environmental Law and Policy, 3rd ed. (N.Y.: Foundation Press, 2008), p. 370.

[17] P.K. Rao, International Environmental Law and Economics (Maiden, M.A.: Blackwell Publisher, 2007).

第三章　國際環境問題之檢視

壹、經濟發展與環境資源之利用共生

　　地球之提供人類進步發展的「能量」（Capacity），在人類歷史進程的任何一個時間點都可以很清楚的看出來。所謂的「利用厚生」，大概就是這個意思。而人類追求經濟發展的基礎，亦不可否認的建立在科技進步的前提之下。如眾所周知，人類幾千年的歷史演進，不如工業革命後的兩三百年的進展成果。由於人類長期追求經濟發展結果，雖然滿足發展上的需求，然而大量利用各種科技及工程技術對自然資源漫無限制的加以開發，結果造成地球資源無法挽救的破壞。

　　如前所述，全球性的工業革命與科技進步，使得國際相互依存程度為之提高，箇中關鍵一是功能取向的經濟整合，二是跨國通訊網絡的建立及發展。此外，在另一個比較間接的層面，工業化也加深國家間的依存關係，此即工業化對自然生產的影響。今天，任何國家的行動都可能影響其他國家繼續取得自然資源的機會。質言之，會對生態環境造成衝擊；當前全球生態環境受到不同來源的威脅，國家間的相互依存因此得到新而重要的動力[1]。

　　一旦生態受到破壞，影響層面將非常廣泛。此外，通常會造成長期性衝擊。由於產生的效應很容易蔓延，因此環境生態保護引發棘手的公共財問題。基本上，一個能夠永續發展的自然環境是項公共財。各國理應討論如何分攤維護成本。環境保護涉及複雜的技術、科學與道德問題。毋庸置疑各國在環保方面具有共同利益。公共財的問題出在環境、人口及自然資

---

[1] 歐信宏與胡祖慶合譯，Joshua S. Goldstein, International Relations，國際關係，台北，雙葉書廊，2003年，第436頁。

源等方面[2]。

　　舉例來說明[3]：全球各個主要漁場並不屬於任何國家所有，它們是項公共財。因此，從事漁撈的國家必須合作，以免漁業資源枯竭。在這方面，相關國家或須對跨國企業等非國家成員進行管理。如果太多國家決定抱持不合作與竭澤而漁態度，漁業資源將迅速減少，每個國家的漁獲量也將隨著降低。事實上，在過去幾十年當中，許多重要的漁場相繼遇到這種情形。因此，到了1990年代初期，全球漁獲總量銳減。從事漁撈的業者每年損失超越500億美元，相關國家提供的補貼金額跟著水漲船高。

　　無論如何，直到近四十年環境生態才逐漸成為國際談判及國際關係學術領域中的重要課題[4]：之前，在這方面只見到零星的研究。1970年，環保人士首次提倡所謂「地球日」，學者對於環保問題的研究興趣迅速增加，1970年代的能源危機更加突顯相關問題的重要性。一夕之間，工業國家的能源儲存量似乎已經是捉襟見肘。與此同時，愈來愈多的環境生態問題被搬上國際舞台，包括原油的漏油事件、都會地區的空氣污染、殺蟲劑殘留問題，以及核能發電廠的安全性等等。

　　自1970年代起，聯合國召開一系列與環境相關之會議[5]：設立「人與生物圈計畫」（Man and Biosphere Program），並將每年6月5日規定為世界環境日。1972年6月12日，聯合國在斯德哥爾摩（Stockholm）召開了「人類環境會議」（United Nation Conference on the Human Environment）。此次會議通過屬於聯合國第一個關於保護人類生存環境的原則聲明，即「人類環境宣言」（Declaration on the Human Environment）。[6]該

[2] 同前註。
[3] 同前註。
[4] 同前註，第438頁。
[5] 蔡育岱與熊武合著，國際關係之理論與實際，台北，鼎茂圖書出版公司，2010年，第169頁至170頁。
[6] 1987「聯合國環境與發展世界委員會」（UN World Commission on Environment and Development, WCED）發表《我們的共同未來》（*Our Common Future*）報告書，為永續發展訂立了一個廣為公眾接受的定義，即「既能滿足吾人現今的需求，又不會損害子孫後代滿足他們需求的發展模式」。其定義雖然籠統，但基本原則已清楚表明人類不該為了任何一項資源的開

宣言象徵人類對環境問題的自覺，對推動各國後來的保護和改善環境工作有著重要影響。此後到1992年里約（Rio de Janerio）「環境與發展會議」（United Nations Conference on Environment and Development）的二十年間，環境議題開始為國際政治中的一個重要領域。其中，里約環境與發展會議的召開突顯了環境問題對人類社會經濟發展的重要性，世人開始意識到唯有在「永續發展」（Sustainable Development）的前提下[7]，經濟活動的成長與人類後代的繁衍才可能獲得確保。而地球及其上所附之一切資源均並非可取之不盡，用之不竭的資產。

2002年8月26日聯合國在南非約翰尼斯堡（Johannesburg）召開永續發展世界高峰會議（World Summit on Sustainable Development, WSSD）[8]。並針對水、能源、健康、農業以及生物多樣性與生態系經營（Biodiversity and Ecosystem Management）等五大議題，研究如何落實永續發展。此外，與會代表亦針對消滅貧窮、改變不永續之消費及製造型態、健康與傳染疾病、小島國家之永續發展等問題交換意見。此次會議，雖然在不少國家的爭議聲中閉幕，但通過了《約堡執行計畫》（Plan of Implementation），作為各國政府推動永續發展政策之參考架構。2007年在德國舉辦的「八大工業國高峰會議」（G8 Summit）上，各國達成共同合作以適應氣候變遷的協議[9]。相較於國際層次對於抑制環境惡化的努力，在某些國家內部也開始醞釀起相關訴求。例如西德的「綠黨」（Green Party）在1980年至1983年間即透過選舉方式進入議會，成為該國的環保主力，其他

發或使用，而犧牲其他。至於永續發展的內涵應包含公平性（fairness）、永續性（sustainability）及共同性（commonality）三個原則。永續發展的層面則為：(1)社會層面，主張公平分配，以滿足當代及後代全體人民的基本需求；(2)經濟層面，主張建立在保護地球自然系統基礎上的持續經濟成長；(3)自然生態層面，主張人類與自然和諧相處。綜言之，永續發展的觀念已成為未來全球環保的極重要理念。

[7] 此協議係起於G8所啟動的對話機制，即「海爾利根達姆進程」（Heiligendamm Process）；參與對話機制的國家除G8成員外，尚包含中國、巴西、印度、墨西哥與南非等新興經濟體。除了美俄兩國外，G8的其他六國同意採取共同措施促使2050年前全世界二氧化碳排放量達到減半的目標，並讓這個目標成為聯合國進程的一部分。

[8] 同前揭註5，第170頁。

[9] 同前註。

國家如芬蘭、瑞典、義大利和比利時也均有綠黨組織先後入閣的實例，進入1990年代，綠黨在其他地區也開始蓬勃的發展，據研究指出，至2005年為止，世界至少有87個綠色政治運動團體，廣泛分布於歐洲、非洲、美洲和亞太地區[10]。

貳、國際環境問題之關鍵性特徵

追根究柢的探討國際環境問題之所以會呈現目前之面貌，不可否認的是因為環境問題的本身與國際社會中人類的追求生活水平的提升目標，有著息息相關的結果；造成了人類行為之作法影響到人類之生產與消費行為之模式，進而對整個人類周遭的環境發生了「無限大」（Unlimited）的效果，同時對於人類生活的本身造成了「無止境」（No-Limitation）的衝擊。

研究國際環境問題，大致上可以看到下列三個關鍵性特徵：

一、經濟發展之優位

環境問題與人類行為密切相關，特別是人類的生產與消費行為。目前學界的研究成果已越來越清楚且肯定的指出[11]：當代環境惡化肇因於人類社會的經濟行為模式。一味追求效率的生產和無所節制的消費現象不但說明何以環境問題日益嚴重，也透露出為何環境問題無法有效獲得解決，蓋兩者間是一種彼竭我盈的牽連關係，很難找到共生雙贏的解決之法。

經濟與環境間的關係是彼此交互的，一方面自然資源是經濟活動中生產階段的泉源與基礎，另一方面經濟活動的結果往往對環境造成負面的衝

---

[10] 綠黨是二十世紀後半葉隨著西方生態運動的發展而出現的左翼政治社群。經過多年的發展，綠黨從單純的、激進的環境保護力量發展成為在歐洲政壇和社會中占有一席之地的政治勢力，致力促使歐洲朝向生態合理和公正。

[11] 同前揭註5，第171頁。

擊。生產與消費導致環境品質的下滑，但人類多半認為此乃維繫經濟持續成長的必要之「惡」。有三個與此相關的事實吾人應予注意[12]：（一）經濟發展過程中固有的環境惡化問題長期以來並未獲得應有的重視；（二）當代國家多以追求經濟成長為目標，間接鼓勵政府對於環境議題的漠視，或是政策上採取敷衍的態度；（三）國際經貿的互賴是加速環境持續惡化的關鍵因素。

環境惡化是人類經濟活動所帶來的副產品，即使目前多數國家已有所謂的環境保護相關政策，但實踐上仍舊是以經濟發展為先，例如補貼政策即是一例[13]。某些國家的補貼政策往往是最終加速環境惡化的幫助犯，主要原因是類此補貼容易造成廠商過多的投入與產出，從而加重環境壓力。簡言之，政府有時不但沒有即時糾正市場錯誤，反而因補貼導致既有的環境問題更加惡化[14]。至於低度發展國家更是不可能（同時也沒有能力）去採取必要的環境改善措施，因為一來沒有足夠的資金與技術，二來擺脫貧窮才是這些國家眼前唯一在乎的事情。實踐上，多數發展中或低度發展國家將其出口天然物資的所得用以支付國際貸款的利息（George, 1990: 16-34）；又如「國際貨幣基金」（International Monetary Fund, IMF）過度強調要求發展中國家增加出口和召募外資，導致國家更多的自然資源剝削行為和對環境惡化問題的輕忽。

此外，造成環境惡化還有所謂的「外部經濟因素」（External Economic Factor）現象。一般商品都可以在經濟市場上進行交換，並有反應其成本的市場價值，但像環境這樣的「公共財」（Public Goods）卻無法進行市場交換，因此不具有一般經濟學所謂的市場價值。惟事實上，生態環境提供給人類的諸多好處，如涵養水源、提供氧氣、孕育物種的溼地等

---

[12] 同前註。

[13] 經濟合作暨發展組織（Organization for Economic Co-operation and Development, OECD）將有害環境的補貼定義為包括所有租稅體系的財務支援，目的在於提高某特定產品、製造程序或地區的競爭力，但也導致環境品質受損。這些有害環境的補貼主要是在工業、交通、農業、能源、水、森林、漁業等部門。

[14] 此種補貼又稱為惡化環境的補貼（environmentally harmful subsidies）。

都屬於極具經濟價值的事物，它們無法進入市場取得相應的市場價值，以致即便客觀上公共財的數量已呈現銳減，但在經濟市場上依然極為地廉價，使得消費量居高不下，最終形成資源耗竭[15]。

二、資本主義之盛行

資本主義與當代生態環境迅速惡化有著十分密切的關係，在資本主義普遍流行和發達的人類社會裡，四個關鍵性的變化讓環境品質下降成為必然的宿命：（一）人類對於自然資源較過往更為廣泛和密集的使用與開發；（二）追求方便、效率、省時的心態讓許多無法被自然過程分解或代謝的物質（例如塑膠、氟氯碳化物）被人類的商業行為所廣泛接受；（三）資本主義間接刺激區域性或全球性的貿易活動，讓許多環境問題成為跨疆界的國際事件，加大解決問題的難度[16]；（四）短時間快速累積財富成為個人與國家一致追求的目標，而負面影響多半要相當時間後才會被感受到，環境問題自然被忽略。

上述四個關鍵變化可由下列事例獲得進一步的證明。首先，受到資本主義的影響，發展中國家基於經濟上的需要，有時會將擁有的重要天然資源（例如雨林）開發出來作為出口財，以換取所需的資本。短期來看，發展中國家和向他們購買這些天然資源的國家（多半是工業國家）經由貿易行為各取所需而互利，但長期來看，這些天然資源會很快的被開採殆盡，在當地形成所謂的「生態陰影」（the Shadow of Ecology）。其次，以全球暖化而言，溫室氣體的主要排放國是經濟與貿易繁榮的國家（例如美

---

[15] 外部經濟是指不經由市場交換過程，一個經濟主體卻受到其他經濟主體的影響；之中效益為有利者，稱為外部經濟（external economics），如觀光產業景氣時，服務業多半也受益。若其效益為有害者，稱為外部不經濟（external diseconomics），如礦石業者濫墾山坡區域導致水土流失，間接促成果農和當地旅遊的經濟損失。自然環境中的豐富資源能帶給人類社會許多好處，例如水源、適當的二氧化碳濃度、遊憩空間、可食用的野生動植物等，因此生態環境是典型的外部經濟因素。

[16] 也促使原本僅存於當地或某區域的「局部性」環境問題得不到有效的處理，或適用於A國（區域）的解決方法，在B國（區域）未必適用。

國、中國），他們透過高度的工業化與商業化來賺取世界的財富，成為最大的受益者。但其促成與遺留下的暖化問題卻必須由全地球人共同承擔，特別是那些經濟弱者往往優先承擔暖化的苦果[17]。

　　簡言之，當代環境問題無法與資本主義切割開來討論，而這又與人口增長的壓力、科技創新的需要、和國家追求經濟成長與發展等現象有著牢不可破的聯繫。因為維護和發展資本主義是國家權力的主要內容，資本主義在全世界已具有支配性地位，而目前全球經貿發展就是資本主義的世界經濟彰顯。從傳統「馬克思主義」（Marxism）立場來看，國家是資本階級對無產階級實施階級統治的機器，由這樣所構成的國際關係體系，即意味經濟差別的社會關係，並形成支配與從屬的階級結構，這些因素便是造成環境問題的根本性原因[18]。

三、環境管理系統之推動

　　「環境管理」為近年來先進國家積極發展推動的環境保護策略，以配合過去行之以久的「行政管制」方式。環境管理的目的，在於鼓勵產業界從組織內部開始規畫其環保改善及污染預防措施，以期達到永續發展的目標。環境管理系統以往大都由業界各別自行設計並執行，針對其企業性質執行不同的環境管理系統[19]：英國在1992年3月，首先提出英國標準「BS 7750環境管理系統」。歐洲聯盟也在1993年7月訂定環境管理及稽核制度（EMAS）。為避免國際間不重視環保之惡性競爭，也避免因標準不一，造成環保貿易障礙，以及保證環境管理系統的一致性，「國際標準組織」（International Organization for Standardization, ISO）第207技術委員會（ISO/TC 207）成立於1993年1月，著手制訂並推動ISO 14000環境管理系列國際標準，已在全球各地形成世界性風潮。其訂定國際環境管理標準相

---

[17] 同前揭註5，第173頁。

[18] 或有學者認為在中國大陸的「走資」方面的實踐，便是一個適當的例子。

[19] 洪正中、杜正榮與吳天基編著，環境生態學，二版，新北市蘆洲區，國立空中大學，2003年，第230頁。

關工作分配之組織架構包括六個「次委員會」（Subcommittee，簡稱SC）
及一個工作小組（work group，簡稱WG）。

　　國際社會的先進國家很明顯地正在努力地從「環境管理」著手，推動
一個具有國際公信力的標準化管理系統之建立；認為如此的作法才是一個
客觀的可長可久之計，用以達成國際社會共有共榮與互利共生之「永續發
展」。

參、二十一世紀國際環境問題之現況

　　關於國際環境問題之面對以及發展中的一個重大里程碑，乃是1972年
的「聯合國人類環境會議」（United Nations Conference on Human Environ-
ment）之召開，而且以「只有一個地球」為主題，在瑞典首都斯德哥爾摩
舉行，會後提出人類環境宣言明示：「各國家，依據聯合國憲章和國際法
的原則，有權力在遵守其國內環境政策下，開發其所屬之資源，也有義務
保證在其轄下領域內的開發活動不會破壞其他國家或他屬領域的環境」。
聯合國於1992年6月在巴西里約熱內盧召開「聯合國環境與發展會議」，
表達對全球環境問題的關切，並以「我們共同的未來」（Our Common
Future）為主題，喚醒全球環保意識，以達到資源永續發展之目的。

　　1988年6月，於加拿大多倫多市，召開「變遷的大氣」之國際會議，
會議結論指出：人類正在從事一項毫無計畫、無法控制、而且又廣被全球
的實驗，其嚴重後果僅次於全球核子戰爭。由於人類活動的污染，低效率
而且又浪費地使用化石燃料，再加上許多地區人口的快速成長，這些情形
均使地球的大氣成份產生了重大的改變，這些改變會對國際間環境品質造
成巨大的威脅，事實上，在許多地區確實已造成了重大災害。

　　在二十一世紀初期，如何冷靜思考全球的環境問題，並謀求解決之
道，已是世界各國所關切的焦點。

　　當前全球共同的環境生態問題，可列舉如下：一、臭氧層的破壞，
二、溫室效應，三、熱帶雨林的破壞，四、酸雨的危害，五、人口增加之

糧食問題，六、耕地擴大的限界，七、人口都市化及過分集中，八、土地過度利用及沙漠化，九、表土流失及鹽類的蓄積，十、單位土地面積生產量增加之困難，十一、能源之消耗，十二、持久性有機毒性污染物及環境荷爾蒙之散布，十三、日益嚴重之海洋污染，十四、濕地的消滅，十五、野生動植物的絕滅，十六、有害廢棄物之越境轉移等等。

現僅就上述其中重要環境生態問題，包括臭氧層破洞、溫室效應、酸雨、熱帶林的破壞、土地沙漠化、野生動植物的滅絕及環境荷爾蒙等加以闡述[20]。

一、臭氧層之破壞

地球表面上空的大氣層稱為對流層，對流層上方的氣層離地面約17～48公里範圍內稱為平流層。平流層內的臭氧層替人類抵擋了具有危害性的太陽輻射，特別是紫外線，對地球上生物的保護扮演重要角色[21]：因為臭氧能吸收太陽光中的紫外線，能將這些波長很短而且有致命危險的輻射線轉換成熱能，使之只有極少量能到達地表而紫外線會破壞包括DNA在內的生物分子，其結果將增加罹患皮膚癌、白內障的機率，而且和許多免疫系統的疾病有關。此外，紫外線對於農作物，甚至海洋生態系都會造成負面影響；所以臭氧層具有能屏蔽地球表面生物不受紫外線侵害的功能。

長期以來，全球除熱帶地區之外的大部分區域，平流層臭氧都有稀薄化的傾向。南極和北極地區人煙稀少，臭氧洞對人類所造成的影響尚不明顯，但如果臭氧減少的範圍擴及全球，則包括東北亞、歐洲和北美洲等人口密集的地區，有害紫外線就會大量增加，對人類的危害亦將相應擴大[22]。

臭氧層破壞有兩個特性[23]：其不論直接或間接，臭氣層之破壞都會危

---

[20] 同前註，第272頁。

[21] 同前註，第273頁。

[22] 同前註。

[23] 同前註，第274頁。

及地球上的所有國家，可能引起地球大規模的環境變化，而且像氟氯碳化合物這種，如果直接暴露在大氣當中，也可能引起公害問題。

臭氧層可吸收對生物有害的β－紫外線，以免地球生物遭受其輻射之危害，如果此保護層破壞了，將會造成人類及自然生態的一場浩劫。歸納其所造成之影響有二[24]：

（一）使人類罹患皮膚癌和白內障之機率大為提高：因為紫外線具突變性和致癌性，會使表面細胞的基因產生病變。據估計，臭氧如果減少1%，則紫外線到達地面之機率就增加2%，使得罹患皮膚癌之機率增加5～7%，其中1%是致死性的惡性腫瘤。

（二）植物受損、農作物減產：紫外線會破壞葉綠素，會造成基因突變，阻礙葉片生長，進而影響產量。也可能因紫外線之照射增加作物之病蟲害，而導致減產。

二、地球溫室效應

在地球的熱環境中，溫室氣體相當於溫室外面的玻璃窗，它可以讓10%的陽光透進來，並且吸收掉85%來自地表向外輻射的紅外線，而使地表的年平均溫度維持在攝氏15度左右。如果沒有溫室效應，來自陽光的能量將會很快的釋放出去，地表的溫度將陡降至零下攝氏18度左右。但溫室氣體增多，反而會帶來地球溫暖化的危機[25]。

在工業革命以前，大氣中的二氧化碳濃度約280ppm，但是自二十世紀以來，濃度就開始急速增加。近年來全球的二氧化碳排放量每年約有56億噸（碳量）來自燃燒，而因熱帶雨林破壞導致綠色植物減少二氧化碳排出量每年約為10～26億噸。從十八世紀以後，二氧化碳濃度已經提高31%，二氧化碳增加所引起的溫室效應，將使全球的平均氣溫上升，在二十世紀中全球平均地表溫度已經增加了$0.6 \pm 0.2°C$。根據氣候變遷政府間專家委員會（IPCC）2001年的第三次評估報告，自1861年有儀器紀錄

---

[24] 同前註。
[25] 同前註，第278頁。

以來二十世紀90年代是最溫暖的十年，其中1998年是最溫暖的一年[26]。

　　二氧化碳可以說是溫室效應最大之因素（約占50%）[27]：通常大氣中二氧化碳含量僅占全部大氣體積之0.03%。此外，從稻田和天然氣中釋放的甲烷占20%，氟氯碳化物占15%，一氧化碳占10%，而接近地球表面的臭氧占5%，這些氣體共同形成溫室效應的另一半比例。

　　其次，燃燒煤炭等石化產物均會產生二氧化碳。根據統計顯示，北美居民每人每年平均二氧化碳排放為4.5公噸，而全球每人每年平均產量則僅為0.9公噸。二氧化碳排放增加率和工業化、現代化的速度有密切關係，今天溫室效應中75%的氣體是由工業化國家所製造。

　　再者，甲烷是溫室層中大量和持續增加的氣體，每年有機物經由細菌分解——特別在垃圾掩埋場、水稻田、牛羊牲口和白蟻消化道以及燃燒木柴和石化燃料所產生的甲烷即多達3億8,500萬公噸之多。其增加速度隨人口增加而穩定成長，平均每十年以1%的速度成長。

　　最後，用在冰箱、汽車冷氣、家用絕緣體和許多其它日常用品中的氟氯碳化物也是溫室層的一員。在1987年簽定的蒙特婁協定書強制停止繼續製造此類化合物，希望藉以減緩其破壞的效果，然而氟氯碳化物的壽命卻高達一百年。

　　另外，氧化亞氮的排放量也在增加之中，其中三分之一主要來自人類的活動，由於其能在大氣中長期保持穩定狀態，亦是造成溫室效應之主要氣體之一。

　　反而，所要注意的是，從1880年到現在，全球的平均氣溫大約上升0.5℃。但專家預測在二十一世紀此種氣溫變化將會加速，而可明顯感覺出來。根據2001年IPCC所提出第三次評估報告，在2100年時地球的平均氣溫會上升1.4～5.8℃。地球變得暖和，乍聽之下似乎滿好的，可節省禦寒之費用，可提高作物產量，可降低平流層溫度而延緩臭氧之分解；但壞處還是很多，如天氣熱冷氣用得兇，會增加都市熱島效應；冷氣需要電，

---

[26] 同前註，第279頁。
[27] 同前註。

火力發電增加二氧化碳之排放量;另外提高氮氧化物和硫氧化物濃度,使地表的臭氧、光化學煙霧、酸雨之情形增加。整體而言,溫室效應會影響生態環境(包括地球、海洋及人類的經濟、社會等)及全球氣候[28]。

三、酸雨之危害[29]

pH值是用來表示溶液酸鹼度之指標,水的酸鹼度介於0及14之間,pH值每下降一單位,酸度就增加十倍,下降二單位,酸度就增加百倍,依此類推;例如pH5之酸度是pH7的100倍。

水一般來說是中性的,亦即pH值為7;但未受污染的正常雨水,本身則是微酸性的,其pH值大約是5.6。因為大氣中所含之二氧化碳有一部分會溶解在雨水中,而形成酸性的碳酸,所以pH值會下降而使雨水略帶酸性,如果雨水pH值小於5.6,我們就稱為「酸雨」(Acid Rain)或「酸沈降」(Acid Deposition)。

自然界因為地形、地質及土壤之差異,常會影響雨水的酸鹼度,使雨水的自然背景pH值常介於4.9~6.5之間,例如風吹塵土會使雨水變鹼,而沼澤及火山氣體使雨水變酸;因此,有些報告認為,在考慮自然的條件下,在大氣清潔的場所,所測得的雨水pH值是5.0,而以pH5.0作為酸雨的臨界值,低於此值才稱為「酸雨」。

酸雨形成的原因,主要是酸性物質和雨水作用的結果,而這些物質部分為自然產生,部分為人為產生。前者如火山爆發噴出的硫化物、水域排放的硫化氫及動植物分解產生的有機酸等;後者則由硫氧化物、氮氧化物經大氣的光化學反應而產生硫酸、硝酸。硫氧化物主要來源是工廠、火力發電廠燃燒煤炭、石油等石化燃料,或工業製程中所排放出來的物質。氮氧化物是高溫燃燒所排放之物質,如汽車之排氣及鍋爐和燃燒爐燃料的高溫燃燒;大都會區人口集中經濟活動頻繁,氮氧化物主要來源則是汽車內燃機燃燒排放之廢氣。

---

[28] 同前註,第280頁。
[29] 同前註,第284頁,節錄。

　　這些硫氧化物及氮氧化物排放到大氣中，隨著大氣的流動而擴散，加上陽光之照射，水分和氧氣之交互作用，產生硫酸鹽及硝酸鹽等酸性粒子，最後以濕的形式（酸雨）或乾的形式（固體顆粒）下降至地表。這些物質常會隨著氣流，飄離原來發生地約500至1,000公里處，才形成酸雨，因而成為全球性之環境生態問題。

　　雨水的酸鹼度常受到許多因素的影響，如人為或自然之排放源、大氣中之化學物質以及氣象條件等；因此，各地區雨水之pH值常會不同，有時甚至同一地點不同時間之降水，其pH值也常不同。

　　而酸雨對全球環境之影響，大致上有下列四方面[30]：

（一）對湖泊之影響

　　酸雨會降低湖水之pH值，溶解湖底之有害金屬如鋁，會阻塞魚貝類之鰓而導致魚貝類之死亡，殺死水生植物及微生物，破壞生態系，使湖泊變成「死湖」。

（二）對森林之影響

　　酸雨降落到森林中，不但會造成土壤之酸化，溶解出有毒的鋁離子，殺死土壤微生物，降低植物根部的吸收能力，也會阻礙樹葉的新陳代謝，抑制樹木之生長，造成「森林死亡」。

（三）對材料之影響

　　酸雨會腐蝕大理石和金屬，所以建築物如住宅和橋樑等，都會受到酸雨之侵蝕；許多具有歷史價值之古蹟、石刻雕像等以及汽車，都會因酸雨而剝落銹蝕。

（四）對人類健康之影響

　　酸雨直接可以引起人們眼睛、皮膚之疼痛，除此之外，多為間接之影

---

[30] 同前註，第286頁。

響。酸化的土壤會使水中或食物鏈中溶入更多的有毒金屬,人吃了之後會聚積在體內,對人體健康造成危害。

四、熱帶雨林之破壞與減少[31]

森林生態系統孕育及維持全世界陸地上80%的生物多樣性,同時提供木材與生質能源。然而,全世界的森林正受到無法控制的退化和任意改作其他土地用途的威脅。根據評估,目前僅剩下約五分之一的原始森林還未遭到破壞。此外,森林消失最快的地方係在孕育生物種類最多的熱帶地區,自從1960年以後,約有五分之一的熱帶森林已經不見了。

另外,熱帶地區因為局部的自然條件有所不同,也會有不同型態的森林出現。例如生長在高山的山岳林、生長在濕地的濕地林、生長在特殊母岩的石南林,以及生長在潮間帶的紅樹林等。

熱帶林分布於中南美洲、非洲及東南亞。熱帶林若區分成密林和疏林,其中密林以亞洲為最高,非洲較低。此外,熱帶雨林則集中在南美洲的亞馬遜河流域、非洲的剛果河流域,以及東南亞各島嶼等赤道區及南北緯十度之間。

熱帶林面積減少之直接原因,是因為人口增加而國家貧窮,使得森林過度的火耕,將森林地轉為農地,或是過度放牧、濫伐薪柴和用材,以及森林大火等所造成的,在這些直接原因中,以火耕所占的比例最高達45%,此外,還有移居遷入等問題。開發中國家多以薪柴當燃料,約占所有燃料的80%;用材之砍伐,都是一些特定林木,但林道的開闢以及伐木量較多時,也會影響周遭之林木。除此之外,一些間接的因素,如空氣污染和酸雨等也會使熱帶林的面積日益減少。

地球上的生質,有一半是來自熱帶林,從當中可獲取各種資源,包括薪柴、食品以及工業原料等。熱帶林最大的功能是孕育生物,保護及調節地球生態環境;尤其是熱帶雨林在地球上具有最多物種的一個生態系,雖

---

[31] 同前註,第287頁至288頁,節錄。

然其面積只占地球陸地面積的6%，但卻有一半以上的地球生物生長在這裡。

　　熱帶林因物極豐沛，可當成生物之「基因庫」，在醫藥的開發以及農作物的品種改良上幫助很大。熱帶林因本身具備多樣性，因此人們會依不同地區和民族特性，孕育出特殊的森林文化。

　　大片的森林，由於光合作用的結果，吸收二氧化碳放出氧氣，可調節大氣中的溫室氣體二氧化碳之濃度，使其維持恆定，避免地球氣溫上升造成危害。同時森林可以減低風速並減少風害，增高大氣的濕度，又能潔淨空氣。

　　森林因為空氣清潔、場地幽靜、無強烈的氣候變化並有多樣性的動植物，對於尋求休憩的人們，是一處很理想的地方，因此森林又具有遊樂之功能。

　　在熱帶雨林中，有90%的土壤養分被植物所吸收截留，具有水土保持及防洪之功效，如果熱帶雨林遭受破壞而減少，那麼這些土地就會變得貧瘠且復原不易，一旦下雨則會引爆洪患，並且也使得燃料供應有短缺現象，嚴重影響居民的生活，也會使固有的森林文化喪失。同時熱帶林減少會使棲息於其中之動植物滅絕，危及人類和其他生物之生存，生物多樣性之基因庫也將會永久消失，影響爾後生物適應地球環境大變遷之能力。熱帶林減少，大氣中之二氧化碳濃度會增加，使地球溫室效應擴大而影響到全球或局部氣候之變遷，進而使農業生產降低。景觀少了森林，風容易形成，加速土壤水分之蒸發及土壤侵蝕作用。

五、土地之過度利用及沙漠化[32]

　　原本是農地或草地等可供耕種與放牧之土地，逐漸使生物生產力減退乃至破壞最後變成無法利用之沙漠，這種情形稱為「土地沙漠化」（Desertification）。其中以非洲地區最為嚴重，地球上之沙漠地區有347,500萬

---

[32] 同前註，第291頁至292頁，節錄。

公頃，每年以600萬公頃的面積在增加（約為台灣面積的1.67倍），光是非洲的撒哈拉沙漠，每年往南擴大約150萬公頃，若不及早阻止，後果將不堪設想。

造成沙漠化的原因可略分為三：一是氣候因素，二是人為因素，三是二次人為因素。氣候因素是因為地球大氣循環產生變化，使得氣流下降或降雨量及水源減少，造成持續乾旱的現象而引起土地沙漠化。人為因素是因為人類在乾燥及半乾燥地區等脆弱生態系中，進行超限的活動，如過度放牧（即家畜放牧超出草地再生能力）、過度耕作（休耕期短所引起的地力耗損）、過度伐木等，因而導致的沙漠化。這個主要是源於人口增加及經濟貧困等社會、人文以及經濟上的因素。二次人為因素是因為耕地灌溉所引起的問題。如灌溉水含鹽分高會使農地有鹽化現象；又如灌溉過剩，會使渠道漏水，造成地下水位上升；在土地基礎脆弱的乾燥地區進行耕作，容易導致風蝕、水蝕和土蝕，加速土地之沙漠化。

由於開發中國家最常用的能源是木材，一旦發生沙漠化，林地就會減少，木材取得不足，將會造成周邊居民生活上發生困難。此種狀況在乾燥、半乾燥地區尤其顯著。而且情況還在繼續惡化中。

另外還有一種說法，就是持續進行中的沙漠化作用，將導致乾燥地區繼續擴大，乾燥情況也會加劇，目前地球上大約有三分之一的陸地是屬於通稱乾燥區或半乾燥區。如此一來，沙漠化將更加惡化，我們可利用的土地資源就會愈來愈少，因而造成各種嚴重的影響，如糧食生產不足等，也會因糧食不足而衍生其他問題。

如果把沙漠化地區和非洲嚴重缺糧的國家做一比較，可發現其間有許多相似的地方，可見沙漠化是如何影響糧食之生產。在沙漠化地區的人民，經常發生飢餓、營養不良等問題。

沙漠化之結果，將使該地區以前所形成的農業、水利、能源等體系完全崩潰，進而嚴重影響糧食之生產與人類之生活。

土地沙漠化長期來看，會導致氣候變化和植被減少，使得二氧化碳濃度增加，溫室效應加劇。

六、野生動植物之瀕臨絕種[33]

大約三、四十億年以前,簡單的生命就在地球上誕生,由於經年累月的進化過程,才有今日地球上所看到的形形色色的生物,這些生物小至土壤微生物、水中的浮游生物,大至陸地大象、海中鯨魚。後來由於氣候之變化和其他環境因素之影響,加上生物個體間的生存競爭,而有自然淘汰發生,此時能夠適應環境的生物才能生存下來,否則就有絕跡滅種之虞。

在這種自然演化的過程中,生物的滅絕是必然的,而且也持續不斷地進行著;但現在野生動植物快速絕跡的現象,並非是這種自然演化過程所造成的,而是人類行為所導致的結果。所以目前生物之絕種與過去最大的區別有三:(一)目前之生物絕種肇因於人;(二)發生的時間很短,只有數十年;(三)植物絕種之速率與動物一樣快。

地球上之物種究竟有多少呢?有人說是150～160萬種,有些專家估計約有500～1,000萬種,也有估計超過3,000萬種。這些生物的分布情形,根據國際自然保護聯盟(International Union for Conservation of Nature, IUCN)之估計,物種以熱帶地區的74～86%為最高,其中的熱帶雨林面積只占地球陸地的6%,物種卻占40%以上;其次,才是溫帶地區約占13～24%;最少的是寒帶地區只占1～2%。

根據國際自然保護聯盟的報告,發現野生動植物絕種的原因有六點,依其重要性來分,依序是:[34]

(一)生態環境破壞及惡化

在生態環境破壞及惡化方面,以生物量豐富的熱帶雨林、濕地、珊瑚礁、島嶼等之破壞最為嚴重,野生生物棲息地之破壞,是造成這些生物被毀滅的主要原因,而罪魁禍首居然是具有高度文明的人類。

---

[33] 同前註,第294頁至295頁,節錄。
[34] 同前註,第296頁。

（二）大肆捕獲

捕殺動物販賣皮毛或其他具有商業價值的部位，而獲取商業利益，有些是合法捕獵，有些則是盜獵，因此許多動物瀕臨滅絕，如美洲虎、印度豹、孟加拉虎、大象及犀牛等。許多植物也同樣面臨絕種之危機，如蘭花因價格昂貴，盜採者為了私利，從野外大量採集，造成蘭花面臨絕種危機。

（三）外來物種之影響

當人們到世界各地旅遊，經常有意或無意地將某些植物和動物，從甲地帶到乙地；有益方面，可作為食物、觀賞、生物控制等；有害方面，外來物種在新環境中因為沒有掠奪者與競爭者，使得它們得以支配新的生態系，而造成當地生物族群之滅絕。

（四）食物不足

當地自然環境不適於耕作或畜牧，為了生活而捕食當地之野生動植物。

（五）因危害作物及家畜而遭殺害

將那些與人類競爭食物和空間的生物清除或撲殺，也會造成生物之絕種。非洲象大肆捕殺，只因其危及作物，其他如美國的卡羅萊納州鸚鵡、猶他犬鼠、野狼等。

（六）偶然捕獲

此種偶然情形的發生，是難以避免的；所幸，所占之比例相當地低。

野生動植物對人類來說，絕對不可或缺，因為它牠們至少具有四大功用如下[35]：

1.是人類生存之必需品

可作為食物、衣料、燃料、醫藥、飾品等之原料。今日之糧食作物有90%是由野生種培育而來；植物纖維及動物皮毛可做成衣料；世界75%的人是以植物作為其藥品之來源，而美國用藥主成分中來自於動植物的占了41%；木雕藝術品及動物皮毛等亦可做成裝飾品。

2.可提供人類觀光休閒，增加生活情趣

如狩獵、觀賞、拍照、垂釣等可由野生動植物提供。另據一位野生生物經濟學者指出在肯亞一頭活獅子每年可從觀光客賺取大約7萬美元的消費額，但若將其殺死，則獅皮只值1,000美元，加上獅肉等也不過3,000美元，因此野生動植物對開發中國家相當重要。

3.可維持自然生態系之平衡

野生植物在生物鏈中扮演生產者，是人類及其他生物之食物來源，而土壤中之動物及微生物則為分解者，分解動物屍骸及植物落葉等，對營養素如氮、磷、鉀之循環有直接之貢獻。

4.具備倫理學上之重要性，可教育人類對生命之尊重

前三項功用多以人為中心（Human-centered）的資源觀念出發；長此以往，野生動植物消失的速率就會很快。因此只有對生命加以尊重，尊重每一種生物的生存權，不論任何動植物都有平等的生存競爭權，對於不同種之野生動植物，人類不可強加定義其在倫理學上之特性，分別其中之尊卑貴賤，這就是以生命為中心（Life-centered）的觀念。

野生動植物之保護，不應該以對人類有用或有害的基礎觀點出發，而

---

[35] 同前註，第295頁。

應聯想到每種生物都歷經長時間的演化而來，在生態系中均有其地位，複雜多樣的生態系，才是一個穩定的生態系，且不可以人為的力量，去滅絕其他動植物，否則終將造成地球的浩劫。

國際間亦對野生動植物之滅絕問題感到重視，並深刻體認唯有透過國際間各國政府的合作，共同致力降低所有有關加速動植物種滅絕之原因。因此乃有1973年「瀕臨絕種野生動植物國際貿易公約」（Convention on International Trade in Endangered Species of Wild Fauna and Flora, CITES）（簡稱華盛頓公約）之出現。其目標就是要以管制國際間野生動植物貿易為手段，來達成保護稀有或瀕臨絕種動植物的目的。

七、生物多樣性之保存

（一）生物多樣性保育之重要性[36]

「生物多樣性」（Biological Diversity，有時可簡寫為Biodiversity）可簡單解釋為「生物之間的多樣性和變異性及物種生境的生態複雜性」。

生物多樣性包括植物、動物和微生物的所有種類和生態系統，以及物種所在的生態系統中的生態過程；也即是說，它把生態系統、物種或基因的數量和頻度這兩方面包含在一個組合之內。我們也可將生物多樣性區分成三個層次：即遺傳多樣性（Genetic Diversity）、物種多樣性（Species diversity）和生態多樣性（Ecosystem Diversity）。遺傳多樣性是指遺傳信息的總和，包括在棲居於地球的植物、動物和微生物個體內的基因，也即是所有生物體中遺傳物質DNA和RNA中所攜帶之所有密碼。物種多樣性是指地球上生命有機體的多樣性，估計地球上約有500～5,000萬種之間，但實際描述者約140萬種。生態系多樣性則與生物圈中的生物群落和生態過程等的多樣化有關。

一個健康的生態環境，應該是資源豐富，而孕育出各式各樣的生物。不但種類眾多，而且所保留在細胞內遺傳基因之變異潛能亦高，不論其變

---

[36] 同前註，第311頁。

異結果是優是劣，也即是其演化及突變能力相當旺盛。同時在其生態環境中，其生態過程例如群眾、物質循環、對環境因子的反應、遷徙、消長等生態現象都是多樣化，表現出生物多樣性的優美景象。然而，環境因污染或開發而受破壞，漸漸生物物種無法生存而減少，同種之稀少幾類或許個體數雖增加，但眾多種類的美景絕然消失，同時也使得遺傳單純化以及生態現象寂靜化，可見生物多樣性對環境生態之重要性。

（二）生物多樣性保育之狀況[37]

「生物多樣性」（Biodiversity）是指地球上存在難以計算的動植物種。無論就全球、區域與地區生態系統而言，多樣性是個普遍現象。生物學者相信，截至目前為止，他們已經為140萬個物種做好命名工作，然而，這些只占全球物種的一小部分。大多數微生物至今尚未被發現和命名。像人類這樣的物種分布在世界各個角落，有些物種只生存在特定地區。

　　由於人類對生態系統的破壞，許多生物已經遭到絕種命運，與此同時，還有許多生物受到絕種的威脅。已經絕種的生物無法復育，造成這些生物絕種的原因包括過度捕撈以及外來物種入侵，就後者而言，當地生物的生存空間會被奪走，終於步上絕種道路。棲息地的喪失（loss of habitat）是導致生物絕種最重要的一項因素，這其中牽涉到的現象包括雨林濫伐、湖泊溪流遭到污染，以及可耕地面積因為都會地區發展而縮減。生態系統平衡繫於不同生物間的複雜互動關係，這樣的平衡既微妙又脆弱。若干生物絕種往往導致環境的重大變化。例如，微生物的絕種可能降低土壤生產力、污染河川，甚至將良田變成荒漠。

---

[37] 同前揭註1，第446頁。

（三）保護生物多樣性進展的主要障礙

影響保護生物多樣性獲得較大進展的六種主要障礙為[38]：

1.國家發展目標忽視了自然資源的價值

生物多樣性是維持國家整體財富所必需的，但是它很少被考慮在國家發展政策中。發展政策傾向於賺取收益或外匯，而不是對生物自然資源的長期持續利用。

2.生物自然資源之開發是為了獲取利潤，而非為了滿足人民合法的需要

比如非洲犀牛或熱帶森林的情況，實際上對當地人民並未帶來利益。

3.對人類生存所依賴的物種和生態系統仍然知道很少

目前相關的專家人數不足，對於物種和生態系統無法充分了解，但仍努力應用既有的技能去作出有關生物資源持續利用的工作上。世界上的科學家和技術人員僅有6%生活在熱帶國家，這些國家幾乎沒有足夠的研究能力去闡明當前的自然保護需要。

4.可用的科學未能充分應用於管理上

近幾十年來進行的許多科學研究已經為管理資源提供了一極好的基礎，但仍需要將生物和社會科學應用到管理物種和生態系統中。

5.大多數組織從事的保護活動範圍太狹窄

大多數自然保護的努力僅致力於少量的物種，比如哺乳類、鳥類、植物等，但不是整個生物多樣性。除了注意物種的保護外，還要研究導致生物資源非持續利用的人類行為方面的原因。

6.委以保護生物多樣性責任的機構缺乏足夠財力、物力

在多數國家這些機構資金很少，沒有充分的發展機會，缺乏專業化訓練，並且威望不高，因此造成保護工作的最大障礙。

---

[38] 同前揭註19，第329頁。

（四）全球保護生物多樣性之推動[39]

　　早在1970年代，生物學家已經向決策者和一般大眾發出生物多樣性快速消失的警訊，世界資源研究所也指出全球熱帶雨林在1960～1990年間已消失了五分之一，而聯合國糧農組織更指出全世界75%左右的作物品系已經滅絕，且每年約有50,000個品系消失。這些訊息確實讓全世界各國感到震驚，聯合國因此積極地尋求解決對策，更扮演了整合及推動之角色。

　　1972年在瑞典首都斯德哥爾摩舉行的「聯合國人類環境大會」（United Nations Conference on Humam Environment）中，已將生物多樣性議題列為重點。翌年「聯合國環境規畫署」（UNEP）在其指導委員會第一屆會議上也把「自然、野生動物和遺傳資源的保育」列為重點，而在1970年代紛紛成立的生態保育公約亦均與生物多樣性保育有關。由於眾多的保育公約先後出籠，許多國際專家開始提出締訂有關全球生物多樣性國際公約的構想，而在1984～1987年間「世界保育聯盟」（International Union for Conservation of Nature, IUCN）亦積極草擬相關之保育公約，間接為往後世界性公約之形成有催生的作用。直到1987年，聯合國環境規畫署意識到經過多年的努力，生物多樣性的消失不但沒有減緩，而且每況愈下，保育行動迫在眉睫，乃成立了「專家工作小組」（ad hoc working group）來調查是否有必要形成一個大公約，涵蓋當時及未來所有的生態保育公約。該小組終於在1990年達成共識：在既有公約之上建立一個新綱要公約，以保護全球生物多樣性。

　　聯合國經過一段努力的協商及籌畫，終於在1992年6月5日巴西里約熱內盧舉行的「聯合國環境及開發大會」（United Nations Coference on Environment and Development），亦即「世界高峰會議」（World Summit）期間通過「生物多樣性公約」（Convention on Biological Diversity），並開啟各國簽署。該公約亦在1993年12月29日正式生效。

---

[39] 同前註，第330頁。

第四章　國際環境法之歷史發展

壹、歷史發展之軌跡

　　人類社會文明演進的軌跡在過去幾千年的發展下來，依稀可以找尋到：在各種不同的文化形成過程之中，存在有某些被寬鬆的定義或形容為與環境問題有關的「法律」。然而，必須要不客氣地指出：一直要到二十世紀才能確切地發現幾乎所有的國際環境法原理——那些有實質效力之核心原理或指導原理，才真正地開始發展。這種現象的發展，在國際社會裡反映出了一個各國所逐漸了解到的認識而自然而然地產生了「共識」（Consensus），那就是：在任何單一國家境內的任一活動，有可能對另外一個國家的環境發生「破壞性的效果」（Detrimental Effects）。各國亦進而認識到有必要去保護它管轄領域以外的地區，例如：月球、極地（Antarctica）以及公海，用以避免任何其他國家行為或活動的「傷害效果」（Harmful Effects）。它也同時反映了國際社會開始去考慮將「環境資源」（Environmental Resources）當作人類利用自然資源的一般準則，要加以管理及保育，這是為了人類社會當前及未來世代的福利之緣故，而不是僅僅把這些資源為了消費及利潤而加以剝削運用；國際社會之環境保護（育）分子更是認知到對於環境[1]的保護與保育，應該是為了保護（育）環境的本身，而不是有其他的想法。除此之外，一個現象讓環境保護的問題處理從單一的單元如空氣、水、土地，擴大到一個複雜的「生態系」（Ecosystem）之「環境整體」（Environment As a Whole）去加以面對。到了二十一世紀的今天，很清楚地發現國際環境法有必要去處理與「永續發展原理」，彼此之間的共續共榮的關係。

---

[1] Sam Blay, Ryszard Piotrowicz and B. Martin Tsamenyi eds., Public International Law (Oxford, Oxford University Press, 1997), p. 357.

　　所以國際環境法之能夠發展到今天的追求「永續發展」的最後總目標，是全人類社會進步的經驗軌跡所累積出來的「成果」。這樣的發展歷史之組成，從關心環境保護議題的法界人士的檢視，大概可以從具有「里程碑」（Milestone）意義的「畫時代」（Landmark）貢獻的三大國際性有關環境保護與發展議題之會議。此三大國際性會議乃是指：「1972年聯合國人類環境會議」（1972 United Nations Conferences on the Human and Environment），又被稱為「斯德哥爾摩會議」（Stockholm Conference）、「1992年聯合國環境與發展會議」（1992 United Nations Conference on Environment and Development），又被稱為「里約會議」（Rio Conference）或「地球高峰會」（Earth Summit），以及「2002年聯合國永續發展世界高峰會」（2002 United Nations World Summit on Sustainable Development, WSSD），又被稱為「約翰尼斯堡高峰會」（Johannesburg Summit）。

　　本章之結構將依「年序」（Chronological）及「地理政治」（Geopolitical）之背景，來說明國際環境問題在聯合國的主導下，各次國際會議之召開及成果。之所以會作這樣的安排，乃是因為國際環境法之形成及政策之主導，有很大的一部分，受到各國所在地的政治因素所影響。具體而言，就「全球的階層」（Global Level）來檢視，在工業國家與發展中國家在發展的「型態」（Pattern）上的主要差別，業已導致了它們這些國家對於處理國際環境問題，在作法上有極大的差異。平心靜氣而論，會有這樣的差異出現，亦有其可以理解的理由存在。工業化的國家像美國、日本、前蘇聯、澳洲、紐西蘭及加拿大等國家，因為科技進步發展的優異，它們國家所追求的是生活品質的提升。這些國家雖然並非全部在北半球；但是二十世紀末以來，一般習慣稱它們為「北方」（North）；而另外的其他「發展中國家」（Developing Countries）則因為多數在南半球，而被稱為「南方」（South）。在全球環境問題的處理上，「南北分裂」（North-South Split）早就是一個事實上存在的問題。北方各國分享著許多共同的性質，例如：比較先進、國家比較富裕，同時享有比較高水準之經濟發展。更重要的是它們在國際社會中是自然資源的主要消費者以及主要的污染者。就這些原因以及這些國家在國際事務上，一般而言，比較有力量，

對於全球環境議題之列入國際議程上，具有特別不成比例的影響力。

　　相對而言，所謂的「南方」，那些「發展中國家」從經濟的角度來檢視，則比「北方」來得貧窮，這些國家中，有許多的人口，且多半居於「窮困」的地位，特別顯著的現象是多半為「文盲」（Illiteracy）、低的（生活期待）（Life Expectancies）、不時會有「飢荒瘟疫」（Famine Plague）的出現。這些情形都不是「北方」國家能夠想像的。然而從另外的一個層面來檢視「南方」這些國家，它們又擁有了「世界財富」（World Wealthy）的絕大部分，例如：最大的熱帶森林、大多數的世界生物多樣性、以及最具價值的礦物質…不勝枚舉。而自二十世紀80年代以來，它們當中的許多國家（至少在非洲地區以外的國家）很迅速地朝工業化的方向去發展；在此同時，這些國家也開始首次發現，必須要面對嚴重的環境污染的問題。水的缺乏及遭受污染的水源，充斥在南方各大城市。也有更多的城市感受到空氣之污染。很明顯的可以發現北京、曼谷、墨西哥城、開羅及聖地牙哥，這些城市的空氣污染均是相當地嚴重。

　　「北方」與「南方」兩相對照之下，在國際環境問題的談判上，雙方立場的對立，就相當地鮮明。「北方」迫切的需要解決全球環境問題，則遇上了南方迫切地去引導全球的經濟發展，來解決或克服「貧窮的循環」（Cycle of Poverty）問題。對某些「南方」國家而言，追求環境保護，是個相當奢侈的工作。就這些南方國家而言，它們質疑環境保護或自然資源的利用問題，應在國際的層級。而南方國家的首要工作應該是放在經濟發展上面。大致上而言，多數的「南方」國家相信經由「環境協議的簽訂」來取得全球性的環境保護標準的一致性，會必然地減緩它們的經濟發展，而且會毫無理由地降低了它們的「經濟成長」（Economic Growth）。其中更有一些國家認為「北方」的環境問題的處理方式與理念，更是對「南方」國家「主權」的攻擊，目的是在掌控「南方」國家脫離了西方殖民時代後的發展的命脈。

　　從以上的「南北分裂」現象，說明了在二十世紀末的一、二十年間，國際環境問題的解決，碰到了「南北差異」的瓶頸問題亟待突破。這就引發了「國際環境外交」（International Environmental Diplomacy）方面

的努力,在1992年的「里約宣言」(Rio Declaration)就提出了「全球夥伴」(Global Partnership)的概念[2];意圖結合「北方」與「南方」在一起,用以達成「永續發展」的目標。此種「合夥」關係的基礎,包括了南北雙方「互相接受」(Mutual Acceptance)環境保護與經濟發展的目標。在這樣共同目標的努力之下,到了2001年「世界觀察學院」(Worldwatch Institute)對於一小群國家及歐洲聯盟的總共九名成員給予一個「E-9」的稱號[3];針對全球環境問題的處理,占有愈來愈重要的地位。此「E-9」包括:歐洲聯盟、南非、日本、印度、印尼、巴西、俄羅斯、德國、美國及中國。就是因為「E-9」是國際社會中的環境問題的「重量級」(Heavy-weight)的成員,它們占有了全球資源的絕大部分,也同時製造了相當比例的污染。它們因此被期待對於全球環境問題要負上相當程度的「責任」,來因應全球環境問題的需求。

貳、國際環境法各階段之發展

一、成長背景

經過幾個世紀以來的演進,在國際社會當中的各種不同的文化之下,某些法律或多或少的被寬鬆的定義成「環境法」;不論它是各個主權國家或區域組織所涉及到的環境相關性的規範,很容易的在一定的「範圍」(Ambit)之內,就會被「描述」(Describe)為環境法規範。然而,不客氣的來說,國際環境法的成長是要一直等到二十世紀,它的原理及運作,成為至今成為國際環境法的主要核心,才開始發展出來。就如同國際人權的發展一樣,國際環境法的主要發展,還是在過去的半個世紀之光景。隨著傳統國際法注意到了各國,對於國際義務之未能充分履行,或根本違反

---

[2] David Hunter, James Salzman and Durwood Zaelke, International Environmental Law and Policy (N.Y.: Foundation Press, 2007), p. 164.

[3] 同前註。

了各國在國際法上所應該履行之義務時，各該國家所應擔負起來的國際責任之意識高漲之下的潮流趨勢之下，也影響到了國際環境法的發展。這樣的發展反映出了國際社會中的主權國家，及相關國際組織或區域組織，逐漸地了解到任何單一國家的活動，有傷害到或「不利於」（Detrimental）另外的或其他的國家之環境。這樣的「活動」就應該要受到某些程度的拘束或限制；同時，國際社會的成員也理解到每一個國家的「活動」，必須要保護到它管轄領域之外，如月球、極地及公海之環境，避免受到「傷害」。這樣的情形也反映出了國際社會的主流思考方向，為了當下及未來世代「利益」或福利之考量，每一個單一主權國家在把環境因素，當作各國「資源」（Resources）來運用時，必須要好好地加以「管理」（Managed）及「保育」（Conserved）；而不是簡單地把「資源」加以「剝削」（Exploited）或是獲利而已。不僅如此，各國對於環境保護的課題，已經跳脫了以往為了其他的原因或因素，而是直接的為了環境保護的本身緣故，而必須做好環境保護的工作。在此新世紀起始之際，國際環境法的發展已經注意到了「永續發展」的人類全體的共同利益。

二、1972年之前

國際環境法早年的發展，大致上均被「定性」（Characterized）為條約，而不是習慣或判例。The Trail Smelter、Corfu Channel，以及Lac Lannoux案例，建立了國際環境法的「一般原則」（General Principle）。那就是各國的「活動」（Activity），不得傷害到其他國家的「環境」，以及各國不得允許讓本身之領域，被使用來作出「環境傷害」（Environmental Harms）的事情。然而，在欠缺由習慣及判例賦予比較更精確而明白的環境保護規範的定義之下，環境保護的「國際規範」（International Norm）經由「條約」的方式，來加以發展，則是一種不錯的管道；至少它能幫助國際社會列舉出哪些是各國在國際環境法規範下，所應該履行的國際義務；同時也能夠對於比較廣泛的「習慣法則」（Customary Rules）給予特

定的內容[4]。

　　再仔細的檢視早期的國際環境法之發展，大致上仍然是透過上百個雙邊條約及多邊條約的簽訂，來拘束各簽約國的「活動」。而且再就條約的規範性質來分析，不難發現牽涉到各國之間的相關「環境資源」的利用及享有的問題，或是特別的「環境權利」的主張，更是受到當時各國的重視。舉例而言，「國際水道」（International Watercourse）之使用即是二十世紀初期，受到當時各海洋國家相當程度的重視。1909年英國（代表加拿大）與美國之間的「邊界水域條約」（Boundary Waters Treaty）就明文規定了邊界水域，不應被污染。此乃源起於承認各國有需要以「合作」的方式，來使用「分享的資源」（Shared Resource）以及著重於對「資源使用」（Resource Use）及「資源分配」（Resource Allocation）的規範之訂定[5]。

　　關於「保育」（Conservation）並沒有把它當作僅是一個概念而加以忽視。然而，早年關於保育的問題，大致上均被當作是「資源管理」（Resource Management）的一環來加以「定義」，用以求取「最大量的使用」（Maximization of Use），而不是從「預作保育」（Preservation）的角度來加以「界定」。因此，以1946年的「有關捕鯨規範之國際公約」（International Convention for the Regulation of Whaling）就明白規定：為了使得鯨魚工業有秩序的發展成為可能之事，對於鯨魚量要做適當的保育。

　　因為科技發展的進步之結果，使得各國也開始注意到了對本國領域內及領域內的資源的保護與海洋污染的防制，均有了初步的「共識」。此一時期國際環境法規範之建制如表4-1。

---

[4]　Sam Blay et al., Public International Law (Melbourne: Oxford University Press, 1997), p. 357.
[5]　同前註。

表4-1

年　份	重點說明
1900	簽署第一個保護瀕臨絕種動物的多邊條約 此條約為當時歐洲殖民強權國家為保護非洲大陸殖民地區的野生物種所簽定的國際性法律文件。
1909	《國際邊境水域條約》（International Boundary Waters Treaty） 美、英兩國自1909年起簽訂此條約，樹立規範並防止污染。該條約執行成效良好，是成功的國際環境合作案例。
1933	《保護自然狀態下之動植物公約》（London Convention on the Preservation and Protection of Fauna and Flora in Their Natural State） 鑑於人類狩獵活動威脅野生動植物的數量，本公約對國家公園及保留區內狩獵及採集訂定行為規範，以保護自然狀態下的動植物。惟該公約保護範圍僅限於國家公園及保留區，簽約國也僅包括美、英等30個國家。
1940	《西半球自然及野生物種保護暨保育公約》（Washington Convention on Nature Protection and Wildlife Preservation in the Western Hemisphere） 1942年5月1日生效 主要締約國為美國和其他西半球國家，希望保護和保存國土範圍內所有種類的當地植物與動物及其自然生態環境。並使動植物的數量保持一定水準，承諾在人為可控制的範圍內，免於瀕臨絕種。
1946	《有關捕鯨規範之國際公約》（International Convention for the Regulation of Whaling） 本公約的宗旨和任務是，調查鯨魚的數量，制定捕撈和保護太平洋海域中鯨魚數量的措施，如確定應予保護之品種、開放期和禁捕期、禁捕水域、捕鯨時間和合法之工具等，並同時對捕鯨業進行嚴格的國際監督。公約中另設有一個國際捕鯨委員會，作為國際捕鯨管理機構，委員會的主要職責為監督評估世界各國捕獲鯨魚之數量及種類，是否合於公約之有關規定，同時嚴格禁止捕捉尚未斷乳的幼鯨及陪同幼鯨的母鯨。
1948	國際海事組織（International Maritime Organization, IMO） 是聯合國負責海上航行安全和防止船舶造成海洋污染的一個專門機構，原名「政府間海事協商組織」，1982年改為現名，目前有172個正式成員。宗旨為促進航運技術合作，維護海上安全，提高船隻航行效率，以及防止和控制船舶對海洋的污染。

年　份	重點說明
1948	世界自然保育聯盟（International Union for Conservation of Nature, IUCN） 影響、鼓勵及協助全球各地的社會，保育自然的完整性與多樣性，並確保任何利用自然資源行為之公平性，及生態上的可持續發展。1999年，聯合國授與世界自然保育聯盟聯合國大會觀察員的地位。而在2001至2004年，IUCN的主要任務為，建立起「貧窮人民的生計有賴於自然資源永續管理」的認知。
1950	世界氣象組織（World Meteorological Organization, WMO） 前身為國際氣象組織，1947年在華盛頓舉行的45國氣象局局長會議決定改為政府間機構，即今日的世界氣象組織。其宗旨是促進觀測天氣的國際合作及資訊交換，促進觀測的標準化及氣象應用於農業、航空、航海等活動，以促進水文與氣象之密切合作和加強相關領域的研究。1951年12月20日成為聯合國的專門機構。
	《國際鳥類保育公約》（International Convention for the Protection of Birds） 鑑於某些鳥類（包括遷徙性鳥類）的生存和數量受到日益嚴重的威脅與滅絕的危險，本公約將這些鳥類在符合科學研究、自然保護和國家經濟的前提和原則下加以保護。
1954	《防治海洋油污染公約》（International Convention for the Prevention of Pollution of the Sea by Oil） 1958年生效。 第一個防止海洋和沿海環境污染的國際公約，國際海事組織從1959年起負責該公約的執行。
1957	國際原子能總署（International Atomic Energy Agency, IAEA） 旨在促進會員國政府間核能科技之和平應用與交流合作。
1961	世界自然基金會（World Wide Fund, WWF） 1961年7月，有16位專家學者集中於瑞士，發表The Morges Manifesto宣言。同年9月11日，正式成立WWF。以貓熊標誌為基金會的象徵，較重視野生動物物種保育，今日則著重整體的生態保育。是目前全球最大的獨立環保機構，亦為目前最具規模的國際非政府間組織之一。

年　份	重點說明
1963	《保護萊茵河免於污染協定》（Agreement Concerning the International Commission for Protection of the Rhine against Pollution）萊茵河流域內國家因彼此經濟發展程度不一，遂於1950年成立萊茵河保護國際委員會（IKSR），旨在全面處理萊茵河流域保護問題，並尋求解決方案。後來逐漸發展成為流域有關國家部長參加的國際協調組織，並於1963年簽署具有法律效力的防制污染協定，奠定此流域日後管理的法律性基礎。

※資料來源：參考蔡育岱與熊武合著，國際關係之理論與實際，第184頁至186頁。

三、1972年

　　1972年在國際環境法的發展，有其重大的意義；它註記了國際環境法「軟法機制」（Soft Law Mechanism）的開始建制。例如：聯合國大會的「決議」（Resolution）及國際會議之「宣言」（Declaration）。它的發生，主要的是因為許多「生態災難」（Ecological Disaster）使得各國有心人士，了解到那一類災難所造成的損害，是巨額的花費來救助，同時也是人類福祉的難以求助的損害。因此乃有113國的政府代表以及與會的環境民間人士在瑞典的首都召開了「聯合國人類環境會議」（United Nations Conference on the Human Environment）。會後共同發表了「聯合國人類環境宣言」（Declaration of the United Nations Conference on the Human Environment; so-called Stockholm Declaration）；所謂的斯德哥爾摩宣言。並決定「聯合國環境計畫署」（United Nations Environment Programme, UNEP）之建立。也同時決定每年之6月5日為世界環境日。

　　該宣言乃是人類社會為了尋求共同的人類環境展望，以及制定環境保護之共同原則，用以解決各種不同環境問題之需要，揭示了七點共同看法以及26個關於環境議題不同面相之原則。宣言中除了對全球環境污染的防止有所宣示外，更強調人類享有生存於適當環境之基本權利（所謂的環境權），並有為後代子孫保護環境之責任。宣言中也注意到了對於自然資源的保護，特別是在資源的利用上，必須要注意到損害回復的確保及資源枯

竭的風險問題。宣言中也首次體認到經濟發展為環境保護的重要基礎。認
為各國應針對經濟發展有所規畫,以使資源能獲得更合理之使用。而且宣
言亦確立了各國有開發內國資源的責任,以及確保他國不會因為其開發資
源而受害之義務。另外,各國並應以雙邊或多邊協定等方式達成各國「地
位平等」下之「國際合作」(International Cooperation);同時,已開發
國家應該提供資金及技術移轉,用以協助及促進開發中國家的發展。

　　總括來說,該宣言的畫時代創舉乃是在訂定於意識型態對立的「冷
戰」(Cold War)時期,但是,仍然能提出「國際合作」的想法,要求
「已開發國家」有義務來協助及促進開發中國家的發展,誠屬難能可貴,
相當地具有前瞻性與啟發性。而另一方面的意義則是「斯德哥爾摩宣言」
為人類歷史上第一個關於環境保護的全球性宣言,具有畫時代的意義,突
顯了人類社會對於國際環境問題的覺醒,表彰了國際社會對於國際環境問
題的關切,與務實的面對國際環境問題的決心,殊屬不易。關於1972年所
發生之國際環境規範之進展,可進一步參見表4-2。

表4-2

年　度	重點說明
1972	聯合國於瑞典斯德哥爾摩召開首次全球環境會議——「人類環境會議」(United Nations Conferences on the Human and Environment, Stockholm Conference) 聯合國第一次就環境議題召開的指標性會議。會中討論了保護全球環境的行動計畫,通過《人類環境宣言》。
	發表《人類環境宣言》(Stockholm Declaration) 保護和改善環境關係到全世界各國人民的幸福和經濟發展,也是全世界各國人民的殷切希望和各國政府的責任。為實現此目標,要求公民和團體及企業和各級機關承擔責任,共同努力。
	《防止傾倒垃圾及其他物質污染海洋公約》(Convention on the Prevention of Marine Pollution by Dumping of Waste and Other Matter, London Dumping Convention, LDC) 1975年生效。 第一個以管制海洋傾倒為目的的全球性公約。多數沿岸國家也依據此公約制定了一系列國內法,作為因應的相關法律和制度,以有效規範海洋傾倒的行為。

年　度	重點說明
1972	聯合國環境計畫署（United Nations Environment Programme, UNEP） 為聯合國架構下負責全球環境事務的代表機構，宗旨是促進環境領域的國際合作，並提出政策建議；透過專業環境資訊的提供，協助並激勵各國政府及其人民踐行環境保育，以改善生活品質，切合永續發展。此外，本機構也在聯合國系統下負責指導和協調環境計畫之整合政策，適時發表世界環境狀況之報告。

※資源來源：參考蔡育岱與熊武合著，國際關係之理論與實際，第187頁。

四、1973至1981年

自從斯德哥爾摩宣言發表之後，經由條約（含公約）的方式來發展國際環境保護的規範，仍然不斷地進行中。有不少的區域性及全球性的國際環境保護的「談判」，到最後都順利的完成了條約的簽訂，其中涵蓋了各種環境保護的「類別」（Sector）。它的範圍，大致上有「防止船舶污染國際公約」（International Convention for the Prevention of Pollution from Ships, MARPOL）、「瀕臨絕種野生動植物國際貿易公約」（Convention for International Trade in Endangered Species of Wild Fauna and Flora, CITES）、「地中海污染防治公約」（Convention for the Protection of the Mediterranean Sea Against Pollution）、「聯合國防治沙漠化會議」（UN Conference on Desertification）、「聯合國潛在有毒化學品登記中心」（International Register of Potentially Toxic Chemicals, IRPTC）、「跨國長程空氣污染公約」（Convention on Long-Range Transboundary Air Pollution, LR-TAP）以及「南極海洋生物資源保育公約」（Convention on the Conservation of Antarctic Marine Living Resources）…不勝枚舉。其中仔細的說明，可參考表4-3。

表4-3

年　度	重點說明
1973	《防止船舶污染國際公約》（International Convention for the Prevention of Pollution from Ships, MARPOL） 1975年生效。 是一個防止船舶造成海洋環境污染的綜合公約，本文有20條，另有2個議定書及5個附錄。經1978年議定書修訂後，以消除作業過程中可能排放之石油、化學品或其他有害物質引起的海洋污染為宗旨。並盡可能減少包括固定或浮動的鑽井平台在內的船舶因碰撞或擱淺而意外洩漏的石油污染問題。
	《瀕臨絕種野生動植物國際貿易公約》（Convention for International Trade in Endangered Species of Wild Fauna and Flora, CITES） 1975年生效 鑑於野生動植物貿易對部分野生動植物族群造成直接或間接的威脅，為能永續使用此等自然資源，遂由世界自然保育聯盟（IUCN）領銜，在1963年公開呼籲各國政府正視此一問題，並著手野生物國際貿易管制的工作。公約精神在於管制而非完全禁止野生物種的國際貿易，以物種分級與許可證的方式，達成野生物市場的永續利用。
1976	《地中海污染防治公約》（Convention for the Protection of the Mediterranean Sea Against Pollution） 制定長期整治計畫並建立長期監測制度，締約國同時投入資金進行海上污染調查和整治工程。例如，法國政府將治理地中海沿岸海域列入國土規畫。80年代中期，此海域整治工程成果漸現，生態環境逐漸恢復，漁業產值也逐年上升。
1977	聯合國防治沙漠化會議（UN Conference on Desertification, UNCOD） 沙漠化的概念最早係由法籍研究人士Aubreville在其1949年的研究中所提出，表達一種土壤失去植被（vegetation）的過程。而沙漠化首次被正式應用於國際政治是在1974年聯合國大會29/337號決議中，此項決議係由布幾納法索（Burkina Faso）倡議，並間接促成後來聯合國沙漠化會議（UNCOD）的召開。UNCOD由94個國家與65個非政府間組織（Non-Governmental Organization, NGOs）共同參與，時間從1977年8月29日到9月9日。預期目標是將先前「對抗沙漠化行動計畫」（Plan of Action to Combat Desertification, PACD）的內容加以具體化，使之

年　度	重點說明
1977	成為全球性的抗沙漠化文本，並將之發展成一項國際性的抗沙漠化機制。
	國際潛在有毒化學品登記中心（International Register of Potentially Toxic Chemicals, IRPTC） 由UNEP所設立，依循1972年聯合國人類與環境會議之宗旨，IRPTC的功能在將現有的全球性化學物質資源做更佳利用，並對發展中國家提供化學物質使用資訊和處理化學製品的技術轉移。
1979	《跨國長程空氣污染公約》（Convention on Long-Range Transboundary Air Pollution, LRTAP） 1983年生效 訂定消除空氣污染的合作原則，建立合作研究的架構，另由公約及其八項議定書之締約國間協商具體的施行辦法。公約關於重金屬的議定書於1998年開放簽署（2003年12月生效）；涵蓋公約之下的三種金屬為鎘、鉛和汞。
1980	《南極海洋生物資源保育條約》（Convention on the Conservation of Antarctic Marine Living Resources） 意識到南極海洋生物資源保育之急迫性，以及增加對本區海洋生態系統的認識，能依科學資訊作出漁獲決策的重要性。因此以國際合作方式保育本區海洋生物資源並尊重《南極條約》之條款及由所有在南極水域從事研究或漁獲活動國家之積極參與。

※資料來源：參考蔡育岱與熊武合著，國際關係之理論與實際，第187頁至189頁。

五、1982年

　　1982年國際社會發生了兩件大事。其一是「聯合國海洋法公約」（United Nations Convention on the Law of the Sea）。其二就是「世界自然憲章」（World Charter for Nature）。二者均是在聯合國長期努力之下所完成的結果。首先，就聯合國海洋法公約而言，國際社會自二十世紀中期以來，各個海洋大國為了保護海上礦藏、漁場，並期望能夠控制污染、區分責任歸屬起見，傳統的海洋規範概念，已不足以因應新世紀海洋規範的

需要。國際社會自1930年代以來，即陸續召開相關國際會議，但成效均不彰。只有在聯合國的主導之下，到了1982年，各國代表終於達成共識而決議出一部整合性的「海洋法公約」。其重點乃是在：（一）便利國際交通與促進海洋之和平用途；（二）海洋資源之公平而有效之利用；（三）海洋生物資源之養護；（四）研究、保護和保全海洋環境。其次，再來檢視「世界自然憲章」，回顧人與自然之關係，自產業革命以來，二者之間的關係是益趨緊張。此種關係延續至二十世紀中期以來，在環境保護意識抬頭之下，人類重新思考對待環境的態度，以及人與自然間所應持有之關係，乃有1982年10月28日，聯合國大會通過了A/RES/37/7號決議，頒布了「世界自然憲章」。

「世界自然憲章」之主旨，乃是在為人與自然的關係作出定位，並且明確表明人類對待自然，以及自然資源應有的態度與行為準則。「世界自然憲章」意識到：人類是自然的一部分，每一種生命形式都具獨特性，不論其對人類的價值為何，均值得受到尊重。而且來自然的持久利益，取決於對生態過程與生命支持系統的維護，也同時取決於生命形式的多樣性。在此基調下，「世界自然憲章」之核心目標，乃是在制定保護自然、科學研究、物種與生態之監測與保護系統等國際合作措施。

關於聯合國海洋法公約及世界自然憲章，可參見表4-4。

六、1983至1991年

國際環境法的成長在這段時間大概可以歸納在兩方面：其一，在環境污染的防治方面，特別是在有關「臭氧層」（Ozone Layer）的保護及禁止有害廢棄物之越境運送及處理。其二，乃是本時期表現的最為特殊的一個現象，即是國際社會中的「開發中國家」（Developing States）與「已開發國家」（Developed States）之間，開始了大規模的對於「發展與環境保護」（Development and Environmental Protection）之間的關係，有了不同立場的爭辯。針對這樣的議題，聯合國大會乃在1983年建置了「環境與發展委員會」（United Nations Commission on the Environment and Development, UNCED）來檢視環境與發展之間的嚴重問題。如此才有「我們共同

表4-4

年　度	重點說明
1982	《聯合國海洋法公約》（United Nations Convention on the Law of the Sea） 本公約於1982年12月10日通過，1994年11月16日生效，目前有160個締約方。本公約之目標：1.便利國際交通與促進海洋和平用途；2.海洋資源之公平且有效的利用；3.海洋生物資源之養護；4.研究、保護和保全海洋環境。藉此等目標之達成，用以特別實現公正與公平之國際經濟秩序。
	《世界自然憲章》（World Charter for Nature） 世界自然憲章除序言外，分為「一般原則」、「功能」與「實施」三大部分。在「一般原則」中，規定了人與自然關係的基本立場。包括尊重及保護大自然、重視及保護各種生命形式及生物棲息地。在「功能」部分，指出人類的行為能夠改變自然，也能耗盡自然資源。在「實施」中，「世界自然憲章」要求國家與國家、個人與集體之間，要採取適當措施，以保護自然及促進這方面的國際合作。「世界自然憲章」認識到人類活動必須注意發展與環境的平衡，將環境因素納為一切人為行動之必要考量；同時必須注意到維持自然的穩定性、保護自然的重要性及養護自然的迫切性。

*資料來源：作者自製。

的未來」（Our Common Future）報告（即布倫特雷報告；The Bruntland Report）在1987年被聯合國大會的一致通過。在經濟發展與環境保護之間，列舉了許多精闢的觀點，用以達成「永續發展」（Sustainable Development）的終極目標。本期之發展可參考表4-5。

七、1992年

1992年在國際環境法規範的成長過程中，代表著相當不平凡的一年。1992這個數字可以當作是個「魔術數字」（Magic Number），在這一年裡完成了過去多少年來所期待完成的工作。當然1992年所發生的事情不是一朝一夕的基因突變所產生的結果。它的近因乃是在1989年聯合國大會決

表4-5

年　度	重點說明
1983	《國際熱帶木材協定》（International Tropical Timber Agreement） 1983年11月18日訂於日內瓦，1985年4月1日生效。 以適當而有效保護和發展熱帶木材森林為宗旨，以達成最適度的利用，同時維持有關區域和生物圈的生態平衡。公約另建立一個在生產國和消費國之間的國際合作機制，以求解決熱帶木材市場所面臨的問題。
1985	《維也納保護臭氧公約》（Vienna Convention for the Protection of the Ozone Layer） 又稱《維也納公約》，1985年3月22日訂於維也納，1988年9月22生效。由聯合國環境計畫署協助制定，以鼓勵國家間全面合作從事維護臭氧之研究，以及資訊交換為目標，目前共有191國締約。
1987	《蒙特婁議定書》（Montreal Protocol on Substances That Deplete the Ozone Layer） 於1989年1月1日經29個國家批准後生效，目前共有187國家批准加入。針對氟氯碳化合物（CFCs）與數種海龍（Halons）物質的停用時程，在定期科學與技術評估基礎下得予以調整及修正，並適時調整其他對破壞臭氧層物質的控制措施或增加清冊中的管制物質。
	世界環境與發展委員會（World Commission on Environment and Development）出版報告 1987年聯合國環境與發展世界委員會發表報告，《我們共同的未來》（亦稱《布倫特蘭報告》（The Bruntland Report），根據委員會主席命名），在經濟發展與環境保護之間提出了永續發展的觀點與定義。
1988	政府間氣候變遷小組（Intergovernmental Panel on Climate Change）成立 由聯合國環境計畫署（UNEP）與世界氣象組織（World Meteorological Organization）所共同成立，募集了世界各國在全球暖化與大氣科學研究領域的頂尖學者及專家。這個小組的任務是評估目前氣候變遷的相關科學知識，以及暖化對於環境及社會經濟的潛在衝擊，並負責制定一套處理暖化問題的實用性策略。

年　度	重點說明
1989	《禁止有害廢棄物越境運送及處理的巴塞爾公約》（The Basel Convention on the Control of Transboundary Movements of the Hazardous Wastes and Their Disposal） 1992年生效 於1989年3月22日在聯合國環境計畫署於瑞士巴塞爾召開的世界環境保護會議上通過，1992年5月正式生效。公約中所指之有害廢棄物係一般國際上普遍認為具有爆炸性、易燃性、腐蝕性、化學反應性、毒性和傳染性等特性中一種或幾種特質之事業廢棄物或家用廢棄物，前者包括廢料、廢渣、廢水和廢氣等，後者包括廢紙、廢瓶罐、廢塑膠和廢舊日用品等。《巴塞爾公約》的目的在於有效管理危險廢棄物，避免非法轉移之情事發生，特別是向發展中國家出口和轉移危險廢棄物。

※資料來源：參考蔡育岱與熊武合著，國際關係之理論與實際，第189頁至190頁。

定要在1992年由「聯合國環境與發展委員會」（United Nations Conference on Environment and Development）召開第二次會議，來鼓勵對於國際環境法發展的「追求」（Pursuit）。它的遠因則是要來延續1972年斯德哥爾摩「人類環境宣言」所揭示的「保護與改善環境品質是人類共同的目標」所應繼續實現的理想。其直接的導火線則是尋求滿足「開發中國家」的特定需要。至此，整個國際社會已經意識到：人類生存的環境應是提供人類享受尊嚴與高水準生活的環境，以及維護與改善人類環境是全人類共同的責任。因此，國際環境問題，已經成為跨越國境的人類共同的危機。各國應該加強合作制定國際法中有關一國（及其國民）因他國（或其國民）的行為或不行為，而遭受到污染及其他環境上的損害時，所得主張之賠償的國際規範。

　　1992年6月，來自全球120幾國元首及代表於里約召開的「地球高峰會議」（Earth Summit），將金球環境議題推到國際政治的舞台，也使全球環保邁入一個嶄新的紀元。然而，人類對全球環保的關懷，並不是在1992年才開始，早在1972年聯合國就已於瑞典斯德哥爾摩舉行「聯合國人類環境會議」（The United Nation Conference on the Human Environment），並發布著名的「聯合國人類環境會議宣言」（Declaration of the United Nations Conference on the Human Environment）。要了解當今全球環境議題的形貌與內涵，有必要對這二十年來全球環境影響的形成與演變有所掌握。

　　1992年里約的「地球高峰會議」（Earth Summit），將全球環境議題的發展推向新的里程碑。固然，有了這一次歷史上為環境所作的最大動員，也難得簽署了包括氣候變化綱要公約、生物多樣性公約、里約宣言、森林原則與21世紀議程這五大文件。但從馬來西亞所表彰的亞洲價值，以及號稱國際環保大國的美國在會中立場曖昧猶豫受到各國圍勦，卻也活生生地讓世人看到全球環境問題背後錯綜複雜的利益糾葛，非短時間靠「地球村」（Global Village）、「我們的共同未來」（Our Common Future）這些高度倫理性的呼籲就能解決問題。於是，在一連串有關全球環境的會議、宣言、條約、世界級領袖人物的呼籲，以及環境全球化的趨勢中，世人隱約看到比以前更錯綜難解的衝突。各國政府在認同全球環保的重要性之餘，也往往基於明示的「國情因素」或隱而不宣的「利益衡量」，而躊躇不前。如何在全球環保浪潮中，採取適當的立場與策略，方不致成為國際上譴責或制裁的對象，但同時也不致因一味配合全球趨勢，而抹殺本國特殊政治、經濟與社會條件，已成為各國政府所關注的焦點。在此一背景下，許多國家或跨國企業，紛紛設立專責單位，職司全球環境問題的研究、規畫與因應，消極上用以避免為潮流所左右，積極上則用以利用潮流，創造有利條件。而對全球環境議題形成背景與發展歷程的了解，則成為全球環境所關懷乃至國家政策規畫的基本要件。

　　1992年6月13日「里約環境與發展宣言」，重申了「人類環境宣言」的追求目標，並試圖在其基礎上更推進一步加以闡釋。關於1992年「里約宣言」，21世紀議程（Agenda 21）、聯合國氣候變遷框架（架構）公約、森林原則及聯合國生物多樣性公約等重要規範，可參考表4-6。

表4-6

年　度	重點說明
1992	聯合國環境與發展會議（里約地球高峰會議）（United Nations Conference on Environment and Development, Rio Earth Summit）高峰會確認永續發展之理念（此定義來自1987年《我們共同的未來》報告）「滿足當代的需要，而同時不損及後代子孫滿足其本身需要之發展」（the needs of the present without compromising the ability of future generations to meet their own needs）會議中並通過五項文件：氣候變化綱要公約、生物多樣性公約、森林原則、里約宣言、21世紀議程。
	發表《里約宣言》（Rio Declaration）、《21世紀議程》（Agenda 21）《里約宣言》又稱《地球憲章》（Earth Charter），目標是通過在國家、社會重要部門和人民之間建立新水平的合作，來建立一種新的和公平的全球夥伴關係，發展體系完整的國際協定。各國根據國際法上的權利按照它們自己的環境和發展政策開發資源，並有責任不在其管轄範圍內的地區製造環境危害。《21世紀議程》是可持續發展的實際執行架構，其內容包括國際社會的經濟、資源、保育與管理、各組織的角色和功能及實施方案等面向，茲將其內容概述於下： (1)社會經濟篇：共七章，包括消除貧窮、改變消費型態、保護並合理使用森林資源、永續性人口動態、保護人類健康、將環境與發展議題納入決策過程、以及促進開發中國家永續發展之國際合作等； (2)資源之維護與管理篇：分為十四章，涵蓋空氣保護、陸地資源之規畫及管理、綜合性土地資源利用、保護並合理使用森林資源、防止沙漠化、保護山區生態系、保護及管理海洋與淡水資源、生物多樣性之維護、生物科技之環保管理、毒化物及廢棄物之管制等； (3)強化主要組織之參與作用篇：計分十章，包括強化主要團體、婦女、兒童，青少年、勞工與工會、農民、企業界、科技界及非政府組織等團體的參與及支持； (4)執行方法篇：計有八章，包括資金來源機制、環保技術轉移、提升環境意識及教育宣導、強化國際機構、制定國際法規、措施及其機制以及建立全球資訊體系等。

年　度	重點說明
1992	《聯合國氣候變遷框架公約》（United Nations Framework Convention on Climate Change, FCCC） 1994年生效 為因應氣候變遷與防制氣候繼續惡化，聯合國於1992年召開的里約會議中通過本公約，對「人為溫室氣體」（anthropogenic greenhouse gases）的排放訂定全球性的管制協議，本公約於1994年3月21日正式生效。
	《聯合國生物多樣性公約》（Convention on Biological Diversity） 1993年生效 以全球為範圍，對生物資源和生物多樣性的維護建立了明確的法律框架和制度。里約會議之後，該公約在保護生物多樣性、利用生物多樣性、及公平分享利用遺傳資源產生之收益等方面有更進一步的發展。
	聯合國永續發展委員會（United Nations Commission on Sustainable Development, CSD） 為有效監督管理各國執行《21世紀議程》，在1993年2月成立了此委員會。現有53個會員國成員，除了以國家身分加入委員會外，CSD亦鼓勵地方政府與非政府組織加入，並設立許多創新性的計畫，包含夥伴關係集會（Partnerships Fair），學習中心（learning center）、圓桌會議（roundtables）等計畫。

※資料來源：參考蔡育岱與熊武合著，國際關係之理論與實際，第191頁至192頁。

八、1993至2001年

從1993至2001年的這段期間，國際社會中關心環境保護的聲浪，雖然不能說響徹雲霄，但是也仍然處於努力不懈的狀態。這期間也完成了許多相當具有畫時代意義的公約與議定書等重要的國際環境法之代表性議題或規範。比較重要的有：1994年之「聯合國抗沙漠化公約」（United Nations Convention to Combat Desertification, UNCCD）、1997年之「聯合國氣候變化架構（框架）公約京都議定書」（Kyoto Protocol to the United Nations Framework Convention on Climate Change, Kyoto Protocol）、1998年之「管

制化學品及農藥進出口之鹿特丹公約」（The Rotterdam Convention on the Prior Informed Consent (PLC) Procedure for Certain Hazardous Chemicals and Pesticides in International Trade）、1999年之「巴賽爾公約議定書」即「危險廢棄物跨境運送及其處置之責任及賠償之巴賽爾公約議定書」（Basel Protocol on Liability and Compensation for Damages Resulting from Trans-boundary Movements of Hazardous Wastes and Their Disposal, Basel Proto-col）、2000年之「生物多樣性公約之卡塔黑納生物安全議定書」（Carta-gena Protocol on Biosafety to the Convention on Biological Diversity）、2000年之「聯合國千禧年宣言」（United Nations Millennium Declaration）以及「消除持久性有機污染物之斯德哥爾摩公約」（Stockholm Convention for the Elimination of the Persistent Organic Pollutants, POPs）。此等公約及議定書之重要內容，可以參考表4-7。

表4-7

年 度	重點說明
1994	《抗沙漠化公約》（Convention to Combat Desertification）1996年生效 1992年12月，第47屆聯合國大會通過47/188號決議，將里約地球高峰會議中希望能抑制沙漠化問題的要求加以落實，於是聯合國抗沙漠化公約（UN Convention to Combat Desertification, UNCCD）的立法工作開始展開，並因此成立一個政府間小組（inter-governmental panel）。這個政府間小組前後一共進行了十次的集會，在1993年5月底至6月初的第一次集會中，成員交換了既有的資訊並就擬定一項具有法律拘束力公約時可能面臨的問題加以討論，同時也對非洲國家的沙漠化情形特別給予關注。接下來的三次集會則是商討公約草案的內容與區域執行辦法的附件。其中一個重要的進展是，南北國家與南南國家間的夥伴合作關係的建立。第五次的集會在1994年6月上旬召開，UNCCD草案的最終版本在這些集會中獲得通過。爾後五次的集會於是開始籌備未來公約通過後首屆締約國家的會議（Conference of the Par-ties, COP）。

年　度	重點說明
1994	本公約旨在透過地方、國家、地區和區域方案以及國際夥伴關係，推動實施具體行動。此外，聯合國決定從1995年起，每年的6月17日訂為防治沙漠化和乾旱日。
1997	《京都議定書》（Kyoto Protocol） 2005年生效 規範工業國家未來溫室氣體排放的標準與時間表，依據共同但有差別的責任原則，締約國家承擔不同的責任，以因應氣候變遷。
1998	《管制化學品及農藥進出口之鹿特丹公約》（The Rotterdam Convention on the Prior Informed Consent (PIC) Procedure for Certain Hazardous Chemicals and Pesticides in International Trade） 2004年正式生效 此公約採用事先通知及同意程序進行各種化學品的輸出入及使用。要求出口禁用或嚴格限用危險化學品和農藥的國家，必須事前通知進口國家，並取得其同意後才能出口。
2000	《卡塔黑納生物安全議定書》（Cartagena Protocol on Biosafety） 2003年生效 聯合國生物多樣性公約締約國按照里約宣言第15條的規定之預防原則（Precautionary Approach）並依據該公約第15條第3項規定，於1995年第2次締約國大會決議訂定本議定書，以因應現代生物技術產生之改造活生物體（Living Modified Organisms, LMOs）可能對生物多樣性保育與永續利用造成之不利影響，特別著重LMOs之越境轉移及提前告知同意程序。
2001	《消除持久性有機污染物之斯德哥爾摩公約》（Stockholm Convention for the Elimination of the Persistent Organic Pollutants, POPs） 2004年生效 涵蓋生產、進口、出口、處理和使用持久性有機污染物的各種管制措施，至於管制的物質，目前總共有三類12項，分別列於附件A至附件C。此外，公約也列有評估機制，做為未來新增管制項目之法源。 在公約管制的物質中，列為附件A者係人為製造與使用的毒性化學物質；附件B為人類刻意製造與使用者，目前僅有DDT一項；附件C所列的化學物質，則是源自非刻意製造的毒性化學物質，共包括戴奧辛（Dioxins）、呋喃（Furans）、六氯苯（Hexachlorobenzene）及多氯聯苯（PCBs）等。

年 度	重點說明
2001	其中附件A之物質在公約生效後，即全面予以禁用。然而對於DDT，則因為許多貧困國家仍利用其撲滅瘧疾病媒蚊，而多氯聯苯則被廣泛使用於變壓器上，故將在取得適當且負擔得起的替代品後，再逐步予以禁用。

※資料來源：參考蔡育岱與熊武合著，國際關係之理論與實際，第192頁至194頁。

九、2002年

　　國際社會僅管自從二十世紀末的二、三十年期間建立了許多新的組織構造，也簽訂了許多新的條約來規範國際環境保護的各種議題；然而從斯德哥爾摩宣言到里約宣言所帶給人類社會的高度期望，漸漸的被各國感覺到並沒有充分被滿足，而有或多或少的失落感。因此整個1990年代國際社會對於「永續發展」的落實感到不足，而且在進展方面也感到「太慢」；更重要的是在環境保護的許多方面反而是惡化了[6]。因此，在2002年由聯合國大會出面在南非約翰尼斯堡（Johannesburg）召開「永續發展世界高峰會」（UN World Summit on Sustainable Development, Johannesburg Summit）。針對水、能源、健康、農業以及「生物多樣性與生態系統經營」（Biodiversity and Ecosystem Management）五大議題，研究如何落實永續發展。整體而言，「約翰尼斯堡高峰會」（Johannesburg Summit）似乎是在強調各個國家與國際組織有必要與「非國家行為者」（Non-State Actors）致力於有意義與有效的合夥關係，永以達成「永續發展」的目標。其內容重點可參閱表4-8。

---

[6] Louis F. Damrosch et al., International Law, 5th ed. (St. Paul, M.N.: West Publishing, 2001), p. 1487.

表4-8

年　度	重點說明
2002	聯合國於南非約翰尼斯堡召開「永續發展世界高峰會」（UN World Summit on Sustainable Development, Johannesburg Summit） 聯合國於2002年8月26日至9月4日在南非約翰尼斯堡召開永續發展世界高峰會。針對水（Water）、能源（Energy）、健康（Health）、農業（Agriculture）以及生物多樣性與生態系經營（Biodiversity and Ecosystem Management）等五大議題（即所謂的WEHAB），研究如何落實永續發展。此外，與會代表亦針對消減貧窮、改變不永續之消費及製造型態、健康與永續發展、小島國家之永續發展、非洲永續發展等廣泛交換意見。
	《約翰尼斯堡永續發展宣言》（Johannesburg Declaration and Plan of Implementation） 擬定永續發展策略與行動方案；以「全球考量，在地行動」的國際共識，由生活環境、消費行為、經營活動，從民間到政府，從每個個人到整體社會，以實際行動，全面落實永續發展。

※資料來源：參考蔡育岱與熊武合著，國際關係之理論與實際，第194頁至195頁。

十、2003年迄今

　　自2003年以來，國際環境法的發展更是不可輕忽。至今可以看到完成了一個相當廣泛的領域，含蓋了數百個多邊與雙邊條約。其內容充滿了各種不同產業下之環境相關規範。雖然可以觀察到國際環保議題，受到各國的關注，但是有更多的問題亦有待國際社會去加以解決。在二十一世紀的最初十年的重要國際環境保護的進展，可參考表4-9。

表4-9

年　度	重點說明
2006	《京都議定書》生效 歐盟率先啟動第一個國際級的碳排放交易體制： 在2004年3月底之前，歐盟各國政府決定將二氧化碳排放量自

年　度	重點說明
2006	2005年起加以分配。各國政府可將二氧化碳排放量的95%免費分配給業者，其餘的5%可以拍賣給業者；核定分配的二氧化碳排放許可量可以在市場上交易，當時歐洲執委會估計每公噸約15歐元，委員會認為執行京都議定書的成本能因此降低35%，每年節省減量投入經費13億歐元。第1階段（2005至2007年）的市場規模限定為歐盟國家，第2階段（2008至2012年）才會擴展到歐盟以外的國家。
2007	IPCC於本年公布第四次氣候變遷評估報告 COP13/CMP3於印尼峇里島召開，通過峇里路線圖
2008	京都機制第一個承諾期開始 COP14/CMP4於波蘭波茲南召開，延續2008年的峇里路線圖決議，希望在2009年年底的COP15/CMP5訂出新的暖化建制協議，作為「後京都機制」，以接續2012年《京都議定書》到期後，全世界對氣候變遷減緩的共識與依規。
2009	COP15/CMP5於丹麥哥本哈根召開，原本預計要在會議中形成的「後京都」全球共識並未形成，取而代之的是一紙不具拘束力的「協議」（Accord）。會前各國期待曾矢言「不能讓氣候變遷的威脅日益增長」的歐巴馬政府，以及2009年9月在聯合國宣布降低碳密度和發展綠能的胡錦濤當局，於關鍵時刻均未能在全球暖化問題上扮演積極的角色。此次會議唯一的貢獻（如果有的話）應是作為日後「公約／議定書」氣候談判模式的參照點和2012年之後全球氣候建制的起始點；它只是一個政治承諾，而不是具有拘束力的最終共識。
2010	《哥本哈根協議》（Copenhagen Accord）的內容中載明，附件一國家承諾將以個別或共同努力的方式達成2020年的減碳目標，而具體方式將於2010年1月31日之前提交給UNFCCC的祕書處。附件一國家的減量承諾與實際提供的資金額度，將會依據現有和未來通過的文件進行檢測、申報和查驗。至於非附件一國家亦將在該期限前，提出其國內所規畫採行的減緩（mitigation）行動。此外，《協議》內容針對減緩森林退化的問題也有論及。依據目前排定的時程，為了達成《協議》中的具體內容，聯合國將會在本年的6月及11月，也就是COP 16之前，舉辦至少兩次的協商。

※資料來源：參考蔡育岱與熊武合著，國際關係之理論與實際，第195頁至196頁。

第五章　國際環境法之法源

壹、國際環境法法源之特殊性與一般性

因為國際環境法所考量的重點，其運作與執行不外是將一般性的國際法原理、法則與規範適用到國際環境問題上面去。所以不必驚訝的是它的法源當然是根基於「國際法院規約」（Statute of the International Court of Justice）所列舉出來的傳統國際法之法源。然而，在這樣的背景之下，有兩點特別值得強調與說明：第一，在當前的國際環境法的規範方面，從「拘束力」的層面來加以審視，「條約」或公約仍然是最重要的法源依據。第二，國際環境法的源起，有個「特別的」（Unique）的「面相」（Feature），那就是在它形成「條約」之前，會先有一些傳統上「不具拘束力」（Non-binding）的源起，例如：「決議」（Resolution）、「建議」（Recommendation）以及國際會議和國際機構的「宣言」（Declaration）。

就第一點而言，條約業已成為具有拘束力的「支配性」（Dominate）的國際環境法之法源。但是，也相當重要的必須要了解條約也只是國際環境法的一個法源而已。從法源的面相來檢視，國際環境法的法源，就如同國際法的法源一樣，它包括：條約、國際習慣、法律一般原理、以及次級法源如司法判決及公法學家的學說論述。就條約這一點來檢視，共識的採納及「包裹條件交換」（Package-Deal）的「作法」（Approach），到最後的條約之「談判」（Negotiation），在國際環境事務的背景下，是特別有助益的，舉例而言[1]，它可以允許各國在下列的事項，如「跨界空污」（Transboundary Air Pollution）、「氣候變遷」（Climate Change）以及「生物多樣性之保育」（Conservation of Biological Diversity）達成一致的

---

[1]　Malcolm D. Evans ed., International Law (Oxford: Oxford University Press, 2006), p. 663.

協議。甚至於在碰到更尖銳的環境保護問題，及爭議事件的解決作法上，協議出共同認可的標準及方案，這是多麼的難能可貴的。

就第二點而言，在許多國際環境條約的具體化形成之初，大概均會以不具有拘束力的「文件」（Instrument）的方式呈現；例如前面所述及之「宣言」、「決議」、「建議」或「指針／指導」（Guideline）等不一而足的名稱引導相關，國際環境公約或條約的繼續研究，走向具體化的結果。這樣的形成過程中的「準規範」，一般均習慣稱為「軟法」（Soft Law）。它們的存在不能因此被誤解為不具有重要性。因為它們雖然就法律上的效力而言，不具有拘束力；但實際上它們讓各國能夠針對某一特定的「議題」，有一個特定的「方向」或「目標」去尋求「共識」，到最後各國終能「同意」而成為具有拘束力的國際條約或公約。在這方面比較具有代表性的例子有[2]：「聯合國環境計畫署指導原則」（UNEP Guidelines）之訂定，才有1989年「巴賽爾公約」（Basel Convention）之完成。聯合國環境計畫署（UNEP）及糧農組織（FAO）之指導原則之訂定，才有1998年之「管制化學品及農藥進出口鹿特丹公約」（The Rotterdam Convention on the Prior Informed Consent (PIC) Procedure for Certain Hazardous Chemical and Pesticides in International Trade）。而事實上「軟法」的普遍性，使得它的廣泛應用之重要性，能夠表現了國際環境法法源上的「獨特性」（Unique），值得關心國際環境法人士特別加以留意。

貳、國際環境法之法源形成

一、習慣國際法

當相當廣泛之有關於環境事件或爭議問題，所引起的各國所可以享有的權利及所應負的義務，是源自於它本身自願的接受它所簽訂的國際公約

---

[2]　同前註。

或雙邊條約；就事論事，這是個事實正確的講法。但是，不能因此就認為「習慣國際法」並不能規範各個單一「國家的行為」（State Conduct）。實際上，國際社會中各國的「實踐」（Practice），早已就形成了許多的習慣國際法之原理與原則。更何況經由條約簽訂的過程與習慣法的「交互運作」（Interaction）的結果，更是突顯了國際社會中各國對於環境法的實踐，與習慣法的相輔相成的作用（所謂的交融整合），形成了今日許許多多的國際環境法的基本原理與要求標準。這其中最重要的例子有：「睦鄰原則」（Good Neighbor Principle）及「不傷害原則」（No Harm Principle）。根據這兩個原則，各國有義務去防止、減少及掌控污染與「跨界環境傷害」（Transboundary Environmental Harm）。這可以從過去的司法判例及各式各樣的軟法宣言或決議中去發現。而且從以往的各國實踐中，也可以證實了各國有義務（習慣法上的義務），去對其他受到不利影響的國家，作諮商與通知潛在、有可能造成的「跨界之傷害」（Transboundary Harm）。至於其他相關之習慣國際法在環境規範上的原理原則有[3]：「污染者付費原則」（Polluter Pays Principle）、「防止行為原則」（Principle of Preventive Action）以及「衡平使用共享資源原則」（Equitable Utilization of Shared Resources Principle）。

　　另外，比較具有爭議性的有下列幾個[4]：「預防原則」（Precautionary Principle）、「永續發展（本身）原則」（Principle of Sustainable per se）以及「世代間衡平資產永續使用原則」（Principle of Sustainable Use Intergeneration Equity）。

二、條約法

　　絕大多數的環境法是包含在「條約本文」（Treaty Text）之中。如此一來，就賦予了環境法規範相當大的動力。其中的一個原因是，那樣的作法能夠提供一個「機關式機制」（Institutional Mechanism），有助於

---

[3]　同前註。

[4]　同前註，第664頁。

日後之「執行」（Implementation）[5]。在這樣的情形下，可以觀察到一個「共同的格式」（Common Format）——對「參加國會議」（Conference of the Parties）提供「定期性會議」（Regular Meeting）；在其下有許多「委員會」（Committee）要對「參加國會議」作出報告。而其中最常見的組成是至少會有一個「科技委員會」（Committee for Scientific and Technical Advice），以及一個「祕書處」（Secretariat）來對這些會議及期間提供必要的行政支援。許多環境條約形成或訂立，就是有背後這樣的「動能力量」（Dynamic Force），來推動源自於要回應實體環境方面的規定之變動需要。這樣的作法，一般稱之為「架構式作法」（Framework Approach）；而這樣的作法，正是許多環境條約所採納的作法。它的優點是可以提供快捷的改變環境變遷，所需的制度性規範的因應對策，與法規方面所需改變的有效作法；這樣的作法比用傳統的「條約修正」（Treaty Amendment）的「正常程序」（Normal Process），要來得省時且有效，能在最短的時間，回應環境規範變動的急迫性需要。

上述的「架構式作法」（Framework Approach）在規範方面最大的實質效益，很明顯的是它可以使得環境法條約，保有一般性之原理與原則，又能明白公告周知，條約當局的組織結構；此乃架構式作法主要的「功能式」（Functional）的特徵。而在此同時更進一步的「議定書」（Protocol）及／或「附件」（Annexes）所涵蓋的「特定標準」（Specific Standards），也可以在通常的情況下，變得更有彈性的加以修正或修改，讓國際環境法侷限於靜態的白紙黑字，而能夠表現出與時並進的具有生命力的國際性規範，能夠適合國際社會的及時需要。最明顯的例子[6]：乃是1979年聯合國旗下的「歐洲經濟委員會」（Economic Commission for Europe）的「跨國長程空氣污染物公約」（Convention on Long-Range Transboundary Air Pollution），至今伴有八個議定書。而另一個不錯的例子，則是1992年「聯合國氣候變遷架構（框架）公約」（United Nations

---

[5]　同前註。
[6]　同前註。

Framework Convention on Climate Change）至今伴隨著1997年「京都議定書」（Kyoto Protocol）。至於最富有彈性的作法，在修正案程序上使用所謂的「默許式修正案程序」（Tacit Amendment Procedures），乃是由「國際海事組織」（International Maritime Organization）在1973年首先使用這樣的方式，在1973/1978之「防止船舶污染國際公約」（International Convention for the Prevention of Pollution from Ships）有六個附件伴隨著該國際公約。其主要的作法如下[7]：任何對於附件的改變，要讓所有的簽約方生效，必須在公約採納之後的16個月內完成，除非在一定期間（通常是10個月）的採納之內，有三分之一的簽約國表示反對或者是由一定數目的簽約方的商船艦隊50%以上的「世界毛噸數」（World Gross Tonnage）的代表，表示反對，如果沒有這兩種情形的任何一種情形發生，對於附件的修正即告完成。一個最近且最好的範例就是1992年的「東北大西洋環境防制公約」（Convention for the Protection of the Environment of the North-East Atlantic; OSPAR），該公約伴隨著五個附件及三個附錄。這些附件與附錄均比公約本身在修正與修改方面都要來得容易得多。

參、國際環境法之法源類別

一、分類之標準

　　國際法的法源一般可以將其區分為「硬法」（Hard Law）與「軟法」（Soft Law）。就「硬法」而言，就如同「國際法院規約第38條」（Article. 38 of the International Court of Justice Statute）所列舉出來的那些種類。在硬法方面對於各國的「拘束力」（Binding Force）乃是指那些原理或法規之拘束各國，僅限於它與其他國家之間的「關係」上面。並不是意指任何關聯之間法律爭議問題的決定。例如：對於「司法審查」的問題，或是

---

[7] 同前註。

保險法的問題就不包含在內。此處再針對國際環境法的法源分類而言，大體上亦是可以分為「硬法」之法源與「軟法」之法源。

　　硬法的例子可以有「1992年東北大西洋海洋環境保護公約」（1992 Convention for the Protection of the Marine Environment of the North-East Atlantic, the Oslo-Paris, or OSPAR, Convention）就要求所有國家去採取所有可能的措施，來防止並且清除污染，而且，這樣的作法就必須適用「污染者付費原理」。這類條文的規定亦僅適用於該公約之簽約國彼此之間。它們這樣的條文規定，並未創造一般性的規範，來拘束所有的國家、個人或其他「公共團體」（Public Body）。

　　在國際環境法之法源發展上，除了上述傳統的法源外，國際環境法的獨特面相，就是它的發展還有經由比較不具傳統及依傳統的標準不具有拘束力的法源，例如：決議（Resolution）、建議（Recommendation）以及國際會議和政府間組織的宣言（Declaration）等。

二、硬法（Hard Law）

（一）國際條約

　　等同於國內社會的立法，在國際社會裡的國際法範疇者應該是指「條約」（Treaty）與「公約」（Convention）。「條約」是指國際法人間所締結而受國際法所規範的具有「書面形式」（Written Form）的「國際協定」（International Agreement）。而「公約」則是指國際組織如聯合國所「主待」（Sponsor）而完成的「國際協定」。二者均對同意而簽訂的國際法人（如：國家）具有法律上的拘束力。這是由於簽訂者均具有分享共同承諾的信念；而且每一個簽約的國際法人，會擔憂如果它不遵守自己所作的承諾，則其他的國際法人也會不遵守它們所作的承諾。雖然或許不是完全的百分之百的正確；但是大致上來說，在幾種各自有特色的國際法產生的淵源當中，國際條約或許是在今天國際社會中，最重要的淵源。

　　條約是用來完成所有不同的國際協定。其中由兩個國際法人所締結者，稱為「雙邊條約」（Bilateral Treaty）；由三個以上的國際法人所締

結者，稱之為「多邊條約」（Multilateral Treaty）。條約之締結、保留、遵守、適用、解釋、修改及效力等主題，已經形成一套複雜而又相當完善的法律規範；國際間於1969年5月23日在維也納外交會議中，簽訂了「條約法公約」（Convention on the Law of Treaties），將條約本身的國際法規範，由條約來規定。國際間對於國家與國際組織之間，或國際組織相互之間的條約規範，更於1986年3月11日簽訂了「關於國家和國際組織間或國際組織相互間之條約法公約」（Convention on the Law of Treaties between State and International Organizations or between International Organizations）。因為在國際社會裡，還沒有真正類似國內社會的立法機關的存在，以致於舉凡立法規範國際社會成員行為準則的工作，均不得不由「條約」來加以完成。

條約的分類方法很多，不一而足，單就其與國際法產生之淵源有關的來分類，可以分成「立法條約」（Law-making Treaties）和「契約條約」（Contractual Treaties或Treaty-Contracts）。前者是國際法產生之真正的重要淵源之一，而後者則僅是締約國之間的特別的權力與義務之規範；是否會成為國際法產先之淵源，學者之間的看法並不一致。有些學者認為「契約條約」僅是締約國之間為了處理彼此的特殊利益或事項所簽訂的條約。例如畫界條約、通商條約、友好同盟條約等，僅是為在條約當事國創造權利義務，而不具有普遍的國際法規範性。因此，「契約條約」並非國際法產生之淵源。而另有一派學者則認為立法條約與契約條約之區別，重心在於條約之內容，有許多條約兼具兩種內容。換句話說，在同一條約內，有些條款固然有契約性質，然而，另外一些條款則具有立法性質，因此，應將一切條約均視為國際法產生之淵源[8]。

立法條約必然是多邊條約，而並非所有的多邊條約均是立法條約。一個多邊條約如果要成為立法條約，必須是其內容為規範一般性的、普遍

---

[8]　Michael Akehurst, A Modern Introduction to International Law, 6th ed. (London: George Alien & Unwin Ltd., 1987) p. 25. Also see Ian Brownlie, Principles of Public International Law, 4th ed. (Oxford: Oxford University Press, 1990), pp. 20-21.

性的或區域性的國際法規則，或設立國際組織的方可。所以有學者認為這類條約也可以稱之為「規範條約」（Normative Treaties）。而美國學者哈德森（Manly O. Hudson）則更直接的稱此種立法條約為「國際立法」（International Legislation）[9]。另外，立法條約幾乎全是「開放性的條約」（Open Treaty），開放給國際社會的成員自由加入。但是立法條約並非一定全是創造或變更國際社會的國際法規則，有甚多的立法條約是將既存習慣國際法規則，加以法典化或成文化。而這一類的立法條約均以「公約」的名稱稱之。例如：1961年「維也納外交關係公約」（Vienna Convention on Diplomatic Relations）以及1963年「維也納領事關係公約」（Vienna Convention on Consular Relations）均是。

每一立法條約都是若干國際法人為了共同的利益而締結，或者藉以制定它們所需要的新規則，事後容許其他國家正式加入或逕加默認和遵行；或者藉以宣示它們所瞭解的特定國際法規則；或者藉以廢除或修改既存的國際習慣或條約規則；或者藉以創立新的國際組織[10]。因此，根據它們的內容和意向，立法條約又可歸納為下列五類[11]：

1.法典化的立法條約

這種條約僅在將現有的習慣法，或某些司法機構所裁示的判例法轉變成「成文立法」。1815年「維也納會議最後（或蕆事）議定書」（Final Act of the Congress of Vienna）將當時規範國際河流之航行自由，及有關外交代表等級的規則加以法典化，便屬較早的此類立法條約。

2.解釋性的立法條約

這種條約旨在就現行習慣或條約規則中加以解釋，並不一定增加新的法律規則。

---

[9] Manly O. Hudso (ed.) International Legislation (Washington D.C.: Carnegie Endowninent for International Peace, 1931-1950), 9 vols, covering period from 1919, is an unofficial compilation of the more important treaties and conventions concluded in that time.9

[10] 俞寬賜，新世紀國際法，台北，三民書局，1994年，第56、57頁。

[11] 同前註。

*3.*創法性的立法條約

這種條約旨在藉國際協議，創造新的法律原則或規則。例如1944年的「國際民用航空公約」（Convention on International Civil Aviation）便是。

*4.*綜合性的立法條約

這種條約則兼具上述兩種或更多種功能。例如1949年的四種日內瓦公約（Geneva Conventions）、1969年的「條約法公約」（Vienna Convention on the Law of Treaties）、1982年的「聯合國海洋法公約」（United Nations Convention on the Law of the Sea）等。

*5.*國際組織基本法

乃是指以創設新的國際組織為宗旨而締結的條約，例如：聯合國憲章、創立歐洲共同市場的1957年羅馬條約，及歐市各國求貨幣、國防安全及外交政策之整合而於1992年簽訂的「馬斯垂克條約」（the Maastricht Treaty）等，也都是立法條約。

基本上，條約只能拘束締約國。因此，立法性條約通常也只能對締約國產生國際法上的效力。如果簽字批准的國家不夠多，那該條約所創造出來的國際法則當然不具有普遍性，而僅只是特別或區域性的規則；其後，若有相當多的國家相繼批准或默示遵行，則該條約中的新規則或對於某種國際法規則的新解釋，就可能因為普遍性的增加而成為國際法的一部分。或者可以直接的說，新的國際法因而產生。國際法大師奧本海（Lassa Froncis Lawrence Oppenheim, 1858-1919）曾將前面所述只有少數締約國的立法條約中之國際法規，稱之為「特別國際法」（Particular International Law）；將包括主要國家在內的多數國家間的立法條約所決定的國際法規則，稱之為「普遍國際法」（General International Law）；將國際社會全體或幾乎全體國家所締結或加入及接受的立法條約所規定之國際法規則，稱之為「世界國際法」（Universal International Law）[12]。另外，立法條約

---

[12] 同前註，第58頁。

對於習慣國際法的形成，有相當密切的關係。在現今的國際社會之中，除了聯合國憲章以外，真正為全體國際社會成員或幾乎全體國際社會成員所批准或加入的國際公約，其實也不多；而原則上國際條約又對非締約國不生國際法的效力；但是一旦一個國際公約達到大多數國家都批准或加入，則該公約（立法條約）就可以逐漸轉變成國際習慣規則。也就是說新的「國際習慣法」（或稱之為國際慣例法）（Customary International Law）就因而產生了。

　　至2010年為止，各方估計有超過500個與環境規範相關的國際條約或公約。重要的國際條約在此整理如下：

年　度	說　明
1946	1946.12.2　國際捕鯨管制公約（International Convention for the Regulation of Whaling）
1956	1956.11.19　1946年捕鯨管制公約之1956年議定書（Protocol to the International Convention for the Regulation of Whaling）
1959	1959.12.1　南極條約（The Antarctic Treaty, ATS）
1963	1963.5.21　關於核損害民事責任之維也納公約（Vienna Convention on Civil Liability for Nuclear Damage）
1969	1969.11.29　國際干預公海油污事故公約（International Convention Relating to Intervention on the High Seas in Cases of Oil Pollution Casualties）
	1969.11.29　國際油污損害民事責任公約（International Convention on Civil Liability for Oil Pollution Damage (1992 Civil Liability Convention)）
1971	1971.2.2　國際重要濕地保護公約（拉姆薩公約）（Convention on Wetlands of International Importance Especially as Waterfowl Habitat (Ramsar Convention)）
	1971.12.18　設立國際油污損害賠償基金公約（International Convention on Civil Liability for Oil Pollution Damage）
1972	1972.6.16　聯合國人類環境會議宣言（斯德哥爾摩宣言）（Declaration of the UN Conference on the Human Environment）

年　度	說　明
1972	1972.11.13　聯合國防止傾倒廢棄物污染海洋公約（倫敦海拋公約）（Convention on the Prevention of Marine Pollution by Dumping of Wastes and Other Matter (London Convention 1972)）
	1972.11.16　保護世界文化與自然遺產公約（世界遺產公約）（Convention concerning the Protection of the World Cultural and Natural Heritage (World Heritage Convention)）
1973	1973.3.3　瀕臨絕種野生動植物國際貿易公約（華盛頓公約）（Convention on International Trade in Endangered Species of Wild Fauna and Flora, CITES）
	1973.11.2　干預公海非油類物質污染議定書（Protocol relating to Intervention on the High Seas in Cases of Marine Pollution by Substances Other Than Oil）
	1973.11.2　國際防止船舶造成污染公約（International Convention for the Prevention of Pollution from Ships, 1973）
1976	1976.11.19　1971年設立國際油污損害賠償基金公約之1976年議定書（Prtocol of 1976 to the International Convention on the Establishment of An International Fund for Compensation for Oil Pollution Damage, 1971）
1978	1978.02.17　關於1973年國際防止船舶造成污染公約之1978年議定書（Protocol of 1978 Relating to the International Convention for Prevention of Pollution From Ships, 1973）
1979	跨國長程空氣污染物公約（Convention on Long Range Transboundary Air Pollution, LRTAP）
1980	南極海洋生物資源保育公約（Convention on the Conservation of Antarctic Marine Living Resources）
1982	1982.10.28　世界自然憲章（World Charter for Nature） 1982.12.10　聯合國海洋法公約（United Nations Convention on the Law of the Sea, UNCLOS）
1985	維也納保護臭氧層公約（Vienna Convention for the Protection of the Ozone Layer）
1987	蒙特婁議定書（Montreal Protocol on Substances That Deplete the Ozone Layer）

年　度	說　明
1989	1989.3.22　控制危險廢棄物跨境轉移及其處置之巴賽爾公約（巴賽爾公約）（Basel Convention on the Control of Transboundary Movements of Hazardous Wastes and Their Disposal (Basel Convention)）
1991	1991.2.25　跨國環境影響評估公約（Convention on Environment Impact Assessment in a Transboundary Context (Espoo Convention)）
1992	1992.5.9　聯合國氣候變化綱要公約（Framework Convention on Climate Change）
	1992.6.5　生物多樣性公約（Convention on Biological Diversity）
	1992.6.14　關於環境與發展之里約熱內盧宣言（里約宣言）（Rio Declaration on Environment and Development (Rio Declaration)）
	1992.6.14　21世紀議程（Agenda 21）
	1992.6.14　關於所有類型森林之管理、保存及永續發展之無法律拘束力之全球協商一致意見之權威性原則聲明（森林原則）（Non-legally Binding Authoritative Statement of Principles for a Global Consensus on the Management, Conservation and Sustainable Development of All Types of Forests (Forest Principles)）
1994	1994.10.14　聯合國關於在發生嚴重旱災及（或）沙漠化之國家（特別是在非洲）防治沙漠化之國際公約（聯合國防治沙漠化公約）（United Nations Convention to Combat Desertification in Those Countries Experiencing Serious Drought and/or Desertification, Particularly in Africa, UNCCD））
1997	1997.9.29　修正1963年關於核損害民事責任之維也納公約之議定書（Protocol to Amend the 1963 Vienna Convention on Civil Liability for Nuclear Damage）
	1997.12.11　聯合國氣候變化綱要公約京都議定書（京都議定書）（Kyoto Protocol to the United Nations Framework Convention on Climate Change, Kyoto Protocol）
1998	1998.6.25　環境決策之資訊取得、公民參與及司法訴訟公約（Convention on Access to Information, Public Participation in Decision-Making and Access to Justice in Environmental Matters (The Aarhus Convention)）

年　度	說　明
1999	1999.12.10　危險廢棄物跨境轉移及其處置之責任及賠償之巴爾賽公約議定書（Basel Protocol on Liability and Compensation for Damage resulting from Transboundary Movements of Hazardous Wastes and Their Disposal, Basel）
2000	2000.1.21　生物多樣性公約之卡塔赫納生物安全議定書（Cartagena Protocol on Biosafety to the Convention on Biological Diversity, Montreal）
	2000.9.8　聯合國千禧年宣言（United Nations Millennium Declaration）
	2000.10.18　1992年國際油污損害民事責任公約議定書之2000年修正條款（The 2000 Amendments of the International Convention on Civil Liability for Oil Pollution Damage, 1969）
2001	2001.5.22　關於持久性有機污染物之斯德哥爾摩公約（Stockholm Convention on Persistent Organic Pollutants, Stockholm）
	2001.11.2　保護水下文化遺產公約（Convention on the Protection of the Underwater Cultural Heritage, Paris）
	2001.11.3　糧食及農業植物遺傳資源國際條約（International Treaty on Plant Genetic Resources for Food and Agriculture, Rome）
2003	2003.5.16　1992年設立國際油污損害賠償基金公約之2003年議定書（Protocol of 2003 to the International Convention on the Establishment of an International Fund for Compensation for Oil Pollution Damage, 1992）
	2003.5.21　跨國環境影響評估公約之政策環評議定書（Protocol on Strategic Environmental Assessment to the Convention on Environmental Impact Assessment in a Transboundary Context）
2009	2009.12.18　哥本哈根協定（Copenhagen Accord）

（二）國際習慣

　　國際法上所謂的「習慣」是指：「從事某些行為的明顯而繼續的習性，而這種習性乃源起於行為者堅信：依照國際法，這些行為是基於義務或權利而從事的。」（A clear and continuous habit of doing certain actions has grown up under the aegis of the conviction that these actions are, according to international law, obligatory or right.）[13]此與通常所稱之「習尚」（Usage）有所不同。「習尚」也是從事某些行為的習性，但其從事此等行為時並無堅信：依照國際法，這些行為是基於義務或權利而從事的[14]；或者可以如此說：「習尚是國際交往的一種例常行為，尚未完全具有法律性質；習慣則是具有法律效力的習尚」[15]。習尚自何時開始可以成為習慣？此為事實認定的問題，難以作概括的說明。習尚一旦經過普遍的承認或接受後，便具有其特性存在，亦即此後它便在國際社會中「實踐」而發生法律的效力，而且繼續發展。

國際習慣所形成的法理基礎，依大多數學者的見解，主要學說有二[16]：

1.默示同意說

傳統國際法學者將習慣（慣例）建立在國際默示同意的基礎之上。英美國內法院判決亦採納此種理論。1871年美國聯邦最高法院對史科西亞（The Scotia）號船案和1900年對哈巴那船案（The Paquete Habana）的判決，揭示了某些規則因為國家默認而具有普遍拘束力。此外，「常設國際法院」（Permanent Court of International Justice）在1927年蓮花號案（Lotus case）為了查明在公海上船隻碰撞案件，船旗國是否有專屬刑事管轄權時，表示：「拘束國家法律規則源自於國家意志之表示。此等意志表示於公約或為國家所普遍接受為法律原則之習尚」。

2.共同法律信念說

習慣乃是指國家對於既存法律確信的表示，而非國家意志行為的結果。「法律信念」（Opinion Juris）是國家在法律上堅持其行為應符合既

---

[13] Lauterpacht-Oppenheim, Vol. 1. 8th ed. (London: Longmans, Green, 1955), p. 27.
[14] 同前註，第26頁。
[15] 蘇義雄著，平時國際法，台北，三民書局，1993年，第31頁。
[16] 同前註，第31、32頁。

存法則。國家之遵守習慣規則，乃因確信這些規則符合正義觀念、客觀法則、社會經濟的依存性或人類法律感。因此，國家並不能任意拒絕國際習慣。

國際習慣之成為國際法產生之淵源，比國際條約要早得多。在國際條約未成為國家行為的規範之前，國際習慣幾乎是國際法規則的全部。而國際習慣至少要經過三個階段，方可形成：第一，要先有國際社會成員（國家）彼此的交往，在特定地區於特定的情況下，採取特定的行為模式，按照特定的規則，為其交往的行為。第二，再有相同的情況時，仍然按相同的規則，進行相同的行為，並且反覆為相同之行為。而國際社會內的其他成員，也繼起效尤，使那些行為規則，演進成習尚。第三，習尚在國際社會內經過一段時間的持續，而各國際社會成員均願意遵守而普遍化後，各成員在心態上認為遵守習尚，才符合國際社會成員的行為準則——法律，否則即違反作為國際社會成員對國際社會所應盡之義務。

另外，「國際法院規約」指示法院在國際條約法之後適用國際習慣法。規約之規定：法律應適用國際習慣，作為通例之證明而經接受為法律者。此項指明至少顯示習慣本身不是在法律上有拘束力的成例。只有當各國所做的是通例「經接受為法律者」，習慣始成為一項在法律上有拘束力的規範的證明。雷維（Warner Levi）教授認為：從時間上來說，就是須各國慣常從事於某一種行為，這種行為才成為習慣；如果它們繼續這種習慣行為，是因為它們承認這是法律效力的「認定」（Opinion juris sive necessitates），這一習慣就代表了一項法律規範，如果它們繼續這一習慣行為，但並不認為它們在法律上有義務這樣做；那麼，按照多數國際法學家的看法，這樣做只不過是道德問題，或是方便、禮貌或彼此遷就的問題。在後一種作法就成為「國際禮讓」（International Comity）[17]。

國際習慣之產生須經複雜的程序，大致上來說「國際習慣的形成」（Evolution of Custom），不僅須具有一致的「國家實踐」（State Prac-

---

[17] Werner Levi, Contemporary International Law: A Concise Introduction (Boulder, Colo.: West View Press, 1979), p. 38.

tices）的客觀行為，更須具有「法的信念」（Legal Conviction）的主觀意識。也就是說必須同時具有「事實的」要件與「心理的」要件，如此方能產生「國際習慣」。而事實的要件，則包含兩個要素：（一）時間上的永續性：即在同一情形下的同一行為（或實踐）被國際社會成員不斷地接受而一再予以適用；（二）空間上的普遍性：即上述的行為或實踐被大多數的國際社會成員，或具代表性國際社會成員的普遍「一致」的採行。至於心理的要件，則是指國際社會成員的從事前述行為，或實踐時具有「法的信念」或「法的確信」（Opinion juris sive necessitates）。也就是認為就國際社會成員而言，在心理上深信此種行為或實踐的必要性，而在採行和遵守之同時，認為唯有採行和遵守，才符合國際法的要求。是身為國際社會成員所應盡的法律義務。國際法院在1969年「北海大陸礁層案」（North Sea Continental Shelf Cases）判決中揭示：「不僅行為必須表示一致的通例；更須證明此種通例是一種法律規則，而必須遵守的信念；當事國必須有履行一種法律義務的感覺，而非僅單純地出於禮讓或傳統的考慮」[18]。國際法學者之所以區別「習尚」和「習慣」，以及國際法院的判決之所以強調「國家實踐」的「一慣性」及「連續性」，都在在說明了國際習慣之產生，各國在心理上必須認定該「習慣」之採行和遵守是一項國際法義務之履行，必須如此方能符合國際社會的要求。而國際法院規約第38條之規定「國際習慣」須經「接受為法律者」（as accepted as law），即是在強調心理上的「法的確性」。

（三）一般法律原則

　　一般法律原則，是國際條約與國際習慣所定規則以外的原則，為國際法院規約第38條所明訂的國際法第三種淵源。規約中指出：國際法院在判決時……應該適用「一般法律原則為文明各國所承認者」（the general principle of law recognized by civilized nations），然而此一條款規定的實在具有相當的爭議。學者間的爭論基本上在詢問：所謂「一般」究竟何

---

[18] C.I.J. Rep. 1969, p. 44.

指？所謂「文明國家」（Civilized Nations）又以何種標準來決定？更重要的是所適用的原則又是何指？是原則本身呢？抑或是從原則中演繹出的具體規範？不論怎麼說，主要的爭論是圍繞著從什麼法律制度中去找法律原則。當然，條款中既明白指出必須是「文明國家」，也就是至少是任何具有一相當完備的法律制度的國家。換句話說，基本上這些原則可以取自國內法律制度，但是必須要能適用於國際社會中的交往關係上。正如麥克奈余爾勛爵（Lord McNair）在「西南非國際地位案」（International Status of South West Africa Case）中所稱：「在此事上國際法庭的責任是：應該將任何可令人想到的私法規則和制度之處或其定義名稱看作為政策和原則的指點，而不是直接把這些規則和制度硬生生地遷運進來」（The duty of international tribunals in this matter is to regard any features or terminology which are reminiscent of the rules and institutions of private law as an indication of policy and principles rather than as dire fly importing these rules and institutions.）[19]。

另外，一種法律制度比照另一種法律制度現有的規範去制定規範，一向存在於國際社會之中。例如：現在國際間所公認的國際法中有很多就是源自於「羅馬法」（Roman Law）。而且長久以來，「仲裁法庭」（Arbitration Tribunal）就經常沿用這樣的方法。法官只有在國際條約及國際習慣均不能提供適當的規範時，才必須去求助於「一般法律原則」。國際法院規約之所以如此規定，主要的即是要讓法官運用他們的創造性想像力來填補法律的「空隙」（Gap），以免因為沒有可以適用的「法律規範」（Legal Norm）而無法作出判決。需要激發各國對國際法的尊重，所以對於國際法院規約第38條所授予法官的可斟酌情形創造或產生法律的權力，並不濫用行使。在實際審判上，國際法庭均特別的慎重其所選取及適用的國際法所依據的原則，往往是在國際社會裡早已確立的原則；而且多半與管轄、程序及證據等有關，而與案件的實質問題牽涉甚少。

何謂「一般法律原則之性質」？學者之間的意見，相當紛歧，比較具

---

[19] I.C.J. Rep. 1950, p. 128.

有代表性的例子，有卜力格（Herbert W. Briggs）教授的認為，一般法律原則包含類推適用、自然法、一般正義原則和國際法一般原則；而不同於國際法之具體規律、習慣規則，各國實證法與比較法的一般原則[20]。但索倫森（Max Sorensen）教授則認為，一般法律原則的實質就是自然法，而國際法院規約第30條已把它限制於「為文明國家所承認者」。它既經「承認」，就不再是自然法，而成為實證法。因為國際社會的任何規則，只要經過社會中政治組織的承認，便取得了實證法的性質和地位[21]。勞特派特（Hersch Lauterpacht）則又認為，國際法院規約第38條授權該院適用國內法系的一般原則，特別是在私法方面，只要它們可以適用於國際關係上[22]。他並且說，實證法學派只承認條約和習慣是國際法的淵源，顯然已被該條款所否定。自然法學派只容許自然法為國際法的主要淵源，當然也被該條款所摒棄[23]。該條款的規定，頗與格羅秀斯學派的理論相近，因為它一方面相當重視國家意志為國際法的淵源；他方面又不背離國家意志和法律的與一般人類的經驗[24]。因此，根據勞特派特的見解，目前國際法的情況可能和格羅秀斯派的法學思想最為接近。

從以上分析可見，究竟一般法律原則的涵義為何？確實是人言人殊，眾說紛紜。大體而言，針對一般法律原則，在學說上可以歸納如後[25]：

1.類比適用說

指習慣或條約不足以解決問題時，可以訴諸國內法則來處理案件。但是，這種類比適用必須取自所有國內法體制下的共同原則，此說以凡拉里為代表。故此說所強調的不過是技術性原則的運用。換言之，採用類比方法以期達到某種理論。同時，此種方法乃是以兩種不同觀念中已存在之相似觀念為基礎。此類比適用的法律一般原則並不能稱為法律淵源之一。

---

[20] Herbert W. Briggs, The Law of Nations, 2nd ed. (N.Y.: Appleton-Century-Crofts, 1952), p. 48.

[21] Max Sorensen (ed.), Manual of Public International Law (N.Y.: St. Martin's Press, 1968), p. 14.

[22] Lauterpacht-Oppenheim, Vol. 1, p. 29.

[23] 同前註，第38頁。

[24] 同前註，第39頁。

[25] 同前揭註15，第35、36頁。

*2.*自然法說

　　將一般法律原則與自然法原則混為一談，早於1920年常設國際法院規約臨時草案擬訂時，法律學家委員會主席戴思幹（Baron Descamps）就認為法律一般原則是「客觀正義」（La Justice Objective）就得適用。但，「真實」乃是一般法律原則的主要特質。此種單純的理想或客觀法的觀念，未具實在價值，並不足以表示其法律性質。規約第38條所稱「為文明各國所承認」，已表明一般法律原則是各國國內現行法的一部分，且為各國所承認，並具實證法之特質者。

*3.*獨立法源說

　　近代部分實證法學者亦否認一般法律原則是國際法形式上的獨立法源，並進而否認國際判例曾以獨立法源適用之。彼等認為法律一般原則只不過為促進國際法發展而引進的國內法，並具高度技術性。

　　一般法律原則的涵義確實是一個見仁見智的問題，即使是在1920年草擬「常設國際法院規約」（Statute of Permanent Court of Justice）時，對於應否列入「一般法律原則」供法院作為判決時依據之問題，就曾在當時引起激烈的爭論。而根據當代國際法權威英國學者史塔克（J.G. Starke）所作的歸納，法學家分別指出的是：(1)一般正義原則；(2)自然法；(3)從私法演繹的類推；(4)比較法的一般原則；(5)國際法的一般原則（這是一些蘇聯學者的看法）；(6)法律的一般理論；(7)一般法律概念[26]。比較起來，史塔克教授的歸納較為具體，而較少受到爭論。事實上，一般法律原則應是一種自主的、獨立的國際法產生的淵源。國際法院規約第38條所明文列舉於第3項者即為證明。但是在實務上，雖然一般法律原則，已在規約中明文規定，法院可以適用，法官也曾引用，以支持其個別意見或反對意見。但是國際法院卻未曾在任何訴訟案件中作正面的、明白的援用。

　　1927年「常設國際法院」（Permanent Court of International Justice）在著名的「蓮花號案」（Lotus Case）判決中明白揭示：「國際法一般原

---

[26] J.G. Starke, An Introduction to International Law, 10th ed. (London: Butterworths, 1989), p. 31.

則乃是所有獨立國家間所適用之原則」[27]。而國際判例對於某些規則也曾以國際法一般原則加以適用，例如有關的「國家獨立」、「國家責任」、「國家繼承」，以及「用盡當地救濟辦法」等。但是在一般法律原則適用的問題上，應該要有一個基本的認識，即是一般法律原則在國際法產生的淵源上應居於輔助地位。而且法官只有在缺乏條約法與習慣法作為判決的依據時，方能適用一般法律原則。更重要的是雖然一般法律原則在實踐上甚少採用，但是卻在必要時，有所助益[28]。總而言之，國際法得以適用的「一般法律原則」可以歸納為三類：(1)國內法所普遍承認的原則，此包括：A.傷害個人人權的國家應負賠償責任；B.「不當致富」（Unjust Enrichment）者應回復原狀或負補償他人損失之責；C.「拒絕正義」（Denial of Justice）構成國際違法行為；D.時效原則；E.一事不再理原則。(2)導源於國際關係的一般法律原則，此包括：A.主權豁免；B.國際法優先於國內法；C.不干涉他國國內事務之義務；D.公海自由；E.用盡當地救濟原則。(3)可適用於一切關係的一般法律原則，此包括：A.「誠信原則」（Good Faith Principle）；B.「條約必須遵守」（Pacta Sun Servada）；C.「禁止反言」（Estoppel）；D.尊重基本人權；E.和平解決國際爭端。

（四）司法判例

　　根據國際法院規約第38條之規定，「司法判例……可以作為確定法律原則之補助資料」，但在適用上須受規約第59條的限制；也就是說：國際法院之判決除了對「當事國及本案外無拘束力」。易言之，國際法院並未採納英美法系的「遵照先例原則」（Doctrine of Stare Decisis）。但是在事實上，以前的「常設國際法院」以及現在的國際法院雖然均不曾視其過去的歷次判決具有拘束力；但是卻可以發現它們均曾在它們的判決及諮詢意見中利用其以往的判例或諮詢意見，作為法律的指引，以便解說區別國際法的規則或原則及其適用之準據。為此，兩個新舊國際法院均十分重視它

---

[27] 同前註。

[28] Gerhard von Glahn, Law mong Nations (N.Y.: McMillan Publishing Co., Lnc., 1981), p. 24.

們的判例及判例中所裁示或所根據的國際法原則和推理。另外，在國際仲裁的案例中，也不時引述其他仲裁法庭的裁決意見。因此，運用司法判例或仲裁裁決來確定國際法規範，已經成為國際社會中的國際實踐趨勢。

*1.*國際法院判例

不論是「常設國際法院」、抑或是「國際法院」，雖然在它們的規約當中，明文指出不採用英美法系的「遵照先例原則」。但是在實踐上，它們卻均不時引述以往的判決或諮詢意見，來說明國際社會既存的國際法規範。其中的原因，最主要的是因為它們均認為國際法院規約（包含常設國際法院規約）第59條所稱之「判決」（Decisions），乃是指判決中的「主文部分」（the operative portion of the judgment），而不是指判決的推理部分。因此，在實踐上，這兩個國際法院雖不曾有意要使自己受判例所闡釋的任何原則之拘束，但它們通常都遵循一連串的判決和諮詢意見——尤其當這些判決和諮詢意見明顯反映出一般法律趨向時，更是如此[29]。

更進一步研究，可以發現國際司法機構的判決或意見，對於國際習慣法之產生、新國際習慣規則之發展、舊國際習慣規則之修改，均有重大之影響。首先就國際法的產生而言，如果國際法院在某一訴訟案中判決顯示出某項新的國際法規則；判決確定後，便可經由國際間的普遍接受，而演進或產生出新的國際法規則。這樣情形的演進而產生出新國際法規則的過程，即是一般所稱之「司法立法」（Judicial Legislation）或「法官造法」（Judge-Made Law）的最佳說明。例如：1951年12月18日國際法院對「英國挪威漁權案」（Anglo-Norwegian Fisheries Case）中認為：「在畫定領海基線時，除了得考慮到地理上的因素外，還必須去考慮到某個地區的特殊經濟利益」[30]。此裁定領海的「直線基線法」（The Method of Straight Baselines）之合法性的規則，似乎是國際法院所首創。後來被1958年「領海及鄰接區公約」（Convention on Territorial Sea and Contiguous Zone）及

---

[29] 同前揭註26，第47頁。
[30] I.C.J. Rep. 1951, p. 116.

1982年「海洋法公約」（Convention on the Law of the Sea）相繼採納而寫入正式條文。法院雖不參與立法，但其判決卻可以直接引導立法，就是指國際司法判例的此種「司法立法」的功能而言。

　　而另外一例即是1951年5月28日國際法院在「防止及懲治種族滅絕罪公約之保留案」（Reservation to the Convention on the Prevention and Punishment of the Crime of Genocide）的諮詢意見中，認為：「『一國對條約某部分提出之保留須得其他締約國同意』之傳統規則，不適用於某些條約……種族滅絕罪公約便是其一……某甲國如對種族滅絕罪公約提出其某項保留，只要此一保留不牴觸公約之目的和宗旨，則雖有若干締約國反對此項保留，甲國仍可成為該公約之締約國。」[31]此一新規則的提出，後來被國際社會的成員所普遍接受而遵循，並已被1965年5月23日所訂立的「維也納條約法公約」（Vienna Convention on the Law of Treaties）所採納，而成為國際條約的一部分，也就是產生了新的國際法。

　　其次，就國際習慣法之形成而言，國際司法機關之判決，可以一方面確認國家實踐之趨勢，而在另一方面又能找出必要的「法的信念」，以加速國際習慣規則之形成。1982年「突尼西亞與利比亞大陸礁層畫界判決案」（Case Concerning the Continental Shelf）中，國際法院認為「『專屬經濟海域』（Exclusive Economic Zone）已經是國際習慣法。」[32]另外，不論是以前的「常設國際法院」抑或現在的國際法院的判決，若要對國際法的產生與發展有影響，不論是修訂既存國際法規則或是產生新國際法規則，必須在判決時有多數法官的支持，而且在判決後受到各國際社會成員的接受。因為如果不為各國際社會成員所接受，則各國際社會成員可以訂立條約，推翻國際法院判決所修正或創新的國際法規則[33]。最後，應該認識到：由於國際法院乃是最具權威的常設司法機構，其判決及諮詢意見雖然不是國際法產生的直接淵源，但是至少可以成為法院決定國際法規則的

---

[31] I.C.J Rep. 1951, p. 15.

[32] I.C.J Rep. 1982, p. 74.

[33] Louis Henkin, Richard C. Pugh, Oscar Schachter and Hans Smit, International Law 3rd ed. (St. Paul, Minn.: West Publishing Co., 1993), p. 121.

相當重要的資料，可以參考佐證。

2.國際仲裁法庭判例

　　有些國際法學者認為國際仲裁與國際訴訟之間存在著基本性質的差異，在他們看來仲裁著重於「妥協」（Compromise）而非如法院之判決。因此他們不認為仲裁判例可對國際法之產生與發展有相當貢獻。國際性的仲裁判例可對國際法之產生與發展有相當貢獻。國際性的仲裁裁決雖然對該案有效，但是對說明與確認國際法的規則卻有相當大的影響。有些國際仲裁案對國際法的發展，確實有相當大的貢獻。例如[34]：1872年9月14日英美賠償仲裁法庭之圓滿解決「阿拉巴馬索賠仲裁案」（The Alabama Claims Arbitration Case）的裁決[35]，開啟了國際間以和平的方式解決國際爭端的大門，各國開始使用「仲裁」來解決國際間的重大糾紛。其次，1928年4月4日「帕爾馬斯島仲裁案」（The Island of Palmas Case）的裁決[36]，亦對國際法上用「時效」（Prescription）作為取得領土的方式，有所貢獻。最後，我們應認識到國際仲裁與國際司法判決，所適用的國際法原則並無不同。因此，它們在國際法淵源方面的功能也應該無所區別。

3.國內司法判例

　　國內司法判例並非國際法產生之淵源。但是基本上，國內司法判例有兩個功能：其一是導致國際習慣規則之產生；其二是作為國際習慣規則存在之證據。就前者而言，美國聯邦最高法院在「哈巴那號船案」及「史柯希亞號案」（The Scotia Case）等所作之判決，對於國際習慣法的性質加以澄清；對國際法往後的發展，有重大的貢獻。如果許多不同國家的國內法院就同樣類型的訴訟案件，先後作出一致的判決，則此種判決所宣示的規則，就可以形成國際習慣規則。就後者而言，如果各國國內法院對於國

---

[34] Malcolm N. Shaw, International Law, 3rd ed. (Cambridge, England: Grotius Publication Ltd., 1991), pp. 90-91.

[35] William W. Bishop, Jr., International Law, 3rd ed. (Boston: Little, Brown and Co., 1971), pp. 1023-1027.

[36] R.I.A.A., Vol. 2, p. 829.

際規則的某相關論點，相繼作成的司法判決，若具有「一致性」（Conformity）、「連續性」（Continuous），則可以證明某項國際習慣規則的存在，至少有其作為證據的價值。

（五）公法學家之學說

國際法院規約第38條規定：各國權威最高之公法學家的學說，可以作為確定法律原則之補助資料。但是，截至目前為止，不論以往之「常設國際法院」抑或現在「國際法院」，均未曾引用過任何學者之學說。然而在當事國的訴狀中或是在法院的個別與反對意見中，都曾經一再的引述學者的學說，用來支持其主張或見解。公法學家的學說具有三方面的功能：其一是能夠闡明國際法規則；其二是能夠導致國際法規則之產生，以促進國際法之發展；最後，能夠作為國際習慣存在之證據。但是，基本上學說不具有法律性質，必須將它演進至習慣規則，方能產生法律的拘束力。

同時並存的習尚或實例，在經過學者加以研究之後，可以從中發現規則，寫成著作；因之其著作可以用來作為國際法規則之可靠證明。而國際法院規約所述：各國權威最高公法學家之學說，和司法判例一樣，僅能作為確定法律原則之補助資料。此條款之真正意義，亦僅是在強調學說之證據價值。正如美國聯邦最高法院法官葛雷（U.S. Supreme Court, Justice Horace Gray）所述：「遇到缺乏條約、也缺乏行政或立法規則之場合時，法院必須訴之於文明國家間的習慣或習尚；同時也必須訴之於法學家的學說，作為習慣的證據。這些法學家們經年累月的經驗，對他們所處理的國際法知之熟稔。司法機構之所以引用這些著作，不是藉以探悉著作者推斷的法律為何，而是藉以探悉實際法律為何的可靠證據」[37]。

早期由於國際法多半由習慣法所構成，法學家之精心研究，對於確定國際法的規則及國際法的發展，頗有貢獻。其中不乏佼佼者，例如：十七世紀被喻為「國際法之父」的格羅秀斯，以及十九世紀的瓦特爾等對於後世影響至大。但是，晚近由於國際條約法的日益受到重視，而有長足的發

---

[37] The Paquete Habana, 175 U.C. 677 (1900), p. 700.

展，影響之所及，使得學說作為國際習慣規則之證據，在國際淵源方面的地位，已大不如前。然而，無論如何，學說對於現代國際法仍有闡明及解釋的功能，仍然可以有所發揮。因此，法學家的學說在確定國際法的規則，以及其發展方面，仍可提供相當大的貢獻，此點是顯而易見的。

（六）衡平原則（Equity Principle）

國際法院規約第38條第1項規定：「前項規定不妨礙法院經當事國同意本公允及善良原則裁判案件之權。」其條文中指之「公允及善良原則」（Ex aegquoet bono），既非一般法律原則，亦非習慣規則，而是正義原則或衡平原則。而衡平原則應該是公平正義再加上信義原則。因此，可以認為公允便是衡平，但是衡平卻不一定符合任何法律的規定。按公允及善良原則以判決，乃是在法律規定外，依理、依情、依時、依地、依正義與道德等等，來解決國際社會成員之間的事端。國際法院規約第38條第2項之規定，其意義是「公平的解決一個爭端、必要時可以不顧既存法律（equitable settlement of a dispute in disregard, if necessary, of existing law）[38]。國際法中的衡平原則與英美法中的「衡平」（Equity）觀念，有些相近，但不盡相同。因為它不是與現有法律規範平行並加以補充的另一套法律規範，而是表達一種貫穿法律並使之符合正義感的精神或態度。

由於衡平原則實際上並不建立法律規範，但卻可能影響法律的具體意義。因此，有學者懷疑衡平原則是否可以作為法律的淵源，此問題則應視衡平原則用於什麼場合和什麼目的來決定。基本上，有下列三種情況[39]：

1. 一個國家或法律適用的機關容許有自由裁量的空間，則可以用衡平原則來決定怎麼適用這個規則，此即所謂「在法律範圍內決定」（decision within the law），當然是可以用衡平原則的。

2. 如果一個決定與法律衝突，並不能用衡平的原因來不適用法律，此即所謂「違反法律的決定」（decision against the law）：只有在一個法庭被

---

[38] Georg Schwarzenberger and E.D. Brown, A Manual of International Law (South Hackensack, N.J.: Fred B. Rothman & Co., 1976) p. 550.

[39] 同前揭註33，第115頁。

授權適用公允與善良的原則時，才能夠如此做。這就是國際法院規約第38條第2項所述的實況。

3.如果一個問題欠缺相關法律規定，而此種情形似乎是一個空白的情況，即所謂「法律之外的決定」（decision outside the law）：是否可適用衡平原則來作決定，則有不同的意見。有認為不應作出決定，即所謂的「無法裁判」（non liquet）的情形。但著名的國際法學家勞特派特認為：禁止用「無法裁判」為理由來拒絕受理案件已是「一般法律原則為各國所承認者」之一。如此，法庭仍應以衡平原則來作決定。

三、軟法（Soft Law）

在國際環境法制規範的形成與發展的過程當中，國際社會因為普遍的確認源起於羅馬法的「合意必須遵守原則」——即日後國際社會所熟知的金科玉律——「條約必須遵守原則」（Pacta Sunt Servanda）；因此，形成最具有拘束力的「條約法」為基準的「習慣國際法」（Customary International Law）及「條約」（Treaty; Convention; Agreement）作為國際環境法的主要依據，這就是我們所習稱之「硬法」，作為國際環境法制規範之主要起源。而在另外一方面，偶爾或在特別的情況與背景之下，某些環境規範或條約，在形成具體的規範條約之前，會先以「不具拘束力」（Non-binding）的「文件」（Instrument）面貌問世。這一類的「文件」，國際社會把它冠名為「軟法」。這一類的例子有「聯合國環境計畫署指引」（United Nations Environment Programme Guidline）之成為1989年「巴賽爾公約」（Basel Convention）之前導，也就是指聯合國環境計畫署指引在巴賽爾公約之前是具有「軟法」之身分與地位。而「聯合國環境計畫署」及聯合國「糧食農業組織」（U.N. FAD）之指針即成為1998年「管制化學品及農藥進出口鹿特丹公約」（The Rotterdam Convention on the Prior Informed Consent Procedure for Certain Hazardous Chemicals and Pesticides in International Trade）之前的「軟法」。

從國際環境法過去的成長經驗裡，可以檢視到「軟法」的普遍性及重

要性，它是國際環境法在具體化成形之前的「不可或缺」的一個重要階段。軟法之所以會被「實踐」上來加以使用，主要的是它原先並不是一個「法律建立」（Law-Creating）的機制，原因有二：（一）宣布或公告之機構並不具備「法律建立」之「權限」（Authority），或是（二）因為「法律建立」之機構本身選擇那樣的一個「不具拘束力之文件」（Non-binding Instrument），意圖讓文件中涵蓋某一個特別的環境法規範原理，在日後更具體的落實在國際環境法之相關公約之中。易言之，透過這樣的作法，軟法的使用乃是在尋求建立相關國際社會的環境法規範，來讓各個單一國家「同意」它們願意受到拘束，但是那些「軟法」在法律上是不具有拘束力的。然而，「軟法」的作法，其最佳的效果是經由不斷地、定期的、一再的、重複的各國的實際上的自願地服膺這樣的「特定環境法原理」（Particular Environment Principle）或「標準」（Standards），將其「置入」到各國的「國內立法」（Domestic Legislation）之中，假以時日，這樣的「軟法」會形成為「硬法」，或者是達到「習慣國際法」（Customary International Law）的地位。

（一）宣言（Declarations）

在國際環境法的「宣言」方面，有三個「關鍵文件」（Key Document），它們是「聯合國人類環境會議」（UN Conference on the Human Environment）的「1972年斯德哥爾摩宣言」（1972 Stockholm Declaration）、1992年的「關於環境與發展里約宣言」（1992 Rio Declaration on Environment and Development）以及2002年的「約翰尼斯堡永續發展宣言」（Johannesburg Declaration on Sustainable Development）。這樣的宣言，大致上可以執行下列三個功能[40]：

*1.*它們強固以及重申那些已經是「習慣國際法」之下的法則。例如「國家對自然資源之主權」（National Sovereignty over Natural Resources）。

---

[40] Stuart Bell and Donald McGillivray, Environmental Law, 7th ed. (Oxford: Oxford University Press, 2008), p. 143.

*2.*它們有助於將那些法則帶動到「習慣」（Custom）的地位。

*3.*它們反映出了「國際社區」（International Community）所同意的渴望。

「北海會議」（North Sea Conference）的五個「宣言」，就落入到了上面第3個類別，而對歐洲聯盟及英國的「工業廢棄物」（Industrial Waste）及海上污染的「傾倒」（Dumping）之禁止的政策具有及時及深遠的影響。

（二）原則（Principles）

在環境法規範領域內，有許多原則在二、三十年前的形成之初，似乎是很明顯地在挑戰當時的「國家主權」（State Sovereignty），但是曾幾何時，到今天已經成為主流國際社會所接受的原則。以「資訊通知及諮商原則」（Principle of Information and Consultation）為例[41]；該原則通常是指任何一個國家，在從事於任何一個活動之前，或開啟任何一個活動，有可能會造成「跨界污染」（Transfrontier Pollution）之時，有義務告知及諮商其他國家；務必要使得潛在地源起活動之國，必須要考慮到受「暴露國」（Exposed Country）的「利益」（Interest）。從一個更普遍性的觀點來檢視，此原則涵蓋了額外的義務給活動「源起國」（Country of Origin），需要提供合理的及相關的「活動資訊」（Activity Information）以及給所有「有潛在可能」（Potential）「暴露國」，以避免或降低至最低的對於各國國家自然資源，及環境損害的結果之造成。此原則在它被「聯合國環境計畫署」（UNEP）於1978年採納成「自然資源分享行為原則」（Draft Principles of Conduct on Shared Natural Resources）之前，至少有二十年左右的光景，被不同的組織或團體，一再的加以使用或論述。

比較更明顯的例子是1992年「聯合國氣候變遷架構公約」（United Nations Framework Convention on Climate Change）之第3條，列舉出「原則表列」（List of Principle），意圖指引簽約各國去落實條約之規定。

---

[41] 同前註。

其中包括「對於未來世代之相關責任原理，以及對於簽約各國在各自能力之下，負起共同但有區別之責任」（Principles relating to duties owed to futures generations and to the common but differentiated responsibilities and respective capabilities of the parties.）

（三）建議（Recommendations）

如果從整個「軟法」的光譜家族來檢視，「建議」可以算是「最軟性的法」。它可以涵蓋所有原則乃至於條約的最早源起。再以前面所提及之「資訊通知及諮商原則」為例[42]：該原則可以在許多國際會議或國際組織的「決議」（Resolution）中作出「建議」。像是1973年聯合國大會3129案之決議（UN General Assembly resolution 3129）；以及「經濟合作暨發展組織」（Organization for Economic Co-operation and Development; OECD）的許多有關環境政策的建議，在之後，均具體的發展出環境法與政策上，得以展現，例如「污染者付費原理」（Polluter Pays Principle）即是。

---

[42] 同前註。

第六章　國際環境法之原理與原則

壹、原理原則之適用

　　當那些對國際環境問題關心的人士，在面對實際要解決的問題或是針對特定的國際環境議題要作出「決定」（Decision）時，或者是要回應前述的「主題」，不論是當下的抑或是未來的問題時，在通常的情形下，均會有一些原理與概念，加以「作成」（Formulate），如此方能「容納」（Accomodate）至少其中某些部分的問題，作為處理或適用時之「依據」。這樣子的「工程」或作法，當然是有其困難之處。因為它必須具有一定程度的「彈性」（Flexibility）存在，讓這樣子的「原理」得以在事實上以包括一定程度的容許「差異性」來解釋各種不同態樣的環境問題。而這樣的「彈性」解釋的結果，自然會產生「確定性」（Certainty）與「精準性」（Precision）的難以避免的問題。

　　就此等原理本身的「性質」（Nature）來加以檢視，這些原理的適用，原本就必須在「國際社會」（International Commuity）的背景下，橫跨環境法律與政策的基礎上，去解釋與說明超越環境法本身的領域之所有相關「主題」。而這些所強調的「國際環境法原理」即在各種位階的環境法與法律的形成及執行或履行之間產生了相當具有「動力的」（Dynamic）關係。這樣的「動力關係」隨著科技的進步，所衍生出來的環境問題，自然會有「法律規範」（Legal Norm）制定之必要性。事實上，與環境法相關的最常見之「實質原理」（Substantive Principle）最重要的且最具有代表性的，包括：「永續發展原理」（Sustainable Development Principle）、「風險預防原理」（Precautionary Principle）、「損害預防原理」（Preventative Principle）以及「污染者付費原理」（Polluter Pays Principle）。以上這四個原理可以被認定是整個國際環境法最重要之「指導原理」，亦是本章要特別加以說明之核心原理。其中又以「永續發展原

理」與「風險預防原理」尤其重要,它們二者從法律與政策的角度來切入,是在國際的層面、區域的層面及各國國內法的層面,發展的最完整與務實的對於國際環境保護有最有效的貢獻。

　　另外,也有在前述指導原理為最高指針之下的所謂的「附屬原理」用以相互運作與相互呼應,達成國際環境法制體系的完整性。而這些「附屬原理」(Subsidiary Principle)則包括:「自我充足原理」(Self-Sufficiency Principle)、「公共參與原理」(Public Participation Principle)及「替換原理」(Substitution Principle)。最後,還有一些「基礎性作法」(Underpinning Approach)用以支撐前所述及之「實質性原理」在程序所依賴的具有程序性之性質卻又內含「環境評估」(Environmental Assessment),最明顯的即為「程序原理」(Procedural Principle)。以上的許多原理在實質運作上,均被發現是「永續發展原理」為中心的外圍組成體系中的一環。其中也多半被發現於1992年「里約地球高峰會議」(Rio Earth Summit)的關於環境與發展的「里約宣言」(Rio Declaration)之中,其餘的則被使用於「特定背景」(Specific Context)之中。而最後,值得一提的是,「原理」乃是用於對於「行動」(Action),特別是環境行為的「一般指針」(General Guide),而不是「細部規則」(Detailed Rules)。就因此,這些原理放在不同的立法與政策上面,自然就會有「不同的說法」(Different Version)。

　　更進一步必須要順便一提的是,本章所論及的這些原理的定義解釋,不要把它們視為是一成不變的界定;更何況它們的定義在一般的情形下,往往是欠缺「完整的」(Complete)。在不同的背景或是特定的主題下,會作不同的界定,是很自然之事。舉例而言[1]:污染者付費原理並未對「污染者」作出明確的定義,或者明確指出「污染者」是什麼?而它所著重的是這個原理的「背景目的」(Background Purpose)。它所要「提升」(Promote)的是什麼?而它所要提升的「背景目的」是否能達成?

---

[1]　Stuart Bell and Donald McGillivray, Environmental Law, 7th ed. (Oxford: Oxford University Press, 2008), p. 54.

又相當程度仰賴於「污染者付費原理」，所賦與這個「背景目的」的「分量」（Weight）為基準，是「如何」？因此，「污染者付費原理」並不是在一個「全拿或全丟」（All-or-Nothing）的態樣之下。所以「污染者付費原理」的重點是在於指出：「所期待的目標」（Desired Objective），但是將這些目標的「實現」（Fulfillment）留給個別的法律或「政策決定者」（Policy Maker）。最後，不得不提及的是，這些原理並非是彼此必然地「相互支援的」（Mutually Supportive）。它們雖然均屬於國際環境問題上的原理，但是基本上因為環境法制形成的技術背景及時間序列的不同，所以在彼此之間，很自然的會是相互獨立的。同樣的邏輯，這些原理當中的某些原理要比其他原理要來得「脆弱」（Fragile）；其中的原因，乃是隨著「政策」方向的改變，某些原理就失去了它原先的「力道」。

貳、國際環境法之原理與原則

一、指導原理

（一）永續發展原理（Sustainable Development Principle）

　　「永續發展」的概念在近代及未來的環境法與政策方面，無須諱言的，占有「核心」地位的一席。此處之「永續」（Sustainable）的概念，所著重的是「永續能力」（Sustainability）。而此「永續能力」則是指一種狀態在長期來看，是「永續」的。而在各單一國家來檢視，大概均是著重於「資源」（Resource）的利用。而在國際法方面，對於「永續發展原理」的精確發展及取得國際公信力則是近幾十年來的事情。雖然它的「全面性特質」（All-Pervasive Characteristic），可以在許多不同的「主題」（Topic）領域內，在許多國際環境法與政策的「文件」（Document）中，明明白白的發現它的存在。但是就因為它的「全面性特質」，得以出現在許多不同的「主題」領域內，因此針對它的「內涵」，自然就會有相當程度的「不確定性」（Uncertainty）。

　　那麼「永續發展」所指為何呢？雖然這個概念至少可以回溯到1972年的「聯合國斯德哥爾摩人類環境會議」（United Nations Stockholm Conference on the Human Environment）所發表的「人類環境宣言」（Stockholm Declaration）。而一般所常見的「共通定義」（Common Definition）則是源自於1987的聯合國「世界環境與發展委員會」（World Commission on Environment and Development）的「布倫特蘭報告」（Brundtland Report）——我們的共同未來（Our Common Future）。報告中對於「永續發展」有明確的建議，該語彙涵蓋了「發展是要能滿足現在的需要，而不要犧牲了未來各世代滿足他們本身需要的能力」（Development that meets the needs of the present without compromising the ability of future generations to meet their own needs.）。

　　上面這樣的定義，從文字的本身觀之，似乎清楚易懂；但是如果從執行面來檢視，則流於「模糊」（Vague），而需要進一步加以描述與釐清[2]：首先，永續發展原理的主要目標乃是要滿足當前及未來的「需要及渴望」（Needs and Aspirations）；而這裡也有何謂「需要與渴望」的問題有待解決。雖然很清楚地碰到了「人為宇宙中心主導者」（Anthropocentric）的思考重心的問題，暫且擱置；在「布倫特蘭報告」（Brundtland Report）的定義之下，環境被認定是人類福利的核心部分，有其一定的意義存在。第二，在「發展」的態樣下，存在有一個所要強調的所謂的「公平」之目標。而此一公平之目標則是要適用在當下的這個世代內貧窮國與富庶國不同的產業之間，以及在當下這個世代與未來世代之間的各種社會階層之間，把它定名成「代間衡平」（Intergeneration Equity）。簡單的說，那就是指未來世代與我們這一代一樣，有相同的「權利來發展」（Right to Develop），而且防止那樣的發展即是「不公平」。最後，現存的一個「潛在的假定」（Inherent Assumption）——就「資源枯竭」（Resource Depletion）而言，我們能夠「指出」（Identify）當前活動的影響，以及「環境吸收污染的能力」（Ability of the Environment to absorb pollu-

---

2　同前註，第57頁。

tion）。對於風險性質所存在的任何懷疑，將會無可避免地對於有必要去達成「永續發展」目標之決定，布上黑雲。

所有的環境規範原理，永續發展原理是最有爭議性的定義；直截了當的說，「它對於不同的人意指不同的事情」（It means different things to different people.）。在「布倫特蘭報告」定義下的永續發展的重心，乃是在改進人類生活的品質，而無須增加自然資源的使用，無限範圍地超越了環境所能供給的能力（The focus of sustainable development under the Brundtland definition is on improving the quality of life for humans without increasing the use of natural resources beyond the capacity of the environment to supply them indefinitely.）。

（二）風險預防原理（Precautionary Principle）

對於「風險預防原理」的認知與解釋，在學者專家之間仍呈現著不一致的看法。但是，就一般而言，大家可以接受的說法則是在描述對於環境與人類健康保護的「作法」（Approach）。這樣的作法乃植基於在源起於一項「活動」（Activity）與「物質」（Substance），縱使是欠缺充分或明顯的證據，有「傷害」（Harm）或「傷害之風險」（Risk of Harm），必須要採取適當的措施，預防其發生。舉例而言[3]：「風險預防原理」就建議要禁止可疑的「污染物」，即使在沒有「結論性的科學證據」（Conclusive Scientific Evidence）來證實「污染物」與「傷害物」之間的「關聯」（Link），只要是被懷疑「污染物」會是造成嚴重傷害之原因，在那樣的情形之下，「污染物」——所謂的「污染源」（Pollutant）就應該被「禁止」（Ban）。換句話說，科學證據雖然從來均不會到達「最後階段」（Final Stage），但是它的「結論性」只要到達尚未被「推翻」（Overturned），即是一個有效的證據。就實務上而言，即是仰賴「直覺」（Instinct）來判斷是否該採取適當的「預防措施」（Pricautionary Measures）。

---

[3] 同前註，第63頁。

　　「風險預防原理」往往會與相當高度被公共人士們所關心的「領域」，特別是社會大眾對於與環境風險及人類健康有關之「未知的」（Unknown）或「難以知悉的」（Unknowable）的風險，結合在一起，因而，引起社會大眾之注意或「考量」（Concern），既而成為公共議題。繼而，使得「風險預防原理」的使用「風險的科學分析」是否得以適用在「環境風險」（Environmental Risk）及「政策決定」（Policy Decision）的作成上面的正反雙方的「爭辯」當中。從這個角度來檢視「風險預防原理」可以了解到此原理之妥適運用，應當適度地考慮到其他的因素，例如：社會大眾對於風險的「認知」（Perception）以及對於「傷害」的潛在可能。更進一步的作深層的考量，不難了解「風險預防原理」是多多少少地有必要的受制於各方人士對於該原理之「解釋」（Interpretation）。例如，對於風險的重要性，以及對於科學證據當作證明之「接受性」（Acceptable），有其存在的價值，自然因為科技的不斷進步，其「不確定性」（Uncertainty）也就會有不同的「解釋」而引起爭論。

　　具體而言，「風險預防原理」乃是指在環境傷害與人類健康遭受嚴重損害或減損的「威脅」時，不應以缺乏充分的科學「定論」作為依據，或作為藉口來推遲採取那些用意在儘量避免，或減輕或降低傷害或危險之措施。換句話說，該原理的重心乃是放在「風險」的預防其發生或是「威脅」之存在為滿足。儘管大多數的國際環境法規範，並未對風險預防原則的含義作任何解釋，但是，這些規範對風險預防原則的理解是一致的，實現了風險預防原則兩個核心思想[4]：第一，都強調風險預防原則的對象——環境風險的不確定性。即風險預防原則必須是以環境風險的存在為前提，危險物質或危險行為將導致的危害後果，是科學知識尚未能作出確切無疑的結論，科學知識或者存在爭論，或者對此種因果關係的認識比較粗淺。第二，此種不確定性不能成為不行動或延遲行動的理由。該定義的核心是一旦存在一定的環境風險，就採取各種防範性的措施，科學不確定性不是不行動的合法根據。

---

[4]　秦天寶，生物多樣國際法導論，台北，元照出版公司，2010年，第119頁。

（三）污染者付費原理（Polluter Pays Principle）

1.污染者付費原理之形成

　　「污染者付費原理」可以被視為是國際社會中各國在其經濟發展與環境保護議題上出現最早，也歷時最久的一個銜接國際經貿投資與環境保護的逐漸形成的「國際法原理」，其重要性及其對未來「地球村」（Earth Village）的影響力，自不待言。回顧它的形成過程，比較具體的被提出，應該是在60年代的後期；而它首次確定的具體提案，是在1971年由「國際貿易經濟與投資政策委員會」（Commission on International Trade and Investment Policy）在其所謂的「威廉斯委員會報告書」（Williams Commission Report）中提及下列的文句：「本委員會強烈建議就現實而論，美國應積極地尋求國際間共同採納一個原理：污染的減除應該給予財務支付的方式為之，該方法即是要確保控制污染的成本，必須反應在生產出來的貨品價格上。」[5]雖然從「威廉斯委員會報告書」當中並未出現「污染者付費」這樣的名稱，但是「污染者付費原理」的基本理念，卻已表露無遺。而實際上該原理的正式產生，則是由「經濟合作暨發展組織」於1972年5月26日以「指導原理」（Guiding Principle）發布的方式出現[6]。其後，「經濟合作暨發展組織」更於1974年11月14日以「執行建議書」（Implementation Recommendation）的方式對「污染者付費原理」作進一步釐清[7]。至於該原則之落實在區域性組織，則是由「歐洲聯盟」（European Union）首先於1975年3月3日透過「部長理事會」（Council of Ministers）以「成本分配建議書」（Cost Allocation Recommendation）的方式正式發布而成為

---

[5] Williams Commission Report State: "The United States actively seek international adoption of the Principle that pollution abatement be financed, so far as practical, by methods which assure that the costs of control are reflected in the prices of the goods produced."

[6] 吳嘉生，當代國際法（上），台北，五南圖書公司，2009年，第77頁。

[7] Recommendation of the Council on the Implementation of the Polluter-Pays Principle, OECD Doc. C (74) 223 (Nov. 14, 1974).

「歐洲聯盟」的「環境事務政策」（Environmental Matters Policy）[8]。

一項大約可以認定的事實，就是「污染者付費原理」被國際間承認為「實證環境法原理」（Principle of Positive Environmental Law）應該是源自於1987年以西歐各國為主所簽署的「單一歐洲法案」時，即被引入此原則，而為各國所接受且認可。在此之前該原則即早已被「歐洲經濟共同體」發布給會員國的多項「指令」（Directive）中引用提及；到了1987年，簽署「單一歐洲法案」只是一個水到渠成的工作的完成；到了1990年，「污染者付費原理」就被直接的引進全球性的條約之中。其最明顯之例證，是1990年11月在倫敦召開並簽訂之「石油污染準備、反應及合作國際公約」（International Convention on Oil Pollution Preparedness, Response and Cooperation）即認可「污染者付費原理」為「國際環境法普遍原理」（General Principle of the International Environmental Law）[9]。

其後在1992年3月，於「聯合國歐洲經濟委員會」（U.N. Economic Commission for Europe）之組織架構之下，各國於芬蘭首都赫爾辛基召開並簽訂了「保護及使用跨越疆界水道及國際湖泊公約」（Convention on the Protection and Use of Transboundary Watercourses and International Lakes）。該公約明文指出：「簽約當事國各方應該以『污染者付費原理』作為採取各項措施的指導原則。也就是指，在污染防止、控制與減少的工作成本支付，應由污染者來負擔。」[10]

再者，1992年9月所簽訂的「東北大西洋海洋環境保護公約」，由14個西歐國家部長代表及「歐洲聯盟」執行委員會的代表共同簽署該公約並強調：正式採納「污染者付費原理」的重要性。該公約於條文中宣稱：「簽約各方應該適用……污染者付費原則，以使污染防治的成本、控制與

---

[8] Council Recommendation of 3 March 1975. Regarding Cost Allocation and Action by Public Authorities on Environment Matters, 1975 O.J. (L.194) 1.

[9] The Preamble of the International Convention on Oil Pollution Preparedness, Response and Cooperation (London, November 1990) contains the following recital "Taking account of the Polluter Pays Principle as a general Principle of international environmental law".

[10] See Art. 2.5 of the ECE Convention on the Protection and Use of Tran boundary Watercourse and International Lakes.

減低污染之措施等花費，應該由污染者來負擔」[11]。如此一來，使得東北大西洋海洋環境的污染者必須承擔「污染防治」（Pollution Prevention）的成本，變成一項無可推諉的義務與責任。

最後值得一提的是籌備經年，而於1992年年中由聯合國負責召開的環境發展會議，在巴西的里約熱內盧（Rio de Janeiro），完成了一項經由全球176個國家經過數次的談判、討論所獲得共識的「里約宣言」（Declaration of the UN Conference on Environment and Development）。「里約宣言」的完成相當不易，可以說明世界各國對於環境保護的觀念，逐漸統一而取得相當程度的共識。其中「里約宣言」對於全球環境保護，最重要的貢獻是引進以往未能讓各國取得一致協議的幾項環境保護措施與原則，例如：環境影響評估、公共參與、「預警行動」（Precautionary Action）等之外，更將「污染者付費原理」引介給世界各國，獲得與會各國的普遍支持。

2.污染者付費原理之意義與內涵

實際上，直到目前為止，國際間並不存在著一個各國所公認或一致同意的「污染者付費原理」的定義。不僅如此，國際間亦從未對該原則的「適用範疇」（The Scope of Applicaton）加以「精確地」（Precisely）界定。同時國際間也未就該原則是否允許任何例外情形，達成任何協議或簽訂任何「協定」（Agreement）。除此之外，「污染者付費原理」在近年來已被各國的傳播媒體大肆使用到近乎濫用的程度。它對不同使用該原則的人，似乎代表著不同的意義與內涵。因此，對該原理之呈現今天的紊亂狀況，勢必應該加以澄清與研究之必要。

然而，如果要對該原理的意義做徹底的認識與了解，則必須從它的歷史層面去著手，考量它產生背景及歷史演變，即不難知悉其意義與內涵。該原則之嚆矢應可回溯至1972年之「經濟合作暨發展組織」之「對環境政策之國際經濟指導原則推薦書」（Recommendation on Guiding Principles

---

[11] Art 2.2b of the Convention for the Protection of the Marine Environment of the North-East Atlantic States that "the Contracting Parties undertook to apply the PPP."

Concerning International Economic Aspects of Environmental Policies）已直接地將「污染者付費原理」視為「環境政策原則」（Principle of Environment Policy）發展而出。緊接著在1974年「經濟合作暨發展組織」再次的在其「推薦書」中提出主張將「污染者付費原理」作為其會員國的「污染防治及控制措施」（Pollution Prevention and Control Measures）之成本分配的「基本原理」（Fundamental Principle）。

　　「污染者付費原理」在「經濟合作暨發展組織」的背景層面上，具有特定的定義與內涵。它對「污染者付費原理」的「權威性解釋」（Authorizing Interpretation）是由其所有的24個會員國家經過一段長期的研擬與磋商，所達成的一致「協議」（Consensus）。基本上，它是被各國認定為一個規範會員國政府，在處理各國國內環境污染問題的「成本分配原則」（Cost Allocation Principle）或「非補貼原則」（Non-Subsidization Principle）。而該原則在最初形成時，曾被賦予下列的定義：「本原則之旨意乃是為了確保各國的環境保護，能維持在一個可以令人接受的狀態，污染者應該負擔起各國權責機構所決定之環境保護措施，在付諸實施時的開支」[12]。

　　從上面所述之「污染者付費原理」的「功能性定義」（Functional Definition），可以得知它的「政策性意義」（Policy Meaning）如下：除非在「非常特別的情形」（Exceptional Circumstances）下，或許可以容許些微的偏離該原則，否則在「一般情況」（Normal Situation）之下，各國政府均不可以經由「補貼」（Subsidization）、「課稅優惠」（Tax Advantage）或其他任何方式，來協助污染者擔負「污染防治」（Pollution Control）的成本。因此，污染者因為其「生產」（Production）或「消費」（Consumption）之行為所導致之污染，其「防治成本」（Prevention Costs）就應該反映在「產品」（Goods）及「服務」（Services）的價格上[13]。

---

[12] 同前揭註6，第84頁。
[13] 同前註。

「污染者付費原理」基本上是指任何造成污染及其後續影響的個人或群體，應該擔負起清除污染及其後續污染效果成本支付的責任。雖然該原則的「精確意義」（Precise Meaning）及其在特定的情況及案例的適用上，仍然沒有準確的定義，仍然有解釋的空間。但無論如何，該原則仍然受到國際間大多數國家，及環保團體的普遍支持與歡迎。尤其在發展民事的賠償法規，及環境損害的國家賠償兩大領域方面，更受到國際間法律界人士的廣泛注意與重視。而該原理在國際間逐漸發展出來的實質上意義，無庸置疑的是側重在經濟效益的分配上，特別是任何與環境保護有關的活動，污染者所應擔負的責任與其對環境的破壞應該呈現出合理的分配。

「污染者付費原理」在環境保護這樣的主題上，在國際間有其一定的分量與地位；但美中不足的是，就長遠的觀點來看，該原則在經歷過90年代的各次相關國際環保公約的簽訂，雖然已經晉身為國際環境法方面的一項基本的普遍原則；但是非常遺憾的是，仍然未能提升至更崇高的「習慣國際法」（Customary International Law）的國際法地位的層次。因此，僅就此點而言，「污染者付費原理」要成為「習慣國際法」的一部分或成為國際法之基本原理，仍有待國際間環保人士、團體及國際環境法學者共同的繼續努力。唯有如此，才能使各國在注重經濟發展的同時，也能注意到國家賴以生存的環境保護的「永續發展」（Sustainable Development）。

（四）污染預防原理（Pollution Prevention Principle）

污染預防原理與不得引起或造成環境傷害之各國的國際義務，是非常緊密的相連在一起。而且事實上當環境問題或環境傷害包括了兩個國家之間的關係，這往往是意味著相同的事情。因此，例如依據國際法委員會的「2001年的來自於危險活動之越境防範草案」（2001 Draft Articles on the Prevention of Transboundary Harm from Hazardous Activities）的第3條即表示：各國應該採取所有的適當措施，來防範重要的越境傷害或在任何情事下，來減低那樣的風險（States shall take all appropriate measure to prevent significant transboundary harm or at any event to minimize the risk thereof.）。當然，從上述條文所述看不出來它與當代各國的國際義務——不可造成環

境傷害,有什麼重大的區別,但是很明顯的可以理解到「污染預防原理」
在特別強調有必要對於「預期之環境損害賠償」(Anticipate Environmental Damage)以及對於那樣的損害賠償事件,要預作「行動」,用以避免
或防止它的發生[14]。從這一點,反映出對於污染預防之類的環境保護,最
好的作法即是在第一時間就能預防「環境傷害」的發生,而不是仰賴在
「環境傷害」發生之後的「損害救濟」(Remedy)或是作出「賠償」或
「補償」(Compensation)。而且進一步來作具體的分析,防範「環境傷
害」的損害賠償,所支出的「成本」,要比無論在任何情形下的「環境
傷害」的損害賠償,及其他補償作法的支出來得低。作為一個「指導原
理」,在國際談判及各國執行環境保護規範的作法上,「污染預防原理」
非常偏好於「環境管理政策」(Environmental Management Policies)的推
展,來清除與減低「發生損害」之後,所作出的額外支出之「環境風險」
(Environmental Risk)。

　　「污染預防原理」往往被簡稱為「預防原理」,這主要的是因為相關
人士很清楚地理解到所謂「預防」即是指「污染預防」。回顧國際社會對
於「環境污染」的重視,於1972年在斯德哥爾摩召開了「聯合國人類環境
會議」(United Nations Conference On the Human Environment)會議發表
「斯德哥爾摩宣言」(Stockholm Declaration),其「第六原則」(Principle 6)即以「全面性之用語」(Sweeping Term)表示:「為確保生態環
境不會遭到嚴重或不可回復之損害,排放有毒物質或其他物質及散熱時,
若其排放量或濃度超過環境能涵容的限度,應立即停止之。」(The dis-
charge of toxic substances or of other Substances and the release of heat, in such
quantities or concentrations as to exceed the capacity of the environment to render them harmless, must be halted in order to ensure that serious or irreversible
damage in not inflicted upon ecosystem.)。一般而言,「污染預防原理」
之「落實」(Implement),可以經由「污染預防」或「廢棄物最小化政

---

[14] David Hunter, James Salzman and Dirwood Zaelke, International Environtrental Law and Policy
(N.Y.: Foundation Press, 2007), p. 507.

策」（Waste Minimization Policies）去完成，以及「改善的環境管理」（Improved Environmental Management）包括：定期督導、「環境影響評估」（Environmental Impact Assessments）等作法去實現「污染預防原理」的指導目標。

此外，根據1992年「關於環境與發展之里約宣言」（Rio Declaration on Environment and Development）原則二（Principle 2），對於各國的義務特別是在「資源開發」（Exploit Resoures）及「損害預防」（Damages Prevention）作出了明確的指導性要求。它明文規定：依據「聯合國憲章」及國際法則，各國擁有按照本國環境與發展政策，開發本國自然資源之主權權利，並負有確保在其管轄範圍內或在其控制下之活動，不致損害其他國家或在各國管轄範圍以外地區之環境責任（States have, in accordance with the Charter of the United Nations and the principles of international law, the sovereign right to exploit their own resources pursuant to their own environmental and developmental policies, and the responsibility to ensure that activities within their jurisdiction or control do not cause damage to the environment of other States or of areas beyond the limits of national jurisdiction.）。

此處之污染預防原理往往與前面所述之「風險預防原理」連結在一起。事實上，二者之間是有所區別的。本原則的作用或功能主要是放在提升對於環境傷害之「預防」；而在實務上將它當作對於已經造成之傷害的「救濟替代」（Remedy Alternative）。此處的一個最好的範例即是使用「最好的可能技術」（Best Available Technique, BAT），在現行的整合污染機制之下，來防止污染的發生可能[15]。

二、基本原則

（一）整合原則（Integration Principle）

基本而言，對於環境保護的要求與要件之構成，在環境政策的形成

---

[15] 同前揭註1，第55頁。

上，有必要在定義與執行兩方面加以整合。而這樣的整合則必須顧慮到「永續發展」的提升。

　　整合原則在實務上乃是要在所有的政策領域上，去尋求對於環境因素的應用。其目的乃是要去避免一個相互矛盾的政策目標，因為未能考量到環境保護或「資源保育」（Resource Conservation）所造成的結果[16]。

（二）公眾參與原則（Public Participation Principle）

　　關於本原則的提出，最具體的出現在1992年的「關於環境與發展之里約宣言」（Rio Declaration on Environment and Development）的原則10，它的文字說明如下：環境問題的處理，最好是能夠在相關層次環節上，讓所有受到影響的人均能參與。在國家層次環節上，任何人皆應能夠適當地取用公共部門所持有之環境相關資料；此包括在其社區內之危險物質及活動之資料，並應有機會參與各項決策程序。各國應經由廣泛之資料提供，以便利及鼓勵公眾之認知及參與。各國應規定人人皆能有效利用司法與行政程序，包括補償及救濟之程序[17]。

　　里約宣言之後，國際社會已經對於「人民」參與環境決策程序及資訊獲得等的重要性，特別有所關注。至此，乃有1998年之「奧爾胡斯公約」（Aarhus Convention; The UNELE Convention on Access to Information, Public Participation in Decision-Making and Access to Justice in Environmental Matters）之出現。其目標乃是要透過國際公約，承認人民享有資訊取得、公眾參與及訴諸司法途徑等的權利；不僅如此，此等權利應該受到保護。其第15條即明白規定：締約各方之會議應於共識之基礎上，為審查本公約之公項規定之遵守情況，制定非衝突性質與非司法性質之協商性任擇條款之安排，此等安排應允許適當之「公民參與」。

16　同前註，第56頁。
17　同前註。

（三）替換原則（Substitution Principle）

替換原則是一個新興的愈來愈重要的「萌芽」（Emerging）原則。基本上來說，該原則之適用，是在鼓勵危險之物質或製造程序，應該以比較不具有那麼大傷害性的物質或製造程序加以取代[18]。本原則源起於2001年針對「新化學物政策策略」（Strategy for a New Chemical Policy）所提出之歐洲委員會「白皮書」（White Paper）所引起的報告書中，指出：所要考量的化學物應該要被比較安全的化學物或物質所替換，或者是使用不包含那種化學物的比較安全的技術，特別是比較安全的替代作法已經存在時，在選擇最好的替代作法時，要考量到社會經濟的層面。此一原則其實就是「歐洲化學物策略」（European Chemicals Strategy）。進一步去研究本原則的發生背景，不難發現它是「風險預防原則」（Precautionary Principle）的延伸。也就是說，此原則主要是將重點放在提升「促進科技」（Technology-Driven）之改變，而不等待「傷害」後之證明。最好的一個替換原則的執行作法就是歐洲委員會針對化學物及它們之安全使用，所頒布的EC REACH法規[19]。該法規明白規定：在比較一般性的措施上，在適當的「替代」作法業已被找出時，要使用進步的「危險化學物」（Dangerous Chemicals）的「替代」方案或物質。

三、作用原則

（一）共同負擔原則

共同負擔原則[20]係與污染者負責原則為相對立的環境基本原則。原則上，環境一旦遭受污染，應由造成該污染的人來負責，但若污染者不明，則必須由社會共同來負擔此社會成本。換言之，環境的損害或污染若無法確定的歸責予某特定之污染者，就必須利用團體的費用加以排除之，亦表

---

[18] 同前註。

[19] 同前註。

[20] 陳慈陽，環境法總論，台北，元照出版公司，2012年，第333頁。

示在這種情形下，環境損害成本的負擔是透過「公」的力量，所以國家在此應採取不同利益之衡平考量，例如經濟、社會、財政及環境法益等要素，基於憲法價值決定來為之。

綜上所述，共同負擔原則乃係具有填補污染者負責原則漏洞的功能，但其並非只具有補充的地位。假設污染是可以預期的，但究竟是由何人所造成，不得而知，則社會就必須以公權力的介入，在沒有污染之前進行預防措施，而此項預防措施之費用，當然應由整個社會來負擔，所以共同負擔原則是可能衍生至預防的階段或擴展至最後的整治階段。

（二）集體負擔原則

集體負擔原則是共同負擔原則與污染者負責原則的折衷，故一方面既是污染者負責，另一方面亦是共同負擔，亦即環境污染的成本及費用是由共同的污染者來負擔。例如化學工廠所造成的污染，由所有的化學工廠共同來負擔，而不限縮以國家的力量或某特定之污染源負擔，轉以某團體整體的力量代之，所以又稱團體負擔原則[21]或污染者團體負責原則。最顯著的例證，就是空氣污染防制費或廢棄物清除處理費中所成立之基金，在污染造成時，應由造成同一污染類型之污染者全體來負擔防制、處理及費用的支付。這種不由個別污染者，而由集體類型相同之污染者負擔的原則，可以達成免除社會成本的效果。

（三）全過程控制原則

該原則源起於美國環境法上發展出來的環境保護政策；所要求的對於有關環境保護的「全面性」（from cradle to Grave）的掌握。具體而言，它包含與環境污染或傷害有關的產品之生產、使用及「排除」或之後的「禁止」，均應作出適當之「監控」，並在適當之情形完全排除之。

---

[21] 同前註，第334頁。

四、特定原則

（一）可持續發展原則

　　1980年10月30日聯合國大會通過A/RES/35/7號決議，認知到自然的運行機制與多樣性的生物形成，能為全人類帶來共同的利益。與此同時，在1980年又制定了「世界自然保護大綱」，其中第一次提及「可持續發展」之概念。更重要的是聯合國大會在1982年10月28日通過了「世界自然憲章」（World Charter for Nature）。在它的第一章一般原則之下，即明文提及：對人類所利用之生態系統與生物及陸地、海洋及大氣資源，應設法使其達到並維持最適宜之永續生產率，但不得危及與其共存之其他生態系統或物種之完整性。到了1987年「聯合國世界環境與發展委員會」（U.N. World Commission on Environment and Development）更提交了一份「布倫特蘭報告」（Bruntland Report）以「我們共同的未來」（Our Common Future）為主題，文中對「可持續發展」作出具體的定義，認為「可持續發展」是「既滿足當代人的需要，又不會對後代人滿足其需要的能力，構成危害的發展」（the needs of the present without compromising the ability of future generations to meet their own needs.）。到了1992年在巴西的里約熱內盧所召開的「聯合國環境與發展會議」（United Nations Conference on Environment and Development）又稱為「里約地球高峰會議」（Rio Earth Summit）。發表了著名的「里約宣言」（Rio Declaration）其原則一即指明：人類為永續發展關懷之核心。人類有權順應自然，過健康而有生產能力之生活。更在原則四提出如下之說明：為實現永續發展，環境保護應為發展進程不可缺之部分，不能脫離此進程予以「孤立」之考量。

（二）共同但有區別之責任原則

　　所謂「共同但有區別之責任」（common but differentiated responsibilities），是指由於地球生態系統的整體性和各國導致全球環境退化的各種不同作用，它們對保護全球環境負有共同但是又有區別的責任。共同但有區別的責任是國際環境法特有的原則，它在1992年的聯合國環境與發展大

會上得以初步確立，並被認為是開發中國家鬥爭的勝利成果之一，此後逐漸成為指導各國參與全球環境保護事業的一項重要原則。該原則包括兩個各自獨立，但又緊密關聯的方面，即共同的責任和有區別之責任。說明如下[22]：

首先，國家之國際社會要承擔保護共同關切事項的共同責任。人類共同關注事項概念的價值之一在於它為國際社會集體行動提供了合法性，克服了共同關切問題只應在國內加以解決的理論假定。

其次，國際社會中發達國家和開發中國家成員對保護共同關切事項承擔有區別的責任。國際社會對共同關切事項承擔共同責任並不意味著「平均主義」。開發中國家與發達國家雖然負有保護共同關切事項的共同責任，但發達國家應當比開發中國家承擔更大的或是主要的責任。這種限制是由共同關切事項問題形成的歷史和現實原因所決定的。

（三）協同合作原則

國際合作是國際法的一項基本原則，它同樣構成了生物多樣性國際法的基石。不過，在生物多樣性國際法領域，該原則被拓展為協同合作原則，國際社會的全體成員（包括各類治理主體）應當進行廣泛密切的合作，透過合作而非對抗的方式、協調一致，來持續保育和持續利用全球生物多樣性[23]。

與傳統的國際合作原則相比，協同合作原則最大的發展就是它雖然依然強調國家間主體在生物多樣性領域合作的主導性，但它同樣重視國家間主體與其他主體和利益相關者之間，以及後者內部之間的國際合作。可以說，生物多樣性的全球治理可能不是由民族國家權威所組成的單一生物多樣性國際法架構，而是國家、政府間國際組織、非政府組織、跨國公司乃至個人等不同主體和利益相關方達成協同的產物。而這種治理的基本形式和有效機制就是多主體的協同合作[24]。

---

[22] 同前揭註4，第114頁。

[23] 同前註，第120頁。

[24] 同前註，第121頁

　　協同合作作為生物多樣性國際法的基本原則有其發生的必然性。當今世界，生物多樣性問題已經由一國的內部事物和國內公害發展為全球性的公害，成為人類共同面臨的威脅。如前所述，全球生物多樣性問題的規模之大、影響範圍之廣、危害之烈、持續之久、發生發展機制之複雜，遠非單個國家的經濟、技術和防治能力所能解決。在環境問題的嚴重程度與各國有限能力間存在尖銳衝突的情況下，各國唯有攜手合作、共同努力，才有拯救世界環境和整個人類之可能。國際合作遂成為生物多樣性國際法用來解決全球生物多樣性問題的必然途徑[25]。

---

[25] 同前註。

第七章　國際環境法之運作

壹、運作背景

　　從前面幾章的內容，一般人所可以注意到的是條約的重要性以及「多邊環境協定」（Multinational Environmental Agreements, MEAs）在國際環境問題上所能發揮的效力。但是更深層的問題，乃在於國際環境法與多邊環境協定之間相輔相成的角色地位，如何在國際社會的大環境之下，各自是如何運作的？它們彼此又是如何解決所共同面對的國際環境的各種問題？在當下的各種重要的國際議題上，二者是如何能發揮它們各自所被設定的功能？或者更進一步地指出：國際環境法與多邊環境協定有沒有更「好」的實現它們所預定的角色。

　　要回答上面的問題，就必須注意到兩個「關鍵措施」（Key Measures）：「遵守措施」（Compliance Measures）及「效果措施」（Effectiveness Measures）[1]。就「遵守措施」而言，那就是要來衡量「多邊環境協定」是如何地成功的改變了法律（國際環境法）所針對的國家及公司企業的「行為」（Behavior），使它們如夠「遵守」法律對它們的要求。而相對的來講，「效果措施」則是要來衡量上述因「遵守措施」而改變的「行為」，是如何成功地實際上的解決了「多邊環境協定」所針對的各種特定的環境問題。而此處有一個很基本的認識必須要加以釐清。那就是任何一個「多邊環境協定」如果運用的不得當，或是任何其他的原因，有可能會造成一個「空心的」（Shallow）的情形，而不具有任何實質的意義或效果。也有可能僅有對締約國產生最小的實質義務而已；在這樣的情形下，縱使是達到「高層度的遵守」（High Compliance），對於所要強調的

---

[1] Daniel Bodansky, Jutta Brunnee and Ellen Hey, The Oxford Handbook of International Environmental Law, (Oxford: Oxford University Press, 2007), p. 894.

環境問題，也不會有什麼「效果」（Effect）的產生。

　　而相對照的來檢視，另外一個「多邊環境協定」，也許就會有一個「深層的義務」（Deep Obligation）要求「改變」（Change），這就因此在國際社會中的各個國家或成員，作出更多的努力以及在「行為」上有更大的「改變」；縱使不具有高度或深層的「遵守」（Compliance），但是對於所面對的環境問題，卻能夠產生比較「強」（Strong）的效果。可以如此的作一個簡要的「預先認定」（Presumption）[2]：在通常的情形下，「遵守措施」與「效果措施」並不相同，但卻會是一個很好的「代理者」（Surrogate），所以愈多的「遵守」，在一般的狀況下，就意味著會有更多的「效果」（It is a good surrogate, so that more compliance generally will mean more effectiveness.）。

　　一個具有代表性的傳統國際法學者韓肯（Louis Henkin）對於國際法的遵守有下面一段話的說明：「幾乎所有的國家會遵守所有的國際法原理以及在幾乎所有的時間下，會遵守所有的它們的義務」（Almost all nations observe almost all principles of international law and almost all of their obligations almost all of the time.）[3]。而另外一位學者史配思（Gus Speth）則毫不客氣的指出：儘管有那麼多的「多邊環境協定」，但是卻一直未能充分的發生它們的效力。他在2004年為文直接指出：「在美國的國內立法上成功地阻止了國內的很多環境上的濫權，然而，在努力保護全球的環境上，大致上卻是是失敗的。那就是在環境惡化的趨勢上並未改善，以及更多的那樣的情形，在沒有前例的環境的時代，沒有辦法把我們及時地帶往我們所要達到的境界。」（Whereas our national legislation [in the U.S.] was successful in curbing many environmental abuses domestically, efforts to protect the global environment have largely failed in the sense that the trends in environmental deterioration have not improved and that more of the same will not get us where we want to be in time to head off an era of unprecedented envi-

---

[2]　同前註，第895頁。
[3]　同前註，第894頁。

ronmental decline.）[4]。我們姑且認定史配思教授的看法或見解是正確的評估；那麼，一個簡單的結論就是「多邊環境協定」一直未能有「效果」的產生，原因在哪？是不是因為各國未能好好地去「執行」（Implement）國際環境協定？抑或是國際環境協定的要求，本身過於軟弱？所以可以知道「遵守措施」與「效果措施」根本是兩個截然不同的東西。

貳、運作之理論基礎

國際環境法之要能有效運作，到了二十世紀末，多數學者專家大致上會同意，「遵守理論」（Compliance Theory）才是主要的支撐基礎。他們大多會同意，任何一個國家的「遵守」國際環境法規範或國際環境協定，而不必去詢問它背後的「動機」（Motivation）為何？或其他因素之考量。進一步而言，要了解「遵守」意旨為何？那就有必要去了解有什麼樣的「特定規則」（Specific Rule）是那樣的「協定」或「規範」使得「遵守」的主體、公司或個人，有「義務」去加以落實；以及這樣的落實作法針對不同的「行為者」，會有什麼樣不同的義務去加以落實。就國際層面而言，任何一個國家當它加入了一個「國際機制」（International Regime）（那是指它簽訂或加入了某一個國際環境協定或公約），那個國家即承擔起了「國際義務」去執行其中的規定，這就是「遵守」。而就「內國」（Domestic）的情形而論，國家內的個人或公司實體有「義務」去遵守它的國家的環境法律或法規，這當然是「遵守」之本意。如果有任何不遵守或違反之情事發生，將會有「責任」去擔負或「損害賠償」的責任，去受到懲罰或其他不同程度的法律責任要擔負起來。

國際環境法的發展至今，已經顯現出許多種不同的「策略」（strategy）來改善落實或「遵守」的效果。一般而言，大致上有兩種「作法」（Approach）：一、經由執行的努力，用「制裁」（Sanction）的方式，

---

[4] 同前註，第895頁。

來達到「阻卻」(Deterrence)的效果;以及二、「遵守之協助」(Compliance Assistance)[5]。

一、阻卻之作法

「阻卻之作法」(Deterrence Approach)是假定在一個國際或國內社會中,國家、公司實體、以及個人均是一個「理性的」(Rational)行為者。它(他)們相信任何違反或不遵守「協定」或規範的結果,會帶來一個迅速即刻的「可預測的」(Predictable)「回應」(Response),而這樣的「回應」則包括制裁或懲罰;因此,在絕大多數的情形下,它(他)們很自然會受到「阻卻」。而「阻卻」的作法,其重點乃是放在或是強調「檢視與監督」(Inspection and Monitoring)來「偵測」(Detect)「不遵守」的情事是否發生。其後,再跟隨著「適當的執行反應」(Appropriate Enforcement Response),例如:行政或司法的「起訴」(Prosecution),來作出制裁或其他的懲罰措施[6]。

二、遵守之協助

「遵守之協助」之作法,乃是在尋求自願的遵守,那就是藉由創造出一個「規範性的國內或國際社區」(Regulated Domestic or International Community)之中的一種「義務的氣息」(Sense of Obligation)。例如:在一個「制定法律的過程」(Law-Making Process)當中,有一個「高程度」(High Degree)的「參與」(Participation)及「透明化」(Transparency),這樣就會導致「合法性及公平性」(Legitimacy and Fairness)的「認知」(Perception),然後就能導引出有義務去遵守的感覺;之後,就有比較高的意願去「遵守」協定或規範。而「遵守之協助」也包括採取教育的、技術的、以及財務合作的方式,去幫忙那些「行為者」或潛在的

---

[5] 同前註,第225頁。
[6] 同前註,第227頁。

行為者，去提升它（他）們的行為「能量」（Capacity），去「遵守」協定或規範之作為或不作為。

參、運作之法則分析

一、預防原則之適用[7]

　　預防原則，簡單而言，主要是在說明環境政策與環境法非僅是對具體環境破壞之「反應」（Reaction），亦即不僅限於抗拒對於環境具有威脅性之危害，及排除已產生之具體損害；而是更進一步積極地，在一定危險性產生之前，就預先去防止對環境及人類生物之危害性的產生，並持續地致力於基本自然生態的保護及美化。

　　所謂的「預防原則」，不是在對環境產生具體危險時，對具體危險做出立即反應，此並非是本原則主要目的，而是如有潛在危害可能性出現時，或毫無危害性，而是事先且預防性地對「人」加以保護，或對生態環境加以美化，使其免於因為環境品質喪失，或環境破壞而遭到損害。此處所謂的危害，並非具體的危險，而是有可能危及生態環境，並造成人之損害的徵兆，便視為預防原則下的危害。基於此原則，相關單位對於資源使用時，應事先規畫其使用，預防資源因不當利用而枯竭，此稱為資源預防。

　　綜上所述，預防原則應包含「危險性的預防」及「未來的預防」。前者則必須從具體危險排除之危險定義為解釋之基準，此時所謂危險係指在事件發展過程中明顯可以得知，無法阻止其造成損害，其結果就是違法或法益保護被降低。就警察法而言，此為客觀明顯可知且迫近的損害出現可能性。依此，預防原則上之危險性應比具體危險出現在時間及空間上更有距離，換言之，就是「危險尚未逼近」，也就是預防措施必須在危險出現

---

[7]　陳慈陽，環境法總論，台北，元照出版公司，2011年，第309頁。

門檻外或危害出現之前採取。此時其要件應是[8]：

（一）時間及空間上尚為遙遠的危險：其內容首先包含未來世代可能產生危險的預防，而且此種環境迫害可能長期或永遠無法再度回復，因此可稱為國家預防事先規畫的危險性控制任務。

（二）其狀態包含了出現可能性非常低及至危險性之嫌疑或僅是危險性事先的預防：此時損害出現可能性的要件，無須如具體危險出現般的嚴格，甚至縱使未經證實的危險嫌疑就已足夠。易言之，只要損害出現可能性、可預期或可想像即可；而無須有此可能性之證明依據。所以預防原則有時被稱為謹慎原則。潛在污染環境行為存在，雖屬不確定，且損害雖不能被證明，但並非不可能就屬之。國家在此之國家保護義務具有憲法正當性之依據。

（三）對環境的污染在此階段與其他污染共同作用時是可能造成損害，但科技上是可以降低其危害或甚至可避免的。

（四）此乃在保護對污染產生可能性有感受之居民。

而對未來預防，可以是資源預防，此乃認為立法者基於預防原則，來對環境資源基於世代永續使用之利益，來為環境規畫的基本決定。此時所規畫的，為未來世代環境空間的規畫及保留，如人口居住空間或工商發展區域之規畫等。不過預防原則並非課與國家排除所有污染可能性，也就是無所謂「零風險」（Zero Risk）的國家義務存在。

二、環境傷害保護原則之適用

環境傷害保護原則亦有學者將其指為「危險防禦原則」。二者所指為對於環境之傷害，即是一種「危險」之發生，而有必要在危險或風險發生之前，即予以「防禦」其發生，亦就是指：對於環境之傷害的危險或風險應預先採取「保護」之作法或措施，以免一旦危險發生或傷害造成，所要付出之代價，就難以計數。

---

[8] 同前註，第314頁。

　　危險防禦或傷害保護之危險，或傷害之對抗的客體，或傷害之客體，必須是具體之危險或傷害，也就是說此類危險或傷害必須會達到明確且顯著之危險或傷害，也就是指對造成環境、生命、身體、健康危險的抵抗。例如抵抗有威脅性的火災、爆炸、水災，或又如防禦人類或是動植物經由水、土壤、空氣接觸有害物質受到的危害。在實務上亦可見到此原則之實現，例如防治水或空氣污染，便規定如遇污染情形應為何種應變措施之時、地、人與行為之規定。此即是一種明顯的對具體環境危害之抵抗或排除，而這些規範一一視為對行為人的規範[9]。

　　但此原則相較於前述之「預防原則」，就環境目標的達成上，應是次要或相較下顯得較不重要之原則。因為環境永續經營及發展著重在事前的預防，例如經由環境影響評估程序或各該環境法中之環境標準，來使污染行為得以避免，使其不發生。然而，「危險防禦原則」則是在管制的階段，就具體造成環境危害時，才有其適用。因此其非是環境法及環境政策上主要之期待。又「預防原則」和「危險防禦原則」雖然在適用上屬於不同階段，但兩者仍是相輔相成的，必須配合使用。例如相關單位在事先計畫時，一個排放污水的設施，其關於放流口的設計、相關設備的設置、損害可能性的評估及發生損害的應變計畫，其內容及數據都應合於基於「預防原則」及「危險防禦原則」所制定之環境及污染標準。而其最終要達到的目的是現存在環境品質之保障，及未來改善可能性的確保；亦即人民及政府的作為不可使環境更加惡化，以及若已發生污染損害，便要使其恢復原狀[10]。

三、合作原則之適用

　　廣義的合作原則，是指包括政府、人民、產業界等所有的環境使用者，都應該負有保護環境的責任。更進一步而言，國家與所有社會的力量，在環境保護的領域之中，必須共同合作。此原則首先分配國家、人

---

[9] 同前註，第317頁。

[10] 同前註，第317頁至318頁。

民、產業及社會之任務及責任，其次要求國家來達成合作性質的任務執行。環境保護就是公共任務，國家、社會及產業是不容許逃脫此任務及責任的承擔，更何況國家任務就在於保障國民團體安全及福祉。所以雖稱合作原則，但國家有整合及達成合作原則的「獨占」義務及責任。基本上，此一原則是屬於政治上之程序原則，係以達成環境政策之內容為目標，但在必要時，方可作為法規之內涵。例如屬於環境協商之以往公害協定與現在的環境保護協定或行政契約，前者是透過協商的方式，達到合作原則的表現。後者是透過對等地位的契約簽訂，而不以國家之強制力來達成一定之目的。此原則首先具體化在我國環境基本法第4條第1項中，要求國民、事業及各級政府應共負環境保護之義務及責任[11]。

　　合作原則最重要的一點內容是「公眾參與」（Public Participation），例如環境影響評估之公開說明會，及行政程序法中有關聽證之舉行等。特別是在工業設施的執照發給，在未進行實質的審查之前，更應該踐行這個程序。其另一個內涵是「資訊的合作」，假設沒有資訊的公開及資訊的取得，任何政府要進行環境保護的工作，都是不可能的。所以，政府在資訊方面亦應與其他之力量，共同來合作，達成環境保護之任務[12]。

　　合作原則本身實為在環境政策上較不具有強制性，而且是一種較溫和達成環境保護的措施及要求。此一原則之內容主要在說明環境保護並非僅是國家的責任，也非僅靠經濟或社會單一方面的力量可以達成的，欲達成此目的主要還是需要所有相關之力量的共同合作。只有相關當事人之共同負責及共同參與於環境保護的事務上，如此才能達到個人自由及社會需求一定的平衡關係。這也就是合作原則在環境保護上所要達成之最基本之目的，就其積極面亦可認為：它是給予國家機關、產業界及人民應為有利於環境保護行為之義務性。此正如我國現階段環境保護政策綱領在第二章策略部分第3款明確的要求，國民及產業界應有與政府共同致力於環境保護之責任。如其並未以法規強制形式出現，而僅是政策綱領之宣示，則應視

---

[11] 同前註，第335頁。
[12] 同前註。

為一環境政策上基本原則，因此，它可以只是一種對立法者或在某種狀況下對司法權之行使指示方針，對人民而言亦不可作為具體侵入行為之授權依據[13]。

肆、運作之流程

一、問題之普遍化

科技為人類社會創造了高度的物質文明，帶來了各國的經濟成長，這是正面的善果；但是，每件事有正面就必然會有負面。科技的發展對人類社會的負面的惡果，最明顯而直接的「結果」，就是環境保護問題的惡化，所謂的「環境危機」（Enironmental Crisis）就是由此而來的。二十世紀以來，這樣的「環境危機」，不再局限於某一個國家或某一個地區，而成為了國際社會所要面對的「共同問題」，必須去面對它、處理它、乃至於去解決它。這就是國際環境法之解決問題的第一步——問題之普遍化，用以證明環境保護問題之必要性與急迫性。

二、問題之共識化

環境保護的「工程」，不是在哪一個單一國家或單一地區，所能夠獨立完成的，也不是「一蹴可幾」的。而各國也都體認到真正的解決，不是哪一個國家的政府可以獨立完成。必須透過「國際合作」的方式，政府、民間、非政府組織等各方面的群策群力，相互配合，方能在正確的方向，帶領到國際社會對於國際環保問題的解決，形成一個得以解決的方案。將環境保護的觀念予以制度化、標準化、合理化，以期望國際社會能夠形成共同的理念，讓全體人類能夠在科技發展及經濟成長之餘，也能同時有個健康、潔淨與高品質的生活環境。這也是聯合國在1970年代積極主動的帶

---

[13] 同前註，第336頁。

領各個單一國家，召開各種環境保護會議、簽訂國際公約，以及發表各種類型之宣言及議定書之前，國際社會對於解決環境問題之「共識」（Consensus）。

三、問題之規範化

國際社會對於國際環境問題之解決，在形成共識之後的下一步，乃是要將問題，超越主觀的認同或言詞討論的階段，期待能達到客觀的接受及書面的認可之層次。然後，再經由宣言的發布、議定書的簽署，最後再透過正式或非正式的雙邊或多邊的「協商」，建立客觀的標準或原則的確定，以完成雙方條約或多邊公約之簽訂。

從以上的「規範化」流程中不難發現，國際環境問題之規範化，其內涵乃是意指，該「環境問題」從來就不曾為人們所察覺，經過科學探究，到最後才能達成國際環境法之規範。當然，並非所有「國際環境議題」都會有「規範化」的現象，而且一般而言，不同的議題，大致上會處於不同的規範程度，或層次的差異上面[14]。

四、問題之實效化[15]

國際環境議題規範化的發展，固然是人類社會解決全球環境問題的重要里程碑，但如此並不必然的能真正解決問題。事實上，許多國際法規範仍未被國際社會所遵行，使該等國際法規範空有規範的軀殼，而無規範的實效。如以氣候變遷此一國際環境議題的因應為例，雖然有綱要公約的出現，但未來仍有許多規範化的路要走，國際社會是否會真誠地遵守公約的規定，仍然存有許多變數。因此，如何在規範的動態發展過程中，同時發展規範的實效性，更是國際社會所應重視的課題。

國際環境法規範的實效性，可從程序理性與規範強化兩方面觀察。前

---

[14] 葉俊榮，全球環境議題——臺灣觀點，台北，巨流圖書公司，1999年，第31頁。
[15] 同前註，第54頁。

者強調規範形成過程中照顧到程序價值，後者則強調於規範形成後，進行規範的反覆審查與回饋，藉著內涵的日漸明確可行，則可以強化規範強度。

　　國際環境法規範，其規範強度，透過規範設定、規範執行與規範審查等階段，循環辯證的結果，往往能由弱轉強。在程序面向上，愈能強化程序理性，讓相關當事國（人）所信服與認同的規範，愈能建立它的實效性。反之，若僅是少數國家基於特殊利益之考量，以相當封閉的決策程序所運作出來，而不考慮到整個規範社群的立場與利益的規範，就很難真正發揮實效性。又規範的執行過程中，往往更能看出內涵的曖昧不清，或規定不實之處，透過合乎事理的解釋與反省，逐漸強化規範的實質理性，就有可能進而強化其實效性。

第八章　國際環境法實質問題研究

壹、基本認識

　　國際環境問題，隨著各國經濟發展及科技進步的結果，所產生的問題變成比任何的一個時期及任何的一門領域，都要來得更加多元化與更加複雜化，而在最近二十年來顯然變成了媒體報導的焦點。舉凡一般人所熟知的臭氧破裂、溫室效應、酸雨問題、瀕臨絕種生物問題、空氣污染、土地污染、海洋污染等問題，不勝枚舉。環境問題，難以否認的是它包羅萬象，是各國最近這些年來相當關心的重要議題。其中最主要的一個特性就是各國在發展經濟的過程中，隨著經濟活動的進行，無論生產或消費活動均會不斷地製造出環境問題。在生產方面，隨著生產單位的增加及生產工具的改良，使得生產品的種類多樣化及產量不斷地成長，景觀的破壞及污染等公害均會與日俱增而日趨嚴重。在消費方面，噪音、廢水、垃圾等也同時不斷地增加而惡化。各國在經濟發展的過程當中，大致上均會碰到相同的問題。這也就是環境保護的另一個特性，也就是它不再局限單一國家本身的問題，往往是跨國之間彼此必須共同面對，協力合作，採取統一而一致的作法，才能有效解決。所謂「地球只有一個」、「給下一代一個乾淨的空間」等等，不再是「口號」，而必須有徹底的認識而積極地去處理地球上的環境保護問題，建立一個客觀的可以接受的規範，讓大家真正地去「愛地球」。在這樣的理念之下，本章將以下列幾個議題，作為研究的對象：一、大氣及外太空；二、海洋及淡水資源；三、生物資源；四、危險物質及危險活動。

貳、大氣之環境保護

就有關於「大氣的環境保護」（The Envirotection Protection of the Atmosphere），大致上可以分為三大「國際規範活動」（International Regulatory Activity）：一、「越境之大氣污染」（Transboundary Air Pollution）、二、「Ozone Depletion」（臭氧層破壞）及三、「全球暖化」（Global Warming）。此三種類別均共同「分享」、「越境」或「全球」層面的共同特質；而且在現行的「習慣法」（Customary Law）之下，並不存在充分的規範性法規（包含傳統國際法之「國家責任」在內）來因應此三種環境保護的問題。而且就目前的情形來檢視有關此三大類型的大氣環境的問題之「持續存在性」（Persistence）及「範圍的涵蓋面」，尚有不少的存疑。

一、越境之大氣污染

國際社會很快就注意到了污染源所造成的「大氣污染」。就國際環境法規範的角度切入這樣的問題，就是污染源「跨越」了國界之後的「責任」負擔的問題，這在早年相當程度的引起了國與國之間的緊張關係。有案可稽的是1941年的Trail Smelter Case（United States v. Canada），此一案例在國際環境法的領域內相當具有代表性。此一案例最後仲裁庭的判決文指出：沒有任何一個國家有權使用或允許在它的領域內的使用，以油煙造成傷害到其他國家之內的人民財產上的損失。本案相當有意義，在某種程度上在「大氣污染」的國際環境保護規範上，占有相當重要的一席之地。

其次，到了1979年，國際社會針對越境之大氣污染簽訂了「跨境長程空氣污染物公約」（Convention on Long Range Transboundary Air Pollution, LRTAP），主要的是訂定了清除空氣污染物的「合作原則」，並且建立了各國合作研究的架構。注意到了「污染問題」的解決，要由各國採取合作研究的方式才能達成環境保護的目標。

二、臭氧層破壞之環境問題

除了溫室效應之外，「臭氧層」（Ozone Layer）破壞是世界各國密切注意與討論的另一項與大氣層有關的重要問題。臭氧層分布在大氣層高處，可以過濾陽光中有害的紫外線，問題是工業廢氣中的微粒會飄到大氣層頂端，並且與那裡的臭氧分子起化學作用，臭氧便隨之分解；在各種懸浮微粒當中，氟氯碳化合物對於臭氧層的破壞程度最為嚴重，這類物質廣泛運用在冷凍設備與噴霧容器當中。值得注意的是，燃燒化石燃料也會產生臭氧，然而，只會對海拔較低的大氣層造成污染，無法飄到高處補充臭氧層的損失[1]。

隨著臭氧層變薄，到達地球表面的紫外線數量增加。南極圈上方的臭氧層原本薄於其他地方。每年有幾個月時間，當地會出現一個臭氧層的破洞。跡象顯示，這個破洞越來越大，出現時間也越來越長。到了1990年代初期，臭氧層破洞已經蔓延到北美洲上空。專家提醒人們做好防曬措施，以便降低罹患皮膚癌的機率。臭氧層的破壞遲早會對環境生態造成嚴重衝擊，紫外線輻射增加可能導致綠色植物大量死亡、農地生產力銳減，以及其他環境生態的浩劫[2]。

1972年，聯合國在瑞典首都斯德哥爾摩首度召開以環境生態為主題的國際會議，會中通過若干一般性原則。例如，甲國採取的行動不應對乙國環境生態造成破壞。相關討論指出環境污染源有可能來自國外的事實，值得各國注意。1982年，類似會議在肯亞首都奈洛比（也是聯合國環保計畫總部所在地）召開，該會受到國際媒體的報導程度不如斯德哥爾摩會議。1992年的地球高峰會（下文簡稱地球峰會）是這類會議的第三度召開。這次會議不僅規模較大，企圖心也比前兩次會議強烈[3]。

針對臭氧層破壞的問題，其解決的作法，也是急不得的，必須循序

---

[1] 歐信宏與胡祖慶合譯，Joshua S. Goldstein, International Relations，國際關係，台北，雙葉書廊，2003年，第445頁。

[2] 同前註。

[3] 同前註。

漸進；從相鄰國家之間的雙邊問題（例如Trail Smelter Case之處理），到區域性問題的解決；然後才進一步到達「全球的層面」（Global Dimension）。臭氧層破壞的影響太大了，它直接影響到地球上全人類的生活環境，必須要確確實實的面對它，在科技允許的範疇下，以一切可能的作法去處理它，才是正確的因應之道。

三、全球暖化之問題

「全球暖化」（Global Warming），也有學者稱之為「全球溫室效應」（Global Warming），乃是指地球上各地的平均氣溫緩慢卻穩定地升高。不過，截至目前科學家仍然無法斷言這種現象是否正在發生。即使真有其事，氣溫上升的速度又有多快？無論如何，愈來愈多證據顯示溫室效應的確是個問題。它的起因是過多二氧化碳及其他氣體排放進入大氣層。在未來幾十年當中，溫室效應將日漸惡化。許多科學家相信及早處理會是個明智決定，一旦等到症候明顯，再做任何補救措施都將無濟於事，人類也將陷入一場浩劫[4]。

然而，要判斷誰先倒楣或災變會來得多快並非易事。根據多數科學家的推算，如果人類坐視溫室效應問題不去處理，五十年後世界各地平均氣溫將升高華氏兩度到九度。如果真的升高華氏九度，這就相當於今天與上個冰河時期間的溫差，也就是明顯的氣候變化。到了一定程度，或許在幾十年以後，南北極的冰帽可能會開始融化，即使只融化一小部分，某些地區的海平面可能會升高好幾英尺。果真如此，許多濱海城市都將沉入海底，與此同時，諸如孟加拉等低窪地區的平原也會被海水淹沒。目前，若干地處太平洋的島國用盡各種手段提醒世人溫室效應的嚴重性。箇中原因不難理解，當海平面升高的時候，他們都將從地圖上消失[5]。

全球氣候變化也可能改變許多地區的天氣型態，從而造成乾旱、洪水及自然生態系統失調的不良後果。當然，溫和的氣候變化也可能帶給某些

---

[4] 同前註，第442頁。
[5] 同前註。

地區好處。例如，當地農業生產力會因此提高。不過，沒有人敢保證不出問題。一般而言，氣候變化對於環境生態來說是弊多於利[6]。

溫室效應令各國面臨三項挑戰[7]：第一，其使得國家陷入左右為難的困境。如果要認真解決問題，各國勢必得在短時間付出代價。雖然就長期而言，他們理應得到回報，但是「報酬率」的高低難以預料。第二，當國家付出代價的時候，某些部門必須負擔較大責任。例如，石油公司與工廠作業員可說是首當其衝，相對地，換來的好處則是由全體國人共享。第三，國家間存在「公共財」的問題。相關工作由個別國家承擔，利益則由全人類共享。

受到南北國家對立的影響，第三項挑戰變得更加難以解決。怎樣分攤成本才算公平？雙方的期待與主張可說是南轅北轍。其中有項問題至為關鍵。如果南方國家承諾將廢氣排放數量控制在可以接受的程度，何年何月他們才能達到北方國家的工業化規模？各國排放溫室氣體的數量大致與其工業活動多寡成正比，目前，百分之八十的廢氣來自工業國家。其中美國一個國家排放的溫室氣體便占全球總量的四分之一。然而，就溫室效應造成的負面影響而言，南方國家或須面對若干最為嚴重的問題。誰應該承擔減少溫室效應的責任？國家間經常為此爭執不休。

「聯合國氣候變化架構公約」（United Nations Framework Convention on Climate Change, UNFCCC）乃是由聯合國大會擔任幕後的推手。其主要內容如下：

公約的目標為「為防止對氣候系統進行人為的有害干擾，應將大氣中非蒙特婁議定書管制溫室氣體的濃度穩定至一定水準。此一水準必須使生態系統有足夠的時間自然地適應氣候變遷，並且不影響食物的生產與經濟發展的永續進行」。

為了達成公約的目標，公約訂定了五個原則以供遵循，重點如下[8]：

---

[6] 同前註。

[7] 同前註。

[8] 葉俊榮，全球環境議題——臺灣觀點，台北，巨流圖書公司，1999年，第235頁至236頁。

（一）共同但有差別的責任

締約國應為了人類這一代及未來世代的利益保護氣候系統，而在公平的基礎上，各締約國依照其不同的能力，對保護氣候系統應負擔不同的責任。因此，已開發國家在對應氣候變遷及其不利影響上，應擔負主要的責任。

（二）考量開發中國家的需要

特別考量易受氣候變遷影響的開發中國家，以及公約是否會對開發中國家帶來不合比例及不正常的負擔。

（三）預防原則

各締約國應採行預先防止措施，以降低氣候變遷的成因與防治負面效果。在有嚴重或不可逆轉性損害的威脅時，不應因為在科學上的不確定性，而延遲採行措施。

（四）永續發展

締約國應該致力於永續發展，管制溫室效應的政策與措施，也必須配合各國特別的狀況並與各國的發展計畫結合。

（五）開放的國際經濟體系

各國應合作致力建立開放的國際經濟體系，以邁向永續性的經濟成長與發展。各項對應氣候變遷的措施，包括單方措施，不應以國際貿易上恣意或不正當的差別待遇或隱藏性限制的方式為之。

參、海洋環境之污染

關於「海洋環境的污染」（Pollution of the Marine Environment）可以來自於各種不同的活動源由，所謂的「污染源」大致上可以分為

一、來自於船舶的污染（Vessel-resource Pollution）；二、來自「傾倒」（Dumping）之污染；三、來自海底活動造成之污染；四、來自陸源之污染（Land-based Pollution Resources）；以及五、來自大氣或通過大氣之污染。而就海洋環境污染的整體性來檢視，聯合國並沒有忽略，依照時序的先後，有下列幾個公約。一、1972年之「防止傾倒垃圾及其物質污染海洋公約」（Convention on the Prevention of Marine Pollution by Dumping of Waste and Other Matter）簡稱「倫敦海拋公約」（London Dumping Convention, LDC）；二、1973年之「防止船舶污染國際公約」（International Convention for the Prevention of Pollution from Ship, MARPOL）；三、1982年之「聯合國海洋法公約」（United Nations Convention on the Law of the Sea, UNCLOS）；四、1989年之「禁止有害廢棄物越境運送及處理之巴塞爾公約」（The Basel Convention on the Control of Transboundary Movements of the Hazardous Wastes and Their Disposal）。分別說明如下。

一、海拋──倫敦海拋公約

　　本公約的管制對象為所有海洋及其沿海國領水範圍內的船隻、飛機等正常操作之外的一切有意傾棄廢物。本公約的目的在於防止隨意傾棄於海洋的廢棄物有害人體健康、危害生物資源及海洋生物、損害舒適或妨礙海洋的其他合法利用[9]。

　　本公約的管制工具係禁止某些廢棄物任意傾棄於海洋，對於特定廢棄物傾棄前，則建立特別許可的要求以及一般廢棄物的普通許可。因此係採取「禁止──許可」式的管制工具[10]。

　　此外，各締約國並承諾[11]：

　　（一）個別及集中地促進所有海洋環境污染來源的有效控制，並採取所有可行步驟防止廢棄物或其他物質傾棄所引起的污染。

---

[9] 同前註，第259頁。
[10] 同前註。
[11] 同前註。

（二）採取有效措拖以個別及集中地防止傾棄所引起的海洋污染並調和其政策。

（三）禁止除了表列以外廢棄物及其他物質的傾棄。

（四）指派一個主管機關發出許可證、保持傾棄的記錄、監測海洋的狀況，以及向國際海事組織報告以上這些事務。

（五）對所有在其領土內註冊及以其旗幟航行，以及在其領土或領海內裝載貨物而傾棄，或被相信在其管轄範圍內傾棄的船隻及航空器，有權執行公約的措施。採取措施以預防及懲罰違反公約的情形，並發展有效適用於公海的程序。

本公約並無制裁措施。締約國是否遵守公約的規定，係由諮商會議監測及評量。諮商會議可藉由傾棄活動及監測報告的通知以了解遵守的情形，但是並沒有建立正式的非遵守認定程序、前期通知義務或多邊諮商程序[12]。

二、油污──國際船污預防公約

本公約乃是一個防止船舶造成海洋環境污染的綜合性公約。本公約經1978年議定書修訂後，以消除作業過程中，可能排放之石油、化學品或其他有害物質，所引起之海洋污染為宗旨，並盡可能減少包括固定或浮動的鑽井平台在內的船舶，因碰撞或擱淺而意外洩漏的石油污染問題。

公約的管制對象為船隻排出對海洋造成污染的油品、化學品及其他有害物質。而公約的目的在於[13]：

（一）防止海洋遭到油品、化學品及其他有害物質的污染。

（二）盡量減少船隻、固定或浮動平台因意外碰撞或擱淺而溢出的油污量。

（三）進一步預防或控制船隻，特別是油輪造成的海洋污染。

---

[12] 同前註。

[13] 同前註，第260頁。

公約還包括了對400種以上有毒液體污染及污水、垃圾處理的特別控制措施。目前公約對於不遵守規範的情形並沒有正式的制裁程序。

三、海洋──聯合國海洋法公約

本公約的管制對象為國家管轄範圍以內及以外的海洋。公約的管制目的在於[14]：

（一）建立一套法秩序，以便利國際交通、促進海洋的和平用途、海洋資源的公平有效利用、海洋生物資源的養護，以及海洋環境的研究及保護。

（二）在全球及區域合作、科技協助、監測、環境影響評估、國際規範及標準，以及有關於海洋污染來源的內國立法方面，建立一套基本的環境保護原則與規範。

基於以上目的，公約規定各締約國應：

（一）密切監督其所允准或所從事活動產生的效果，以決定該項活動是否易於污染海洋環境。自該項監督所獲結果應通報國際組織，以便其提供資訊給所有締約國。

（二）在其管轄範圍內，繼續實施關於所有污染來源的內國及可應用的國際標準的主動執行。

（三）有關公約相關規定解釋及適用的爭議，應以和平的方式解決；並且確保受其管轄人民所導致海洋環境的損害，可在其法院系統下獲得救濟。

（四）採取保育生物資源的措施，並且合作採取保育公海漁業資源的措施。

---

[14] 同前註，第257頁至258頁。

四、有害廢棄物之跨國運送──巴賽爾公約

許多國家在處理廢棄物問題時，也已注意到有害廢棄物的潛在危害，為了保持其周圍的自然環境不受到破壞，而從立法及行政上加強有害廢棄物的管制。於是，或基於內國的管制標準較嚴格，處理費用較高；或基於場址選擇困難等因素，漸漸的將廢棄物送往遠處處理，以尋求較少成本的處理方式，解決其所產生的有害廢棄物。因此，廢棄物製造者往往有意無意將有害廢棄物運往外國處理。然而，由於不同的國家對有害廢棄物的處理技術與管制法令差異甚大，廢棄物的跨國境運送，往往引起許多環境生態與人體健康的疑慮，而跨國運送背後的商業動機，更引發許多國際倫理與正義的爭執[15]。

巴賽爾公約規範的對象在於限制管制物質的跨國境移動，故締約國具有以下的義務[16]：

（一）禁止輸出有害廢棄物到已禁止該種廢棄物輸入之國家，當締約國禁止廢棄物輸入時，必須通知其他締約國。

（二）締約國應致力於有害廢棄物的減量，並對其作最佳的處置，防止處理過程中可能產生的污染。各締約國應使有害廢棄物的跨國境移動減至最少。

（三）各締約國應採取各項法律和行政措施，執行公約的規定。

（四）各締約國應禁止輸出有害廢棄物至非締約國，也禁止自非締約國輸入有害廢棄物。

（五）有害廢棄物禁止運送至南緯六十度以南地區。

（六）輸入國應對輸入的有害廢棄物做到周全的環境管理（Environmentally Sound Management）。

（七）各締約國應採取各項措施，使有害廢棄物在以下兩種情況下才能允許輸出：1.本國沒有適當的處理場地或處理必須的設施。2.輸出的有

---

[15] 同前註，第262頁。
[16] 同前註。

害廢棄物可作為輸入國回收、循環再利用的原料。

　　所要注意的是巴賽爾公約中所指之有害廢棄物係指一般國所普遍認為具有爆炸性、易燃性、腐蝕性、化學反應性、毒性和傳染性特性中，一種或幾種特質之事業廢棄物或家用廢棄物。

肆、生物資源之保育與保護

一、瀕臨絕種之生物

　　1960年代，蓬勃之野生動植物國際貿易行為，對於部分的野生動植物的「族群」的生存與繁衍，已經造成相當程度的威脅。為了能使各種野生動植物「物種」得以「永續發展」免於滅絕的危機，乃由「國際自然保育聯盟」（World Conservation Union; IUCN）發起，公開呼籲各國政府正視此一問題之嚴重性，同時也開始著手野生物國際貿易管制工作。該「公約」之簽訂乃係國際社會的共同重視野生動植物「永續發展」的重要性；有多達80個國家的代表在1973年3月3日於美國首都華盛頓所簽署。公約之精神在於管制而非完全禁止野生物種的國際貿易。其具體目標係確保野生動植物之國際貿易，不至於威脅物種之生存，著重於保護瀕臨絕種之動植物，並且管制締約各方對公約界定之物種的國際貿易。

　　在野生物的保護上，華盛頓公約具有舉足輕重的角色。然而，相對於其他國際公約或區域協定，華盛頓公約並不對野生物的棲息地或威脅野生物生存的污染活動進行管制，而僅在於規範野生物的國際貿易行為[17]。華盛頓公約所揭示的基本原則在國際上普獲認同，公約對野生物的保育確也發生了實質作用。一般而言，會員大會所作成保育計畫或制裁不法的決

---

[17] 同前註，第277頁。

議，多能發揮成效，公正性也普受推崇[18]。

華盛頓公約的目的，在於如何保育瀕臨絕種的野生動植物，但野生物仍以急遽的速度消失。對保育而言更應關切的是野生物棲息地、生態系的保護，相關的科學研究也刻不容緩。以往所進行的大會，很少論及保育計畫的進行，多偏重在貿易管制的技術，甚至進一步肯認野生物貿易的價值。為積極促使瀕臨滅絕的生物恢復生機，整體性的保育工作將更為重要[19]。

二、生物多樣性之保育

經過多年的研究，人類認知到物種消失的速度，並體認到生物多樣性在生態、基因、社會、經濟、科學、教育、文化、娛樂和美學上的價值，同時亦認知到它在演化及維持生態圈永續生命系統的角色。生物多樣性的保育因而為人類共同關切，國際法上亦肯認每個國家對其境內的生物資源應有管轄權，且國家應負責保育國家境內的生物多樣性，並以永續的方式利用生物資源；但某些人類活動明顯地降低生物多樣性，關於生物多樣性的資訊與知識也非常欠缺，急切需要發展科學的、技術的、制度的能力，以提供計畫和實踐的基礎了解[20]。

基於上述認知，「聯合國環境保護署」（UNEP）自1987年即呼籲各國考慮就生物多樣的保育與合理利用訂定國際性的法律文件。次年，UNEP成立生物多樣性專家工作小組。經過近四年的研擬，生物多樣性公約於1992年5月22日獲得「政府間談判委員會」通過，於1992年6月2日巴西高峰會中正式開放簽署通過「生物多樣性公約」，1993年12月29日生效[21]。

本公約為有史以來國際生態保育上最重要的公約，相較於華盛頓公

---

[18] 同前註。
[19] 同前註，第286頁。
[20] 同前註，第287頁。
[21] 同前註，第288頁。

約，其格局放大至生態系諸多資源的保育與永續利用，且顧及科技、經濟、社會、文化、國際合作諸面向，因此世界對它期望之深不言可喻，唯實際功效如何，尚待努力與觀察[22]。

伍、危險物質及活動

一、巴塞爾公約之背景

國際社會長久以來就相當程度的注意到「國際安全」（International Safety）的問題。特別是自從1960年代以來，各國爭先恐後的實施「核子試爆」，其結果及影響，令國際社會相當的不安。各國開始朝向制定一個共同的規範去研擬國際公約來保障「國際安全」，特別是從1960年代之後，國際環境保護意識的高漲。再加上各國環境主義份子的監督及倡議之下，各國政府紛紛制定各種不同層級的環境管制法規，在民間產業方面也感受到相當程度的壓力，特別是在有危險物質及廢棄物的處理、運送及掩埋上面。因為管制的嚴格要求，使得相關的「成本」提高。在不得已的情況之下，民間企業團體不得不找出比較廉價的作法，那就是規範與管制。

1980年代後，日益高漲的環保意識與嚴格的內國環境管制法規，使得企業及廠商清理危險廢棄物的成本提高，為尋找更便宜的處理方式，企業開始私下將危險廢棄物運送至開發中國家或東歐。此等行為遭揭露後引起國際社會強烈不滿，因此促成了巴塞爾公約的起革及簽署[23]。本公約於1992年生效，直至目前為止已有172個締約方。最初十年，公約致力於立下管制危險廢棄物跨境移轉的法律架構，並發展出「無害環境管理」的標準。1995年，通過「禁運修正條款」（Ban Amendment）。1999年，通過議定書，然兩者皆尚未生效。截至2010年4月，本公約共有173個國家為其

---

[22] 同前註。

[23] 葉俊榮主編，國際環境法：條約選輯與解說，台北，新學林出版公司，第260頁。

締約方[24]。

二、巴塞爾公約之目標

　　公約近期目標為確實執行公約內容,並持續推動危險廢棄物的減量。1999年的部長會議肯認危險廢棄物減量為當前公約執行的首要任務,其具體目標包括[25]:積極推動和利用更乾淨的科技與生產方法、減少危險廢棄物的跨國運送、避免並監控非法的危險廢棄物運輸、提升科技與制度的能力,尤其須協助開發中國眾進行廢棄物處理、發展區域性訓練和技術移轉中心以強化廢棄物處理技術。1995年之修正案,禁止公約中附錄七的國家出口危險廢棄物。1999年之議定書,規範危險廢棄物跨境轉移時意外傾洩的損害賠償。[26]

三、巴塞爾公約之理念[27]

　　(一)本公約締約方,意識到危險廢棄物與其他廢棄物及其跨境轉移對人類與環境可能造成之損害。

　　(二)銘記著危險廢棄物與其他廢棄物之產生,其複雜性與跨境轉移之增長對人類健康與環境所造成之威脅日趨嚴重。

　　(三)又銘記著保護人類健康與環境免受此類廢棄物危害之最有效方法,係使其產生之數量及(或)潛在危害程度減至最低限度。

　　(四)深信各國應採取必要措施,以保證危險廢棄物與其他廢棄物之管現,包括其跨境轉移與處置須符合保護人類健康與環境之目的,不論處置場所位於何處。

　　(五)注意到各國應確保產生者必須以符合環境保護之方式,於危險廢棄物與其他廢棄物之運輸與處置方面履行義務,不論處置場所位於何

---

[24] 同前註。
[25] 同前註。
[26] 同前註,第261頁。
[27] 公約之序言論及。

處。

（六）充分確認任何國家皆享有禁止外國危險廢棄物與其他廢棄物進入其領土或於其領土內處置之主權權利。

（七）確認人們日益盼望禁止危險廢棄物之跨境轉移與其於其他國家，特別是於開發中國家之處置。

（八）深信危險廢棄物與其他廢棄物盡量於符合對環境無害之有效管理下，於廢棄物產生國之國境內處置。

（九）又意識到此類廢棄物自產生國到任何其他國家之跨境轉移，只有在進行此種轉移不致危害人類健康與環境、並遵照本公約各項規定之情況下才予以許可。

（十）認為加強對危險廢棄物與其他廢棄物跨境轉移之控制，將為環境無害管理與減少跨境轉移量帶來正面誘因。

（十一）深信各國應採取措施，適當交流有關危險廢棄物與其他廢棄物來往於相關國家之跨境轉移資訊，並控制此種轉移。

（十二）注意到一些國際與區域協定已處理關於危險物品過境時，保護與維護環境之問題。

四、巴塞爾公約之主要內容

公約內容大致可分為七部分，其分別為[28]：公約範圍與定義、締約國義務（合法的跨國危險廢棄物運送）、防免非法運輸、推動無害環境管理（Environmental Sound Management, ESM）、爭端解決與責任歸屬、國際公約間合作、公約運作方式與主要機構。公約最重要的無害環境管理，可從第4、5、6、7、10、11條中推導出，其最重要的宗旨在建立一完整的控制鏈，從危險廢棄物的儲存、運輸、處理、再利用、回收到棄置，都有完善的監控機制，以保護人類健康及環境，並盡量減少危險廢棄物的產生。而由於危險廢棄物對人體健康與環境極具威脅，其應盡可能在出產處就地

---

[28] 見前揭註23。

處理，因此，第4條規定，任何危險廢棄物的跨國移轉只有在先前以書面通知進口國並獲得其同意時，始可為之。第4條及第6條進而規定，危險廢棄物的運輸過程，從啟程處至最後棄置處，須附隨運輸移轉文件，以清楚危險廢棄物之內容及確保責任之歸屬，未附有該文件的危險廢棄物移轉行為即是非法。第4條並明示某些區域，例如南緯六十度以南，無論如何皆不可棄置危險廢棄物。第4條第9項規定若出口國無能力處理危險廢棄物時，得將廢棄物出口至其他有能力的國家，且同條第2項也對開發中國家明文加以保障，降低已開發國家將有害廢棄物出口到經濟弱勢國家的可能。公約第10條並規定國際合作，要求各締約方彼此提供貨料，建立廢棄物的環境無害管理機制，協調相關措施與標準，有能力的國家並應協助開發中國家進行技術升級，以便達成管制廢棄物的同一標準並實質減少有害廢棄物之產生。

第九章 國際環境法經典案例解析

案例一：The Trail Smelter Arbitration

壹、案例檢選

United States v. Canada

American-Canadian Joint Commission, Arbitral Tribunal, 1938 and 1941.

United Nations Reports of International Arbitral Awards, vol. 3, p. 1905.

　　At the beginning of this century, a Canadian company built a lead and zinc smelting plant at Trail, British Columbia, about ten miles north of the state of Washington border. Beginning in the 1920s, production was increased and by 1930 more than 300 tons of sulfur, including large quantities of sulfur dioxide, were being emitted daily. Some of the emissions were being carried down the Columbia River valley and allegedly causing damage to land and other property in the state of Washington. After negotiations between the US and Canada, the latter agreed in 1928 to refer the matter to the American-Canadian Joint Commission that the two countries had established in the Boundary Waters Treaty of 1909. In 1931, the Commission's Arbitral Tribunal reported that damage had occurred in the amount of $350,000. Canada did not dispute its liability and agreed to pay this amount. The smelter continued to operate, however, and continued to emit pollutants into the air over Washington. In 1938, the US claimed $2 million in damages for the years 1931 to 1937. The Tribunal allowed the claim only in part, awarding damages of just $78,000. In 1941, the US sought to have the operation of the smelter enjoined. The following question was submitted to the Tribunal: "whether the Trail Smelter should be required to refrain from causing damage in the state of Washington in the future and, if so, to what extent?"

1941 REPORT OF THE TRIBUNAL

The first problem which arises is whether the question should be answered on the basis of the law followed in the United States or on the basis of international law. The Tribunal, however, finds that this problem need not be solved here as the law followed in the United States in dealing with quasi-sovereign rights of the states of the Union, in the matter of air pollution, whilst more definite, is in conformity with the general rules of international law.

Particularly in reaching its conclusions as regards this question ... , the Tribunal has given consideration to the desire of the high contracting parties "to reach a solution just to all parties concerned."

As Professor Eagleton puts it: "A state owes at all times a duty to protect other states against injurious acts by individuals from within its jurisdiction." A great number of such general pronouncements by leading authorities concerning the duly of a state to respect other states and their territory have been presented to the Tribunal .... But the real difficulty often arises rather when it comes to determine what, *pro subjecta materie*, is deemed to constitute an injurious act.

A case concerning, as the present one does, territorial relations decided by the Federal Court of Switzerland between the Cantons of Soleure and Argovia, may serve to illustrate the relativity of the rule. Soleure brought a suit against her sister state to enjoin use of a shooting establishment which endangered her territory. The court, in granting the injunction, said: "This right (sovereignty) excludes ... not only the usurpation and exercise of sovereign rights (of another state) ... but also an actual encroachment which might prejudice the natural use of the territory and the free movement of its inhabitants." As a result of the decision, Argovia made plans for the improvement of the existing installations. These, however, were considered as insufficient protection by Soleure. The

Canton of Argovia then moved the Federal Court to decree that the shooting be again permitted after completion of the projected improvements. This motion was granted. "The demand of the government of Soleure," said the court, "that all endangerment be absolutely abolished apparently goes too far." The court found that all risk whatever had not been eliminated, as the region was flat and absolutely safe shooting ranges were only found in mountain valleys; that there was a federal duty for the communes to provide facilities for military target practice and that "no more precautions may be demanded for shooting ranges near the boundaries of two Cantons than are required for shooting ranges in the interior of a Canton."

No case of air pollution dealt with by an international tribunal has been brought to the attention of the Tribunal nor does the Tribunal know of any such case. The nearest analogy is that of water pollution. But, here also, no decision of an international tribunal has been cited or has been found.

There are, however, as regards both air pollution and water pollution, certain decisions of the Supreme Court of the United States which may legitimately be taken as a guide in this field in international law, for it is reasonable to follow by analogy, in international cases, precedents established by that court in dealing with controversies between states of the Union or with other controversies concerning the quasi-sovereign rights of such states, where no contrary rule prevails in international law and no reason for rejecting such precedents can be adduced from the limitations of sovereignty inherent in the Constitution of the United States ....

The Tribunal, therefore, finds that the above decisions, taken as a whole, constitute an adequate basis for its conclusions, namely that, under the principles of international law, as well as the law of the United States, no state has the right to use or permit the use of its territory in such a manner as to cause injury by fumes in or to the territory of another or the properties or persons therein, when the case is of serious consequences and the injury is established by clear and convincing evidence.

The decisions of the Supreme Court of the United States which are the basis of these conclusions are decisions in equity and a solution inspired by them, together with the regime hereinafter prescribed, will, in the opinion of the Tribunal, be "just to all parties concerned," as long, at least, as the present conditions in the Columbia River Valley continue to prevail.

Considering the circumstances of the case, the Tribunal holds that the Dominion of Canada is responsible in international law for the conduct of the Trail Smelter. Apart from the undertakings in the Convention, it is, therefore, the duty of the government of the Dominion of Canada to see to it that this conduct should be in conformity with the obligation of the Dominion under international law as herein determined.

The Tribunal, therefore, answers [the question submitted] as follows: ... So long as the present conditions in the Colombia River Valley prevail, the Trail Smelter shall be required from causing any damage through fumes in the state of Washington; the damage herein referred to and its extent being such as would be recoverable under the decisions of the courts of the United States in suits between private individuals. The indemnity for such damage should be fixed in such manner as the governments, acting under Article XI of the Convention, should agree upon.

貳、案例說明

一、任何一個國家有義務要採取措施，在那樣的情況下，可能是必要的、務實的到那樣的程度來確保在它的管轄領域內或掌控之下：

（一）遵守一般可以接受的國際法規及標準，為了防止、減少及對損害的掌握，特別是對於他國的環境保護必須如此，以及在本國管轄權範圍之外的環境保護亦是如此。

（二）本國活動的進行不要引起對於其他國家在環境上的重大傷害，或是本國管轄權以外地區環境的傷害。

二、任何一個國家對於其他國家前述一之（一）活動的違反要負起責任。

三、任何一個國家對於違反環境保護法規，所造成的對於其他國家的環境、財產、或人民的傷害，有義務要負起責任。

■案例二：Corfu Channel Case (Merits)

壹、案例檢選

United Kingdom v. Albania

International Court of Justice, 1949.

International Court of Justice Reports, vol. 1949, p. 4 (1949);

International Law Reports, vol. 16, p. 155 (1955).

JUDGMENT OF THE COURT: ...

In the Second part of the Special Agreement, the following question is submitted to the Court:

(2) Has the United Kingdom under international law violated the sovereignty of the Albanian People's Republic by reason of the acts of the Royal Navy in Albanian waters on October 22nd and on November 12th and 13th, 1946 and is there any duty to give satisfaction?

On May 15th, 1946, the British cruisers Orion and Superb, while passing southward through the North Corfu Channel, were fired at by an Albanian battery in the vicinity of Saranda ....

The United Kingdom government at once protested to the Albanian government, stating that innocent passage through straits is a right recognized by international law. There ensued a diplomatic correspondence in which the Albanian government asserted that foreign warships and merchant vessels had no right to pass through Albanian territorial waters without prior notification to, and the permission of, Albanian authorities. This view was put into effect by a communication of the Albanian Chief of Staff, dated May 17, 1946, which purported to subject the passage of foreign warships and merchant vessels in Albanian territorial waters to previous notification to and authorization by the Albanian government. The diplomatic correspondence continued and culminated in a United Kingdom note on August 2, 1946, in which the United Kingdom government maintained its view with regard to the right of innocent passage through straits forming routes for international maritime traffic between two parts of the high seas. The note ended with the warning that if the Albanian coastal batteries in the future opened fire on any British warship passing through the Corfu Channel, the fire would be returned.

...

It was in such circumstances that ... [the British cruisers *Mauritius and Leander*] together with the destroyers *Saumarez* and *Volage* were sent through the North Corfu Strait on ... [October 22, 1946].

The Court will now consider the Albanian contention that the United Kingdom violated Albanian sovereignty by sending the warships through this strait without the previous authorization of the Albanian government.

It is the opinion of the Court, generally recognized and in accordance with international custom that states in time of peace have a right to send their warships through straits used for international navigation between two parts of the high sea without the previous authorization of a coastal state, provided that the passage is *innocent*. Unless otherwise prescribed in an international convention, there is no right for a coastal state to prohibit such passage through straits in time of peace.

The Albanian government does not dispute that the North Corfu Channel is a strait in the geographical sense; but it denies that this Channel belongs to the class of international highways through which a right of passage exists, on the grounds that it is only of secondary importance, and not even a necessary route between two parts of the high seas, and that it is used almost exclusively for local traffic to and from the ports of Corfu and Saranda.

It may be asked whether the test is to be found in the volume of traffic passing through the strait or in its greater or lesser importance for international navigation. But in the opinion of the Court the decisive criterion is rather its geographical situation as connecting two parts of the high seas and the fact of its being used for international navigation. Nor can it be decisive that this strait is not a necessary route between two parts of the high seas, but only an alternative passage between the Aegean and the Adriatic Seas. It has nevertheless been a useful route for international maritime traffic .... The Court is further informed that the British Navy has regularly used this Channel for eighty years or more, and that it has also been used by the navies of other states.

One fact of particular importance is that the North Corfu Channel constitutes a frontier between Albania and Greece, that a part of it is wholly within the territorial waters of these states, and that the strait is of special importance to Greece by reason of the traffic to and from the port of Corfu.

Having regard to these various considerations, the Court has arrived at the conclusion that the North Corfu Channel should be considered as belonging to the class of international highways through which passage cannot be prohibited by a coastal state in time of peace.

On the other hand, it is a fact that the two coastal states did not maintain normal relations, that Greece had made territorial claims precisely with regard to a part of Albanian territory bordering on the Channel, that Greece had declared that she considered herself technically in a state of war with Albania, and that Albania, invoking the danger of Greek incursions, had considered it necessary to take certain measures of vigilance in this region. The Court is of the opinion that Albania, in view of these exceptional circumstances, would have been justified in issuing regulations in respect of the passage of warships through the strait, but not in prohibiting such passage or subjecting it to the requirement of special authorization.

For these reasons the Court is unable to accept the Albanian contention that the government of the United Kingdom has violated Albanian sovereignty by sending the warships through the strait without having obtained the previous authorization of the Albanian government.

...

The Albanian government has further contended that the sovereignty of Albania was violated because the passage of British warships on October 22nd, 1946 was not an *innocent passage* ....

It is shown by the Admiralty telegram of September 21st ... that the object of sending the warships through the strait was not only to carry out a passage for purposes of navigation, but also to test Albania's attitude. As mentioned above, the Albanian government, on May 15th, 1946, tried to impose by means of gunfire its view with regard to the passage. As the exchange of diplomatic notes did not lead to any clarification, the government of the United Kingdom wanted to ascertain by other means whether the Albanian government would maintain its illegal attitude and again impose its view by firing at passing ships. The legality of tins measure taken by the government of the United Kingdom cannot be disputed provided that it was carried out in a manner consistent with the requirements of international law. The "mission" was designed to affirm a right which had been unjustly denied. The government of the United Kingdom was not bound to abstain from exercising its right of passage, which the Albanian government had illegally denied.

...

It remains, therefore, to consider whether the *manner* in which the passage was carried out was consistent with the principle of innocent passage and to examine the various contentions of the Albanian government insofar as they appear to be relevant.

...

In the ... telegram of October 26th, the Commander-in-Chief reported that the passage "was made with ships at action stations in order that they might be able to retaliate quickly if fired upon again." In view of the firing from the Albanian battery on May 15th, this measure of precaution cannot, in itself, be regarded as unreasonable. But four warships-two cruisers and two destroyers-passed in this manner, with crews at action stations, ready to retaliate quickly if fired upon. They passed one after another through this narrow channel close to the Albanian coast, at a time of political tension in this region. The intention must have been, not only to test Albania's attitude, but at the same time to demonstrate such force that she would abstain from firing again on passing ships. Having regard, however, to all the circumstances of the case, as described above, the Court is unable to characterize these measures taken by the United Kingdom authorities as a violation of Albania's sovereignty.

... In a report of the commander of *Volage*, dated October 23rd, 1946－a report relating to the passage on the 22nd－it is stated: "The most was made of the opportunities to study Albanian defenses at close range ...."

...

With regard to the observations of coastal defenses made after the explosions, these were justified by the fact that two ships had just been blown up and that, in this critical situation, their commanders might fear that they would be fired on from the coast, as on May 15th.

Having thus examined the various contentions of the Albanian government insofar as they appear to be relevant, the Court has arrived at the conclusion that the United Kingdom did not violate the sovereignty of Albania by reason of the acts of the British Navy in Albanian waters on October 22nd, 1946.

***

In addition to the passage of the United Kingdom warships on October

22nd, 1946, the second question in the Special Agreement relates to the acts of the Royal Navy in Albanian waters on November 12th and 13th, 1946. This is the minesweeping operation called "Operation Retail."

After the explosions of October 22nd, the United Kingdom government sent a note to the Albanian government, in which it announced its intention to sweep the Corfu Channel shortly. The Albanian reply, which was received in London on October 31st, stated that the Albanian government would not give its consent to this ....

...

After this exchange of notes, "Operation Retail" ... was carried out under the protection of an important covering force composed of an aircraft carrier, cruisers, and other war vessels. This covering force remained throughout the operation at a certain distance to the west of the Channel .... The area swept was in Albanian territorial waters ....

The United Kingdom government does not dispute that "Operation Retail" was carried out against the clearly expressed wish of the Albanian government. It recognizes that the operation had not the consent of the international mine clearance organizations, that it could not be justified as the exercise of a right of innocent passage, and lastly that, in principle, international law does not allow a state to assemble a large number of warships in the territorial waters of another state and to carry out minesweeping in those waters. The United Kingdom government states that the operation was one of extreme urgency, and that it considered itself entitled to carry it out without anybody's consent.

...

The United Kingdom Agent, in his speech ... [to this Court], has ... classified "Operation Retail" among methods of self-protection or self-help. The Court cannot accept this defense .... Between independent states, respect for territorial sovereignty is an essential foundation of international relations. The Court recognizes that the Albanian government's complete failure to carry out its duties after the explosions, and the dilatory nature of its diplomatic notes, are extenuating circumstances for the action of the United Kingdom government. But to ensure respect for international law, of which it is the organ, the Court must declare that the action of the British Navy constituted a violation of Albanian sovereignty.

...

For these reasons, the Court ... by fourteen votes to two gives judgment that the United Kingdom did not violate the sovereignty of the People's Republic of Albania by reason of the acts of the British Navy in Albanian waters on October 22nd, 1946; and unanimously, gives judgment that by reason of the acts of the British Navy in Albanian waters in the course of the Operation of November 12th and 13th, 1946, the United Kingdom violated the sovereignty of the People's Republic of Albania, and that this declaration by the Court constitutes in itself appropriate satisfaction.

貳、案例說明

　　國際社會會在一般的情形下承認，根據國際習慣，在和平時期，每一個國家有權派出它們的戰艦通過公海兩端的國際航行水域，而無須事先獲得沿岸國的授權。但是這樣的航行乃是所謂的「無害通過」；除非國際公約（會議）另有規定。

■案例三：The Case Of Lake Lanoux Arbitration (Spain v. Fr.), 12 U.N.R.I.A.A. 281 (1957)

壹、案例檢選

In this dispute, wherein Spain unsuccessfully objected to a French hydroelectric power plan on the grounds that, if effectuated, it would alter the natural flow of a river crossing from France into Spain, the decision turned, as noted above, on the interpretation of an 1866 treaty. However, because Spain claimed, beyond the treaty, that customary international law requires prior agreement among co-riparians whenever a substantial alteration of a transboundary system of waters is contemplated, the Tribunal considered itself obliged to take "international common law" into account. It did so, at 308 and 316, echoing all the above-summarized cases, as follows:

International practice reflects the conviction that States ought to strive to conclude ... agreements [regarding the industrial use of international rivers] .... But international practice does not so far permit more than the following conclusion: the rule that States may utilize the hydraulic power of international watercourses only on condition of a prior agreement between the interested States cannot be established as a custom, even less a general principle of law ....

...

As a matter of form, the upstream State has, procedurally, a right of initiative; it is not obliged to associate the downstream State in the elaboration of its schemes. If, in the course of discussions, the downstream State submits schemes to it, the upstream State must examine them, but it has the right to give preference to the solution contained in its own scheme provided that it takes into consideration in a reasonable manner the interests of the downstream State.

The Tribunal then held that, although the State Parties had failed to reach agreement, France had sufficiently involved Spain in the preparation of its hy-droelectric scheme.

貳、案例說明

一、國際實務上反映出下面這個信念，就是有關於國際河流的使用，應該努力完成國際協議的簽訂。

二、各國可以使用國際水道的「水力」，但有個先行條件，那就是必須在相關有興趣的國家間，先有個「協定」方可。

■案例四：Nuclear Tests Case

壹、案例檢選

Australia v. France

International Court of Justice, 1973.

International Court of Justice Reports, vol. 1973, p. 99 (1973);

International Law Reports, vol. 57, p. 350 (1980).

Australia and New Zealand brought suit in the International Court of Justice seeking to stop France from conducting atmospheric tests of its nuclear weapons in the South Pacific near Fangataufa Atoll. Shortly after filing their suit, they asked the Court to order－in the "interim"－that France halt its atmospheric tests. The Court granted the request.

DISSENTING OPINION OF Judge IGNACIO-PINTO:

To my regret, I am unable to support the Order of the Court upholding Australia's request for the indication of interim measures of protection pending the settlement on the merits of the dispute between that state and France with re-gard to the nuclear tests which the French government wishes to carry out in the South Pacific.

I voted against the grant of those interim measures because I find this deci-sion legally unjust, or in any event without sufficient basis. But I wish to em-phasize that my negative vote does not mean that I am in favor of nuclear tests-on the contrary, I am strongly opposed to all such tests, and align myself with those who wish to see the prohibition of all these experiments which are danger-ous for our planet, and of which the least one can say is that we do not yet fully know what harmful consequences they may have, and how long the effects of atomic tests last in the atmosphere.

In the dispute brought before the Court by Australia, however, we must not be swayed by sentiment, and still less must we permit ourselves to be affected by the feelings－which in fact are very understandable－prompted by the deci-sion of the French government to carry out nuclear tests, just as other states, in exercise of their rights of sovereignty, have carried out such tests, and a further state, and no minor one at that, still continues to do so, using devices which pro-duce explosions which give rise to still greater pollution ....

There is an ... important point which does not seem to have been suffi-ciently taken into account in the arguments put forward by the French govern-ment. I refer to its reiterated request to the Australian government, expressed in its Ambassador's letter of 7 February 1973 to the Australian Prime Minister and Foreign Minister, that it be given some indication of the precise rules of interna-tional law which France is said to violate:

But the French government finds it hard to see what is the precise rule on whose existence Australia relies. Perhaps Australia could enlighten it on this point.

In reality, it seems to the French government that this complaint of the vio-lation of international law on account of atomic pollution amounts to a claim that atmospheric nuclear experiments are automatically unlawful. This, in its view, is not the case. But here again the French government would appreciate having its attention drawn to any points lending color to the opposite opinion.

This request for specific enlightenment has received no reply, and Australia has confined itself to presuming the existence of a right which in my view does not really exist, alleging moreover more or less hypothetical damage, the assessment of which is difficult in the extreme. Nevertheless the majority of the Court has seen fit to recognize that such damage, however uncertain or imprecise it may be, is sufficient to justify acceding to the request for the indication of provisional measures without any clear statement of the nature of the rights which have to be protected or preserved.

Of course, Australia can invoke its sovereignty over its territory and its right to prevent pollution caused by another state. But when the French government also claims to exercise its right of territorial sovereignty, by proceeding to carry out tests in its territory, is it possible legally to deprive it of that right, on account of the mere expression of the will of Australia?

In my opinion, international law is now, and will be for some time to come, a law in process of formation, and one which contains only a concept of responsibility after the fact, unlike municipal law, in which the possible range of responsibility can be determined with precision a priori. Whatever those who hold the opposite view may think, each state is free to act as it thinks fit within the limits of its sovereignty, and in the event of genuine damage or injury, if the said damage is clearly established, it owes reparation to the state having suffered that damage.

There is, so far as I am aware, in international law no hierarchy in the exercise of the right of sovereignty, and the Order issued by the Court has-at least, for the moment-no legal ground for preventing the French government from making use of its right of sovereignty and exploding an atomic device, as other states have done before it, and as one other state is still doing at the present time, in order to obtain the means of ensuring their own security.

Is Australia's right, in the exercise of its sovereignty, to be regarded as superior to the identical right possessed by France, which would thus rank second when it came to exercise of its own right?

By directing the French government to "avoid nuclear tests causing the deposit of radio-active fall-out in Australian territory" (*operative clause of the Order; emphasis added*), the Court certainly oversteps the limits of its powers, and appears thereby to be innovating in declaring unlawful the exercise of a right which up to now has been regarded as falling within the sovereignty of a state. The Court is not yet a supreme court as in municipal law, nor does it have legislative powers, and it has no right to hand down a decision against a state which by a formal declaration excludes its jurisdiction over disputes concerning activities connected with national defense.

I entirely agree with Australia that that country runs considerable risk by seeing atomic fall-out descend upon its territory and seeing its people suffer the harmful effects thereof, and for my own part, I would like to see that risk finally exorcised, but I see no existing legal means in the present state of the law which would authorize a state to come before the Court asking it to prohibit another state from carrying out on its own territory such activities, which involve risks to its neighbors ....

... The question of the illegality of nuclear tests exceeds the competence of the Court and becomes, as I see it, a political problem. No further proof is in my view needed than the statements of the Prime Minister and Foreign Minister himself in his Note to the Minister for Foreign Affairs of the French government, dated 13 February 1973, in winch we find the following words:

In my discussion with your Ambassador on 8 February 1973, I referred to the strength of public opinion in Australia about the effects of French tests in the Pacific. I explained that the strength of public opinion was such that, whichever political party was in office, it would be under great pressure to take action. The

Australian public would consider it intolerable if the nuclear tests proceeded during discussions to which the Australian government had agreed.

By way of conclusion, I am inclined to think that the decidedly political character of the case ought, or so it seems to me, to have prompted the Court to exercise greater circumspection and to have caused it to take the decision of purely and simply rejecting the request of Australia for the indication of provisional measures. It is not for the Court to declare unlawful the act of a state exercising its sovereignty within its own territorial limits, or at least to lend credence by its decision to the proposition that the act in question is unlawful. It was therefore wrong for Australia to have secured the benefit of the provisional measures which it sought, and a violation of Article 2, paragraph 7, of the Charter.

Despite Judge Ignacio-Pinto's argument, the international Court of Justice acceded to Australia's request for interim measures and ordered France to cease its nuclear testing until the case could be considered by the full court. When France announced in 1973 that it was permanently discontinuing its testing, the Court took the case off its list without a decision ever being given on its merits.

貳、案例說明

一、在本案中，雖然沒有明文成為判決文的一部分，但語意中很清楚的表示：領域管轄權不是「絕對的」（Absolute），至少反映出在國際環境保護方面，國際社會為了全體人類的福祉是如此。

二、所有的國家為了環境保護之緣故，有義務默示的限制了它的權利；直言之，任何一個國家在其管轄領域範圍內權利之行使是受制於環境保護的限制。

第十章　國際環境法之未來

壹、國際環境法現況之啟示

　　一般而言，國際環境問題之產生，多半是因為各國的追求經濟成長而產生。在開放的國際競爭社會之下，在經濟成長的競賽中爭取領先，無可厚非的更是各國設定的目標之一。各國政府為了提高人民的生活水準，乃以經濟成長的追求作為手段，而如此一來就必須利用環境資源，來作為發展經濟的基礎。其結果難免會伴隨著資源耗損及資源破壞的情形。如果以國際社會的整體層面來檢視，其結果自然會使得國際環境問題變得更為嚴重。但是我們所必須注意到的是除此之外的更為重要的認知乃是各國追求經濟成長，固然是造成國際環境問題日趨嚴重的原因之一；但是停止經濟成長的追求，並不能解決國際環境問題。何況經濟成長的追求，提高人民的生活水準，本身並沒有錯，更何況一個能為人民服務的政府，原本就應該追求經濟成長。因為在一個現代經濟社會中，資本財是生產力的重要來源，而資本財是會折舊的，如不以適當成長來補充資本財，則整個社會只好退回成長前的原始經濟狀態。因此，因應環境問題應非是停止經濟成長，而是積極認識環境問題的內容，才能對症下藥。

　　第一類環境問題是生活素質的破壞。因經濟成長而產生的生活素質破壞可分為主觀及客觀兩種。在主觀方面，隨著相對富裕程度提高，許多屬於個人資產的物品逐漸轉變或為社會負債的物品。例如，音響設備是個人的資產，在人人都擁有音響設備時，它很可能就會成為噪音的來源。再如，轎車是個人的資產，在大部分人都擁有轎車時，它就成為交通擁擠及停車困難的原因。在客觀方面，隨著工業發展程度提高，許多公害成為工業產品的副產品。例如，工廠增加後，空氣及水資源污染、噪音都會增加。再如，因工業發展而產生的都市化後，自來水、下水道、廢棄物處理等需要也會增加。面對這種性質的問題，最重要的是調整公共財觀念，研

訂足以克服問題的制度及政策，一方面制止民間對公共財的破壞，他方面則設法增加公共財的投資，才能達成改善生活素質的目標。

　　第二類環境問題是資源的消耗。生活素質的評估多少會因偏好因素而有不同的感受，而資源消耗則是具體而可以客觀評估的。經濟成長是生產的增加，為增加生產而投入生產資源所產生的資源消耗分為兩種，一種是再生資源使用過度。例如，砍伐森林超過樹木再生能力，就會導致森林面積的減少。一種是非再生資源的消耗，例如，煤、石油等地下礦產的使用。面對這種性質的問題有三種因應方法，一種是積極研究開發替代品。不過，通常替代品有時會隱藏副作用，在應用之前必須認真評估。一種是節約資源使用。這種對策須合理計算資源的機會成本或再生成本。一種是加強資源探勘。因為人類對可用資源的知識仍受可用科技的限制，加強探勘可減少對資源消耗的恐懼。

　　第三類環境問題是景觀的破壞。自然景觀屬非再生資源的一種，其主要特性是可供直接滿足怡情益性的願望，一旦經人力破壞便不易恢復舊觀，但其實際上的效益不容易評估。基於這種特性，景觀資源是爭論最多的環境問題，因為開闢道路、建造港口、興築水壩等都可提出具體經濟效益，而這些工程所造成的景觀破壞則難以估出機會成本。面對這種問題應有消極及積極兩種對策，在消極方面，經濟建設及生產投資應盡可能避免直接破壞景觀資源，使景觀資源得以繼續存在。在積極方面，政府應寬籌經費，開發已知景觀資源，使之發揮應有的經濟貢獻，乃至於產生應有的經濟收益。

　　總之，隨著經濟發展程度的提高，環境意識自然會抬頭。各國政府財經官員既然自以為經濟成長是經濟政策正確的成果，就不宜將環境問題視為社會的無能，而應積極面對問題，以追求經濟成長的同樣態度來面對國際社會中的各種環境問題，來務實的提出解決之道。

貳、國際環境法現況之省思

　　當人類逐漸在生態環境保育觀念上有所覺醒時，我們的確應注意酸雨、臭氣、核能等污染會對人類生命、生態平衡構成何種直接或間接的威脅。國際間對環境污染防治更應共同合作，致力減少危害生態環境的各項重大危機。而關於「環境危機」的處理，自然應該從「污染防治」做起。而對於「污染防治」應該要有下列幾點之體認。

一、經濟掛帥生後遺症

　　回顧過去的經濟發展，四條龍中的台灣一夜之間，名噪宇內，經濟起飛的結果，邁進了開發國家之林，在驕傲驚人的成就，憧憬生活品質的提升之際，已先嚐到了經濟起飛的時代產物——空氣污染、水污染、環境污染等——緊接著阻道、擋路、遊行示威、請願風潮也隨之展開。這種不調和的現象，說明了大家在經濟發展前提下所做的犧牲，已經到了忍無可忍的地步，也顯示這群受害者所能發出的微弱的抵抗聲勢，雖如螳臂擋車，但多少表示民眾之覺醒與厭憎。

二、廠商以社會為芻狗

　　經濟運動蓬勃發展是國家與國民共同追求的目標。目標達成，不但可增強經濟競爭能力，更可改善人民生活，本意至善。在發展之初，由於忽略經濟發展帶來的副作用程度，及低估社會大眾的環保意識，而只求降低生產成本提高利潤，不去投資防治污染的設備，把環境污染的社會成本移轉給整個社會負擔。由於時代進步，教育普及，民智益蒸，環境保護的意識日漸覺醒；這是一股無法阻擋的洪流，決非過去「拖延」戰術與「太極拳」功夫能奏效的。政府不應沿襲以前的老大作風，一味蠻幹，所謂「民之所惡惡之，民之所好好之」。

三、環保與經濟難兼得

環境保護與經濟發展猶如魚與熊掌，不可得兼。仰賴外資至深的海島型經濟，政府的經濟措施是無可厚非的，台灣為彈丸之地，尋找優良的工業發展環境，諸如土地、交通、港口、勞動人口及其他配合條件實是煞費苦心，在經濟發展的追求中多少犧牲一點環境品質在所難免，在這兩難的抉擇時，政府宜與有關單位如環保單位，並邀請專家學者、民眾代表等多方面評估後再作決策，以期尋找出一條利多弊少的途徑，使犧牲減少到最低的程度。筆者建議宜「思患預防」與「亡羊補牢」齊頭並進，所謂「思患預防」即防患未然，政府運用立法，強制新廠商設廠時，須具備防治污染設施，經有關單位檢查合格後始能生產，為提高工商企業對防治污染設備投資之意願，應在投資方面予以獎勵，或在稅負上予以抵減，以求事半功倍。所謂「亡羊補牢」，即已有的工商企業由於過去無防治污染設施，或有此設施而不盡理想、規模不足者，政府應予以輔導，編列此項預算，或優惠貸款，逐漸促使工商企業達到應有的要求，進而達成經濟成長與環境保護的雙重目標。

四、防治污染待建共識

環境保護的工作非一蹴可幾，亦非政府之力所能達成。必須社會大眾、工商企業與政府多方面配合；透過教育使全民皆能體認環境保護對全民健康、生活品質的重要性，進而造成全民共識，共同維護環境的整齊清潔；工商企業在追求利潤之餘，必須兼具社會道德的觀念及使命感，共同為促進健康的環境而付出其應有的代價，即投資污染環境設備，政府更應發揮監督功能，制定有關法律，將污染環境的觀念予以制度化、標準化、合理化，以期在共同的理念，與群策群力的維護下，有個健康、潔淨、高品質的生活環境。

參、國際環境法之發展趨勢評估

　　1970年代在國際環境法的發展上，以酸雨及有害廢棄物之跨國運送為代表之區域環境問題，開始受到國際社會的關注，而成為國際環境法的主要議題。因而促成了「聯合國人類環境會議」的召開，並發表了人類歷史上有關環境保護的第一個「全球性宣言」──斯德哥爾摩宣言。聯合國人類環境會議在國際環境保護方面，在國際社會具有指標性的意義。顯示出國際社會對於國際環境的保護已經開始從「關心」進入到「行動」的階段。而斯德哥爾摩宣言更是對於國際環境議題訂定了26個不同面相的原則，更強調了人類享有生存於適當環境的基本權利，更要為後代子孫負起保護環境的責任。同時提出以「國際合作」的方式，來協助與促進開發中國家的發展。

　　到了1990年代，為了保護全球環境並健全人類發展，聯合國乃在1992年6月於里約熱內盧舉行「聯合國環境與發展會議」，並以1972年的斯德哥爾摩宣言為基礎，通過了「關於環境與發展之里約熱內盧宣言」，意圖在國家、社會重要部門與人民之間，建立新的合作模式，尋求一種創新且公平之全球夥伴關係，同時致力於發展尊重各方利益並能維護全球環境與人類發展的國際協定，用以達成永續的目標。里約會議的召開及里約宣言的發布是國際社會對於1970年至1990年的國際環境保護議題的進展，並要預測國際社會在未來的年代裡又會碰到哪些議題需要加以解決。1992年之後的二十年，在2012年的今天，國際社會所面臨的問題，包括：一、臭氧層的破壞；二、地球溫室效應；三、酸雨；四、海洋污染；五、有害廢棄物之跨境運送；六、熱帶雨林之減少；七、野生動植物之瀕臨絕種；八、土地沙漠化；以及九、開發中國家之公害問題等，不一而足。回顧過去半個世紀左右，國際環境法的演進與發展，可以看得出來，在環境法的世界秩序的建立，約略可以很清楚的看到新的方向正在開展出來。此等發展趨勢，大致上可以將其歸類成一、立即地狹窄界面；二、長遠地寬廣界面。

將二者詳細說明如下[1]：

一、立即地狹窄界面

在「可預見的未來」（Foreseeable Future），環境保護與經濟發展將會整合。環境與貿易的萌芽出來之新領域，反映出了這樣的「聯結」（Linkage）。就以此為例，環境與貿易的問題朝向兩個方向去發展——環境保護的作法影響到貿易行為，而貿易的作法也影響到環境保育／保護。因此，很重要的一點是環境與貿易均應給予「相對應的合法性」（Comparable Legitimacy），而且應該將二者均視為「永續發展」的重要元素。更一般性的說法就是：在尋求環境上的「永續發展」，其核心重點就是各國在「工業化過程」（Industrializing Process）之同時，必須要考量到「環境因素」，來防止污染的造成、減低「環境惡化」（Environmental Degradation）、以及更有效地利用資源。因此，就國際環境法未來的短期而立即的演進趨勢來看，就是：第一，未來的「經濟發展」，在生產過程上會愈來愈重視與考量到整個的「生產體系」（System of Production）的「環境上的完善」（Environmentally Sound）。如此則國際環境法將會反映出國際社會所強調的防止污染與減低環境惡化的環境保護的標準及程序，而不是將重點放在環境保護的損害賠償責任及提供產業界的誘因，來使用環境保護健全的生產製程上面。

第二，對於「不具拘束力之法制文件」（Non-binding Legal Instrument）之形成（即軟法）要比談判正式的國際公約，更具有加速增加的效果。這是因為當國際文件是不具拘束力之協議，通常是比較容易達成交換意見的成本比較低、談判策略使用的機會比較有彈性，其成功的機會就比較大，而且以現有對於環境與發展的科技上的了解，如果加以回應，自然是迅速改變的能力要比以往來得大，而且可以解決的環境與發展的爭議問題，也就涵蓋的更為廣泛。

---

[1] Lakshman D. Guruswamy et al., International Environmental Law and World Order (St. Paul, Minn.: West Publishing 1994), p. 1152.

　　第三，對於國際環境保護的新「作法」（Approach）之採納，將更為迅速的成長，同時對於國際環境法制規範所定之責任、義務及程序的接受也會繼續的發展下去。這其中所涵蓋的內容相當廣泛，例如：風險預防原理之應用、與環境保護受到影響的國家之諮商的義務、在採取任何「專案計畫」（Project）之前，要預備好「環境影響評估」（Environment Impact Assessment）、要對於環境意外事件或災難提供「緊急協助」（Emergency Assistance），以及監督活動之進行，並且使得相關活動資訊得以提供（所謂的環境決策之資訊取得即是一例）。

　　最後，「聯合國環境與發展會議」（UNCED）及「1992里約宣言」（1992 Rio Declaration）也許可以將之視為「公眾參與」（Public Participation）環境決策及讓社會大眾取得相關環境保護資訊的「合法化」的依據。更進一步而言，許多國際文件（國際會議與國際公約）所植基之國際機構體系（如聯合國之下的大會及聯合國附屬機構）將繼續變得更為廣泛而多元，而且會包括各種不同種類的「非政府組織」（Non-governmental Organizations）。半世紀之前國際社會中有關國際環境保護相關事宜的推動與執行，絕大多數為各國政府及其下屬機關；而時至今日的國際體系則包括各國政府（含地方政府）、「政府間組織」（Intergovernmental Organization）以及「非政府組織」（Non-governmental Organization）。而且可以這麼說，「非政府組織」在未來的幾十年內將繼續在有關國際環境法制的談判、執行以及遵守規範上扮演愈來愈重要的角色，以及不可或缺的「推手」。

二、長遠地寬廣界面

　　在傳統國際法上，國際法學者所習以為常的使用「國家利益」（National Interest）的概念，來解釋「外交政策」（Foreign Policy）的決定。但是此一「國家利益」的概念，如果要用來分析國際環境問題的「長期」（Long-Term）作法，就顯得格格不入而行不通了。國家利益可以把它定義成國家之「偏好」（Preference）或者是一個國家的「決定作成者」

（Decision-maker）的偏好。而在「全球尺度上」（Global Scale）這些利益（國家利益）往往是以「零合」（Zero-Sum）「取得」（Gain）的角度，來加以認定。在這樣的情形下，就存在著「潛在的假定」（Implicit Assumption），那就是一個國家的「國家利益」，往往必然是另外的國家之不利益。但是，一旦遇到國際環境爭議問題時，「利益」就變成了「共同的」（Common）一個利益——國際環境體系整體的維繫（the overall maintenance of the International Environmental System）。這樣的情形，在當今的世界就變得非常明顯，因為在環境問題方面所面對的未來，沒有任何一個國家有能力來保育整個「國際體系」整體的利益；甚至於就算為它自己的未來子孫，均達不成；更遑論為全體人類的未來。

因為當今的全體人類社會，每一個人均是被緊緊的綁在一起，在可預見的未來，所面對的是一個共同的全球性的國際環境。這句話乃是指：長期下來在環境問題上面，一個國家的「國家利益」，將會是另一個國家的不利益，這是不成立的「結論」或「預先的假定」（Presumption）。在此二十一世紀之初，我們所看到的「國際合作」（International Cooperation）特別是表現在國際環境法制規範上，是全世界各個國家及其人民所共知共見之事實。這也反映出了國際社會中絕大多數的國家，已經開始默默的承認或接受：在國際環境問題的處理上，每一個國家就長遠的利益來檢視，彼此之間有必要開始進行「合作」，提升全體人類的共同利益，而不是某一國家本身的利益。

或許各國逐漸承認或接受在維持整個國際社會的環境保護與保育的議題上，彼此正在分享著「共同的利益」（Commonality of Interest）。這可以見諸於「21世紀議程」（Agenda 21）的序言中所述：人類正站在歷史的關鍵時刻，我們面對國家之間與各國內部長期存在的懸殊差距……我們福祉所依賴的生態系統持續惡化中。然而，整合對環境與發展的關懷，並給予這些問題更多關注，將可滿足基本需要，提高所有人的生活水準，改進對生態系統的保護與管理，創造更安全與更繁榮的未來。沒有任何一個國家能單獨實現這樣的目標；但只要我們共同努力，建立永續發展的全球夥伴關係，就可以達成這樣的目標。

　　開發中國家與已開發國家在面對環境保護與經濟發展的「優先順位」（Priorities）時，必須要排除「本位主義」的想法與作法，來面對「我們的共同未來」，在經濟發展與環境保護上面，取得「平衡點」，尋找共同的利益，彼此協力合作，已開發國家更有義務協助開發中國家，彼此同心協力，相互合作，不僅滿足當代的需要，同時更要能夠不損及後代子孫的滿足其本身需要之發展能力。因為現在的國際環境保護的工作，已經不再局限於保育我們眼前的「全球環境」（Global Environment），更要能夠為未來的世世代代確保「永續發展」的終極目標。在這樣的理念之下，國家利益已經被全體人類的利益所吸收，這就是國際環境法與其他國際法制最大的不同之處。

參考文獻

一、中文部分

王樹義等著，環境法前沿問題研究，台北，元照出版公司，2012年。

王樹義等著，環境法基本理論研究，台北，元照出版公司，2012年。

王曦著，美國環境保護法，台北，漢興書局有限公司，1995年。

石鳳城編著，環境保護法規概論，新北市，新文京開發公司，2004年。

行政院研考會編，公害糾紛處理政策與法制之研究，台北，行政院研考會，1995年。

洪正中、杜正榮與吳天基編著，環境生態學（二版），新北市，國立空中大學，2003年。

洪德欽著，WTO法律與政策專題研究，台北，學林文化公司，2002年。

吳嘉生著，環保糾紛解決之研究，台北，中興法學，1998年。

吳嘉生著，當代國際法（下），台北，五南圖書公司，2009年。

吳嘉生著，國際貿易法析論，台北，翰蘆圖書公司，2004年。

胡祖慶譯，Fred. S. Pearson & J. Martin Rochester, International Relations，國際關係，台北，
　　　麥格羅希爾出版公司，2006年。

秦天寶著，生物多樣性國際法導論，台北，元照出版公司，2010年。

陳慈陽著，環境法總論，台北，元照出版公司，2011年。

曾隆興著，公害糾紛與民事救濟，台北，三民書局，1995年。

黃錦堂著，台灣地區環境法之研究，台北，月旦出版社，1994年。

葉俊榮著，環境政策與法律，台北，元照出版公司，2010年。

葉俊榮主編，國際環境法條約選輯與解說，台北，新學林出版公司，2010年。

葉俊榮著，全球環境議題——臺灣觀點，台北，巨流圖書公司，1999年。

蔡育岱與熊武合著，國際關係之理論與實際，台北，鼎茂圖書出版公司，2010年。

二、英文部分

Albert, Colin M., "Technology Transfer and It's Role in International Environmental Law: A Structural Dilemma." 6 *Harvard Journal of Law & Technology* 63 (1992).

Asiedu-Akrofi, Derek, "Debt-for-Nature SwaPS: Extending the Frontires of Innovation Financing in Support of the Global Environment." 25 *International Lawyer* 557 (1992).

Baldock, David and Edward Keene, "Incooperating Environmental Considerations in Common Market Arrangements." 23 *Environment Law* 575 (1993).

Bell, Stuart and Donald McGillivray, *Environmental Law* (Oxford: Oxford University Press, 2008).

Blay, Sam, *Public International Law* (Melbourne: Oxford University Press, 1997).

Bodansky, Daniel, et al., *The Oxford Handbook of International Environmental Law* (N.Y.: Oxford University Press, 2007).

Carter, Barry E. and Phillip R. Trimble, *International Law*, 2nd ed. (Boston: Litter Brown and Comp, 1995).

Charnovitz, Steve, "The Environment vs. Trade Rules Defogging the Debate." 23 *Environmental Law 475* (1993).

Chen, Lung-Chi., *An Introduction to Contemporary International Law* (New Haven: Yale Univ. Press, 1989).

Crubb, Miichael, Matthias Koch, Abby Munson, Francis Sullivan and Koy Thomson, *The Earth Summit Agreements: A Guide and Assement. The Royal Institute of International Affairs* (1993).

Dixon, Martin and Robert McCorquodale, *International Law* (London: Blackstone Press, 1995).

Doremus, Holly, et al., *Environmental Policy Law* (N.Y.: Thomson/Foundation Press, 2008).

Esty, Daniel C., "Beyond Rio: Trade and Environment." 23 *Environmental Law* 390 (1993).

Esty, Daniel C., "Unpacking the 'Trade and Environment' Conflict." 25 *Law & Policy in International Business* 1259 (1994).

Evans, Malcolm D., *International Law*, 2nd ed. (Oxford: Oxford University Press, 2006).

Farber, Daniel A., et al., *Environmental Law* (St. Paul, M.N.: Thomson/West, 2003).

Grubb, Michael, "Seeking Fair Weather: Ethics and the International Debate on Climate Change." 71 *International Affairs* 463 (1995).

Guruswamy, Lakshman, et al., *International Environmental Law and World Order* (St. Paul, M.N.: West Publishing Co., 1994).

Hunter, David, James Salzman and Durwood Zaelke, *International Environmental Law and Policy* (N.Y.: Foundation Press, 2007).

Janis, Mark W. and John E. Noyes, *International Law* (St. Paul, M.N.: West Publishing Co., 2001).

Kuokkanen, Tuomas, *International Law and the Environment* (The Hague: Kluwer Law International, 2002).

O'Neill, Catherine A. and Cass R. Sunstein, "Economics and the Environment: Trading Debt and Technology for Nature." 17 *Columbia Journal of Environmental Law* 93 (1992).

Porter, Gareth and Janet Welsh Brown, *Global Environmental Politics* (West View Press, 1996).

Rao, P.K., *International Environmental Law and Economics* (Malden, M.A.: Blackwell, Publishers, 2007).

Revesz, Richard L., *Foundations of Environmental Law and Policy* (N.Y.: Foudation Press, 1997).

Salzman, James and Barton H. Thompson, Jr., *Environmental Law and Policy* (N.Y.: Foundation Press, 2007).

Shaw, Malcolm N., *International Law*, 6th ed. (Cambridge: Cambridge University Press, 2009).

Shue, Henry, "Ethics, The Environment and the Change International Order." 71 *International Affairs* 453 (1996).

Sprinz, Detlef and Tapani Vaahtoranta, "The Interest-based Explanation of International Environmental Policy." 48 *International Organization* 77 (1994).

Weiss, Edith Brown, "International Environmental Law: Contemporary Issues and the Emergence of a New World Order." 81 *Georgetown Law Journal* 675 (1993).

Wirth, David A., "A Matchmaker's Challenge: Marrying International Law and American Environmental Law." 32 *Virginia Journal of International Law* 377 (1992).

Yamin, Farhana, "Biodiversity, Ethics, and International Law." 71 *International Affairs* 529 (1995).

名詞索引

附錄一：斯德哥爾摩宣言

STOCKHOLM DECLARATION OF THE UNITED NATIONS CONFER-
ENCE ON THE HUMAN ENVIRONMENT. Adopted by the U.N.
Conference on the Human Environment at Stockholm, 16 June
1972. *Report of the UN Conference on the Human Environment,
Stockholm, 5–16 June 1972,* U.N.Doc. A/CONF.48/14/Rev. 1 at 3
(1973), U.N.Doc. A/CONF.48/14 at 2–65, and Corr. 1 (1972), 11 I.L.M.
1416 (1972)

THE UNITED NATIONS CONFERENCE ON THE HUMAN ENVIRONMENT.

HAVING MET at Stockholm from 5 to 16 June 1972.

HAVING CONSIDERED the need for a common outlook and for common
principles to inspire and guide the peoples of the world in the preservation
and enhancement of the human environment.

I

PROCLAIMS THAT:

1. Man is both creature and moulder of his environment, which gives
him physical sustenance and affords him the opportunity for intellectual,
moral, social and spiritual growth. In the long and tortuous evolution of the
human race on this planet a stage has been reached when, through the rapid
acceleration of science and technology, man has acquired the power to
transform his environment in countless ways and on an unprecedented scale.
Both aspects of man's environment, the natural and the man-made, are
essential to his well-being and to the enjoyment of basic human rights—even
the right to life itself.

2. The protection and improvement of the human environment is a
major issue which affects the well-being of peoples and economic development
throughout the world; it is the urgent desire of the peoples of the whole world
and the duty of all Governments.

3. Man has constantly to sum up experience and go on discovering,
inventing, creating and advancing. In our time, man's capability to transform his surroundings, if used wisely, can bring to all peoples the benefits of
development and the opportunity to enhance the quality of life. Wrongly or
heedlessly applied, the same power can do incalculable harm to human beings
and the human environment. We see around us growing evidence of man-
made harm in many regions of the earth: dangerous levels of pollution in
water, air, earth and living beings; major and undesirable disturbances to the
ecological balance of the biosphere; destruction and depletion of irreplaceable
resources; and gross deficiencies harmful to the physical, mental and social
health of man, in the man-made environment, particularly in the living and
working environment.

4. In the developing countries most of the environmental problems are caused by under-development. Millions continue to live far below the minimum levels required for a decent human existence, deprived of adequate food and clothing, shelter and education, health and sanitation. Therefore, the developing countries must direct their efforts to development, bearing in mind their priorities and the need to safeguard and improve the environment. For the same purpose, the industrialized countries should make efforts to reduce the gap between themselves and the developing countries. In the industrialized countries, environmental problems are generally related to industrialization and technological development.

5. The natural growth of population continuously presents problems on the preservation of the environment, and adequate policies and measures should be adopted, as appropriate, to face these problems. Of all things in the world, people are the most precious. It is the people that propel social progress, create social wealth, develop science and technology and, through their hard work, continuously transform the human environment. Along with social progress and the advance of production, science and technology, the capability of man to improve the environment increases with each passing day.

6. A point has been reached in history when we must shape our actions throughout the world with a more prudent care for their environmental consequences. Through ignorance or indifference we can do massive and irreversible harm to the earthly environment on which our life and well-being depend. Conversely, through fuller knowledge and wiser action, we can achieve for ourselves and our posterity a better life in an environment more in keeping with human needs and hopes. There are broad vistas for the enhancement of environmental quality and the creation of a good life. What is needed is an enthusiastic but calm state of mind and intense but orderly work. For the purpose of attaining freedom in the world of nature, man must use knowledge to build, in collaboration with nature, a better environment. To defend and improve the human environment for present and future generations has become an imperative goal for mankind—a goal to be pursued together with, and in harmony with, the established and fundamental goals of peace and of world-wide economic and social development.

7. To achieve this environmental goal will demand the acceptance of responsibility by citizens and communities and by enterprises and institutions at every level, all sharing equitably in common efforts. Individuals in all walks of life as well as organizations in many fields, by their values and the sum of their actions, will shape the world environment of the future. Local and national governments will bear the greatest burden for large-scale environmental policy and action within their jurisdictions. International cooperation is also needed in order to raise resources to support the developing countries in carrying out their responsibilities in this field. A growing class of environmental problems, because they are regional or global in extent or because they affect the common international realm, will require extensive co-

operation among nations and action by international organizations in the common interest. The Conference calls upon Governments and peoples to exert common efforts for the preservation and improvement of the human environment, for the benefit of all the people and for their posterity.

II
Principles

STATES THE COMMON CONVICTION THAT:

Principle 1

Man has the fundamental right to freedom, equality and adequate conditions of life, in an environment of a quality that permits a life of dignity and well-being, and he bears a solemn responsibility to protect and improve the environment for present and future generations. In this respect, policies promoting or perpetuating apartheid, racial segregation, discrimination, colonial and other forms of oppression and foreign domination stand condemned and must be eliminated.

Principle 2

The natural resources of the earth including the air, water, land, flora and fauna and especially representative samples of natural ecosystems must be safeguarded for the benefit of present and future generations through careful planning or management, as appropriate.

Principle 3

The capacity of the earth to produce vital renewable resources must be maintained and, wherever practicable, restored or improved.

Principle 4

Man has a special responsibility to safeguard and wisely manage the heritage of wildlife and its habitat which are now gravely imperilled by a combination of adverse factors. Nature conservation including wildlife must therefore receive importance in planning for economic development.

Principle 5

The non-renewable resources of the earth must be employed in such a way as to guard against the danger of their future exhaustion and to ensure that benefits from such employment are shared by all mankind.

Principle 6

The discharge of toxic substances or of other substances and the release of heat, in such quantities or concentrations as to exceed the capacity of the environment to render them harmless, must be halted in order to ensure that serious or irreversible damage is not inflicted upon ecosystems. The just struggle of the peoples of all countries against pollution should be supported.

Principle 7

States shall take all possible steps to prevent pollution of the seas by substances that are liable to create hazards to human health, to harm living resources and marine life, to damage amenities or to interfere with other legitimate uses of the sea.

Principle 8

Economic and social development is essential for ensuring a favourable living and working environment for man and for creating conditions on earth that are necessary for the improvement of the quality of life.

Principle 9

Environmental deficiencies generated by the conditions of underdevelopment and natural disasters pose grave problems and can best be remedied by accelerated development through the transfer of substantial quantities of financial and technological assistance as a supplement to the domestic effort of the developing countries and such timely assistance as may be required.

Principle 10

For the developing countries, stability of prices and adequate earnings for primary commodities and raw material are essential to environmental management since economic factors as well as ecological processes must be taken into account.

Principle 11

The environmental policies of all States should enhance and not adversely affect the present or future development potential of developing countries, nor should they hamper the attainment of better living conditions for all, and appropriate steps should be taken by States and international organizations with a view to reaching agreement on meeting the possible national and international economic consequences resulting from the application of environmental measures.

Principle 12

Resources should be made available to preserve and improve the environment, taking into account the circumstances and particular requirements of developing countries and any costs which may emanate from their incorporating environmental safeguards into their development planning and the need for making available to them, upon their request, additional international technical and financial assistance for this purpose.

Principle 13

In order to achieve a more rational management of resources and thus to improve the environment, State should adopt an integrated and co-ordinated approach to their development planning so as to ensure that development is compatible with the need to protect and improve the human environment for the benefit for their population.

Principle 14

Rational planning constitutes an essential tool for reconciling any conflict between the needs of development and the need to protect and improve the environment.

Principle 15

Planning must be applied to human settlements and urbanization with a view to avoiding adverse effects on the environment and obtaining maximum social, economic and environmental benefits for all. In this respect projects which are designed for colonialist and racist domination must be abandoned.

Principle 16

Demographic policies, which are without prejudice to basic human rights and which are deemed appropriate by Governments concerned, should be applied in those regions where the rate of population growth or excessive population concentrations are likely to have adverse effects on the environment or development, or where low population density may prevent improvement of the human environment and impede development.

Principle 17

Appropriate national institutions must be entrusted with the task of planning, managing or controlling the environmental resources of States with the view to enhancing environmental quality.

Principle 18

Science and technology, as part of their contribution to economic and social development, must be applied to the identification, avoidance and control of environmental risks and the solution of environmental problems and for the common good of mankind.

Principle 19

Education in environmental matters, for the younger generation as well as adults, giving due consideration to the underprivileged, is essential in order to broaden the basis for an enlightened opinion and responsible conduct by individuals, enterprises and communities in protecting and improving the environment in its full human dimension. It is also essential that mass media of communications avoid contributing to the deterioration of the environment, but, on the contrary, disseminate information of an educational nature, on the need to protect and improve the environment in order to enable man to develop in every respect.

Principle 20

Scientific research and development in the context of environmental problems, both national and multinational, must be promoted in all countries, especially the developing countries. In this connection, the free flow of up-to-date scientific information and transfer of experience must be supported and assisted, to facilitate the solution of environmental problems; environmental technologies should be made available to developing countries on terms which would encourage their wide dissemination without constituting an economic burden on the developing countries.

Principle 21

States have, in accordance with the Charter of the United Nations and the principles of international law, the sovereign right to exploit their own resources pursuant to their own environmental policies, and the responsibility to ensure that activities within their jurisdiction or control do not cause damage to the environment of other States or of areas beyond the limits of national jurisdiction.

Principle 22

States shall co-operate to develop further the international law regarding liability and compensation for the victims of pollution and other environmental damage caused by activities within the jurisdiction or control of such States to areas beyond their jurisdiction.

Principle 23

Without prejudice to such criteria as may be agreed upon by the international community, or to standards which will have to be determined nationally, it will be essential in all cases to consider the systems of values prevailing in each country, and the extent of the applicability of standards which are valid for the most advanced countries but which may be inappropriate and of unwarranted social cost for the developing countries.

Principle 24

International matters concerning the protection and improvement of the environment should be handled in a co-operative spirit by all countries, big or small, on an equal footing. Co-operation through multilateral or bilateral arrangements or other appropriate means is essential to effectively control, prevent, reduce and eliminate adverse environmental effects resulting from activities conducted in all spheres, in such a way that due account is taken of the sovereignty and interests of all States.

Principle 25

States shall ensure that international organizations play a co-ordinated, efficient and dynamic role for the protection and improvement of the environment.

Principle 26

Man and his environment must be spared the effects of nuclear weapons and all other means of mass destruction. States must strive to reach prompt agreement, in the relevant international organs, on the elimination and complete destruction of such weapons.

附錄二：世界自然憲章

WORLD CHARTER FOR NATURE.　Adopted by the U.N. General Assembly, 28 October 1982.　G.A. Res. 37/7 (Annex), U.N. GAOR, 37th Sess., Supp. No. 51, at 17, U.N. Doc. A/37/51, 22 I.L.M. 455 (1983)

The General Assembly,

Reaffirming the fundamental purposes of the United Nations, in particular the maintenance of international peace and security, the development of friendly relations among nations and the achievement of international cooperation in solving international problems of an economic, social, cultural, technical, intellectual or humanitarian character,

Aware that:

(*a*) Mankind is a part of nature and life depends on the uninterrupted functioning of natural systems which ensure the supply of energy and nutrients,

(*b*) Civilization is rooted in nature, which has shaped human culture and influenced all artistic and scientific achievement, and living in harmony with nature gives man the best opportunities for the development of his creativity, and for rest and recreation,

Convinced that:

(*a*) Every form of life is unique, warranting respect regardless of its worth to man, and, to accord other organisms such recognition, man must be guided by a moral code of action,

(*b*) Man can alter nature and exhaust natural resources by his action or its consequences and, therefore, must fully recognize the urgency of maintaining the stability and quality of nature and of conserving natural resources,

Persuaded that:

(*a*) Lasting benefits from nature depend upon the maintenance of essential ecological processes and life support systems, and upon the diversity of life forms, which are jeopardized through excessive exploitation and habitat destruction by man,

(*b*) The degradation of natural systems owing to excessive consumption and misuse of natural resources, as well as to failure to establish an appropriate economic order among peoples and among States, leads to the breakdown of the economic, social and political framework of civilization,

(*c*) Competition for scarce resources creates conflicts, whereas the conservation of nature and natural resources contributes to justice and the maintenance of peace and cannot be achieved until mankind learns to live in peace and to forsake war and armaments,

Reaffirming that man must acquire the knowledge to maintain and enhance his ability to use natural resources in a manner which ensures the preservation of the species and ecosystems for the benefit of present and future generations,

Firmly convinced of the need for appropriate measures, at the national and international, individual and collective, and private and public levels, to protect nature and promote international co-operation in this field,

Adopts, to these ends, the present World Charter for Nature, which proclaims the following principles of conservation by which all human conduct affecting nature is to be guided and judged.

I. General Principles

1. Nature shall be respected and its essential processes shall not be impaired.

2. The genetic viability on the earth shall not be compromised; the population levels of all life forms, wild and domesticated, must be at least sufficient for their survival, and to this end necessary habitats shall be safeguarded.

3. All areas of the earth, both land and sea, shall be subject to these principles of conservation; special protection shall be given to unique areas, to representative samples of all the different types of ecosystems and to the habitats of rare or endangered species.

4. Ecosystems and organisms, as well as the land, marine and atmospheric resources that are utilized by man, shall be managed to achieve and maintain optimum sustainable productivity, but not in such a way as to endanger the integrity of those other ecosystems or species with which they coexist.

5. Nature shall be secured against degradation caused by warfare or other hostile activities.

II. Functions

6. In the decision-making process it shall be recognized that man's needs can be met only by ensuring the proper functioning of natural systems and by respecting the principles set forth in the present Charter.

7. In the planning and implementation of social and economic development activities, due account shall be taken of the fact that the conservation of nature is an integral part of those activities.

8. In formulating long-term plans for economic development, population growth and the improvement of standards of living, due account shall be taken of the long-term capacity of natural systems to ensure the subsistence and settlement of the populations concerned, recognizing that this capacity may be enhanced through science and technology.

9.　The allocation of areas of the earth to various uses shall be planned, and due account shall be taken of the physical constraints, the biological productivity and diversity and the natural beauty of the areas concerned.

10.　Natural resources shall not be wasted, but used with a restraint appropriate to the principles set forth in the present Charter, in accordance with the following rules:

(*a*) Living resources shall not be utilized in excess of their natural capacity for regeneration;

(*b*) The productivity of soils shall be maintained or enhanced through measures which safeguard their long-term fertility and the process of organic decomposition, and prevent erosion and all other forms of degradation;

(*c*) Resources, including water, which are not consumed as they are used shall be reused or recycled;

(*d*) Non-renewable resources which are consumed as they are used shall be exploited with restraint, taking into account their abundance, the rational possibilities of converting them for consumption, and the compatibility of their exploitation with the functioning of natural systems.

11.　Activities which might have an impact on nature shall be controlled, and the best available technologies that minimize significant risks to nature or other adverse effects shall be used; in particular:

(*a*) Activities which are likely to cause irreversible damage to nature shall be avoided;

(*b*) Activities which are likely to pose a significant risk to nature shall be preceded by an exhaustive examination; their proponents shall demonstrate that expected benefits outweigh potential damage to nature, and where potential adverse effects are not fully understood, the activities should not proceed.

(*c*) Activities which may disturb nature shall be preceded by assessment of their consequences, and environmental impact studies of development projects shall be conducted sufficiently in advance, and if they are to be undertaken, such activities shall be planned and carried out so as to minimize potential adverse effects;

(*d*) Agriculture, grazing, forestry and fisheries practices shall be adapted to the natural characteristics and constraints of given areas;

(*e*) Areas degraded by human activities shall be rehabilitated for purposes in accord with their natural potential and compatible with the well-being of affected populations.

12.　Discharge of pollutants into natural systems shall be avoided and:

(*a*) Where this is not feasible, such pollutants shall be treated at the source, using the best practicable means available;

(b) Special precautions shall be taken to prevent discharge of radio-active or toxic wastes.

13. Measures intended to prevent, control or limit natural disasters, infestations and diseases shall be specifically directed to the causes of these scourges and shall avoid adverse side-effects on nature.

III. Implementation

14. The principles set forth in the present Charter shall be reflected in the law and practice of each State, as well as at the international level.

15. Knowledge of nature shall be broadly disseminated by all possible means, particularly by ecological education as an integral part of general education.

16. All planning shall include, among its essential elements, the formulation of strategies for the conservation of nature, the establishment of inventories of ecosystems and assessments of the effects on nature of proposed policies and activities; all of these elements shall be disclosed to the public by appropriate means in time to permit effective consultation and participation.

17. Funds, programmes and administrative structures necessary to achieve the objective of the conservation of nature shall be provided.

18. Constant efforts shall be made to increase knowledge of nature by scientific research and to disseminate such knowledge unimpeded by restrictions of any kind.

19. The status of natural processes, ecosystems and species shall be closely monitored to enable early detection of degradation or threat, ensure timely intervention and facilitate the evaluation of conservation policies and methods.

20. Military activities damaging to nature shall be avoided.

21. States and, to the extent they are able, other public authorities, international organizations, individuals, groups and corporations shall:

(a) Co-operate in the task of conserving nature through common activities and other relevant actions, including information exchange and consultations;

(b) Establish standards for products and manufacturing processes that may have adverse effects on nature, as well as agreed methodologies for assessing these effects;

(c) Implement the applicable international legal provisions for the conservation of nature and the protection of the environment;

(d) Ensure that activities within their jurisdictions or control do not cause damage to the natural systems located within other States or in the areas beyond the limits of national jurisdiction;

(e) Safeguard and conserve nature in areas beyond national jurisdiction.

22.　Taking fully into account the sovereignty of States over their natural resources, each State shall give effect to the provisions of the present Charter through its competent organs and in co-operation with other States.

23.　All persons, in accordance with their national legislation, shall have the opportunity to participate, individually or with others, in the formulation of decisions of direct concern to their environment, and shall have access to means of redress when their environment has suffered damage or degradation.

24.　Each person has a duty to act in accordance with the provisions of the present Charter; acting individually, in association with others or through participation in the political process, each person shall strive to ensure that the objectives and requirements of the present Charter are met.

附錄三：里約宣言

RIO DECLARATION ON ENVIRONMENT AND DEVELOPMENT.
Adopted by the U.N. Conference on Environment and Development (UNCED) at Rio de Janeiro, 13 June 1992.　U.N.Doc. A/CONF.151/26 (vol. I) (1992), 31 I.L.M. 874 (1992)

The United Nations Conference on Environment and Development,

Having met at Rio de Janeiro from 3 to 14 June 1992,

Reaffirming the Declaration of the United Nations Conference on the Human Environment, adopted at Stockholm on 16 June 1972, and seeking to build upon it,

With the goal of establishing a new and equitable global partnership through the creation of new levels of cooperation among States, key sectors of societies and people,

Working towards international agreements which respect the interests of all and protect the integrity of the global environmental and developmental system,

Recognizing the integral and interdependent nature of the Earth, our home,

Proclaims that:

Principle 1

Human beings are at the centre of concerns for sustainable development. They are entitled to a healthy and productive life in harmony with nature.

Principle 2

States have, in accordance with the Charter of the United Nations and the principles of international law, the sovereign right to exploit their own resources pursuant to their own environmental and developmental policies, and the responsibility to ensure that activities within their jurisdiction or control do not cause damage to the environment of other States or of areas beyond the limits of national jurisdiction.

Principle 3

The right to development must be fulfilled so as to equitably meet developmental and environmental needs of present and future generations.

Principle 4

In order to achieve sustainable development, environmental protection shall constitute an integral part of the development process and cannot be considered in isolation from it.

Principle 5

All States and all people shall cooperate in the essential task of eradicating poverty as an indispensable requirement for sustainable development, in order to decrease the disparities in standards of living and better meet the needs of the majority of the people of the world.

Principle 6

The special situation and needs of developing countries, particularly the least developed and those most environmentally vulnerable, shall be given special priority. International actions in the field of environment and development should also address the interests and needs of all countries.

Principle 7

States shall cooperate in a spirit of global partnership to conserve, protect and restore the health and integrity of the Earth's ecosystem. In view of the different contributions to global environmental degradation, States have common but differentiated responsibilities. The developed countries acknowledge the responsibility that they bear in the international pursuit of sustainable development in view of the pressures their societies place on the global environment and of the technologies and financial resources they command.

Principle 8

To achieve sustainable development and a higher quality of life for all people, States should reduce and eliminate unsustainable patterns of production and consumption and promote appropriate demographic policies.

Principle 9

States should cooperate to strengthen endogenous capacity-building for sustainable development by improving scientific understanding through exchanges of scientific and technological knowledge, and by enhancing the development, adaptation, diffusion and transfer of technologies, including new and innovative technologies.

Principle 10

Environmental issues are best handled with the participation of all concerned citizens, at the relevant level. At the national level, each individual shall have appropriate access to information concerning the environment that is held by public authorities, including information on hazardous materials and activities in their communities, and the opportunity to participate in decision-making processes. States shall facilitate and encourage public awareness and participation by making information widely available. Effective access to judicial and administrative proceedings, including redress and remedy, shall be provided.

Principle 11

States shall enact effective environmental legislation. Environmental standards, management objectives and priorities should reflect the environmental and developmental context to which they apply. Standards applied by some countries may be inappropriate and of unwarranted economic and social cost to other countries, in particular developing countries.

Principle 12

States should cooperate to promote a supportive and open international economic system that would lead to economic growth and sustainable development in all countries, to better address the problems of environmental degradation.　Trade policy measures for environmental purposes should not constitute a means of arbitrary or unjustifiable discrimination or a disguised restriction on international trade.　Unilateral actions to deal with environmental challenges outside the jurisdiction of the importing country should be avoided.　Environmental measures addressing transboundary or global environmental problems should, as far as possible, be based on an international consensus.

Principle 13

States shall develop national law regarding liability and compensation for the victims of pollution and other environmental damage.　States shall also cooperate in an expeditious and more determined manner to develop further international law regarding liability and compensation for adverse effects of environmental damage caused by activities within their jurisdiction or control to areas beyond their jurisdiction.

Principle 14

States should effectively cooperate to discourage or prevent the relocation and transfer to other States of any activities and substances that cause severe environmental degradation or are found to be harmful to human health.

Principle 15

In order to protect the environment, the precautionary approach shall be widely applied by States according to their capabilities.　Where there are threats of serious or irreversible damage, lack of full scientific certainty shall not be used as a reason for postponing cost-effective measures to prevent environmental degradation.

Principle 16

National authorities should endeavor to promote the internalization of environmental costs and the use of economic instruments, taking into account the approach that the polluter should, in principle, bear the cost of pollution, with due regard to the public interest and without distorting international trade and investment.

Principle 17

Environmental impact assessment, as a national instrument, shall be undertaken for proposed activities that are likely to have a significant adverse impact on the environment and are subject to a decision of a competent national authority.

Principle 18

States shall immediately notify other States of any natural disasters or other emergencies that are likely to produce sudden harmful effects on the environment of those States.　Every effort shall be made by the international community to help States so afflicted.

Principle 19

States shall provide prior and timely notification and relevant information to potentially affected States on activities that may have a significant adverse transboundary environmental effect and shall consult with those States at an early stage and in good faith.

Principle 20

Women have a vital role in environmental management and development. Their full participation is therefore essential to achieve sustainable development.

Principle 21

The creativity, ideals and courage of the youth of the world should be mobilized to forge a global partnership in order to achieve sustainable development and ensure a better future for all.

Principle 22

Indigenous people and their communities and other local communities have a vital role in environmental management and development because of their knowledge and traditional practices. States should recognize and duly support their identity, culture and interests and enable their effective participation in the achievement of sustainable development.

Principle 23

The environment and natural resources of people under oppression, domination and occupation shall be protected.

Principle 24

Warfare is inherently destructive of sustainable development. States shall therefore respect international law providing protection for the environment in times of armed conflict and cooperate in its further development, as necessary.

Principle 25

Peace, development and environmental protection are interdependent and indivisible.

Principle 26

States shall resolve all their environmental disputes peacefully and by appropriate means in accordance with the Charter of the United Nations.

Principle 27

States and people shall cooperate in good faith and in a spirit of partnership in the fulfilment of the principles embodied in this Declaration and in the further development of international law in the field of sustainable development.

附錄四：21世紀議程

AGENDA 21. Adopted by the U.N. Conference on Environment and Development (UNCED) at Rio de Janeiro, 13 June 1992. U.N. Doc. A/CONF. 151/26 (vols. I, II, & III) (1992): *Table of Contents & Chs. 5, 15, 17, 20, 33*

Agenda 21 was adopted by the U.N. Conference on Environment and Development (UNCED) at Rio de Janeiro, 13 June 1992. The complete text is too lengthy for publication in this volume. The following table of contents provides a summary of its provisions. The full text may be found in the above-cited source.

SECTION III. STRENGTHENING THE ROLE OF MAJOR GROUPS

SECTION IV. MEANS OF IMPLEMENTATION

* * *

Chapter 5

DEMOGRAPHIC DYNAMICS AND SUSTAINABILITY

5.1. This chapter contains the following programme areas:

(a) Developing and disseminating knowledge concerning the links between demographic trends and factors and sustainable development;

(b) Formulating integrated national policies for environment and development, taking into account demographic trends and factors;

(c) Implementing integrated, environment and development programmes at the local level, taking into account demographic trends and
factors.

PROGRAMME AREAS

A. *Developing and disseminating knowledge concerning the links between
demographic trends and factors and sustainable development*

Basis for action

5.2.　Demographic trends and factors and sustainable development have
a synergistic relationship.

5.3.　The growth of world population and production combined with
unsustainable consumption patterns places increasingly severe stress on the
life-supporting capacities of our planet.　These interactive processes affect the
use of land, water, air, energy and other resources.　Rapidly growing cities,
unless well-managed, face major environmental problems.　The increase in
both the number and size of cities calls for greater attention to issues of local
government and municipal management.　The human dimensions are key
elements to consider in this intricate set of relationships and they should be
adequately taken into consideration in comprehensive policies for sustainable
development.　Such policies should address the linkages of demographic
trends and factors, resource use, appropriate technology dissemination, and
development.　Population policy should also recognize the role played by
human beings in environmental and development concerns.　There is a need
to increase awareness of this issue among decision makers at all levels and to
provide both better information on which to base national and international
policies and a framework against which to interpret this information.

5.4.　There is a need to develop strategies to mitigate both the adverse
impact on the environment of human activities and the adverse impact of
environmental change on human populations.　The world's population is
expected to exceed 8 billion by the year 2020.　Sixty per cent of the world's
population already live in coastal areas, while 65 per cent of cities with
populations above 2.5 million are located along the world coasts; several of
them are already at or below the present sea level.

Objectives

5.5.　The following objectives should be achieved as soon as practicable:

(a) To incorporate demographic trends and factors in the global
analysis of environment and development issues;

(b) To develop a better understanding of the relationships among
demographic dynamics, technology, cultural behaviour, natural resources
and life support systems;

(c) To assess human vulnerability in ecologically sensitive areas and
centres of population to determine the priorities for action at all levels,
taking full account of community defined needs.

Activities

Research on the interaction between demographic trends and factors and sustainable development

5.6. Relevant international, regional and national institutions should consider undertaking the following activities:

(a) Identifying the interactions between demographic processes, natural resources and life support systems, bearing in mind regional and subregional variations deriving from, *inter alia,* different levels of development;

(b) Integrating demographic trends and factors into the ongoing study of environmental change, using the expertise of international, regional and national research networks and of local communities, first, to study the human dimensions of environmental change and, second, to identify vulnerable areas;

(c) Identifying priority areas for action and developing strategies and programmes to mitigate the adverse impact of environmental change on human populations, and vice versa.

Means of implementation

(a) *Financing and cost evaluation*

5.7. The Conference secretariat has estimated the average total annual cost (1993–2000) of implementing the activities of this programme to be about $10 million from the international community on grant or concessional terms. These are indicative and order-of-magnitude estimates only and have not been reviewed by Governments. Actual costs and financial terms, including any that are non-concessional, will depend upon, *inter alia,* the specific strategies and programmes Governments decide upon for implementation.

(b) *Strengthening research programmes that integrate population, environment and development*

5.8. In order to integrate demographic analysis into a broader social science perspective on environment and development, interdisciplinary research should be increased. International institutions and networks of experts should enhance their scientific capacity, taking full account of community experience and knowledge, and should disseminate the experience gained in multidisciplinary approaches and in linking theory to action.

5.9. Better modelling capabilities should be developed, identifying the range of possible outcomes of current human activities, especially the interrelated impact of demographic trends and factors, per capita resource use and wealth distribution, as well as the major migration flows that may be expected with increasing climatic events and cumulative environmental change that may destroy people's local livelihoods.

(c) *Developing information and public awareness*

5.10. Socio-demographic information should be developed in a suitable format for interfacing with physical, biological and socio-economic data. Compatible spatial and temporal scales, cross-country and time-series information, as well as global behavioural indicators should be developed, learning from local communities' perceptions and attitudes.

5.11. Awareness should be increased at all levels concerning the need to optimize the sustainable use of resources through efficient resource management, taking into account the development needs of the populations of developing countries.

5.12. Awareness should be increased of the fundamental linkages between improving the status of women and demographic dynamics, particularly through women's access to education, primary and reproductive health care programmes, economic independence and their effective, equitable participation in all levels of decision-making.

5.13. Results of research concerned with sustainable development issues should be disseminated through technical reports, scientific journals, the media, workshops, forums or other means so that the information can be used by decision makers at all levels and increase public awareness.

(d) *Developing and/or enhancing institutional capacity and collaboration*

5.14. Collaboration and exchange of information should be increased between research institutions and international, regional and national agencies and all other sectors (including the private sector, local communities, non-governmental organizations and scientific institutions) from both the industrialized and developing countries, as appropriate.

5.15. Efforts should be intensified to enhance the capacities of national and local governments, the private sector and non-governmental organizations in developing countries to meet the growing needs for improved management of rapidly growing urban areas.

B. *Formulating integrated national policies for
environment and development, taking into account
demographic trends and factors*

Basis for action

5.16. Existing plans for sustainable development have generally recognized demographic trends and factors as elements that have a critical influence on consumption patterns, production, lifestyles and long-term sustainability. But in future, more attention will have to be given to these issues in general policy formulation and the design of development plans. To do this, all countries will have to improve their own capacities to assess the environment and development implications of their demographic trends and factors. They will also need to formulate and implement policies and action programmes where appropriate. Policies should be designed to address the consequences of population growth built into population momentum, while at the same time incorporating measures to bring about demographic transition. They should combine environmental concerns and population issues within a holistic view of development whose primary goals include the alleviation of poverty; secure livelihoods; good health; quality of life; improvement of the status and income of women and their access to schooling and professional training, as well as fulfilment of their personal aspirations; and empowerment of individuals and communities. Recognizing that large increases in the size and number of cities will occur in developing countries under any likely population scenario, greater attention should be given to preparing for the needs, in particular of women and children, for improved municipal management and local government.

Objective

5.17. Full integration of population concerns into national planning, policy and decision-making processes should continue. Population policies and programmes should be considered, with full recognition of women's rights.

Activities

5.18. Governments and other relevant actors could, *inter alia,* undertake the following activities, with appropriate assistance from aid agencies, and report on their status of implementation to the International Conference on Population and Development to be held in 1994, especially to its committee on population and environment.

(a) *Assessing the implications of national demographic trends and factors*

5.19. The relationships between demographic trends and factors and environmental change and between environmental degradation and the components of demographic change should be analysed.

5.20. Research should be conducted on how environmental factors interact with socio-economic factors as a cause of migration.

5.21. Vulnerable population groups (such as rural landless workers, ethnic minorities, refugees, migrants, displaced people, women heads of household) whose changes in demographic structure may have specific impacts on sustainable development should be identified.

5.22. An assessment should be made of the implications of the age structure of the population on resource demand and dependency burdens, ranging from educational expenses for the young to health care and support for the elderly, and on household income generation.

5.23. An assessment should also be made of national population carrying capacity in the context of satisfaction of human needs and sustainable development, and special attention should be given to critical resources, such as water and land, and environmental factors, such as ecosystem health and biodiversity.

5.24.　The impact of national demographic trends and factors on the traditional livelihoods of indigenous groups and local communities, including changes in traditional land use because of internal population pressures, should be studied.

(b) *Building and strengthening a national information base*

5.25.　National databases on demographic trends and factors and environment should be built and/or strengthened, disaggregating data by ecological region (ecosystem approach), and population/environment profiles should be established by region.

5.26.　Methodologies and instruments should be developed to identify areas where sustainability is, or may be, threatened by the environmental effects of demographic trends and factors, incorporating both current and projected demographic data linked to natural environmental processes.

5.27.　Case-studies of local level responses by different groups to demographic dynamics should be developed, particularly in areas subject to environmental stress and in deteriorating urban centres.

5.28.　Population data should be disaggregated by, *inter alia,* sex and age in order to take into account the implications of the gender division of labour for the use and management of natural resources.

(c) *Incorporating demographic features into policies and plans*

5.29.　In formulating human settlements policies, account should be taken of resource needs, waste production and ecosystem health.

5.30.　The direct and induced effects of demographic changes on environment and development programmes should, where appropriate, be integrated, and the impact on demographic features assessed.

5.31.　National population policy goals and programmes that are consistent with national environment and development plans for sustainability and in keeping with the freedom, dignity and personally held values of individuals should be established and implemented.

5.32.　Appropriate socio-economic policies for the young and the elderly, both in terms of family and state support systems, should be developed.

5.33.　Policies and programmes should be developed for handling the various types of migrations that result from or induce environmental disruptions, with special attention to women and vulnerable groups.

5.34.　Demographic concerns, including concerns for environmental migrants and displaced people, should be incorporated in the programmes for sustainable development of relevant international and regional institutions.

5.35. National reviews should be conducted and the integration of population policies in national development and environment strategies should be monitored nationally.

Means of implementation
(a) *Financing and cost evaluation*

5.36. The Conference secretariat has estimated the average total annual cost (1993–2000) of implementing the activities of this programme to be about $90 million from the international community on grant or concessional terms. These are indicative and order-of-magnitude estimates only and have not been reviewed by Governments. Actual costs and financial terms, including any that are non-concessional, will depend upon, *inter alia*, the specific strategies and programmes Governments decide upon for implementation.

(b) *Raising awareness of demographic and sustainable development interactions*

5.37. Understanding of the interactions between demographic trends and factors and sustainable development should be increased in all sectors of society. Stress should be placed on local and national action. Demographic and sustainable development education should be coordinated and integrated in both the formal and non-formal education sectors. Particular attention should be given to population literacy programmes, notably for women. Special emphasis should be placed on the linkage between these programmes, primary environmental care and the provision of primary health care and services.

(c) *Strengthening institutions*

5.38. The capacity of national, regional and local structures to deal with issues relating to demographic trends and factors and sustainable development should be enhanced. This would involve strengthening the relevant bodies responsible for population issues to enable them to elaborate policies consistent with the national prospects for sustainable development. Cooperation among government, national research institutions, non-governmental organizations and local communities in assessing problems and evaluating policies should also be enhanced.

5.39. The capacity of the relevant United Nations organs, organizations and bodies, international and regional intergovernmental bodies, non-governmental organizations and local communities should, as appropriate, be enhanced to help countries develop sustainable development policies on request and, as appropriate, provide assistance to environmental migrants and displaced people.

5.40. Inter-agency support for national sustainable development policies and programmes should be improved through better coordination of population and environment activities.

(d) *Promoting human resource development*

5.41.　The international and regional scientific institutions should assist Governments, upon request, to include concerns regarding the population/environment interactions at the global, ecosystem and micro-levels in the training of demographers and population and environment specialists.　Training should include research on linkages and ways to design integrated strategies.

C.　*Implementing integrated environment and development programmes at the local level, taking into account demographic trends and factors*

Basis for action

5.42.　Population programmes are more effective when implemented together with appropriate cross-sectoral policies.　To attain sustainability at the local level, a new framework is needed that integrates demographic trends and factors with such factors as ecosystem health, technology and human settlements, and with socio-economic structures and access to resources. Population programmes should be consistent with socio-economic and environmental planning.　Integrated sustainable development programmes should closely correlate action on demographic trends and factors with resource management activities and development goals that meet the needs of the people concerned.

Objective

5.43.　Population programmes should be implemented along with natural resource management and development programmes at the local level that will ensure sustainable use of natural resources, improve the quality of life of the people and enhance environmental quality.

Activities

5.44.　Governments and local communities, including community-based women's organizations and national non-governmental organizations, consistent with national plans, objectives, strategies and priorities, could, *inter alia*, undertake the activities set out below with the assistance and cooperation of international organizations, as appropriate.　Governments could share their experience in the implementation of Agenda 21 at the International Conference on Population and Development, to be held in 1994, especially its committee on population and environment.

(a) *Developing a framework for action*

5.45.　An effective consultative process should be established and implemented with concerned groups of society where the formulation and decision-making of all components of the programmes are based on a nationwide consultative process drawing on community meetings, regional workshops and national seminars, as appropriate.　This process should ensure that views of women and men on needs, perspective and constraints are equally well reflected in the design of programmes, and that solutions are rooted in specific experience.　The poor and underprivileged should be priority groups in this process.

5.46. Nationally determined policies for integrated and multifaceted programmes, with special attention to women, to the poorest people living in critical areas and to other vulnerable groups should be implemented, ensuring the involvement of groups with a special potential to act as agents for change and sustainable development. Special emphasis should be placed on those programmes that achieve multiple objectives, encouraging sustainable economic development, and mitigating adverse impacts of demographic trends and factors, and avoiding long-term environmental damage. Food security, access to secure tenure, basic shelter, and essential infrastructure, education, family welfare, women's reproductive health, family credit schemes, reforestation programmes, primary environmental care, women's employment should, as appropriate, be included among other factors.

5.47. An analytical framework should be developed to identify complementary elements of sustainable development policies as well as the national mechanisms to monitor and evaluate their effects on population dynamics.

5.48. Special attention should be given to the critical role of women in population/environment programmes and in achieving sustainable development. Projects should take advantage of opportunities to link social, economic and environmental gains for women and their families. Empowerment of women is essential and should be assured through education, training and policies to accord and improve women's rights and access to assets, human and civil rights, labour-saving measures, job opportunities and participation in decision-making. Population/environment programmes must enable women to mobilize themselves to alleviate their burden and improve their capacity to participate in and benefit from socio-economic development. Specific measures should be undertaken to close the gap between female and male illiteracy rates.

(b) *Supporting programmes that promote changes in demographic trends and factors towards sustainability*

5.49. Reproductive health programmes and services, should, as appropriate, be developed and enhanced to reduce maternal and infant mortality from all causes and enable women and men to fulfil their personal aspirations in terms of family size, in a way in keeping with their freedom and dignity and personally held values.

5.50. Governments should take active steps to implement, as a matter of urgency, in accordance with country-specific conditions and legal systems, measures to ensure that women and men have the same right to decide freely and responsibly on the number and spacing of their children, to have access to the information, education and means, as appropriate, to enable them to exercise this right in keeping with their freedom, dignity and personally held values taking into account ethical and cultural considerations.

5.51. Governments should take active steps to implement programmes to establish and strengthen preventive and curative health facilities that include women-centred, women-managed, safe and effective reproductive health care and affordable, accessible services, as appropriate, for the responsible planning of family size, in keeping with freedom, dignity and personally held values and taking into account ethical and cultural considerations. Programmes should focus on providing comprehensive health care, including pre-natal care, education and information on health and responsible parenthood and should provide the opportunity for all women to breast-feed fully, at least during the first four months post-partum. Programmes should fully support women's productive and reproductive roles and well being, with special attention to the need for providing equal and improved health care for all children and the need to reduce the risk of maternal and child mortality and sickness.

5.52. Consistent with national priorities, culturally based information and education programmes that transmit reproductive health messages to men and women that are easily understood should be developed.

(c) *Creating appropriate institutional conditions*

5.53. Constituencies and institutional conditions to facilitate the implementation of demographic activities should, as appropriate, be fostered. This requires support and commitment from political, indigenous, religious and traditional authorities, the private sector and the national scientific community. In developing these appropriate institutional conditions, countries should closely involve established national machinery for women.

5.54. Population assistance should be coordinated with bilateral and multilateral donors to ensure that population needs and requirements of all developing countries are addressed, fully respecting the overall coordinating responsibility and the choice and strategies of the recipient countries.

5.55. Coordination should be improved at local and international levels. Working practices should be enhanced in order to make optimum use of resources, draw on collective experience and improve the implementation of programmes. UNFPA and other relevant agencies should strengthen the coordination of international cooperation activities with recipient and donor countries in order to ensure that adequate funding is available to respond to growing needs.

5.56. Proposals should be developed for local, national and international population/environment programmes in line with specific needs for achieving sustainability. Where appropriate, institutional changes must be implemented so that old-age security does not entirely depend on input from family members.

Means of implementation

(a) *Financing and cost evaluation*

5.57. The Conference secretariat has estimated the average total annual cost (1993–2000) of implementing the activities of this programme to be about

$7 billion, including about $3.5 billion from the international community on grant or concessional terms. These are indicative and order-of-magnitude estimates only and have not been reviewed by Governments. Actual costs and financial terms, including any that are non-concessional, will depend upon, *inter alia,* the specific strategies and programmes Governments decide upon for implementation.

(b) *Research*

5.58. Research should be undertaken with a view to developing specific action programmes; it will be necessary to establish priorities between proposed areas of research.

5.59. Socio-demographic research should be conducted on how populations respond to a changing environment.

5.60. Understanding of socio-cultural and political factors that can positively influence acceptance of appropriate population policy instruments should be improved.

5.61. Surveys of changes in needs for appropriate services relating to responsible planning of family size, reflecting variations among different socio-economic groups and variations in different geographical regions should be undertaken.

(c) *Human resource development and capacity-building*

5.62. The areas of human resource development and capacity-building, with particular attention to the education and training of women, are areas of critical importance and are a very high priority in the implementation of population programmes.

5.63. Workshops to help programme and projects managers to link population programmes to other development and environmental goals should be conducted.

5.64. Educational materials, including guides/workbooks for planners and decision makers and other actors of population/environment/development programmes, should be developed.

5.65. Cooperation should be developed between Governments, scientific institutions and non-governmental organizations within the region, and similar institutions outside the region. Cooperation with local organizations should be fostered in order to raise awareness, engage in demonstration projects and report on the experience gained.

5.66. The recommendations contained in this chapter should in no way prejudice discussions at the International Conference on Population and Development in 1994, which will be the appropriate forum for dealing with population and development issues, taking into account the recommendations of the International Conference on Population, held in Mexico City in 1984, and the Forward-looking Strategies for the Advancement of Women, adopted by the World Conference to Review and Appraise the Achievements of the United Decade for Women: Equality, Development and Peace, held in Nairobi in 1985.

* * *

Chapter 15
CONSERVATION OF BIOLOGICAL DIVERSITY
INTRODUCTION

15.1.   The objectives and activities in this chapter of Agenda 21 are intended to improve the conservation of biological diversity and the sustainable use of biological resources, as well as to support the Convention on Biological Diversity.

15.2.   Our planet's essential goods and services depend on the variety and variability of genes, species, populations and ecosystems. Biological resources feed and clothe us and provide housing, medicines and spiritual nourishment. The natural ecosystems of forests, savannahs, pastures and rangelands, deserts, tundras, rivers, lakes and seas contain most of the Earth's biodiversity. Farmers' fields and gardens are also of great importance as repositories, while gene banks, botanical gardens, zoos and other germplasm repositories make a small but significant contribution. The current decline in biodiversity is largely the result of human activity and represents a serious threat to human development.

PROGRAMME AREA
Conservation of biological diversity

Basis for action

15.3.   Despite mounting efforts over the past 20 years, the loss of the world's biological diversity, mainly from habitat destruction, over-harvesting, pollution and the inappropriate introduction of foreign plants and animals, has continued. Biological resources constitute a capital asset with great potential for yielding sustainable benefits. Urgent and decisive action is needed to conserve and maintain genes, species and ecosystems, with a view to the sustainable management and use of biological resources. Capacities for the assessment, study and systematic observation and evaluation of biodiversity need to be reinforced at national and international levels. Effective national action and international cooperation is required for the *in situ* protection of ecosystems, for the *ex situ* conservation of biological and genetic resources and for the enhancement of ecosystem functions. The participation and support of local communities are elements essential to the success of such an approach. Recent advances in biotechnology have pointed up the likely potential for agriculture, health and welfare and for the environmental purposes of the genetic material contained in plants, animals and microorganisms. At the same time, it is particularly important in this context to stress that States have the sovereign right to exploit their own biological resources pursuant to their environmental policies, as well as the responsibility to conserve their biodiversity and use their biological resources sustainably, and to ensure that activities within their jurisdiction or control do not cause damage to the biological diversity of other States or of areas beyond the limits of national jurisdiction.

Objectives

15.4.   Governments at the appropriate level, with the cooperation of the relevant United Nations bodies and regional, intergovernmental and non-governmental organizations, the private sector and financial institutions, and taking into consideration indigenous people and their communities, as well as social and economic factors, should:

(a) Press for the early entry into force of the Convention on Biological Diversity, with the widest possible participation;

(b) Develop national strategies for the conservation of biological diversity and the sustainable use of biological resources;

(c) Integrate strategies for the conservation of biological diversity and the sustainable use of biological resources into national development strategies and/or plans;

(d) Take appropriate measures for the fair and equitable sharing of benefits derived from research and development and use of biological and genetic resources, including biotechnology, between the sources of those resources and those who use them;

(e) Carry out country studies, as appropriate, on the conservation of biological diversity and the sustainable use of biological resources, including analyses of relevant costs and benefits, with particular reference to socio-economic aspects;

(f) Produce regularly updated world reports on biodiversity based upon national assessments;

(g) Recognize and foster the traditional methods and the knowledge of indigenous people and their communities, emphasizing the particular role of women, relevant to the conservation of biological diversity and the sustainable use of biological resources, and ensure the opportunity for the participation of those groups in the economic and commercial benefits derived from the use of such traditional methods and knowledge;

(h) Implement mechanisms for the improvement, generation, development and sustainable use of biotechnology and its safe transfer, particularly to developing countries, taking account the potential contribution of biotechnology to the conservation of biological diversity and the sustainable use of biological resources;

(i) Promote broader international and regional cooperation in furthering scientific and economic understanding of the importance of biodiversity and its functions in ecosystems;

(j) Develop measures and arrangements to implement the rights of countries of origin of genetic resources or countries providing genetic resources, as defined in the Convention on Biological Diversity, particularly developing countries, to benefit from the biotechnological development and the commercial utilization of products derived from such resources.

Activities

(a) *Management-related activities*

15.5. Governments at the appropriate levels, consistent with national policies and practices, with the cooperation of the relevant United Nations bodies and, as appropriate, intergovernmental organizations and, with the support of indigenous people and their communities, non-governmental organizations and other groups, including the business and scientific communities, and consistent with the requirements of international law, should, as appropriate:

(a) Develop new or strengthen existing strategies, plans or programmes of action for the conservation of biological diversity and the sustainable use of biological resources, taking account of education and training needs;

(b) Integrate strategies for the conservation of biological diversity and the sustainable use of biological and genetic resources into relevant sectoral or cross-sectoral plans, programmes and policies, with particular reference to the special importance of terrestrial and aquatic biological and genetic resources for food and agriculture;

(c) Undertake country studies or use other methods to identify components of biological diversity important for its conservation and for the sustainable use of biological resources, ascribe values to biological and genetic resources, identify processes and activities with significant impacts upon biological diversity, evaluate the potential economic implications of the conservation of biological diversity and the sustainable use of biological and genetic resources, and suggest priority action;

(d) Take effective economic, social and other appropriate incentive measures to encourage the conservation of biological diversity and the sustainable use of biological resources, including the promotion of sustainable production systems, such as traditional methods of agriculture, agroforestry, forestry, range and wildlife management, which use, maintain or increase biodiversity;

(e) Subject to national legislation, take action to respect, record, protect and promote the wider application of the knowledge, innovations and practices of indigenous and local communities embodying traditional lifestyles for the conservation of biological diversity and the sustainable use of biological resources, with a view to the fair and equitable sharing of the benefits arising, and promote mechanisms to involve those communities, including women, in the conservation and management of ecosystems;

(f) Undertake long-term research into the importance of biodiversity for the functioning of ecosystems and the role of ecosystems in producing goods, environmental services and other values supporting sustainable development, with particular reference to the biology and reproductive capacities of key terrestrial and aquatic species, including native, cultivated and cultured species; new observation and inventory techniques; ecological conditions necessary for biodiversity conservation and continued evolution; and social behaviour and nutrition habits dependent on natural ecosystems, where women play key roles. The work should be undertaken with the widest possible participation, especially of indigenous people and their communities, including women;

(g) Take action where necessary for the conservation of biological diversity through the *in situ* conservation of ecosystems and natural habitats, as well as primitive cultivars and their wild relatives, and the maintenance and recovery of viable populations of species in their natural surroundings, and implement *ex situ* measures, preferably in the source country. *In situ* measures should include the reinforcement of terrestrial, marine and aquatic protected area systems and embrace, *inter alia,* vulnerable freshwater and other wetlands and coastal ecosystems, such as estuaries, coral reefs and mangroves;

(h) Promote the rehabilitation and restoration of damaged ecosystems and the recovery of threatened and endangered species;

(i) Develop policies to encourage the conservation of biodiversity and the sustainable use of biological and genetic resources on private lands;

(j) Promote environmentally sound and sustainable development in areas adjacent to protected areas with a view to furthering protection of these areas;

(k) Introduce appropriate environmental impact assessment procedures for proposed projects likely to have significant impacts upon biological diversity, providing for suitable information to be made widely available and for public participation, where appropriate, and encourage the assessment of the impacts of relevant policies and programmes on biological diversity;

(*l*) Promote, where appropriate, the establishment and strengthening of national inventory, regulation or management and control systems related to biological resources, at the appropriate level;

(m) Take measures to encourage a greater understanding and appreciation of the value of biological diversity, as manifested both in its component parts and in the ecosystem services provided.

(b) *Data and information*

15.6. Governments at the appropriate level, consistent with national policies and practices, with the cooperation of the relevant United Nations bodies and, as appropriate, intergovernmental organizations, and with the support of indigenous people and their communities, non-governmental organizations and other groups, including the business and scientific communities, and consistent with the requirements of international law, should, as appropriate:

(a) Regularly collate, evaluate and exchange information on the conservation of biological diversity and the sustainable use of biological resources;

(b) Develop methodologies with a view to undertaking systematic sampling and evaluation on a national basis of the components of biological diversity identified by means of country studies;

(c) Initiate or further develop methodologies and begin or continue work on surveys at the appropriate level on the status of ecosystems and establish baseline information on biological and genetic resources, including those in terrestrial, aquatic, coastal and marine ecosystems, as well as inventories undertaken with the participation of local and indigenous people and their communities;

(d) Identify and evaluate the potential economic and social implications and benefits of the conservation and sustainable use of terrestrial and aquatic species in each country, building upon the results of country studies;

(e) Undertake the updating, analysis and interpretation of data derived from the identification, sampling and evaluation activities described above;

(f) Collect, assess and make available relevant and reliable information in a timely manner and in a form suitable for decision-making at all levels, with the full support and participation of local and indigenous people and their communities.

(c) *International and regional cooperation and coordination*

15.7. Governments at the appropriate level, with the cooperation of the relevant United Nations bodies and, as appropriate, intergovernmental organizations, and, with the support of indigenous people and their communities, non-governmental organizations and other groups, including the business and scientific communities, and consistent with the requirements of international law, should, as appropriate:

(a) Consider the establishment or strengthening of national or international capabilities and networks for the exchange of data and information of relevance to the conservation of biological diversity and the sustainable use of biological and genetic resources;

(b) Produce regularly updated world reports on biodiversity based upon national assessments in all countries;

(c) Promote technical and scientific cooperation in the field of conservation of biological diversity and the sustainable use of biological and genetic resources. Special attention should be given to the development and strengthening of national capabilities by means of human resource development and institution-building, including the transfer of technology and/or development of research and management facilities, such as herbaria, museums, gene banks, and laboratories, related to the conservation of biodiversity;

(d) Without prejudice to the relevant provisions of the Convention on Biological Diversity, facilitate for this chapter the transfer of technologies relevant to the conservation of biological diversity and the sustainable use of biological resources or technologies that make use of genetic resources and cause no significant damage to the environment, in conformity with chapter 34, and recognizing that technology includes biotechnology;

(e) Promote cooperation between the parties to relevant international conventions and action plans with the aim of strengthening and coordinating efforts to conserve biological diversity and the sustainable use of biological resources;

(f) Strengthen support for international and regional instruments, programmes and action plans concerned with the conservation of biological diversity and the sustainable use of biological resources;

(g) Promote improved international coordination of measures for the effective conservation and management of endangered/non-pest migratory species, including appropriate levels of support for the establishment and management of protected areas in transboundary locations;

(h) Promote national efforts with respect to surveys, data collection, sampling and evaluation, and the maintenance of gene banks.

Means of implementation

(a) *Financing and cost evaluation*

15.8.　The Conference secretariat has estimated the average total annual cost (1993–2000) of implementing the activities of this chapter to be about $3.5 billion, including about $1.75 billion from the international community on grant or concessional terms. These are indicative and order-of-magnitude estimates only and have not been reviewed by Governments. Actual costs and financial terms, including any that are non-concessional, will depend upon, *inter alia,* the specific strategies and programmes Governments decide upon for implementation.

(b) *Scientific and technological means*

15.9.　Specific aspects to be addressed include the need to develop:

(a) Efficient methodologies for baseline surveys and inventories, as well as for the systematic sampling and evaluation of biological resources;

(b) Methods and technologies for the conservation of biological diversity and the sustainable use of biological resources;

(c) Improved and diversified methods for *ex situ* conservation with a view to the long-term conservation of genetic resources of importance for research and development.

(c) *Human resource development*

15.10.　There is a need, where appropriate, to:

(a) Increase the number and/or make more efficient use of trained personnel in scientific and technological fields relevant to the conservation of biological diversity and the sustainable use of biological resources;

(b) Maintain or establish programmes for scientific and technical education and training of managers and professionals, especially in developing countries, on measures for the identification, conservation of biological diversity and the sustainable use of biological resources;

(c) Promote and encourage understanding of the importance of the measures required for the conservation of biological diversity and the sustainable use of biological resources at all policy-making and decision-making levels in Governments, business enterprises and lending institutions, and promote and encourage the inclusion of these topics in educational programmes.

(d) *Capacity-building*

15.11.　There is a need, where appropriate, to:

(a) Strengthen existing institutions and/or establish new ones responsible for the conservation of biological diversity and to consider the development of mechanisms such as national biodiversity institutes or centres;

(b) Continue to build capacity for the conservation of biological diversity and the sustainable use of biological resources in all relevant sectors;

(c) Build capacity, especially within Governments, business enterprises and bilateral and multilateral development agencies, for integrating biodiversity concerns, potential benefits and opportunity cost calculations into project design, implementation and evaluation processes, as well as for evaluating the impact on biological diversity of proposed development projects;

(d) Enhance the capacity of governmental and private institutions, at the appropriate level, responsible for protected area planning and management to undertake intersectoral coordination and planning with other governmental institutions, non-governmental organizations and, where appropriate, indigenous people and their communities.

* * *

Chapter 17

PROTECTION OF THE OCEANS, ALL KINDS OF SEAS, INCLUDING
ENCLOSED AND SEMI-ENCLOSED SEAS, AND COASTAL AREAS
AND THE PROTECTION, RATIONAL USE AND DEVELOPMENT OF
THEIR LIVING RESOURCES

INTRODUCTION

17.1. The marine environment—including the oceans and all seas and
adjacent coastal areas—forms an integrated whole that is an essential component of the global life-support system and a positive asset that presents
opportunities for sustainable development. International law, as reflected in
the provisions of the United Nations Convention on the Law of the Sea,
referred to in this chapter of Agenda 21, sets forth rights and obligations of
States and provides the international basis upon which to pursue the protection and sustainable development of the marine and coastal environment and
its resources. This requires new approaches to marine and coastal area
management and development at the national, subregional, regional and
global levels, approaches that are integrated in content and are precautionary
and anticipatory in ambit, as reflected in the following programme areas:

(a) Integrated management and sustainable development of coastal
areas, including exclusive economic zones;

(b) Marine environmental protection;

(c) Sustainable use and conservation of marine living resources of
the high seas;

(d) Sustainable use and conservation of marine living resources
under national jurisdiction;

(e) Addressing critical uncertainties for the management of the marine environment and climate change;

(f) Strengthening international, including regional, cooperation and
coordination;

(g) Sustainable development of small islands.

17.2. The implementation by developing countries of the activities set
forth below shall be commensurate with their individual technological and
financial capacities and priorities in allocating resources for development
needs and ultimately depends on the technology transfer and financial resources required and made available to them.

PROGRAMME AREAS

A. *Integrated management and sustainable development of coastal
and marine areas, including exclusive economic zones*

Basis for action

17.3. The coastal area contains diverse and productive habitats important for human settlements, development and local subsistence. More than

half the world's population lives within 60 km of the shoreline, and this could rise to three quarters by the year 2020. Many of the world's poor are crowded in coastal areas. Coastal resources are vital for many local communities and indigenous people. The exclusive economic zone (EEZ) is also an important marine area where the States manage the development and conservation of natural resources for the benefit of their people. For small island States or countries, these are the areas most available for development activities.

17.4. Despite national, subregional, regional and global efforts, current approaches to the management of marine and coastal resources have not always proved capable of achieving sustainable development, and coastal resources and the coastal environment are being rapidly degraded and eroded in many parts of the world.

Objectives

17.5. Coastal States commit themselves to integrated management and sustainable development of coastal areas and the marine environment under their national jurisdiction. To this end, it is necessary to, *inter alia:*

(a) Provide for an integrated policy and decision-making process, including all involved sectors, to promote compatibility and a balance of uses;

(b) Identify existing and projected uses of coastal areas and their interactions;

(c) Concentrate on well-defined issues concerning coastal management;

(d) Apply preventive and precautionary approaches in project planning and implementation, including prior assessment and systematic observation of the impacts of major projects;

(e) Promote the development and application of methods, such as national resource and environmental accounting, that reflect changes in value resulting from uses of coastal and marine areas, including pollution, marine erosion, loss of resources and habitat destruction;

(f) Provide access, as far as possible, for concerned individuals, groups and organizations to relevant information and opportunities for consultation and participation in planning and decision-making at appropriate levels.

Activities

(a) *Management-related activities*

17.6. Each coastal State should consider establishing, or where necessary, strengthening, appropriate coordinating mechanisms (such as a high-level policy planning body) for integrated management and sustainable devel-

opment of coastal and marine areas and their resources, at both the local and
national levels. Such mechanisms should include consultation, as appropriate, with the academic and private sectors, non-governmental organizations,
local communities, resource user groups, and indigenous people. Such national coordinating mechanisms could provide, *inter alia,* for:

(a) Preparation and implementation of land and water use and siting
policies;

(b) Implementation of integrated coastal and marine management
and sustainable development plans and programmes at appropriate levels;

(c) Preparation of coastal profiles identifying critical areas, including
eroded zones, physical processes, development patterns, user conflicts and
specific priorities for management;

(d) Prior environmental impact assessment, systematic observation
and follow-up of major projects, including the systematic incorporation of
results in decision-making;

(e) Contingency plans for human induced and natural disasters,
including likely effects of potential climate change and sealevel rise, as
well as contingency plans for degradation and pollution of anthropogenic
origin, including spills of oil and other materials;

(f) Improvement of coastal human settlements, especially in housing,
drinking water and treatment and disposal of sewage, solid wastes and
industrial effluents;

(g) Periodic assessment of the impacts of external factors and phe-
nomena to ensure that the objectives of integrated management and
sustainable development of coastal areas and the marine environment are
met;

(h) Conservation and restoration of altered critical habitats;

(i) Integration of sectoral programmes on sustainable development
for settlements, agriculture, tourism, fishing, ports and industries affecting the coastal area;

(j) Infrastructure adaptation and alternative employment;

(k) Human resource development and training;

(*l*) Public education, awareness and information programmes;

(m) Promoting environmentally sound technology and sustainable
practices;

(n) Development and simultaneous implementation of environmental
quality criteria.

17.7. Coastal States, with the support of international organizations,
upon request, should undertake measures to maintain biological diversity and
productivity of marine species and habitats under national jurisdiction. *Inter*

alia, these measures might include: surveys of marine biodiversity, inventories of endangered species and critical coastal and marine habitats; establishment and management of protected areas; and support of scientific research and dissemination of its results.

(b) *Data and information*

17.8.　Coastal States, where necessary, should improve their capacity to collect, analyse, assess and use information for sustainable use of resources, including environmental impacts of activities affecting the coastal and marine areas.　Information for management purposes should receive priority support in view of the intensity and magnitude of the changes occurring in the coastal and marine areas.　To this end, it is necessary to, *inter alia:*

(a) Develop and maintain databases for assessment and management of coastal areas and all seas and their resources;

(b) Develop socio-economic and environmental indicators;

(c) Conduct regular environmental assessment of the state of the environment of coastal and marine areas;

(d) Prepare and maintain profiles of coastal area resources, activities, uses, habitats and protected areas based on the criteria of sustainable development;

(e) Exchange information and data.

17.9.　Cooperation with developing countries, and, where applicable, subregional and regional mechanisms, should be strengthened to improve their capacities to achieve the above.

(c) *International and regional cooperation and coordination*

17.10.　The role of international cooperation and coordination on a bilateral basis and, where applicable, within a subregional, interregional, regional or global framework, is to support and supplement national efforts of coastal States to promote integrated management and sustainable development of coastal and marine areas.

17.11.　States should cooperate, as appropriate, in the preparation of national guidelines for integrated coastal zone management and development, drawing on existing experience.　A global conference to exchange experience in the field could be held before 1994.

Means of implementation

(a) *Financing and cost evaluation*

17.12.　The Conference secretariat has estimated the average total annual cost (1993–2000) of implementing the activities of this programme to be about $6 billion, including about $50 million from the international community on grant or concessional terms.　These are indicative and order-of-magnitude estimates only and have not been reviewed by Governments. Actual costs and financial terms, including any that are non-concessional, will depend upon, *inter alia,* the specific strategies and programmes Governments decide upon for implementation.

(b) *Scientific and technological means*

17.13. States should cooperate in the development of necessary coastal systematic observation, research and information management systems. They should provide access to and transfer environmentally safe technologies and methodologies for sustainable development of coastal and marine areas to developing countries. They should also develop technologies and endogenous scientific and technological capacities.

17.14. International organizations, whether subregional, regional or global, as appropriate, should support coastal States, upon request, in these efforts, as indicated above, devoting special attention to developing countries.

(c) *Human resource development*

17.15. Coastal States should promote and facilitate the organization of education and training in integrated coastal and marine management and sustainable development for scientists, technologists, managers (including community-based managers) and users, leaders, indigenous peoples, fisher-folk, women and youth, among others. Management and development, as well as environmental protection concerns and local planning issues, should be incorporated in educational curricula and public awareness campaigns, with due regard to traditional ecological knowledge and socio-cultural values.

17.16. International organizations, whether subregional, regional or global, as appropriate, should support coastal States, upon request, in the areas indicated above, devoting special attention to developing countries.

(d) *Capacity-building*

17.17. Full cooperation should be extended, upon request, to coastal States in their capacity-building efforts and, where appropriate, capacity-building should be included in bilateral and multilateral development cooperation. Coastal States may consider, *inter alia:*

(a) Ensuring capacity-building at the local level;

(b) Consulting on coastal and marine issues with local administrations, the business community, the academic sector, resource user groups and the general public;

(c) Coordinating sectoral programmes while building capacity;

(d) Identifying existing and potential capabilities, facilities and needs for human resource development and scientific and technological infrastructure;

(e) Developing scientific and technological means and research;

(f) Promoting and facilitating human resource development and education;

(g) Supporting "centres of excellence" in integrated coastal and marine resource management;

(h) Supporting pilot demonstration programmes and projects in integrated coastal and marine management.

B. *Marine environmental protection*

Basis for action

17.18.　Degradation of the marine environment can result from a wide range of sources.　Land-based sources contribute 70 per cent of marine pollution, while maritime transport and dumping-at-sea activities contribute 10 per cent each.　The contaminants that pose the greatest threat to the marine environment are, in variable order of importance and depending on differing national or regional situations, sewage, nutrients, synthetic organic compounds, sediments, litter and plastics, metals, radionucleides, oil/hydrocarbons and polycyclic aromatic hydrocarbons (PAHs).　Many of the polluting substances originating from land-based sources are of particular concern to the marine environment since they exhibit at the same time toxicity, persistence and bioaccumulation in the food chain.　There is currently no global scheme to address marine pollution from land-based sources.

17.19.　Degradation of the marine environment can also result from a wide range of activities on land.　Human settlements, land use, construction of coastal infrastructure, agriculture, forestry, urban development, tourism and industry can affect the marine environment.　Coastal erosion and siltation are of particular concern.

17.20.　Marine pollution is also caused by shipping and sea-based activities.　Approximately 600,000 tons of oil enter the oceans each year as a result of normal shipping operations, accidents and illegal discharges.　With respect to offshore oil and gas activities, currently machinery space discharges are regulated internationally and six regional conventions to control platform discharges have been under consideration.　The nature and extent of environmental impacts from offshore oil exploration and production activities generally account for a very small proportion of marine pollution.

17.21.　A precautionary and anticipatory rather than a reactive approach is necessary to prevent the degradation of the marine environment.　This requires, *inter alia,* the adoption of precautionary measures, environmental impact assessments, clean production techniques, recycling, waste audits and minimization, construction and/or improvement of sewage treatment facilities, quality management criteria for the proper handling of hazardous substances, and a comprehensive approach to damaging impacts from air, land and water.　Any management framework must include the improvement of coastal human settlements and the integrated management and development of coastal areas.

Objectives

17.22. States, in accordance with the provisions of the United Nations Convention on the Law of the Sea on protection and preservation of the marine environment, commit themselves, in accordance with their policies, priorities and resources, to prevent, reduce and control degradation of the marine environment so as to maintain and improve its life-support and productive capacities. To this end, it is necessary to:

(a) Apply preventive, precautionary and anticipatory approaches so as to avoid degradation of the marine environment, as well as to reduce the risk of long-term or irreversible adverse effects upon it;

(b) Ensure prior assessment of activities that may have significant adverse impacts upon the marine environment;

(c) Integrate protection of the marine environment into relevant general environmental, social and economic development policies;

(d) Develop economic incentives, where appropriate, to apply clean technologies and other means consistent with the internalization of environmental costs, such as the polluter pays principle, so as to avoid degradation of the marine environment;

(e) Improve the living standards of coastal populations, particularly in developing countries, so as to contribute to reducing the degradation of the coastal and marine environment.

17.23. States agree that provision of additional financial resources, through appropriate international mechanisms, as well as access to cleaner technologies and relevant research, would be necessary to support action by developing countries to implement this commitment.

Activities

(a) *Management-related activities*

Prevention, reduction and control of degradation of the marine environment from land-based activities

17.24. In carrying out their commitment to deal with degradation of the marine environment from land-based activities, States should take action at the national level and, where appropriate, at the regional and subregional levels, in concert with action to implement programme area A, and should take account of the Montreal Guidelines for the Protection of the Marine Environment from Land–Based Sources.

17.25. To this end, States, with the support of the relevant international environmental, scientific, technical and financial organizations, should cooperate, *inter alia*, to:

(a) Consider updating, strengthening and extending the Montreal Guidelines, as appropriate;

(b) Assess the effectiveness of existing regional agreements and action plans, where appropriate, with a view to identifying means of strengthening action, where necessary, to prevent, reduce and control marine degradation caused by land-based activities;

(c) Initiate and promote the development of new regional agreements, where appropriate;

(d) Develop means of providing guidance on technologies to deal with the major types of pollution of the marine environment from land-based sources, according to the best scientific evidence;

(e) Develop policy guidance for relevant global funding mechanisms;

(f) Identify additional steps requiring international cooperation.

17.26. The UNEP Governing Council is invited to convene, as soon as practicable, an intergovernmental meeting on protection of the marine environment from land-based activities.

17.27. As concerns sewage, priority actions to be considered by States may include:

(a) Incorporating sewage concerns when formulating or reviewing coastal development plans, including human settlement plans;

(b) Building and maintaining sewage treatment facilities in accordance with national policies and capacities and international cooperation available;

(c) Locating coastal outfalls so as to maintain an acceptable level of environmental quality and to avoid exposing shell fisheries, water intakes and bathing areas to pathogens;

(d) Promoting environmentally sound co-treatments of domestic and compatible industrial effluents, with the introduction, where practicable, of controls on the entry of effluents that are not compatible with the system;

(e) Promoting primary treatment of municipal sewage discharged to rivers, estuaries and the sea, or other solutions appropriate to specific sites;

(f) Establishing and improving local, national, subregional and regional, as necessary, regulatory and monitoring programmes to control effluent discharge, using minimum sewage effluent guidelines and water quality criteria and giving due consideration to the characteristics of receiving bodies and the volume and type of pollutants.

17.28. As concerns other sources of pollution, priority actions to be considered by States may include:

(a) Establishing or improving, as necessary, regulatory and monitoring programmes to control effluent discharges and emissions, including the development and application of control and recycling technologies;

(b) Promoting risk and environmental impact assessments to help ensure an acceptable level of environmental quality;

(c) Promoting assessment and cooperation at the regional level, where appropriate, with respect to the input of point source pollutants from new installations;

(d) Eliminating the emission or discharge of organohalogen compounds that threaten to accumulate to dangerous levels in the marine environment;

(e) Reducing the emission or discharge of other synthetic organic compounds that threaten to accumulate to dangerous levels in the marine environment;

(f) Promoting controls over anthropogenic inputs of nitrogen and phosphorus that enter coastal waters where such problems as eutrophication threaten the marine environment or its resources;

(g) Cooperating with developing countries, through financial and technological support, to maximize the best practicable control and reduction of substances and wastes that are toxic, persistent or liable to bioaccumulate and to establish environmentally sound land-based waste disposal alternatives to sea dumping;

(h) Cooperating in the development and implementation of environmentally sound land-use techniques and practices to reduce run-off to water-courses and estuaries which would cause pollution or degradation of the marine environment;

(i) Promoting the use of environmentally less harmful pesticides and fertilizers and alternative methods for pest control, and considering the prohibition of those found to be environmentally unsound;

(j) Adopting new initiatives at national, subregional and regional levels for controlling the input of non-point source pollutants, which require broad changes in sewage and waste management, agricultural practices, mining, construction and transportation.

17.29.　As concerns physical destruction of coastal and marine areas causing degradation of the marine environment, priority actions should include control and prevention of coastal erosion and siltation due to anthropogenic factors related to, *inter alia,* land-use and construction techniques and practices. Watershed management practices should be promoted so as to prevent, control and reduce degradation of the marine environment.

Prevention, reduction and control of degradation of the marine environment from sea-based activities

17.30.　States, acting individually, bilaterally, regionally or multilaterally and within the framework of IMO and other relevant international organizations, whether subregional, regional or global, as appropriate, should assess the need for additional measures to address degradation of the marine environment:

(a) From shipping, by:

(i) Supporting wider ratification and implementation of relevant shipping conventions and protocols;

(ii) Facilitating the processes in (i), providing support to individual States upon request to help them overcome the obstacles identified by them;

(iii) Cooperating in monitoring marine pollution from ships, especially from illegal discharges (e.g., aerial surveillance), and enforcing MARPOL discharge, provisions more rigorously;

(iv) Assessing the state of pollution caused by ships in particularly sensitive areas identified by IMO and taking action to implement applicable measures, where necessary, within such areas to ensure compliance with generally accepted international regulations;

(v) Taking action to ensure respect of areas designated by coastal States, within their exclusive economic zones, consistent with international law, in order to protect and preserve rare or fragile ecosystems, such as coral reefs and mangroves;

(vi) Considering the adoption of appropriate rules on ballast water discharge to prevent the spread of non-indigenous organisms;

(vii) Promoting navigational safety by adequate charting of coasts and ship-routing, as appropriate;

(viii) Assessing the need for stricter international regulations to further reduce the risk of accidents and pollution from cargo ships (including bulk carriers);

(ix) Encouraging IMO and IAEA to work together to complete consideration of a code on the carriage of irradiated nuclear fuel in flasks on board ships;

(x) Revising and updating the IMO Code of Safety for Nuclear Merchant Ships and considering how best to implement a revised code;

(xi) Supporting the ongoing activity within IMO regarding development of appropriate measures for reducing air pollution from ships;

(xii) Supporting the ongoing activity within IMO regarding the development of an international regime governing the transportation of hazardous and noxious substances carried by ships and further considering whether the compensation funds similar to the ones established under the Fund Convention would be appropriate in respect of pollution damage caused by substances other than oil;

(b) From dumping, by:

(i) Supporting wider ratification, implementation and participation in relevant Conventions on dumping at sea, including early conclusion of a future strategy for the London Dumping Convention;

(ii) Encouraging the London Dumping Convention parties to take appropriate steps to stop ocean dumping and incineration of hazardous substances;

(c) From offshore oil and gas platforms, by assessing existing regulatory measures to address discharges, emissions and safety and assessing the need for additional measures;

(d) From ports, by facilitating establishment of port reception facilities for the collection of oily and chemical residues and garbage from ships, especially in MARPOL special areas, and promoting the establishment of smaller scale facilities in marinas and fishing harbours.

17.31.　IMO and as appropriate, other competent United Nations organizations, when requested by the States concerned, should assess, where appropriate, the state of marine pollution in areas of congested shipping, such as heavily used international straits, with a view to ensuring compliance with generally accepted international regulations, particularly those related to illegal discharges from ships, in accordance with the provisions of Part III of the United Nations Convention on the Law of the Sea.

17.32.　States should take measures to reduce water pollution caused by organotin compounds used in anti-fouling paints.

17.33.　States should consider ratifying the Convention on Oil Pollution Preparedness, Response and Cooperation, which addresses, *inter alia,* the development of contingency plans on the national and international level, as appropriate, including provision of oil-spill response material and training of personnel, including its possible extension to chemical spill response.

17.34.　States should intensify international cooperation to strengthen or establish, where necessary, regional oil/chemical-spill response centres and/or, as appropriate, mechanisms in cooperation with relevant subregional, regional or global intergovernmental organizations and, where appropriate, industry-based organizations.

(b) *Data and information*

17.35.　States should, as appropriate, and in accordance with the means at their disposal and with due regard for their technical and scientific capacity and resources, make systematic observations on the state of the marine environment. To this end, States should, as appropriate, consider:

(a) Establishing systematic observation systems to measure marine environmental quality, including causes and effects of marine degradation, as a basis for management;

(b) Regularly exchanging information on marine degradation caused by land-based and sea-based activities and on actions to prevent, control and reduce such degradation;

(c) Supporting and expanding international programmes for systematic observations such as the mussel watch programme, building on existing facilities with special attention to developing countries;

(d) Establishing a clearing-house on marine pollution control information, including processes and technologies to address marine pollution control and to support their transfer to developing countries and other countries with demonstrated needs;

(e) Establishing a global profile and database providing information on the sources, types, amounts and effects of pollutants reaching the marine environment from land-based activities in coastal areas and sea-based sources;

(f) Allocating adequate funding for capacity-building and training programmes to ensure the full participation of developing countries, in particular, in any international scheme under the organs and organizations of the United Nations system for the collection, analysis and use of data and information.

Means of implementation

(a) *Financing and cost evaluation*

17.36.　The Conference secretariat has estimated the average total annual cost (1993–2000) of implementing the activities of this programme to be about $200 million from the international community on grant or concessional terms.　These are indicative and order-of-magnitude estimates only and have not been reviewed by Governments.　Actual costs and financial terms, including any that are non-concessional, will depend upon, *inter alia,* the specific strategies and programmes Governments decide upon for implementation.

(b) *Scientific and technological means*

17.37.　National, subregional and regional action programmes will, where appropriate, require technology transfer, in conformity with Chapter 34, and financial resources, particularly where developing countries are concerned, including:

(a) Assistance to industries in identifying and adopting clean production or cost-effective pollution control technologies;

(b) Planning development and application of low-cost and low-maintenance sewage installation and treatment technologies for developing countries;

(c) Equipment of laboratories to observe systematically human and other impacts on the marine environment;

(d) Identification of appropriate oil- and chemical-spill control materials, including low-cost locally available materials and techniques, suitable for pollution emergencies in developing countries;

(e) Study of the use of persistent organohalogens that are liable to accumulate in the marine environment to identify those that cannot be adequately controlled and to provide a basis for a decision on a time schedule for phasing them out as soon as practicable;

(f) Establishment of a clearing-house for information on marine pollution control, including processes and technologies to address marine pollution control, and support for their transfer to developing and other countries with demonstrated needs.

(c) *Human resource development*

17.38.　States individually or in cooperation with each other and with the support of international organizations, whether subregional, regional or global, as appropriate, should:

(a) Provide training for critical personnel required for the adequate protection of the marine environment as identified by training needs' surveys at the national, regional or subregional levels;

(b) Promote the introduction of marine environmental protection topics into the curriculum of marine studies programmes;

(c) Establish training courses for oil- and chemical-spill response personnel, in cooperation, where appropriate, with the oil and chemical industries;

(d) Conduct workshops on environmental aspects of port operations and development;

(e) Strengthen and provide secure financing for new and existing specialized international centres of professional maritime education;

(f) States should, through bilateral and multilateral cooperation, support and supplement the national efforts of developing countries as regards human resource development in relation to prevention and reduction of degradation of the marine environment.

(d) *Capacity-building*

17.39.　National planning and coordinating bodies should be given the capacity and authority to review all land-based activities and sources of pollution for their impacts on the marine environment and to propose appropriate control measures.

17.40.　Research facilities should be strengthened or, where appropriate, developed in developing countries for systematic observation of marine pollution, environmental impact assessment and development of control recommendations and should be managed and staffed by local experts.

17.41.　Special arrangements will be needed to provide adequate financial and technical resources to assist developing countries in preventing and solving problems associated with activities that threaten the marine environment.

17.42.　An international funding mechanism should be created for the application of appropriate sewage treatment technologies and building sewage treatment facilities, including grants or concessional loans from international agencies and appropriate regional funds, replenished at least in part on a revolving basis by user fees.

17.43.　In carrying out these programme activities, particular attention needs to be given to the problems of developing countries that would bear an unequal burden because of their lack of facilities, expertise or technical capacities.

C.　*Sustainable use and conservation of marine living resources of the high seas*

Basis for action

17.44.　Over the last decade, fisheries on the high seas have considerably expanded and currently represent approximately 5 per cent of total world landings.　The provisions of the United Nations Convention on the Law of the Sea on the marine living resources of the high seas sets forth rights and obligations of States with respect to conservation and utilization of those resources.

17.45.　However, management of high seas fisheries, including the adoption, monitoring and enforcement of effective conservation measures, is inadequate in many areas and some resources are overutilized.　There are problems of unregulated fishing, overcapitalization, excessive fleet size, vessel reflagging to escape controls, insufficiently selective gear, unreliable databases and lack of sufficient cooperation between States.　Action by States whose nationals and vessels fish on the high seas, as well as cooperation at the bilateral, subregional, regional and global levels, is essential particularly for highly migratory species and straddling stocks.　Such action and cooperation should address inadequacies in fishing practices, as well as in biological knowledge, fisheries statistics and improvement of systems for handling data. Emphasis should also be on multi-species management and other approaches that take into account the relationships among species, especially in addressing depleted species, but also in identifying the potential of underutilized or unutilized populations.

Objectives

17.46.　States commit themselves to the conservation and sustainable use of marine living resources on the high seas.　To this end, it is necessary to:

　　(a) Develop and increase the potential of marine living resources to meet human nutritional needs, as well as social, economic and development goals;

(b) Maintain or restore populations of marine species at levels that can produce the maximum sustainable yield as qualified by relevant environmental and economic factors, taking into consideration relationships among species;

(c) Promote the development and use of selective fishing gear and practices that minimize waste in the catch of target species and minimize by-catch of non-target species;

* * *

Chapter 20
ENVIRONMENTALLY SOUND MANAGEMENT OF HAZARDOUS WASTES, INCLUDING PREVENTION OF ILLEGAL INTERNATIONAL TRAFFIC IN HAZARDOUS WASTES
INTRODUCTION

20.1. Effective control of the generation, storage, treatment, recycling and reuse, transport, recovery and disposal of hazardous wastes is of paramount importance for proper health, environmental protection and natural resource management, and sustainable development. This will require the active cooperation and participation of the international community, Governments and industry. Industry, as referred to in this paper, shall include large industrial enterprises, including transnational corporations and domestic industry.

20.2. Prevention of the generation of hazardous wastes and the rehabilitation of contaminated sites are the key elements, and both require knowledge, experienced people, facilities, financial resources and technical and scientific capacities.

20.3. The activities outlined in the present chapter are very closely related to, and have implications for, many of the programme areas described in other chapters, so that an overall integrated approach to hazardous waste management is necessary.

20.4. There is international concern that part of the international movement of hazardous wastes is being carried out in contravention of existing national legislation and international instruments to the detriment of the environment and public health of all countries, particularly developing countries.

20.5. In section I of resolution 44/226 of 22 December 1989, the General Assembly requested each regional commission, within existing resources, to contribute to the prevention of the illegal traffic in toxic and dangerous products and wastes by monitoring and making regional assessments of that illegal traffic and its environmental and health implications. The Assembly also requested the regional commissions to interact among themselves and cooperate with the United Nations Environment Programme (UNEP), with a view to maintaining efficient and coordinated monitoring and assessment of the illegal traffic in toxic and dangerous products and wastes.

Overall objective

20.6.　Within the framework of integrated life-cycle management, the overall objective is to prevent to the extent possible, and minimize, the generation of hazardous wastes, as well as to manage those wastes in such a way that they do not cause harm to health and the environment.

Overall targets

20.7.　The overall targets are:

(a) Preventing or minimizing the generation of hazardous wastes as part of an overall integrated cleaner production approach; eliminating or reducing to a minimum transboundary movements of hazardous wastes, consistent with the environmentally sound and efficient management of those wastes; and ensuring that environmentally sound hazardous waste management options are pursued to the maximum extent possible within the country of origin (the self-sufficiency principle).　The transboundary movements that take place should be on environmental and economic grounds and based upon agreements between the States concerned;

(b) Ratification of the Basel Convention on the Control of Transboundary Movements of Hazardous Wastes and their Disposal and the expeditious elaboration of related protocols, such as the protocol on liability and compensation, mechanisms and guidelines to facilitate the implementation of the Basel Convention;

(c) Ratification and full implementation by the countries concerned of the Bamako Convention on the Ban on the Import into Africa and the Control of Transboundary Movement of Hazardous Wastes within Africa and the expeditious elaboration of a protocol on liability and compensation;

(d) Elimination of the export of hazardous wastes to countries that, individually or through international agreements, prohibits the import of such wastes, such as, the contracting parties to the Bamako Convention, the fourth Lomé Convention or other relevant conventions, where such prohibition is provided for.

20.8.　The following programme areas are included in this chapter:

(a) Promoting the prevention and minimization of hazardous waste;

(b) Promoting and strengthening institutional capacities in hazardous waste management;

(c) Promoting and strengthening international cooperation in the management of transboundary movements of hazardous wastes;

(d) Preventing illegal international traffic in hazardous wastes.

PROGRAMME AREAS

A. *Promoting the prevention and minimization of hazardous waste*

Basis for action

20.9.　Human health and environmental quality are undergoing continuous degradation by the increasing amount of hazardous wastes being produced.　There are increasing direct and indirect costs to society and to individual citizens in connection with the generation, handling and disposal of such wastes.　It is therefore crucial to enhance knowledge and information on the economics of prevention and management of hazardous wastes, including the impact in relation to the employment and environmental benefits, in order to ensure that the necessary capital investment is made available in development programmes through economic incentives.　One of the first priorities in hazardous waste management is minimization, as part of a broader approach to changing industrial processes and consumer patterns through pollution prevention and cleaner production strategies.

20.10.　Among the most important factors in these strategies is the recovery of hazardous wastes and their transformation into useful material. Technology application, modification and development of new low-waste technologies are therefore currently a central focus of hazardous waste minimization.

Objectives

20.11.　The objectives of this programme area are:

(a) To reduce the generation of hazardous wastes, to the extent feasible, as part of an integrated cleaner production approach;

(b) To optimize the use of materials by utilizing, where practicable and environmentally sound, the residues from production processes;

(c) To enhance knowledge and information on the economics of prevention and management of hazardous wastes.

20.12.　To achieve those objectives, and thereby reduce the impact and cost of industrial development, countries that can afford to adopt the requisite technologies without detriment to their development should establish policies that include:

(a) Integration of cleaner production approaches and hazardous waste minimization in all planning, and the adoption of specific goals;

(b) Promotion of the use of regulatory and market mechanisms;

(c) Establishment of an intermediate goal for the stabilization of the quantity of hazardous waste generated;

(d) Establishment of long-term programmes and policies including targets where appropriate for reducing the amount of hazardous waste produced per unit of manufacture;

(e) Achievement of a qualitative improvement of waste streams, mainly through activities aimed at reducing their hazardous characteristics;

(f) Facilitation of the establishment of cost-effective policies and approaches to hazardous waste prevention and management, taking into consideration the state of development of each country.

Activities

(a) *Management-related activities*

20.13.　The following activities should be undertaken:

(a) Governments should establish or modify standards or purchasing specifications to avoid discrimination against recycled materials, provided that those materials are environmentally sound;

(b) Governments, according to their possibilities and with the help of multilateral cooperation, should provide economic or regulatory incentives, where appropriate, to stimulate industrial innovation towards cleaner production methods, to encourage industry to invest in preventive and/or recycling technologies so as to ensure environmentally sound management of all hazardous wastes, including recyclable wastes, and to encourage waste minimization investments;

(c) Governments should intensify research and development activities on cost-effective alternatives for processes and substances that currently result in the generation of hazardous wastes that pose particular problems for environmentally sound disposal or treatment, the possibility of ultimate phase-out of those substances that present an unreasonable or otherwise unmanageable risk and are toxic, persistent and bio-accumulative to be considered as soon as practicable.　Emphasis should be given to alternatives that could be economically accessible to developing countries;

(d) Governments, according to their capacities and available resources and with the cooperation of the United Nations and other relevant organizations and industries, as appropriate, should support the establishment of domestic facilities to handle hazardous wastes of domestic origin;

(e) Governments of developed countries should promote the transfer of environmentally sound technologies and know-how on clean technologies and low-waste production to developing countries in conformity with chapter 34, which will bring about changes to sustain innovation.　Governments should cooperate with industry to develop guidelines and codes of conduct, where appropriate, leading to cleaner production through sectoral trade industry associations;

(f) Governments should encourage industry to treat, recycle, reuse and dispose of wastes at the source of generation, or as close as possible thereto, whenever hazardous waste generation is unavoidable and when it is both economically and environmentally efficient for industry to do so;

(g) Governments should encourage technology assessments, for example through the use of technology assessment centres;

(h) Governments should promote cleaner production through the establishment of centres providing training and information on environmentally sound technologies;

(i) Industry should establish environmental management systems, including environmental auditing of its production or distribution sites, in order to identify where the installation of cleaner production methods is needed;

(j) A relevant and competent United Nations organization should take the lead, in cooperation with other organizations, to develop guidelines for estimating the costs and benefits of various approaches to the adoption of cleaner production and waste minimization and environmentally sound management of hazardous wastes, including rehabilitation of contaminated sites, taking into account, where appropriate, the report of the 1991 Nairobi meeting of government-designated experts on an international strategy and an action programme, including technical guidelines for the environmentally sound management of hazardous wastes, in particular in the context of the work of the Basel Convention, being developed under the UNEP secretariat;

(k) Governments should establish regulations that lay down the ultimate responsibility of industries for environmentally sound disposal of the hazardous wastes their activities generate.

(b) *Data and information*

20.14.　The following activities should be undertaken:

(a) Governments, assisted by international organizations, should establish mechanisms for assessing the value of existing information systems;

(b) Governments should establish nationwide and regional information collection and dissemination clearing-houses and networks that are easy for Government institutions and industry and other non-governmental organizations to access and use;

(c) International organizations, through the UNEP Cleaner Production programme and ICPIC, should extend and strengthen existing systems for collection of cleaner production information;

(d) All United Nations organs and organizations should promote the use and dissemination of information collected through the Cleaner Production network;

(e) OECD should, in cooperation with other organizations, undertake a comprehensive survey of, and disseminate information on, experiences of member countries in adopting economic regulatory schemes and incentive mechanisms for hazardous waste management and for the use of clean technologies that prevent such waste from being generated;

(f) Governments should encourage industries to be transparent in their operations and provide relevant information to the communities that might be affected by the generation, management and disposal of hazardous wastes.

(c) *International and regional cooperation and coordination*

20.15.　International/regional cooperation should encourage the ratification by States of the Basel and Bamako Conventions and promote the implementation of those Conventions. Regional cooperation will be necessary for the development of similar conventions in regions other than Africa, if so required. In addition there is a need for effective coordination of international regional and national policies and instruments. Another activity proposed is cooperating in monitoring the effects of the management of hazardous wastes.

Means of implementation

(a) *Financing and cost evaluation*

20.16.　The Conference secretariat has estimated the average total annual cost (1993–2000) of implementing the activities of this programme to be about $750 million from the international community on grant or concessional terms. These are indicative and order-of-magnitude estimates only and have not been reviewed by Governments. Actual costs and financial terms, including any that are non-concessional, will depend upon, *inter alia,* the specific strategies and programmes Governments decide upon for implementation.

(b) *Scientific and technological means*

20.17.　The following activities related to technology development and research should be undertaken:

(a) Governments, according to their capacities and available resources and with the cooperation of the United Nations and other relevant organizations, and industries, as appropriate, should significantly increase financial support for cleaner technology research and development programmes, including the use of biotechnologies;

(b) States, with the cooperation of international organizations where appropriate, should encourage industry to promote and undertake research into the phase-out of the processes that pose the greatest environmental risk based on hazardous wastes generated;

(c) States should encourage industry to develop schemes to integrate the cleaner production approach into design of products and management practices;

(d) States should encourage industry to exercise environmentally responsible care through hazardous waste reduction and by ensuring the environmentally sound reuse, recycling and recovery of hazardous wastes, as well as their final disposal.

(c) *Human resource development*

20.18.　The following activities should be undertaken:

(a) Governments, international organizations and industry should encourage industrial training programmes, incorporating hazardous waste prevention and minimization techniques and launching demonstration projects at the local level to develop "success stories" in cleaner production;

(b) Industry should integrate cleaner production principles and case examples into training programmes and establish demonstration projects/networks by sector/country;

(c) All sectors of society should develop cleaner production awareness campaigns and promote dialogue and partnership with industry and other actors.

(d) *Capacity-building*

20.19.   The following activities should be undertaken:

(a) Governments of developing countries, in cooperation with industry and with the cooperation of appropriate international organizations, should develop inventories of hazardous waste production, in order to identify their needs with respect to technology transfer and implementation of measures for the sound management of hazardous wastes and their disposal;

(b) Governments should include in national planning and legislation an integrated approach to environmental protection, driven by prevention and source reduction criteria, taking into account the "polluter pays" principle, and adopt programmes for hazardous waste reduction, including targets and adequate environmental control;

(c) Governments should work with industry on sector-by-sector cleaner production and hazardous waste minimization campaigns, as well as on the reduction of such wastes and other emissions;

(d) Governments should take the lead in establishing and strengthening, as appropriate, national procedures for environmental impact assessment, taking into account the cradle-to-grave approach to the management of hazardous wastes, in order to identify options for minimizing the generation of hazardous wastes, through safer handling, storage, disposal and destruction;

(e) Governments, in collaboration with industry and appropriate international organizations, should develop procedures for monitoring the application of the cradle to grave approach, including environmental audits;

(f) Bilateral and multilateral development assistance agencies should substantially increase funding for cleaner technology transfer to developing countries, including small- and medium-sized enterprises.

B.   *Promoting and strengthening institutional capacities in hazardous waste management*

Basis for action

20.20.   Many countries lack the national capacity to handle and manage hazardous wastes.   This is primarily due to inadequate infrastructure, deficiencies in regulatory frameworks, insufficient education and training programmes and lack of coordination between the different ministries and institutions involved in various aspects of waste management. In addition, there is a lack of knowledge about environmental contamination and pollution and the associated health risk from the exposure of populations, especially women and children, and ecosystems to hazardous wastes; assessment of risks; and the characteristics of wastes. Steps need to be taken immediately to identify populations at high risk and to take remedial measures, where necessary. One of the main priorities in ensuring environmentally sound management of hazardous wastes is to provide awareness, education and training programmes covering all levels of society. There is also a need to undertake research programmes to understand the nature of hazardous wastes, to identify their potential environmental effects and to develop technologies to safely handle those wastes. Finally, there is a need to strengthen the capacities of institutions that are responsible for the management of hazardous wastes.

Objectives

20.21.　The objectives in this programme area are:

(a) To adopt appropriate coordinating, legislative and regulatory measures at the national level for the environmentally sound management of hazardous wastes, including the implementation of international and regional conventions;

(b) To establish public awareness and information programmes on hazardous waste issues and to ensure that basic education and training programmes are provided for industry and government workers in all countries;

(c) To establish comprehensive research programmes on hazardous wastes in countries;

(d) To strengthen service industries to enable them to handle hazardous wastes, and to build up international networking;

(e) To develop endogenous capacities in all developing countries to educate and train staff at all levels in environmentally sound hazardous waste handling and monitoring and in environmentally sound management;

(f) To promote human exposure assessment with respect to hazardous waste sites and identify the remedial measures required;

(g) To facilitate the assessment of impacts and risks of hazardous wastes on human health and the environment by establishing appropriate procedures, methodologies, criteria and/or effluent-related guidelines and standards;

(h) To improve knowledge regarding the effects of hazardous wastes on human health and the environment;

(i) To make information available to Governments and to the general public on the effects of hazardous wastes, including infectious wastes, on human health and the environment.

Activities

(a) *Management-related activities*

20.22.　The following activities should be undertaken:

(a) Governments should establish and maintain inventories, including computerized inventories, of hazardous wastes and their treatment/disposal sites, as well as of contaminated sites that require rehabilitation, and assess exposure and risk to human health and the environment; they should also identify the measures required to clean up the disposal sites. Industry should make the necessary information available;

(b) Governments, industry and international organizations should collaborate in developing guidelines and easy-to-implement methods for the characterization and classification of hazardous wastes;

(c) Governments should carry out exposure and health assessments of populations residing near uncontrolled hazardous waste sites and initiate remedial measures;

(d) International organizations should develop improved health-based criteria, taking into account national decision-making processes, and assist in the preparation of practical technical guidelines for the prevention, minimization and safe handling and disposal of hazardous wastes;

(e) Governments of developing countries should encourage interdisciplinary and intersectoral groups, in cooperation with international organizations and agencies, to implement training and research activities related to evaluation, prevention and control of hazardous waste health risks. Such groups should serve as models to develop similar regional programmes;

(f) Governments, according to their capacities and available resources and with the cooperation of the United Nations and other relevant organizations as appropriate, should encourage as far as possible the establishment of combined treatment/disposal facilities for hazardous wastes in small- and medium-sized industries;

(g) Governments should promote identification and clean-up of sites of hazardous wastes in collaboration with industry and international organizations. Technologies, expertise and financing should be available for this purpose, as far as possible and when appropriate with the application of the "polluter pays" principle;

(h) Governments should ascertain that their military establishments conform to their nationally applicable environmental norms in the treatment and disposal of hazardous wastes.

(b) *Data and information*

20.23.　The following activities should be undertaken:

(a) Governments, international and regional organizations and industry should facilitate and expand the dissemination of technical and scientific information dealing with the various health aspects of hazardous wastes, and promote its application;

(b) Governments should establish notification systems and registries of exposed populations and of adverse health effects and databases on risk assessments of hazardous wastes;

(c) Governments should endeavour to collect information on those who generate or dispose/recycle hazardous wastes and provide such information to the individuals and institutions concerned.

(c) *International and regional cooperation and coordination*

20.24.　Governments, according to their capacities and available resources and with the cooperation of the United Nations and other relevant organizations, as appropriate, should:

(a) Promote and support the integration and operation, at the regional and local levels as appropriate, of institutional and interdisciplinary groups that collaborate, according to their capabilities, in activities oriented towards strengthening risk assessment, risk management and risk reduction with respect to hazardous wastes;

(b) Support capacity-building and technological development and research in developing countries in connection with human resource development, with particular support to be given to consolidating networks;

(c) Encourage self-sufficiency in hazardous waste disposal in the country of origin to the extent environmentally sound and feasible. The transboundary movements that take place should be on environmental and economic grounds and based upon agreements between all States concerned.

Means of implementation

(a) *Financing and cost evaluation*

20.25.　The Conference secretariat has estimated the average total annual cost (1993–2000) of implementing the activities of this programme to be about $18.5 billion on a global basis with about $3.5 billion related to developing countries, including about $500 million from the international community on grant or concessional terms. These are indicative and order-of-magnitude estimates only and have not been reviewed by Governments. Actual costs and financial terms, including any that are non-concessional, will depend upon, *inter alia,* the specific strategies and programmes Governments decide upon for implementation.

(b) *Scientific and technological means*

20.26. The following activities should be undertaken:

(a) Governments, according to their capacities and available resources and with the cooperation of the United Nations and other relevant organizations and industry as appropriate, should increase support for hazardous waste research management in developing countries;

(b) Governments, in collaboration with international organizations, should conduct research on the health effects of hazardous wastes in developing countries, including the long-term effects on children and women;

(c) Governments should conduct research aimed at the needs of small- and medium-sized industries;

(d) Governments and international organizations in cooperation with industry should expand technological research on environmentally sound hazardous waste handling, storage, transport, treatment and disposal and on hazardous waste assessment, management and remediation;

(e) International organizations should identify relevant and improved technologies for handling, storage, treatment and disposal of hazardous wastes.

(c) *Human resource development*

20.27. Governments, according to their capacities and available resources and with the cooperation of the United Nations and other relevant organizations and industry as appropriate, should:

(a) Increase public awareness and information on hazardous waste issues and promote the development and dissemination of hazardous wastes information that the general public can understand;

(b) Increase participation in hazardous waste management programmes by the general public, particularly women, including participation at grass-roots levels;

(c) Develop training and education programmes for men and women in industry and Government aimed at specific real-life problems, for example, planning and implementing hazardous waste minimization programmes, conducting hazardous materials audits and establishing appropriate regulatory programmes;

(d) Promote the training of labour, industrial management and government regulatory staff in developing countries on technologies to minimize and manage hazardous wastes in an environmentally sound manner.

20.28. The following activities should also be undertaken:

(a) Governments, according to their capacities and available resources and with the cooperation of the United Nations, other organizations and non-governmental organizations, should collaborate in developing and disseminating educational materials concerning hazardous wastes and their effects on environment and human health, for use in schools, by women's groups and by the general public;

(b) Governments, according to their capacities and available resources and with the cooperation of the United Nations and other organizations, should establish or strengthen programmes for the environmentally sound management of hazardous wastes in accordance with, as appropriate, health and environmental standards, and extend surveillance systems for the purpose of identifying adverse effects on populations and the environment of exposure to hazardous wastes;

(c) International organizations should provide assistance to member States in assessing the health and environmental risks resulting from exposure to hazardous wastes, and in identifying their priorities for controlling the various categories or classes of wastes;

(d) Governments, according to their capacities and available resources and with the cooperation of the United Nations and other relevant organizations, should promote centres of excellence for training in hazardous waste management, building on appropriate national institutions and encouraging international cooperation, *inter alia,* through institutional links between developed and developing countries.

(d) *Capacity-building*

20.29. Wherever they operate, transnational corporations and other large-scale enterprises should be encouraged to introduce policies and make commitments to adopt standards of operation with reference to hazardous waste generation and disposal that are equivalent to or no less stringent than standards in the country of origin, and Governments are invited to make efforts to establish regulations requiring environmentally sound management of hazardous wastes.

20.30. International organizations should provide assistance to member States in assessing the health and environmental risks resulting from exposure to hazardous wastes and in identifying their priorities for controlling the various categories or classes of wastes.

20.31. Governments, according to their capacities and available resources and with the cooperation of the United Nations and other relevant organizations and industries, should:

(a) Support national institutions in dealing with hazardous wastes from the regulatory monitoring and enforcement perspectives, with such support including enabling of those institutions to implement international conventions;

(b) Develop industry-based institutions for dealing with hazardous wastes and service industries for handling hazardous wastes;

(c) Adopt technical guidelines for the environmentally sound management of hazardous wastes and support the implementation of regional and international conventions;

(d) Develop and expand international networking among professionals working in the area of hazardous wastes and maintain an information flow among countries;

(e) Assess the feasibility of establishing and operating national, subregional and regional hazardous wastes treatment centres. Such centres could be used for education and training, as well as for facilitation and promotion of the transfer of technologies for the environmentally sound management of hazardous wastes;

(f) Identify and strengthen relevant academic/research institutions or centres for excellence to enable them to carry out education and training activities in the environmentally sound management of hazardous wastes;

(g) Develop a programme for the establishment of national capacities and capabilities to educate and train staff at various levels in hazardous wastes management;

(h) Conduct environmental audits of existing industries to improve in-plant regimes for the management of hazardous wastes.

C. *Promoting and strengthening international cooperation in the management of transboundary movements of hazardous wastes*

Basis for action

20.32. In order to promote and strengthen international cooperation in the management, including control and monitoring, of transboundary movements of hazardous wastes, a precautionary approach should be applied. There is a need to harmonize the procedures and criteria used in various international and legal instruments. There is also a need to develop or harmonize existing criteria for identifying wastes dangerous to the environment and to build monitoring capacities.

Objectives

20.33. The objectives of this programme area are:

(a) To facilitate and strengthen international cooperation in the environmentally sound management of hazardous wastes, including control and monitoring of transboundary movements of such wastes, including wastes for recovery, by using internationally adopted criteria to identify and classify hazardous wastes and to harmonize relevant international legal instruments;

(b) To adopt a ban on or prohibit, as appropriate, the export of hazardous wastes to countries that do not have the capacity to deal with those wastes in an environmentally sound way or that have banned the import of such wastes;

(c) To promote the development of control procedures for the trans-boundary movement of hazardous wastes destined for recovery operations under the Basel Convention that encourage environmentally and econom-ically sound recycling options.

Activities

(a) *Management-related activities*

Strengthening and harmonizing criteria and regulations

20.34. Governments, according to their capacities and available re-sources and with the cooperation of [the] United Nations and other relevant organizations, as appropriate, should:

(a) Incorporate the notification procedure called for in the Basel Convention and relevant regional conventions, as well as in their annex-es, into national legislation;

(b) Formulate, where appropriate, regional agreements such as the Bamako Convention regulating the transboundary movement of hazard-ous wastes;

(c) Help promote the compatibility and complementarity of such regional agreements with international conventions and protocols;

(d) Strengthen national and regional capacities and capabilities to monitor and control the transboundary movement of hazardous wastes;

(e) Promote the development of clear criteria and guidelines, within the framework of the Basel Convention and regional conventions, as appropriate, for environmentally and economically sound operation in resource recovery, recycling reclamation, direct use or alternative uses and for determination of acceptable recovery practices, including recovery levels where feasible and appropriate, with a view to preventing abuses and false presentation in the above operations;

(f) Consider setting up, at national and regional levels, as appropri-ate, systems for monitoring and surveillance of the transboundary move-ments of hazardous wastes;

(g) Develop guidelines for the assessment of environmentally sound treatment of hazardous wastes;

(h) Develop guidelines for the identification of hazardous wastes at the national level, taking into account existing internationally—and, where appropriate, regionally—agreed criteria and prepare a list of haz-ard profiles for the hazardous wastes listed in national legislation;

(i) Develop and use appropriate methods for testing, characterizing and classifying hazardous wastes and adopt or adapt safety standards and principles for managing hazardous wastes in an environmentally sound way.

Implementing existing agreements

20.35. Governments are urged to ratify the Basel Convention and the Bamako Convention, as applicable, and to pursue the expeditious elaboration of related protocols, such as protocols on liability and compensation, and of mechanisms and guidelines to facilitate the implementation of the Conventions.

Means of implementation

(a) *Financing and cost evaluation*

20.36. Because this programme area covers a relatively new field of operation and because of the lack so far of adequate studies on costing of activities under this programme, no cost estimate is available at present. However, the costs for some of the activities related to capacity-building that are presented under this programme could be considered to have been covered under the costing of programme area B above.

20.37. The interim secretariat for the Basel Convention should undertake studies in order to arrive at a reasonable cost estimate for activities to be undertaken initially until the year 2000.

(b) *Capacity-building*

20.38. Governments, according to their capacities and available resources and with the cooperation of [the] United Nations and other relevant organizations, as appropriate, should:

(a) Elaborate or adopt policies for the environmentally sound management of hazardous wastes, taking into account existing international instruments;

(b) Make recommendations to the appropriate forums or establish or adapt norms, including the equitable implementation of the polluter pays principle, and regulatory measures to comply with obligations and principles of the Basel Convention, the Bamako Convention and other relevant existing or future agreements, including protocols, as appropriate, for setting appropriate rules and procedures in the field of liability and compensation for damage resulting from the transboundary movement and disposal of hazardous wastes;

(c) Implement policies for the implementation of a ban or prohibition, as appropriate, of exports of hazardous wastes to countries that do not have the capacity to deal with those wastes in an environmentally sound way or that have banned the import of such wastes;

(d) Study, in the context of the Basel Convention and relevant regional conventions, the feasibility of providing temporary financial assistance in the case of an emergency situation, in order to minimize damage from accidents arising from transboundary movements of hazardous wastes or during the disposal of those wastes.

D. *Preventing illegal international traffic in hazardous wastes*

Basis for action

20.39.　The prevention of illegal traffic in hazardous wastes will benefit the environment and public health in all countries, particularly developing countries.　It will also help to make the Basel Convention and regional international instruments, such as the Bamako Convention and the fourth Lomé Convention, more effective by promoting compliance with the controls established in those agreements.　Article IX of the Basel Convention specifically addresses the issue of illegal shipments of hazardous wastes.　Illegal traffic of hazardous wastes may cause serious threats to human health and the environment and impose a special and abnormal burden on the countries that receive such shipments.

20.40.　Effective prevention requires action through effective monitoring and the enforcement and imposition of appropriate penalties.

Objectives

20.41.　The objectives of this programme area are:

(a) To reinforce national capacities to detect and halt any illegal attempt to introduce hazardous wastes into the territory of any State in contravention of national legislation and relevant international legal instruments;

(b) To assist all countries, particularly developing countries, in obtaining all appropriate information concerning illegal traffic in hazardous wastes;

(c) To cooperate, within the framework of the Basel Convention, in assisting countries that suffer the consequences of illegal traffic.

Activities

(a) *Management-related activities*

20.42.　Governments, according to their capacities and available resources and with the cooperation of the United Nations and other relevant organizations, as appropriate, should:

(a) Adopt, where necessary, and implement legislation to prevent the illegal import and export of hazardous wastes;

(b) Develop appropriate national enforcement programmes to monitor compliance with such legislation, detect and deter violations through appropriate penalties and give special attention to those who are known to have conducted illegal traffic in hazardous wastes and to hazardous wastes that are particularly susceptible to illegal traffic.

(b) *Data and information*

20.43.　Governments should develop as appropriate, an information network and alert system to assist in detecting illegal traffic in hazardous wastes. Local communities and others could be involved in the operation of such a network and system.

20.44.　Governments should cooperate in the exchange of information on illegal transboundary movements of hazardous wastes and should make such information available to appropriate United Nations bodies such as UNEP and the regional commissions.

(c) *International and regional cooperation*

20.45.　The regional commissions, in cooperation with and relying upon expert support and advice from UNEP and other relevant bodies of the United Nations system, taking full account of the Basel Convention, shall continue to monitor and assess the illegal traffic in hazardous wastes, including its environmental, economic and health implications, on a continuing basis, drawing upon the results and experience gained in the joint UNEP/ESCAP preliminary assessment of illegal traffic.

20.46.　Countries and international organizations, as appropriate, should cooperate to strengthen the institutional and regulatory capacities, in particular of developing countries, in order to prevent the illegal import and export of hazardous wastes.

* * *

SECTION IV.　MEANS OF IMPLEMENTATION
Chapter 33
FINANCIAL RESOURCES AND MECHANISMS
INTRODUCTION

33.1.　The General Assembly, in resolution 44/228 of 22 December 1989, *inter alia*, decided that the United Nations Conference on Environment and Development should:

Identify ways and means of providing new and additional financial resources, particularly to developing countries, for environmentally sound development programmes and projects in accordance with national development objectives, priorities and plans and to consider ways of effectively monitoring the provision of such new and additional financial resources, particularly to developing countries, so as to enable the international community to take further appropriate action on the basis of accurate and reliable data;

Identify ways and means of providing additional financial resources for measures directed towards solving major environmental problems of global concern and especially of supporting those countries, in particular developing countries, for which the implementation of such measures would entail a special or abnormal burden, owing, in particular, to their lack of financial resources, expertise or technical capacity;

Consider various funding mechanisms, including voluntary ones, and examine the possibility of a special international fund and other innovative approaches, with a view to ensuring, on a favourable basis, the most effective and expeditious transfer of environmentally sound technologies to developing countries;

Quantify the financial requirements for the successful implementation of Conference decisions and recommendations and identify possible sources, including innovative ones, of additional resources.

33.2. This chapter deals with the financing of the implementation of Agenda 21, which reflects a global consensus integrating environmental considerations into an accelerated development process. For each of the other chapters, the secretariat of the Conference has provided indicative estimates of the total costs of implementation for developing countries and the requirements for grant or other concessional financing needed from the international community. These reflect the need for a substantially increased effort, both by countries themselves and by the international community.

BASIS FOR ACTION

33.3. Economic growth, social development and poverty eradication are the first and overriding priorities in developing countries and are themselves essential to meeting national and global sustainability objectives. In the light of the global benefits to be realized by the implementation of Agenda 21 as a whole, the provision to developing countries of effective means, *inter alia,* financial resources and technology, without which it will be difficult for them to fully implement their commitments, will serve the common interests of developed and developing countries and of humankind in general, including future generations.

33.4. The cost of inaction could outweigh the financial costs of implementing Agenda 21. Inaction will narrow the choices of future generations.

33.5. For dealing with environmental issues, special efforts will be required. Global and local environmental issues are interrelated. The United Nations Framework Convention on Climate Change and the Convention on Biological Diversity address two of the most important global issues.

33.6. Economic conditions, both domestic and international, that encourage free trade and access to markets will help make economic growth and environmental protection mutually supportive for all countries, particularly for developing countries and countries undergoing the process of transition to a market economy (see chapter 2 for a fuller discussion of these issues).

33.7. International cooperation for sustainable development should also be strengthened in order to support and complement the efforts of developing countries, particularly the least developed countries.

33.8. All countries should assess how to translate Agenda 21 into national policies and programmes through a process that will integrate environment and development considerations. National and local priorities should be established by means that include public participation and community involvement, promoting equal opportunity for men and women.

33.9. For an evolving partnership among all countries of the world, including, in particular, between developed and developing countries, sustainable development strategies and enhanced and predictable levels of funding in support of longer term objectives are required. For that purpose, developing countries should articulate their own priority actions and needs for support and developed countries should commit themselves to addressing these priorities. In this respect, consultative groups and round tables and other nationally based mechanisms can play a facilitative role.

33.10. The implementation of the huge sustainable development programmes of Agenda 21 will require the provision to developing countries of substantial new and additional financial resources. Grant or concessional financing should be provided according to sound and equitable criteria and indicators. The progressive implementation of Agenda 21 should be matched by the provision of such necessary financial resources. The initial phase will be accelerated by substantial early commitments of concessional funding.

OBJECTIVES

33.11. The objectives are as follows:

(a) To establish measures concerning financial resources and mechanisms for the implementation of Agenda 21;

(b) To provide new and additional financial resources that are both adequate and predictable;

(c) To seek full use and continuing qualitative improvement of funding mechanisms to be utilized for the implementation of Agenda 21.

ACTIVITIES

33.12. Fundamentally, the activities of this chapter are related to the implementation of all the other chapters of Agenda 21.

MEANS OF IMPLEMENTATION

33.13. In general, the financing for the implementation of Agenda 21 will come from a country's own public and private sectors. For developing countries, particularly the least developed countries, ODA is a main source of external funding, and substantial new and additional funding for sustainable development and implementation of Agenda 21 will be required. Developed countries reaffirm their commitments to reach the accepted United Nations target of 0.7 per cent of GNP for ODA and, to the extent that they have not yet achieved that target, agree to augment their aid programmes in order to reach that target as soon as possible and to ensure prompt and effective implementation of Agenda 21. Some countries have agreed to reach the target by the year 2000. It was decided that the Commission on Sustainable Development would regularly review and monitor progress towards this target. This review process should systematically combine the monitoring of the implementation of Agenda 21 with a review of the financial resources available. Those countries that have already reached the target are to be commended and encouraged to continue to contribute to the common effort to make available the substantial additional resources that have to be mobilized. Other developed countries, in line with their support for reform efforts in developing countries, agree to make their best efforts to increase their level of ODA. In this context, the importance of equitable burden-sharing among developed countries is recognized. Other countries, including those undergoing the process of transition to a market economy, may voluntarily augment the contributions of the developed countries.

33.14. Funding for Agenda 21 and other outcomes of the Conference should be provided in a way that maximizes the availability of new and additional resources and uses all available funding sources and mechanisms. These include, among others:

(a) The multilateral development banks and funds:

(i) *The International Development Association (IDA).* Among the various issues and options that IDA deputies will examine in connection with the forthcoming tenth replenishment of IDA, the statement made by the President of the World Bank at the United Nations Conference on Environment and Development should be given special consideration in order to help the poorest countries meet their sustainable development objectives as contained in Agenda 21;

(ii) *Regional and subregional development banks.* The regional and subregional development banks and funds should play an increased and more effective role in providing resources on concessional or other favourable terms needed to implement Agenda 21;

(iii) *The Global Environment Facility,* managed jointly by the World Bank, UNDP and UNEP, whose additional grant and concessional funding is designed to achieve global environmental benefits, should cover the agreed incremental costs of relevant activities under Agenda 21, in particular for developing countries. Therefore, it should be restructured so as to, *inter alia:*

Encourage universal participation;

Have sufficient flexibility to expand its scope and coverage to relevant programme areas of Agenda 21, with global environmental benefits, as agreed;

Ensure a governance that is transparent and democratic in nature, including in terms of decision-making and operations, by guaranteeing a balanced and equitable representation of the interests of developing countries and giving due weight to the funding efforts of donor countries;

Ensure new and additional financial resources on grant and concessional terms, in particular to developing countries;

Ensure predictability in the flow of funds by contributions from developed countries, taking into account the importance of equitable burden-sharing;

Ensure access to and disbursement of the funds under mutually agreed criteria without introducing new forms of conditionality;

(b) *The relevant specialized agencies, other United Nations bodies and other international organizations,* which have designated roles to play in supporting national Governments in implementing Agenda 21;

(c) *Multilateral institutions for capacity-building and technical cooperation.* Necessary financial resources should be provided to UNDP to use its network of field offices and its broad mandate and experience in the field of technical cooperation for facilitating capacity-building at the country level, making full use of the expertise of the specialized agencies and other United Nations bodies within their respective areas of competence, in particular UNEP and including the multilateral and regional development banks;

(d) *Bilateral assistance programmes.* These programmes will need to be strengthened in order to promote sustainable development;

(e) *Debt relief.* It is important to achieve durable solutions to the debt problems of low- and middle-income developing countries in order to provide them with the needed means for sustainable development. Measures to address the continuing debt problems of low- and middle-income countries should be kept under review. All creditors in the Paris Club should promptly implement the agreement of December 1991 to provide debt relief for the poorest heavily indebted countries pursuing structural adjustment; debt relief measures should be kept under review so as to address the continuing difficulties of those countries;

(f) *Private funding.* Voluntary contributions through non-governmental channels, which have been running at about 10 per cent of ODA, might be increased.

33.15. *Investment.* Mobilization of higher levels of foreign direct investment and technology transfers should be encouraged through national policies that promote investment and through joint ventures and other modalities.

33.16. *Innovative financing.* New ways of generating new public and private financial resources should be explored, in particular:

(a) Various forms of debt relief, apart from official or Paris Club debt, including greater use of debt swaps;

(b) The use of economic and fiscal incentives and mechanisms;

(c) The feasibility of tradeable permits;

(d) New schemes for fund-raising and voluntary contributions through private channels, including non-governmental organizations;

(e) The reallocation of resources at present committed to military purposes.

33.17.　A supportive international and domestic economic climate conducive to sustained economic growth and development is important, particularly for developing countries, in order to achieve sustainability.

33.18.　The secretariat of the Conference has estimated the average annual costs (1993–2000) of implementing in developing countries the activities in Agenda 21 to be over $600 billion, including about $125 billion on grant or concessional terms from the international community.　These are indicative and order-of-magnitude estimates only, and have not been reviewed by Governments.　Actual costs will depend upon, *inter alia,* the specific strategies and programmes Governments decide upon for implementation.

33.19.　Developed countries and others in a position to do so should make initial financial commitments to give effect to the decisions of the Conference.　They should report on such plans and commitments to the United Nations General Assembly at its forty-seventh session, in 1992.

33.20.　Developing countries should also begin to draw up national plans for sustainable development to give effect to the decisions of the Conference.

33.21.　Review and monitoring of the financing of Agenda 21 is essential. Questions related to the effective follow-up of the Conference are discussed in chapter 38 (International institutional arrangements).　It will be important to review on a regular basis the adequacy of funding and mechanisms, including efforts to reach agreed objectives of the present chapter, including targets where applicable.

附錄五：跨國長程空氣污染物公約

CONVENTION ON LONG–RANGE TRANSBOUNDARY AIR POLLUTION (LRTAP) (WITHOUT PROTOCOLS).[1] But see Basic Document 3.19, infra. Concluded at Geneva, 13 November 1979. Entered into force, 16 March 1983. 1302 U.N.T.S. 217, 18 I.L.M. 1442 (1979), T.I.A.S. No. 10541

The Parties to the present Convention,

Determined to promote relations and co-operation in the field of environmental protection,

Aware of the significance of the activities of the United Nations Economic Commission for Europe in strengthening such relations and co-operation, particularly in the field of air pollution including long-range transport of air pollutants,

Recognizing the contribution of the Economic Commission for Europe to the multilateral implementation of the pertinent provisions of the Final Act of the Conference on Security and Co-operation in Europe,

Cognizant of the references in the chapter on environment of the Final Act of the Conference on Security and Co-operation in Europe calling for co-operation to control air pollution and its effects, including long-range transport of air pollutants, and to the development through international co-operation of an extensive programme for the monitoring and evaluation of long-range transport of air pollutants, starting with sulphur dioxide and with possible extension to other pollutants,

Considering the pertinent provisions of the Declaration of the United Nations Conference on the Human Environment, and in particular principle 21, which expresses the common conviction that States have, in accordance with the Charter of the United Nations and the principles of international law, the sovereign right to exploit their own resources pursuant to their own environmental policies, and the responsibility to ensure that activities within their jurisdiction or control do not cause damage to the environment of other States or of areas beyond the limits of natural jurisdiction,

Recognizing the existence of possible adverse effects, in the short and long term, of air pollution including transboundary air pollution,

Concerned that a rise in the level of emissions of air pollutants within the region as forecast may increase such adverse effects,

Recognizing the need to study the implications of the long-range transport of air pollutants and the need to seek solutions for the problems identified,

Affirming their willingness to reinforce active international co-operation to develop appropriate national policies and by means of exchange of information, consultation, research and monitoring, to co-ordinate national action for combating air pollution including long-range transboundary air pollution,

Have agreed as follows:

DEFINITIONS
Article 1

For the purposes of the present Convention:

(a) *"air pollution"* means the introduction by man, directly or indirectly, of substances or energy into the air resulting in deleterious effects of such a nature as to endanger human health, harm living resources and ecosystems and material property and impair or interfere with amenities and other legitimate uses of the environment, and "air pollutants" shall be construed accordingly;

(b) *"long-range transboundary air pollution"* means air pollution whose physical origin is situated wholly or in part within the area under the national jurisdiction of one State and which has adverse effects in the area under the jurisdiction of another State at such a distance that it is not generally possible to distinguish the contribution of individual emission sources or groups of sources.

FUNDAMENTAL PRINCIPLES
Article 2

The Contracting Parties, taking due account of the facts and problems involved, are determined to protect man and his environment against air pollution and shall endeavour to limit and, as far as possible, gradually reduce and prevent air pollution including long-range transboundary air pollution.

Article 3

The Contracting Parties, within the framework of the present Convention, shall by means of exchanges of information, consultation, research and monitoring, develop without undue delay policies and strategies which shall serve as a means of combating the discharge of air pollutants, taking into account efforts already made at national and international levels.

Article 4

The Contracting Parties shall exchange information on and review their policies, scientific activities and technical measures aimed at combating, as far as possible, the discharge of air pollutants which may have adverse effects, thereby contributing to the reduction of air pollution including long-range transboundary air pollution.

Article 5

Consultations shall be held, upon request, at an early stage between, on the one hand, Contracting Parties which are actually affected by or exposed to a significant risk of long-range transboundary air pollution and, on the other hand, Contracting Parties within which and subject to whose jurisdiction a significant contribution to long-range transboundary air pollution originates, or could originate, in connexion with activities carried on or contemplated therein.

AIR QUALITY MANAGEMENT
Article 6

Taking into account articles 2 to 5, the ongoing research, exchange of information and monitoring and the results thereof, the cost and effectiveness of local and other remedies and, in order to combat air pollution, in particular that originating from new or rebuilt installations, each Contracting Party undertakes to develop the best policies and strategies including air quality management systems and, as part of them, control measures compatible with balanced development, in particular by using the best available technology which is economically feasible and low- and non-waste technology.

RESEARCH AND DEVELOPMENT
Article 7

The Contracting Parties, as appropriate to their needs, shall initiate and co-operate in the conduct of research into and/or development of:

(a) existing and proposed technologies for reducing emissions of sulphur compounds and other major air pollutants, including technical and economic feasibility, and environmental consequences;

(b) instrumentation and other techniques for monitoring and measuring emission rates and ambient concentrations of air pollutants;

(c) improved models for a better understanding of the transmission of long-range transboundary air pollutants;

(d) the effects of sulphur compounds and other major air pollutants on human health and the environment, including agriculture, forestry, materials, aquatic and other natural ecosystems and visibility, with a view to establishing a scientific basis for dose/effect relationships designed to protect the environment;

(e) the economic, social and environmental assessment of alternative measures for attaining environmental objectives including the reduction of long-range transboundary air pollution;

(f) education and training programmes related to the environmental aspects of pollution by sulphur compounds and other major air pollutants.

EXCHANGE OF INFORMATION
Article 8

The Contracting Parties, within the framework of the Executive Body referred to in article 10 and bilaterally, shall, in their common interests, exchange available information on:

(a) data on emissions at periods of time to be agreed upon, of agreed air pollutants, starting with sulphur dioxide, coming from grid-units of agreed size; or on the fluxes of agreed air pollutants, starting with sulphur dioxide, across national borders, at distances and at periods of time to be agreed upon;

(b) major changes in national policies and in general industrial development, and their potential impact, which would be likely to cause significant changes in long-range transboundary air pollution;

(c) control technologies for reducing air pollution relevant to long-range transboundary air pollution;

(d) the projected cost of the emission control of sulphur compounds and other major air pollutants on a national scale;

(e) meteorological and physico-chemical data relating to the processes during transmission;

(f) physico-chemical and biological data relating to the effects of long-range transboundary air pollution and the extent of the damage which these data indicate can be attributed to long-range transboundary air pollution;

(g) national, subregional and regional policies and strategies for the control of sulphur compounds and other major air pollutants.

IMPLEMENTATION AND FURTHER DEVELOPMENT OF THE CO–OPERATIVE PROGRAMME FOR THE MONITORING AND EVALUATION OF THE LONG–RANGE TRANSMISSION OF AIR POLLUTANTS IN EUROPE

Article 9

The Contracting Parties stress the need for the implementation of the existing "Co-operative programme for the monitoring and evaluation of the long-range transmission of air pollutants in Europe" (hereinafter referred to as EMEP) and, with regard to the further development of this programme, agree to emphasize:

(a) the desirability of Contracting Parties joining in and fully implementing EMEP which, as a first step, is based on the monitoring of sulphur dioxide and related substances;

(b) the need to use comparable or standardized procedures for monitoring whenever possible;

(c) the desirability of basing the monitoring programme on the framework of both national and international programmes. The establishment of monitoring stations and the collection of data shall be carried out under the national jurisdiction of the country in which the monitoring stations are located;

(d) the desirability of establishing a framework for a co-operative environmental monitoring programme, based on and taking into account present and future national, subregional, regional and other international programmes;

(e) the need to exchange data on emissions at periods of time to be agreed upon, of agreed air pollutants, starting with sulphur dioxide, coming from grid-units of agreed size; or on the fluxes of agreed air pollutants, starting with sulphur dioxide, across national borders, at distances and at periods of time to be agreed upon. The method, including the model, used to determine the fluxes, as well as the method, including the model, used to determine the transmission of air pollutants based on the emissions per grid-unit, shall be made available and periodically reviewed, in order to improve the methods and the models;

(f) their willingness to continue the exchange and periodic updating of national data on total emissions of agreed air pollutants, starting with sulphur dioxide;

(g) the need to provide meteorological and physico-chemical data relating to processes during transmission;

(h) the need to monitor chemical components in other media such as water, soil and vegetation, as well as a similar monitoring programme to record effects on health and environment;

(i) the desirability of extending the national EMEP networks to make them operational for control and surveillance purposes.

EXECUTIVE BODY

Article 10

1. The representatives of the Contracting Parties shall, within the framework of the Senior Advisers to ECE Governments on Environmental Problems, constitute the Executive Body of the present Convention, and shall meet at least annually in that capacity.

2. The Executive Body shall:

(a) review the implementation of the present Convention;

(b) establish, as appropriate, working groups to consider matters related to the implementation and development of the present Convention and to this end to prepare appropriate studies and other documentation and to submit recommendations to be considered by the Executive Body;

(c) fulfil such other functions as may be appropriate under the provisions of the present Convention.

3. The Executive Body shall utilize the Steering Body for the EMEP to play an integral part in the operation of the present Convention, in particular with regard to data collection and scientific co-operation.

4. The Executive Body, in discharging its functions, shall, when it deems appropriate, also make use of information from other relevant international organizations.

SECRETARIAT
Article 11

The Executive Secretary of the Economic Commission for Europe shall carry out, for the Executive Body, the following secretariat functions:

(a) to convene and prepare the meetings of the Executive Body;

(b) to transmit to the Contracting Parties reports and other information received in accordance with the provisions of the present Convention;

(c) to discharge the functions assigned by the Executive Body.

AMENDMENTS TO THE CONVENTION
Article 12

1. Any Contracting Party may propose amendments to the present Convention.

2. The text of proposed amendments shall be submitted in writing to the Executive Secretary of the Economic Commission for Europe, who shall communicate them to all Contracting Parties. The Executive Body shall discuss proposed amendments at its next annual meeting provided that such proposals have been circulated by the Executive Secretary of the Economic Commission for Europe to the Contracting Parties at least ninety days in advance.

3. An amendment to the present Convention shall be adopted by consensus of the representatives of the Contracting Parties, and shall enter into force for the Contracting Parties which have accepted it on the ninetieth day after the date on which two-thirds of the Contracting Parties have deposited their instruments of acceptance with the depositary. Thereafter, the amendment shall enter into force for any other Contracting Party on the ninetieth day after the date on which that Contracting Party deposits its instrument of acceptance of the amendment.

SETTLEMENT OF DISPUTES
Article 13

If a dispute arises between two or more Contracting Parties to the present Convention as to the interpretation or application of the Convention, they shall seek a solution by negotiation or by any other method of dispute settlement acceptable to the parties to the dispute.

SIGNATURE
Article 14

1. The present Convention shall be open for signature at the United Nations Office at Geneva from 13 to 16 November 1979 on the occasion of the High-level Meeting within the framework of the Economic Commission for Europe on the Protection of the Environment, by the member States of the Economic Commission for Europe as well as States having consultative status with the Economic Commission for Europe, pursuant to paragraph 8 of

Economic and Social Council resolution 36 (IV) of 28 March 1947, and by regional economic integration organizations, constituted by sovereign States members of the Economic Commission for Europe, which have competence in respect of the negotiation, conclusion and application of international agreements in matters covered by the present Convention.

2. In matters within their competence, such regional economic integration organizations shall, on their own behalf, exercise the rights and fulfil the responsibilities which the present Convention attributes to their member States. In such cases, the member States of these organizations shall not be entitled to exercise such rights individually.

RATIFICATION, ACCEPTANCE, APPROVAL AND ACCESSION
Article 15

1. The present Convention shall be subject to ratification, acceptance or approval.

2. The present Convention shall be open for accession as from 17 November 1979 by the States and organizations referred to in article 14, paragraph 1.

3. The instruments of ratification, acceptance, approval or accession shall be deposited with the Secretary–General of the United Nations, who will perform the functions of the depositary.

ENTRY INTO FORCE
Article 16

1. The present Convention shall enter into force on the ninetieth day after the date of deposit of the twenty-fourth instrument of ratification, acceptance, approval or accession.

2. For each Contracting Party which ratifies, accepts or approves the present Convention or accedes thereto after the deposit of the twenty-fourth instrument of ratification, acceptance, approval or accession, the Convention shall enter into force on the ninetieth day after the date of deposit by such Contracting Party of its instrument of ratification, acceptance, approval or accession.

WITHDRAWAL
Article 17

At any time after five years from the date on which the present Convention has come into force with respect to a Contracting Party, that Contracting Party may withdraw from the Convention by giving written notification to the depositary. Any such withdrawal shall take effect on the ninetieth day after the date of its receipt by the depositary.

AUTHENTIC TEXTS
Article 18

The original of the present Convention, of which the English, French and Russian texts are equally authentic, shall be deposited with the Secretary–General of the United Nations.

附錄六：維也納保護臭氧層公約

VIENNA CONVENTION FOR THE PROTECTION OF THE OZONE LAYER (WITH ANNEXES I & II).[1] Concluded at Vienna, 22 March 1985. Entered into force, 22 September 1988. UNEP Doc. IG.53/5, 26 I.L.M. 1529 (1987)

ARTICLE 1

DEFINITIONS

For the purposes of this Convention:

1. 'The ozone layer' means the layer of atmospheric ozone above the planetary boundary layer.

2. 'Adverse effects' means changes in the physical environment or biota, including changes in climate, which have significant deleterious effects on human health or on the composition, resilience and productivity of natural and managed ecosystems, or on materials useful to mankind.

3. 'Alternative technologies or equipment' means technologies or equipment the use of which makes it possible to reduce or effectively eliminate emissions of substances which have or are likely to have adverse effects on the ozone layer.

4. 'Alternative substances' means substances which reduce, eliminate or avoid adverse effects on the ozone layer.

5. 'Parties' means, unless the text otherwise indicates, Parties to this Convention.

6. 'Regional economic integration organization' means an organization constituted by sovereign States of a given region which has competence in respect of matters governed by this Convention or its protocols and has been duly authorized, in accordance with its internal procedures, to sign, ratify, accept, approve or accede to the instruments concerned.

7. 'Protocols' means protocols to this Convention.

ARTICLE 2

GENERAL OBLIGATIONS

1. The Parties shall take appropriate measures in accordance with the provisions of this Convention and of those protocols in force to which they are party to protect human health and the environment against adverse effects resulting or likely to result from human activities which modify or are likely to modify the ozone layer.

2. To this end the Parties shall, in accordance with the means at their disposal and their capabilities:

　(a) Co-operate by means of systematic observations, research and information exchange in order to better understand and assess the effects of human activities on the ozone layer and the effects on human health and the environment from modification of the ozone layer;

(b) Adopt appropriate legislative or administrative measures and co-operate in harmonizing appropriate policies to control, limit, reduce or prevent human activities under their jurisdiction or control should it be found that these activities have or are likely to have adverse effects resulting from modification or likely modification of the ozone layer;

(c) Co-operate in the formulation of agreed measures, procedures and standards for the implementation of this Convention, with a view to the adoption of protocols and annexes;

(d) Co-operate with competent international bodies to implement effectively this Convention and protocols to which they are party.

3.　The provisions of this Convention shall in no way affect the right of Parties to adopt, in accordance with international law, domestic measures additional to those referred to in paragraphs 1 and 2 above, nor shall they affect additional domestic measures already taken by a Party, provided that these measures are not incompatible with their obligations under this Convention.

4.　The application of this article shall be based on relevant scientific and technical considerations.

ARTICLE 3

RESEARCH AND SYSTEMATIC OBSERVATIONS

1.　The Parties undertake, as appropriate, to initiate and co-operate in, directly or through competent international bodies, the conduct of research and scientific assessments on:

(a) The physical and chemical processes that may affect the ozone layer;

(b) The human health and other biological effects deriving from any modifications of the ozone layer, particularly those resulting from changes in ultra-violet solar radiation having biological effects (UV–B);

(c) Climatic effects deriving from any modifications of the ozone layer;

(d) Effects deriving from any modifications of the ozone layer and any consequent change in UV–B radiation on natural and synthetic materials useful to mankind;

(e) Substances, practices, processes and activities that may affect the ozone layer, and their cumulative effects;

(f) Alternative substances and technologies;

(g) Related socio-economic matters;

and as further elaborated in annexes I and II.

2.　The Parties undertake to promote or establish, as appropriate, directly or through competent international bodies and taking fully into account national legislation and relevant ongoing activities at both the national and international levels, joint or complementary programmes for systematic obser-vation of the state of the ozone layer and other relevant parameters, as elaborated in annex I.

3.　The Parties undertake to co-operate, directly or through competent international bodies, in ensuring the collection, validation and transmission of research and observational data through appropriate world data centres in a regular and timely fashion.

ARTICLE 4

CO-OPERATION IN THE LEGAL, SCIENTIFIC AND TECHNICAL FIELDS

1.　The Parties shall facilitate and encourage the exchange of scientific, technical, socio-economic, commercial and legal information relevant to this Convention as further elaborated in annex II.　Such information shall be supplied to bodies agreed upon by the Parties.　Any such body receiving information regarded as confidential by the supplying Party shall ensure that such information is not disclosed and shall aggregate it to protect its confiden-tiality before it is made available to all Parties.

2.　The Parties shall co-operate, consistent with their national laws, regulations and practices and taking into account in particular the needs of the developing countries, in promoting, directly or through competent inter-national bodies, the development and transfer of technology and knowledge. Such co-operation shall be carried out particularly through:

(a) Facilitation of the acquisition of alternative technologies by other Parties;

(b) Provision of information on alternative technologies and equip-ment, and supply of special manuals or guides to them;

(c) The supply of necessary equipment and facilities for research and systematic observations;

(d) Appropriate training of scientific and technical personnel.

ARTICLE 5

TRANSMISSION OF INFORMATION

The Parties shall transmit, through the secretariat, to the Conference of the Parties established under article 6 information on the measures adopted by them in implementation of this Convention and of protocols to which they are party in such form and at such intervals as the meetings of the parties to the relevant instruments may determine.

ARTICLE 6

CONFERENCE OF THE PARTIES

1.　A Conference of the Parties is hereby established.　The first meeting of the Conference of the Parties shall be convened by the secretariat designat-ed on an interim basis under article 7 not later than one year after entry into force of this Convention. Thereafter, ordinary meetings of the Conference of the Parties shall be held at regular intervals to be determined by the Conference at its first meeting.

2. Extraordinary meetings of the Conference of the Parties shall be held at such other times as may be deemed necessary by the Conference, or at the written request of any Party, provided that, within six months of the request being communicated to them by the secretariat, it is supported by at least one third of the Parties.

3. The Conference of the Parties shall by consensus agree upon and adopt rules of procedure and financial rules for itself and for any subsidiary bodies it may establish, as well as financial provisions governing the functioning of the secretariat.

4. The Conference of the Parties shall keep under continuous review the implementation of this Convention, and, in addition, shall:

(a) Establish the form and the intervals for transmitting the information to be submitted in accordance with article 5 and consider such information as well as reports submitted by any subsidiary body;

(b) Review the scientific information on the ozone layer, on its possible modification and on possible effects of any such modification;

(c) Promote, in accordance with article 2, the harmonization of appropriate policies, strategies and measures for minimizing the release of substances causing or likely to cause modification of the ozone layer, and make recommendations on any other measures relating to this Convention;

(d) Adopt, in accordance with articles 3 and 4, programmes for research, systematic observations, scientific and technological co-operation, the exchange of information and the transfer of technology and knowledge;

(e) Consider and adopt, as required, in accordance with articles 9 and 10, amendments to this Convention and its annexes;

(f) Consider amendments to any protocol, as well as to any annexes thereto, and, if so decided, recommend their adoption to the parties to the protocol concerned;

(g) Consider and adopt, as required, in accordance with article 10, additional annexes to this Convention;

(h) Consider and adopt, as required, protocols in accordance with article 8;

(i) Establish such subsidiary bodies as are deemed necessary for the implementation of this Convention;

(j) Seek, where appropriate, the services of competent international bodies and scientific committees, in particular the World Meteorological Organization and the World Health Organization, as well as the Co-ordinating Committee on the Ozone Layer, in scientific research, systematic observations and other activities pertinent to the objectives of this Convention, and make use as appropriate of information from these bodies and committees;

(k) Consider and undertake any additional action that may be required for the achievement of the purposes of this Convention.

5. The United Nations, its specialized agencies and the International Atomic Energy Agency, as well as any State not party to this Convention, may be represented at meetings of the Conference of the Parties by observers. Any body or agency, whether national or international, governmental or non-governmental, qualified in fields relating to the protection of the ozone layer which has informed the secretariat of its wish to be represented at a meeting of the Conference of the Parties as an observer may be admitted unless at least one-third of the Parties present object. The admission and participation of observers shall be subject to the rules of procedure adopted by the Conference of the Parties.

ARTICLE 7

SECRETARIAT

1. The functions of the secretariat shall be:

(a) To arrange for and service meetings provided for in articles 6, 8, 9 and 10;

(b) To prepare and transmit reports based upon information received in accordance with articles 4 and 5, as well as upon information derived from meetings of subsidiary bodies established under article 6;

(c) To perform the functions assigned to it by any protocol;

(d) To prepare reports on its activities carried out in implementation of its functions under this Convention and present them to the Conference of the Parties;

(e) To ensure the necessary co-ordination with other relevant international bodies, and in particular to enter into such administrative and contractual arrangements as may be required for the effective discharge of its functions;

(f) To perform such other functions as may be determined by the Conference of the Parties.

2. The secretariat functions will be carried out on an interim basis by the United Nations Environment Programme until the completion of the first ordinary meeting of the Conference of the Parties held pursuant to article 6. At its first ordinary meeting, the Conference of the Parties shall designate the secretariat from amongst those existing competent international organizations which have signified their willingness to carry out the secretariat functions under this Convention.

ARTICLE 8

ADOPTION OF PROTOCOLS

1. The Conference of the Parties may at a meeting adopt protocols pursuant to article 2.

2. The text of any proposed protocol shall be communicated to the Parties by the secretariat at least six months before such a meeting.

ARTICLE 9

AMENDMENT OF THE CONVENTION OR PROTOCOLS

1. Any Party may propose amendments to this Convention or to any protocol. Such amendments shall take due account, *inter alia,* of relevant scientific and technical considerations.

2. Amendments to this Convention shall be adopted at a meeting of the Conference of the Parties. Amendments to any protocol shall be adopted at a meeting of the Parties to the protocol in question. The text of any proposed amendment to this Convention or to any protocol, except as may otherwise be provided in such protocol, shall be communicated to the Parties by the secretariat at least six months before the meeting at which it is proposed for adoption. The secretariat shall also communicate proposed amendments to the signatories to this Convention for information.

3. The Parties shall make every effort to reach agreement on any proposed amendment to this Convention by consensus. If all efforts at consensus have been exhausted, and no agreement reached, the amendment shall as a last resort be adopted by a three-fourths majority vote of the Parties present and voting at the meeting, and shall be submitted by the Depositary to all Parties for ratification, approval or acceptance.

4. The procedure mentioned in paragraph 3 above shall apply to amendments to any protocol, except that a two-thirds majority of the parties to that protocol present and voting at the meeting shall suffice for their adoption.

5. Ratification, approval or acceptance of amendments shall be notified to the Depositary in writing. Amendments adopted in accordance with paragraph 3 or 4 above shall enter into force between parties having accepted them on the ninetieth day after the receipt by the Depositary of notification of their ratification, approval or acceptance by at least three-fourths of the Parties to this Convention or by at least two-thirds of the parties to the protocol concerned, except as may otherwise be provided in such protocol. Thereafter the amendments shall enter into force for any other Party on the ninetieth day after that Party deposits its instrument of ratification, approval or acceptance of the amendments.

6. For the purposes of this article, "Parties present and voting" means Parties present and casting an affirmative or negative vote.

ARTICLE 10

ADOPTION AND AMENDMENT OF ANNEXES

1. The annexes to this Convention or to any protocol shall form an integral part of this Convention or of such protocol, as the case may be, and, unless expressly provided otherwise, a reference to this Convention or its protocols constitutes at the same time a reference to any annexes thereto. Such annexes shall be restricted to scientific, technical and administrative matters.

2. Except as may be otherwise provided in any protocol with respect to its annexes, the following procedure shall apply to the proposal, adoption and entry into force of additional annexes to this Convention or of annexes to a protocol:

(a) Annexes to this Convention shall be proposed and adopted according to the procedure laid down in article 9, paragraphs 2 and 3, while annexes to any protocol shall be proposed and adopted according to the procedure laid down in article 9, paragraphs 2 and 4;

(b) Any party that is unable to approve an additional annex to this Convention or an annex to any protocol to which it is party shall so notify the Depositary, in writing, within six months from the date of the communication of the adoption by the Depositary. The Depositary shall without delay notify all Parties of any such notification received. A Party may at any time substitute an acceptance for a previous declaration of objection and the annexes shall thereupon enter into force for that Party;

(c) On the expiry of six months from the date of the circulation of the communication by the Depositary, the annex shall become effective for all Parties to this Convention or to any protocol concerned which have not submitted a notification in accordance with the provision of subparagraph (b) above.

3. The proposal, adoption and entry into force of amendments to annexes to this Convention or to any protocol shall be subject to the same procedure as for the proposal, adoption and entry into force of annexes to the Convention or annexes to a protocol. Annexes and amendments thereto shall take due account, *inter alia,* of relevant scientific and technical considerations.

4. If an additional annex or an amendment to an annex involves an amendment to this Convention or to any protocol, the additional annex or amended annex shall not enter into force until such time as the amendment to this Convention or to the protocol concerned enters into force.

ARTICLE 11

SETTLEMENT OF DISPUTES

1. In the event of a dispute between Parties concerning the interpretation or application of this Convention, the parties concerned shall seek solution by negotiation.

2.　If the parties concerned cannot reach agreement by negotiation, they may jointly seek the good offices of, or request mediation by, a third party.

3.　When ratifying, accepting, approving or acceding to this Convention, or at any time thereafter, a State or regional economic integration organization may declare in writing to the Depositary that for a dispute not resolved in accordance with paragraph 1 or paragraph 2 above, it accepts one or both of the following means of dispute settlement as compulsory:

(a) Arbitration in accordance with procedures to be adopted by the Conference of the Parties at its first ordinary meeting;

(b) Submission of the dispute to the International Court of Justice.

4.　If the parties have not, in accordance with paragraph 3 above, accepted the same or any procedure, the dispute shall be submitted to conciliation in accordance with paragraph 5 below unless the parties otherwise agree.

5.　A conciliation commission shall be created upon the request of one of the parties to the dispute.　The commission shall be composed of an equal number of members appointed by each party concerned and a chairman chosen jointly by the members appointed by each party.　The commission shall render a final and recommendatory award, which the parties shall consider in good faith.

6.　The provisions of this article shall apply with respect to any protocol except as otherwise provided in the protocol concerned.

ARTICLE 12
SIGNATURE

This Convention shall be open for signature by States and by regional economic integration organizations at the Federal Ministry for Foreign Affairs of the Republic of Austria in Vienna from 22 March 1985 to 21 September 1985, and at United Nations Headquarters in New York from 22 September 1985 to 21 March 1986.

ARTICLE 13
RATIFICATION, ACCEPTANCE OR APPROVAL

1.　This Convention and any protocol shall be subject to ratification, acceptance or approval by States and by regional economic integration organizations.　Instruments of ratification, acceptance or approval shall be deposited with the Depositary.

2.　Any organization referred to in paragraph 1 above which becomes a Party to this Convention or any protocol without any of its member States being a Party shall be bound by all the obligations under the Convention or the protocol, as the case may be.　In the case of such organizations, one or more of whose member States is a Party to the Convention or relevant protocol, the organization and its member States shall decide on their respective responsibilities for the performance of their obligation under the Convention or protocol, as the case may be. In such cases, the organization and the member States shall not be entitled to exercise rights under the Convention or relevant protocol concurrently.

3. In their instruments of ratification, acceptance or approval, the organizations referred to in paragraph 1 above shall declare the extent of their competence with respect to the matters governed by the Convention or the relevant protocol. These organizations shall also inform the Depositary of any substantial modification in the extent of their competence.

ARTICLE 14
ACCESSION

1. This Convention and any protocol shall be open for accession by States and by regional economic integration organizations from the date on which the Convention or the protocol concerned is closed for signature. The instruments of accession shall be deposited with the Depositary.

2. In their instruments of accession, the organizations referred to in paragraph 1 above shall declare the extent of their competence with respect to the matters governed by the Convention or the relevant protocol. These organizations shall also inform the Depositary of any substantial modification in the extent of their competence.

3. The provisions of article 13, paragraph 2, shall apply to regional economic integration organizations which accede to this Convention or any protocol.

ARTICLE 15
RIGHT TO VOTE

1. Each Party to this Convention or to any protocol shall have one vote.

2. Except as provided for in paragraph 1 above, regional economic integration organizations, in matters within their competence, shall exercise their right to vote with a number of votes equal to the number of their member States which are Parties to the Convention or the relevant protocol. Such organizations shall not exercise their right to vote if their member States exercise theirs, and vice versa.

ARTICLE 16
RELATIONSHIP BETWEEN THE CONVENTION AND ITS PROTOCOLS

1. A State or a regional economic integration organization may not become a party to a protocol unless it is, or becomes at the same time, a Party to the Convention.

2. Decisions concerning any protocol shall be taken only by the parties to the protocol concerned.

ARTICLE 17
ENTRY INTO FORCE

1. This Convention shall enter into force on the ninetieth day after the date of deposit of the twentieth instrument of ratification, acceptance, approval or accession.

2. Any protocol, except as otherwise provided in such protocol, shall enter into force on the ninetieth day after the date of deposit of the eleventh instrument of ratification, acceptance or approval of such protocol or accession thereto.

3. For each Party which ratifies, accepts or approves this Convention or accedes thereto after the deposit of the twentieth instrument of ratification, acceptance, approval or accession, it shall enter into force on the ninetieth day after the date of deposit by such Party of its instrument of ratification, acceptance, approval or accession.

4. Any protocol, except as otherwise provided in such protocol, shall enter into force for a party that ratifies, accepts or approves that protocol or accedes thereto after its entry into force pursuant to paragraph 2 above, on the ninetieth day after the date on which that party deposits its instrument of ratification, acceptance, approval or accession, or on the date on which the Convention enters into force for that Party, whichever shall be the later.

5. For the purposes of paragraphs 1 and 2 above, any instrument deposited by a regional economic integration organization shall not be counted as additional to those deposited by member States of such organization.

ARTICLE 18
RESERVATIONS

No reservations may be made to this Convention.

ARTICLE 19
WITHDRAWAL

1. At any time after four years from the date on which this Convention has entered into force for a Party, that Party may withdraw from the Convention by giving written notification to the Depositary.

2. Except as may be provided in any protocol, at any time after four years from the date on which such protocol has entered into force for a party, that party may withdraw from the protocol by giving written notification to the Depositary.

3. Any such withdrawal shall take effect upon expiry of one year after the date of its receipt by the Depositary, or on such later date as may be specified in the notification of the withdrawal.

4. Any Party which withdraws from this Convention shall be considered as also having withdrawn from any protocol to which it is party.

ARTICLE 20

DEPOSITARY

1. The Secretary–General of the United Nations shall assume the functions of Depositary of this Convention and any protocols.

2. The Depositary shall inform the Parties, in particular, of:

(a) The signature of this Convention and of any protocol, and the deposit of instruments of ratification, acceptance, approval or accession in accordance with articles 13 and 14;

(b) The date on which the Convention and any protocol will come into force in accordance with article 17;

(c) Notifications of withdrawal made in accordance with article 19;

(d) Amendments adopted with respect to the Convention and any protocol, their acceptance by the parties and their date of entry into force in accordance with article 9;

(e) All communications relating to the adoption and approval of annexes and to the amendment of annexes in accordance with article 10;

(f) Notifications by regional economic integration organizations of the extent of their competence with respect to matters governed by this Convention and any protocols, and of any modifications thereof;

(g) Declarations made in accordance with article 11, paragraph 3.

ARTICLE 21

AUTHENTIC TEXTS

The original of this Convention, of which the Arabic, Chinese, English, French, Russian and Spanish texts are equally authentic, shall be deposited with the Secretary–General of the United Nations.

ANNEX I

RESEARCH AND SYSTEMATIC OBSERVATIONS

1. The Parties to the Convention recognize that the major scientific issues are:

(a) Modification of the ozone layer which would result in a change in the amount of solar ultra-violet radiation having biological effects (UV–B) that reaches the Earth's surface and the potential consequences for human health, for organisms, ecosystems and materials useful to mankind;

(b) Modification of the vertical distribution of ozone, which could change the temperature structure of the atmosphere and the potential consequences for weather and climate.

2. The Parties to the Convention, in accordance with article 3, shall co-operate in conducting research and systematic observations and in formulating recommendations for future research and observation in such areas as:

(a) *Research into the physics and chemistry of the atmosphere*

(i) Comprehensive theoretical models: further development of models which consider the interaction between radiative, dynamic and chemical processes; studies of the simultaneous effects of various man-made and naturally occurring species upon atmospheric ozone; interpretation of satellite and non-satellite measurement data sets; evaluation of trends in atmospheric and geophysical parameters, and the development of methods for attributing changes in these parameters to specific causes;

(ii) Laboratory studies of: rate coefficients, absorption cross-sections and mechanisms of tropospheric and stratospheric chemical and photochemical processes; spectroscopic data to support field measurements in all relevant spectral regions;

(iii) Field measurements: the concentration and fluxes of key source gases of both natural and anthropogenic origin; atmospheric dynamics studies; simultaneous measurements of photochemically-related species down to the planetary boundary layer, using *in situ* and remote sensing instruments; intercomparison of different sensors, including co-ordinated correlative measurements for satellite instrumentation; three-dimensional fields of key atmospheric trace constituents, solar spectral flux and meteorological parameters;

(iv) Instrument development, including satellite and non-satellite sensors for atmospheric trace constituents, solar flux and meteorological parameters;

(b) *Research into health, biological and photodegradation effects*

(i) The relationship between human exposure to visible and ultra-violet solar radiation and (a) the development of both non-melanoma and melanoma skin cancer and (b) the effects on the immunological system;

(ii) Effects of UV–B radiation, including the wavelength dependence, upon (a) agricultural crops, forests and other terrestial ecosystems and (b) the aquatic food web and fisheries, as well as possible inhibition of oxygen production by marine phytoplankton;

(iii) The mechanisms by which UV–B radiation acts on biological materials, species and ecosystems, including: the relationship between dose, dose rate, and response; photorepair, adaptation, and protection;

(iv) Studies of biological action spectra and the spectral response using polychromatic radiation in order to include possible interactions of the various wavelength regions;

(v) The influence of UV–B radiation on: the sensitivities and activities of biological species important to the biospheric balance; primary processes such as photosynthesis and biosynthesis;

(vi) The influence of UV–B radiation on the photodegradation of pollutants, agricultural chemicals and other materials;

(c) *Research on effects on climate*

(i) Theoretical and observational studies of the radiative effects of ozone and other trace species and the impact on climate parameters, such as land and ocean surface temperatures, precipitation patterns, the exchange between the troposphere and stratosphere;

(ii) The investigation of the effects of such climate impacts on various aspects of human activity;

(d) *Systematic observations on:*

(i) The status of the ozone layer (i.e. the spatial and temporal variability of the total column content and vertical distribution) by making the Global Ozone Observing System, based on the integration of satellite and ground-based systems, fully operational;

(ii) The tropospheric and stratospheric concentrations of source gases for the HO_x, NO_x, $C10_x$ and carbon families;

(iii) The temperature from the ground to the mesosphere, utilizing both ground-based and satellite systems;

(iv) Wavelength-resolved solar flux reaching, and thermal radiation leaving, the Earth's atmosphere, utilizing satellite measurements;

(v) Wavelength-resolved solar flux reaching the Earth's surface in the ultra-violet range having biological effects (UV–B);

(vi) Aerosol properties and distribution from the ground to the mesosphere, utilizing ground-based, airborne and satellite systems;

(vii) Climatically important variables by the maintenance of programmes of high-quality meteorological surface measurements;

(viii) Trace species, temperatures, solar flux and aerosols utilizing improved methods for analysing global data.

3.　The Parties to the Convention shall co-operate, taking into account the particular needs of the developing countries, in promoting the appropriate scientific and technical training required to participate in the research and systematic observations outlined in this annex. Particular emphasis should be given to the intercalibration of observational instrumentation and methods with a view to generating comparable or standardized scientific data sets.

4. The following chemical substances of natural and anthropogenic origin, not listed in order of priority, are thought to have the potential to modify the chemical and physical properties of the ozone layer.

(a) Carbon substances

(i) *Carbon monoxide (CO)*

Carbon monoxide has significant natural and anthropogenic sources, and is thought to play a major direct role in tropospheric photochemistry, and an indirect role in stratospheric photochemistry.

(ii) *Carbon dioxide (CO₂)*

Carbon dioxide has significant natural and anthropogenic sources, and affects stratospheric ozone by influencing the thermal structure of the atmosphere.

(iii) *Methane (CH₄)*

Methane has both natural and anthropogenic sources, and affects both tropospheric and stratospheric ozone.

(iv) *Non-methane hydrocarbon species*

Non-methane hydrocarbon species, which consist of a large number of chemical substances, have both natural and anthropogenic sources, and play a direct role in tropospheric photochemistry and an indirect role in stratospheric photochemistry.

(b) Nitrogen substances

(i) *Nitrous oxide (N₂O)*

The dominant sources of N_2O are natural, but anthropogenic contributions are becoming increasingly important. Nitrous oxide is the primary source of stratospheric NO_x, which play a vital role in controlling the abundance of stratospheric ozone.

(ii) *Nitrogen oxides (NOₓ)*

Ground-level sources of NO_x play a major direct role only in tropospheric photochemical processes and an indirect role in stratospheric photochemistry, whereas injection of NO_x close to the tropopause may lead directly to a change in upper tropospheric and stratospheric ozone.

(c) Chlorine substances

(i) *Fully halogenated alkanes, e.g. CCl₄, CFCl₃ (CFC–11), CF₂Cl₂ (CFC–12), C₂F₃Cl₃ (CFC–113), C₂F₄Cl₂ (CFC–114)*

Fully halogenated alkanes are anthropogenic and act as a source of $C10_x$, which plays a vital role in ozone photochemistry, especially in the 30–50 km altitude region.

(ii) *Partially halogenated alkanes, e.g. CH_3Cl, CHF_2Cl (CFC–22), CH_3CCl_3, $CHFCl_2$ (CFC–21)*

The sources of CH_3Cl are natural, whereas the other partially halogenated alkanes mentioned above are anthropogenic in origin. These gases also act as a source of stratospheric $C10_x$.

(d) Bromine substances

Fully halogenated alkanes, e.g. CF_3Br

These gases are anthropogenic and act as a source of BrO_x, which behaves in a manner similar to ClO_x.

(e) Hydrogen substances

(i) *Hydrogen (H_2)*

Hydrogen, the source of which is natural and anthropogenic, plays a minor role in stratospheric photochemistry.

(ii) *Water (H_2O)*

Water, the source of which is natural, plays a vital role in both tropospheric and stratospheric photochemistry. Local sources of water vapour in the stratosphere include the oxidation of methane and, to a lesser extent, of hydrogen.

ANNEX II

INFORMATION EXCHANGE

1. The Parties to the Convention recognize that the collection and sharing of information is an important means of implementing the objectives of this Convention and of assuring that any actions that may be taken are appropriate and equitable. Therefore, Parties shall exchange scientific, technical, socio-economic, business, commercial and legal information.

2. The Parties to the Convention, in deciding what information is to be collected and exchanged, should take into account the usefulness of the information and the costs of obtaining it. The Parties further recognize that co-operation under this annex has to be consistent with national laws, regulations and practices regarding patents, trade secrets, and protection of confidential and proprietary information.

3. *Scientific information*

This includes information on:

(a) Planned and ongoing research, both governmental and private, to facilitate the co-ordination of research programmes so as to make the most effective use of available national and international resources;

(b) The emission data needed for research;

(c) Scientific results published in peer-reviewed literature on the understanding of the physics and chemistry of the Earth's atmosphere and of its susceptibility to change, in particular on the state of the ozone layer and effects on human health, environment and climate which would result from changes on all time-scales in either the total column content or the vertical distribution of ozone;

(d) The assessment of research results and the recommendations for future research.

4. *Technical information*

This includes information on:

(a) The availability and cost of chemical substitutes and of alternative technologies to reduce the emissions of ozone-modifying substances and related planned and ongoing research;

(b) The limitations and any risks involved in using chemical or other substitutes and alternative technologies.

5. *Socio-economic and commercial information on the substances referred to in annex I*

This includes information on:

(a) Production and production capacity;

(b) Use and use patterns;

(c) Imports/exports;

(d) The costs, risks and benefits of human activities which may indirectly modify the ozone layer and of the impacts of regulatory actions taken or being considered to control these activities.

6. *Legal information*

This includes information on:

(a) National laws, administrative measures and legal research relevant to the protection of the ozone layer;

(b) International agreements, including bilateral agreements, relevant to the protection of the ozone layer;

(c) Methods and terms of licensing and availability of patents relevant to the protection of the ozone layer.

附錄七：蒙特婁議定書

MONTREAL PROTOCOL ON SUBSTANCES THAT DEPLETE THE OZONE LAYER (WITH ANNEX A AND AS ADJUSTED).[1] Concluded at Montreal, 16 September 1987. Entered into force, 1 January 1989. 26 I.L.M. 1550 (1987)

ARTICLE 1. DEFINITIONS

For the purposes of this Protocol:

1. "Convention" means the Vienna Convention for the Protection of the Ozone Layer, adopted on 22 March 1985.

2. "Parties" means, unless the text otherwise indicates, Parties to this Protocol.

3. "Secretariat" means the secretariat of the Convention.

4. "Controlled substance" means a substance listed in Annex A to this Protocol, whether existing alone or in a mixture. It excludes, however, any such substance or mixture which is in a manufactured product other than a container used for the transportation or storage of the substance listed.

5. "Production" means the amount of controlled substances produced minus the amount destroyed by technologies to be approved by the Parties.

6. "Consumption" means production plus imports minus exports of controlled substances.

7. "Calculated levels" of production, imports, exports and consumption means levels determined in accordance with Article 3.

8. "Industrial rationalization" means the transfer of all or a portion of the calculated level of production of one Party to another, for the purpose of achieving economic efficiencies or responding to anticipated shortfalls in supply as a result of plant closures.

ARTICLE 2. CONTROL MEASURES

5. Any Party whose calculated level of production in 1986 of the controlled substances in Group I of Annex A was less than twenty-five kilotonnes may, for the purposes of industrial rationalization, transfer to or receive from any other Party, production in excess of the limits set out in paragraphs 1, 3 and 4 provided that the total combined calculated levels of production of the Parties concerned does not exceed the production limits set out in this Article. Any transfer of such production shall be notified to the secretariat, no later than the time of the transfer.

6. Any Party not operating under Article 5, that has facilities for the production of controlled substances under construction, or contracted for, prior to 16 September 1987, and provided for in national legislation prior to 1 January 1987, may add the production from such facilities to its 1986 production of such substances for the purposes of determining its calculated

level of production for 1986, provided that such facilities are completed by 31 December 1990 and that such production does not raise that Party's annual calculated level of consumption of the controlled substances above 0.5 kilograms per capita.

7. Any transfer of production pursuant to paragraph 5 or any addition of production pursuant to paragraph 6 shall be notified to the secretariat, no later than the time of the transfer or addition.

8. (a) Any Parties which are Member States of a regional economic integration organization as defined in Article 1(6) of the Convention may agree that they shall jointly fulfil their obligations respecting consumption under this Article provided that their total combined calculated level of consumption does not exceed the levels required by this Article.

(b) The Parties to any such agreement shall inform the secretariat of the terms of the agreement before the date of the reduction in consumption with which the agreement is concerned.

(c) Such agreement will become operative only if all Member States of the regional economic integration organization and the organization concerned are Parties to the Protocol and have notified the secretariat of their manner of implementation.

9. (a) Based on the assessments made pursuant to Article 6, the Parties may decide whether:

(i) adjustments to the ozone depleting potentials specified in Annex A should be made and, if so, what the adjustments should be; and

(ii) further adjustments and reductions of production or consumption of the controlled substances from 1986 levels should be undertaken and, if so, what the scope, amount and timing of any such adjustments and reductions should be.

(b) Proposals for such adjustments shall be communicated to the Parties by the secretariat at least six months before the meeting of the Parties at which they are proposed for adoption.

(c) In taking such decisions, the Parties shall make every effort to reach agreement by consensus. If all efforts at consensus have been exhausted, and no agreement reached, such decisions shall, as a last resort, be adopted by a two-thirds majority vote of the Parties present and voting representing at least fifty per cent of the total consumption of the controlled substances of the Parties.

(d) The decisions, which shall be binding on all Parties, shall forthwith be communicated to the Parties by the Depositary. Unless otherwise provided in the decisions, they shall enter into force on the expiry of six months from the date of the circulation of the communication by the Depositary.

10.　(a) Based on the assessments made pursuant to Article 6 of this Protocol and in accordance with the procedure set out in Article 9 of the Convention, the Parties may decide:

(i) whether any substances, and if so which, should be added to or removed from any annex to this Protocol; and

(ii) the mechanism, scope and timing of the control measures that should apply to those substances;

(b) Any such decision shall become effective, provided that it has been accepted by a two-thirds majority vote of the Parties present and voting.

11.　Notwithstanding the provisions contained in this Article, Parties may take more stringent measures than those required by this Article.

Article 2A.　CFCS

1.　Each Party shall ensure that for the twelve-month period commencing on the first day of the seventh month following the date of the entry into force of this Protocol, and in each twelve-month period thereafter, its calculated level of consumption of the controlled substances in Group I of Annex A does not exceed its calculated level of consumption in 1986. By the end of the same period, each Party producing one or more of these substances shall ensure that its calculated level of production of the substances does not exceed its calculated level of production in 1986, except that such level may have increased by no more than ten per cent based on the 1986 level. Such increase shall be permitted only so as to satisfy the basic domestic needs of the Parties operating under Article 5 and for the purposes of industrial rationalization between Parties.

2.　Each Party shall ensure that for the period from 1 July 1991 to 31 December 1992 its calculated levels of consumption and production of the controlled substances in Group I of Annex A do not exceed 150 per cent of its calculated levels of production and consumption of those substances in 1986; with effect from 1 January 1993, the twelve-month control period for these controlled substances shall run from 1 January to 31 December each year.

3.　Each Party shall ensure that for the twelve-month period commencing on 1 January 1995, and in each twelve-month period thereafter, its calculated level of consumption of the controlled substances in Group I of Annex A does not exceed, annually, fifty per cent of its calculated level of consumption in 1986. Each Party producing one or more of these substances shall, for the same periods, ensure that its calculated level of production of the substances does not exceed, annually, fifty per cent of its calculated level of production in 1986. However, in order to satisfy the basic domestic needs of the Parties operating under paragraph 1 of Article 5, its calculated level of production may exceed that limit by up to ten per cent of its calculated level of production in 1986.

4. Each Party shall ensure that for the twelve-month period commencing on 1 January 1997, and in each twelve-month period thereafter, its calculated level of consumption of the controlled substances in Group I of Annex A does not exceed, annually, fifteen per cent of its calculated level of consumption in 1986. Each Party producing one or more of these substances shall, for the same periods, ensure that its calculated level of production of the substances does not exceed, annually, fifteen per cent of its calculated level of production in 1986. However, in order to satisfy the basic domestic needs of the Parties operating under paragraph 1 of Article 5, its calculated level of production may exceed that limit by up to 10 per cent of its calculated level of production in 1986.

5. Each Party shall ensure that for the twelve-month period commencing on 1 January 2000, and in each twelve-month period thereafter, its calculated level of consumption of the controlled substances in Group I of Annex A does not exceed zero. Each Party producing one or more of these substances shall, for the same periods, ensure that its calculated level of production of the substances does not exceed zero. However, in order to satisfy the basic domestic needs of the Parties operating under paragraph 1 of Article 5, its calculated level of production may exceed that limit by up to fifteen percent of its calculated level of production in 1986.

6. In 1992, the Parties will review the situation with the objective of accelerating the reduction schedule.

Article 2B. Halons

1. Each Party shall ensure that for the twelve-month period commencing on 1 January 1992, and in each twelve-month period thereafter, its calculated level of consumption of the controlled substances in Group II of Annex A does not exceed, annually, its calculated level of consumption in 1986. Each Party producing one or more of these substances shall, for the same periods, ensure that its calculated level of production of the substances does not exceed, annually, its calculated level of production in 1986. However, in order to satisfy the basic domestic needs of the Parties operating under paragraph 1 of Article 5, its calculated level of production may exceed that limit by up to ten per cent of its calculated level of production in 1986.

2. Each Party shall ensure that for the twelve-month period commencing on 1 January 1995, and in each twelve-month period thereafter, its calculated level of consumption of the controlled substances in Group II of Annex A does not exceed, annually, fifty per cent of its calculated level of consumption in 1986. Each Party producing one or more of these substances shall, for the same periods, ensure that its calculated level of production of the substances does not exceed, annually, fifty per cent of its calculated level of production in 1986. However, in order to satisfy the basic domestic needs of the Parties operating under paragraph 1 of Article 5, its calculated level of production may exceed that limit by up to ten per cent of its calculated level

of production in 1986. This paragraph will apply save to the extent that the Parties decide to permit the level of production or consumption that is necessary to satisfy essential uses for which no adequate alternatives are available.

3. Each Party shall ensure that for the twelve-month period commencing on 1 January 2000, and in each twelve-month period thereafter, its calculated level of consumption of the controlled substances in Group II of Annex A does not exceed zero. Each Party producing one or more of these substances shall, for the same periods, ensure that its calculated level of production of the substances does not exceed zero. However, in order to satisfy the basic domestic needs of the Parties operating under paragraph 1 of Article 5, its calculated level of production may exceed that limit by up to fifteen per cent of its calculated level of production in 1986. This paragraph will apply save to the extent that the Parties decide to permit the level of production or consumption that is necessary to satisfy essential uses for which no adequate alternatives are available.

4. By 1 January 1993, the Parties shall adopt a decision identifying essential uses, if any, for the purposes of paragraphs 2 and 3 of this Article. Such decision shall be reviewed by the Parties at their subsequent meetings.

ARTICLE 3. CALCULATION OF CONTROL LEVELS

For the purposes of Articles 2 and 5, each Party shall, for each Group of substances in Annex A, determine its calculated levels of:

(a) production by:

(i) multiplying its annual production of each controlled substance by the ozone depleting potential specified in respect of it in Annex A; and

(ii) adding together, for each such Group, the resulting figures;

(b) imports and exports, respectively, by following, *mutatis mutandis,* the procedure set out in subparagraph (a); and

(c) consumption by adding together its calculated levels of production and imports and subtracting its calculated level of exports as determined in accordance with subparagraphs (a) and (b). However, beginning on 1 January 1993, any export of controlled substances to non-Parties shall not be subtracted in calculating the consumption level of the exporting Party.

ARTICLE 4. CONTROL OF TRADE WITH NON–PARTIES

1. Within one year of the entry into force of this Protocol, each Party shall ban the import of controlled substances from any State not party to this Protocol.

2. Beginning on 1 January 1993, no Party operating under paragraph 1 of Article 5 may export any controlled substance to any State not party to this Protocol.

3.　Within three years of the date of the entry into force of this Protocol, the Parties shall, following the procedures in Article 10 of the Convention, elaborate in an annex a list of products containing controlled substances. Parties that have not objected to the annex in accordance with those procedures shall ban, within one year of the annex having become effective, the import of those products from any State not party to this Protocol.

4.　Within five years of the entry into force of this Protocol, the Parties shall determine the feasibility of banning or restricting, from States not party to this Protocol, the import of products produced with, but not containing, controlled substances. If determined feasible, the Parties shall, following the procedures in Article 10 of the Convention, elaborate in an annex a list of such products. Parties that have not objected to it in accordance with those procedures shall ban or restrict, within one year of the annex having become effective, the import of those products from any State not party to this Protocol.

5.　Each Party shall discourage the export, to any State not party to this Protocol, of technology for producing and for utilizing controlled substances.

6.　Each Party shall refrain from providing new subsidies, aid, credits, guarantees or insurance programmes for the export to States not party to this Protocol of products, equipment, plants or technology that would facilitate the production of controlled substances.

7.　Paragraphs 5 and 6 shall not apply to products, equipment, plants or technology that improve the containment, recovery, recycling or destruction of controlled substances, promote the development of alternative substances, or otherwise contribute to the reduction of emissions of controlled substances.

8.　Notwithstanding the provisions of this Article, imports referred to in paragraphs 1, 3 and 4 may be permitted from any State not party to this Protocol if that State is determined, by a meeting of the Parties, to be in full compliance with Article 2 and this Article, and has submitted data to that effect as specified in Article 7.

ARTICLE 5.　SPECIAL SITUATION OF DEVELOPING COUNTRIES

1.　Any Party that is a developing country and whose annual calculated level of consumption of the controlled substances is less than 0.3 kilograms per capita on the date of the entry into force of the Protocol for it, or any time thereafter within ten years of the date of entry into force of the Protocol shall, in order to meet its basic domestic needs, be entitled to delay its compliance with the control measures set out in paragraphs 1 to 4 of Article 2 by ten years after that specified in those paragraphs. However, such Party shall not exceed an annual calculated level of consumption of 0.3 kilograms per capita. Any such Party shall be entitled to use either the average of its annual calculated level of consumption for the period 1995 to 1997 inclusive or a calculated level of consumption of 0.3 kilograms per capita, whichever is the lower, as the basis for its compliance with the control measures.

2. The Parties undertake to facilitate access to environmentally safe alternative substances and technology for Parties that are developing countries and assist them to make expeditious use of such alternatives.

3. The Parties undertake to facilitate bilaterally or multilaterally the provision of subsidies, aid, credits, guarantees or insurance programmes to Parties that are developing countries for the use of alternative technology and for substitute products.

ARTICLE 6. ASSESSMENT AND REVIEW OF CONTROL MEASURES

Beginning in 1990, and at least every four years thereafter, the Parties shall assess the control measures provided for in Article 2 on the basis of available scientific, environmental, technical and economic information. At least one year before each assessment, the Parties shall convene appropriate panels of experts qualified in the fields mentioned and determine the composition and terms of reference of any such panels. Within one year of being convened, the panels will report their conclusions, through the secretariat, to the Parties.

ARTICLE 7. REPORTING OF DATA

1. Each Party shall provide to the secretariat, within three months of becoming a Party, statistical data on its production, imports and exports of each of the controlled substances for the year 1986, or the best possible estimates of such data where actual data are not available.

2. Each Party shall provide statistical data to the secretariat on its annual production (with separate data on amounts destroyed by technologies to be approved by the Parties), imports, and exports to Parties and non-Parties, respectively, of such substances for the year during which it becomes a Party and for each year thereafter. It shall forward the data no later than nine months after the end of the year to which the data relate.

ARTICLE 8. NON-COMPLIANCE

The Parties, at their first meeting, shall consider and approve procedures and institutional mechanisms for determining non-compliance with the provisions of this Protocol and for treatment of Parties found to be in non-compliance.

ARTICLE 9. RESEARCH, DEVELOPMENT, PUBLIC AWARENESS AND EXCHANGE OF INFORMATION

1. The Parties shall co-operate, consistent with their national laws, regulations and practices and taking into account in particular the needs of developing countries, in promoting, directly or through competent international bodies, research, development and exchange of information on:

(a) best technologies for improving the containment, recovery, recycling or destruction of controlled substances or otherwise reducing their emissions;

(b) possible alternatives to controlled substances, to products containing such substances, and to products manufactured with them; and

(c) costs and benefits of relevant control strategies.

2. The Parties, individually, jointly or through competent international bodies, shall co-operate in promoting public awareness of the environmental effects of the emissions of controlled substances and other substances that deplete the ozone layer.

3. Within two years of the entry into force of this Protocol and every two years thereafter, each Party shall submit to the secretariat a summary of the activities it has conducted pursuant to this Article.

ARTICLE 10. TECHNICAL ASSISTANCE

1. The Parties shall, in the context of the provisions of Article 4 of the Convention, and taking into account in particular the needs of developing countries, co-operate in promoting technical assistance to facilitate participation in and implementation of this Protocol.

2. Any Party or Signatory to this Protocol may submit a request to the secretariat for technical assistance for the purposes of implementing or participating in the Protocol.

3. The Parties, at their first meeting, shall begin deliberations on the means of fulfilling the obligations set out in Article 9, and paragraphs 1 and 2 of this Article, including the preparation of workplans. Such workplans shall pay special attention to the needs and circumstances of the developing countries. States and regional economic integration organizations not party to the Protocol should be encouraged to participate in activities specified in such workplans.

ARTICLE 11. MEETINGS OF THE PARTIES

1. The Parties shall hold meetings at regular intervals. The secretariat shall convene the first meeting of the Parties not later than one year after the date of the entry into force of this Protocol and in conjunction with a meeting of the Conference of the Parties to the Convention, if a meeting of the latter is scheduled within that period.

2. Subsequent ordinary meetings of the Parties shall be held, unless the Parties otherwise decide, in conjunction with meetings of the Conference of the Parties to the Convention. Extraordinary meetings of the Parties shall be held at such other times as may be deemed necessary by a meeting of the Parties, or at the written request of any Party, provided that, within six months of such a request being communicated to them by the secretariat, it is supported by at least one third of the Parties.

3. The Parties, at their first meeting, shall:

(a) adopt by consensus rules of procedure for their meetings;

(b) adopt by consensus the financial rules referred to in paragraph 2 of Article 13;

(c) establish the panels and determine the terms of reference referred to in Article 6;

(d) consider and approve the procedures and institutional mechanisms specified in Article 8; and

(e) begin preparation of workplans pursuant to paragraph 3 of Article 10.

4. The functions of the meetings of the Parties shall be to:

(a) review the implementation of this Protocol;

(b) decide on any adjustments or reductions referred to in paragraph 9 of Article 2;

(c) decide on any addition to, insertion in or removal from any annex of substances and on related control measures in accordance with paragraph 10 of Article 2;

(d) establish, where necessary, guidelines or procedures for reporting of information as provided for in Article 7 and paragraph 3 of Article 9;

(e) review requests for technical assistance submitted pursuant to paragraph 2 of Article 10;

(f) review reports prepared by the secretariat pursuant to subparagraph (c) of Article 12;

(g) assess, in accordance with Article 6, the control measures provided for in Article 2;

(h) consider and adopt, as required, proposals for amendment of this Protocol or any annex and for any new annex;

(i) consider and adopt the budget for implementing this Protocol; and

(j) consider and undertake any additional action that may be required for the achievement of the purposes of this Protocol.

5. The United Nations, its specialized agencies and the International Atomic Energy Agency, as well as any State not party to this Protocol, may be represented at meetings of the Parties as observers. Any body or agency, whether national or international, governmental or non-governmental, qualified in fields relating to the protection of the ozone layer which has informed the secretariat of its wish to be represented at a meeting of the Parties as an observer may be admitted unless at least one third of the Parties present object. The admission and participation of observers shall be subject to the rules of procedure adopted by the Parties.

ARTICLE 12.　SECRETARIAT

For the purposes of this Protocol, the secretariat shall:

(a) arrange for and service meetings of the Parties as provided for in Article 11;

(b) receive and make available, upon request by a Party, data provided pursuant to Article 7;

(c) prepare and distribute regularly to the Parties reports based on information received pursuant to Articles 7 and 9;

(d) notify the Parties of any request for technical assistance received pursuant to Article 10 so as to facilitate the provision of such assistance;

(e) encourage non-Parties to attend the meetings of the Parties as observers and to act in accordance with the provisions of this Protocol;

(f) provide, as appropriate, the information and requests referred to in subparagraphs (c) and (d) to such non-party observers;　and

(g) perform such other functions for the achievement of the purposes of this Protocol as may be assigned to it by the Parties.

ARTICLE 13.　FINANCIAL PROVISIONS

1.　The funds required for the operation of this Protocol, including those for the functioning of the secretariat related to this Protocol, shall be charged exclusively against contributions from the Parties.

2.　The Parties, at their first meeting, shall adopt by consensus financial rules for the operation of this Protocol.

ARTICLE 14.　RELATIONSHIP OF THIS PROTOCOL TO THE CONVENTION

Except as otherwise provided in this Protocol, the provisions of the Convention relating to its protocols shall apply to this Protocol.

ARTICLE 15.　SIGNATURE

This Protocol shall be open for signature by States and by regional economic integration organizations in Montreal on 16 September 1987, in Ottawa from 17 September 1987 to 16 January 1988, and at United Nations Headquarters in New York from 17 January 1988 to 15 September 1988.

ARTICLE 16.　ENTRY INTO FORCE

1.　This Protocol shall enter into force on 1 January 1989, provided that at least eleven instruments of ratification, acceptance, approval of the Protocol or accession thereto have been deposited by States or regional economic integration organizations representing at least two-thirds of 1986 estimated global consumption of the controlled substances, and the provisions of paragraph 1 of Article 17 of the Convention have been fulfilled.　In the event that these conditions have not been fulfilled by that date, the Protocol shall enter into force on the ninetieth day following the date on which the conditions have been fulfilled.

2. For the purposes of paragraph 1, any such instrument deposited by a regional economic integration organization shall not be counted as additional to those deposited by member States of such organization.

3. After the entry into force of this Protocol, any State or regional economic integration organization shall become a Party to it on the ninetieth day following the date of deposit of its instrument of ratification, acceptance, approval or accession.

ARTICLE 17. PARTIES JOINING AFTER ENTRY INTO FORCE

Subject to Article 5, any State or regional economic integration organization which becomes a Party to this Protocol after the date of its entry into force, shall fulfil forthwith the sum of the obligations under Article 2, as well as under Article 4, that apply at that date to the States and regional economic integration organizations that became Parties on the date the Protocol entered into force.

ARTICLE 18. RESERVATIONS

No reservations may be made to this Protocol.

ARTICLE 19. WITHDRAWAL

For the purposes of this Protocol, the provisions of Article 19 of the Convention relating to withdrawal shall apply, except with respect to Parties referred to in paragraph 1 of Article 5. Any such Party may withdraw from this Protocol by giving written notification to the Depositary at any time after four years of assuming the obligations specified in paragraphs 1 to 4 of Article 2. Any such withdrawal shall take effect upon expiry of one year after the date of its receipt by the Depositary, or on such later date as may be specified in the notification of the withdrawal.

ARTICLE 20. AUTHENTIC TEXTS

The original of this Protocol, of which the Arabic, Chinese, English, French, Russian and Spanish texts are equally authentic, shall be deposited with the Secretary–General of the United Nations.

ANNEX A
CONTROLLED SUBSTANCES

Group	Substance	Ozone Depleting Potential
Group I		
	$CFCl_3$ (CFC–11)	1.0
	CF_2Cl_2 (CFC–12)	1.0
	$C_2F_3Cl_3$ (CFC–113)	0.8
	$C_2F_4Cl_2$ (CFC–114)	1.0
	C_2F_5Cl (CFC–115)	0.6
Group II		
	CF_2BrCl (halon–1211)	3.0
	CF_3Br (halon–1301)	10.0
	$C_2F_4Br_2$ (halon–2402)	(to be determined)

附錄八：赫爾辛基宣言

HELSINKI DECLARATION ON THE PROTECTION OF THE OZONE LAYER.[1] Adopted at the First Meetings of the Parties to the 1985 Vienna Convention and the 1987 Montreal Protocol at Helsinki, 2 May 1989.　28 I.L.M. 1335 (1989)

The Governments and the European Communities represented at the First Meetings of the Parties to the Vienna Convention and the Montreal Protocol

Aware of the wide agreement among scientists that depletion of the ozone layer will threaten present and future generations unless more stringent control measures are adopted

Mindful that some ozone depleting substances are powerful greenhouse gases leading to global warming

Aware also of the extensive and rapid technological development of environmentally acceptable substitutes for the substances that deplete the ozone layer and the urgent need to facilitate the transfer of technologies of such substitutes especially to developing countries

ENCOURAGE all states that have not done so to join the Vienna Convention for the Protection of the Ozone Layer and its Montreal Protocol

AGREE to phase out the production and the consumption of CFC's controlled by the Montreal Protocol as soon as possible but not later than the year 2000 and for that purpose to tighten the timetable agreed upon in the Montreal Protocol taking due account of the special situation of developing countries

AGREE to both phase out halons and control and reduce other ozone-depleting substances which contribute significantly to ozone depletion as soon as feasible

AGREE to commit themselves, in proportion to their means and resources, to accelerate the development of environmentally acceptable substituting chemicals, products and technologies

AGREE to facilitate the access of developing countries to relevant scientific information, research results and training and to seek to develop appropriate funding mechanisms to facilitate the transfer of technology and replacement of equipment at minimum cost to developing countries.

附錄九：聯合國氣候變遷架構公約

UNITED NATIONS FRAMEWORK CONVENTION ON CLIMATE CHANGE (WITHOUT ANNEXES I & II). Concluded at Rio de Janeiro, 29 May 1992. Entered into force 21 March 1994. 31 I.L.M. 849 (1992)

The Parties to this Convention,

Acknowledging that change in the Earth's climate and its adverse effects are a common concern of humankind,

Concerned that human activities have been substantially increasing the atmospheric concentrations of greenhouse gases, that these increases enhance the natural greenhouse effect, and that this will result on average in an additional warming of the Earth's surface and atmosphere and may adversely affect natural ecosystems and humankind,

Noting that the largest share of historical and current global emissions of greenhouse gases has originated in developed countries, that per capita emissions in developing countries are still relatively low and that the share of global emissions originating in developing countries will grow to meet their social and development needs,

Aware of the role and importance in terrestrial and marine ecosystems of sinks and reservoirs of greenhouse gases,

Noting that there are many uncertainties in predictions of climate change, particularly with regard to the timing, magnitude and regional patterns thereof,

Acknowledging that the global nature of climate change calls for the widest possible cooperation by all countries and their participation in an effective and appropriate international response, in accordance with their common but differentiated responsibilities and respective capabilities and their social and economic conditions,

Recalling the pertinent provisions of the Declaration of the United Nations Conference on the Human Environment, adopted at Stockholm on 16 June 1972,

Recalling also that States have, in accordance with the Charter of the United Nations and the principles of international law, the sovereign right to exploit their own resources pursuant to their own environmental and developmental policies, and the responsibility to ensure that activities within their jurisdiction or control do not cause damage to the environment of other States or of areas beyond the limits of national jurisdiction,

Reaffirming the principle of sovereignty of States in international cooperation to address climate change,

Recognizing that States should enact effective environmental legislation, that environmental standards, management objectives and priorities should reflect the environmental and developmental context to which they apply, and that standards applied by some countries may be inappropriate and of unwarranted economic and social cost to other countries, in particular developing countries,

Recalling the provisions of General Assembly resolution 44/228 of 22 December 1989 on the United Nations Conference on Environment and Development, and resolutions 43/53 of 6 December 1988, 44/207 of 22 December 1989, 45/212 of 21 December 1990 and 46/169 of 19 December 1991 on protection of global climate for present and future generations of mankind,

Recalling also the provisions of General Assembly resolution 44/206 of 22 December 1989 on the possible adverse effects of sealevel rise on islands and coastal areas, particularly low-lying coastal areas and the pertinent provisions of General Assembly resolution 44/172 of 19 December 1989 on the implementation of the Plan of Action to Combat Desertification,

Recalling further the Vienna Convention for the Protection of the Ozone Layer, 1985, and the Montreal Protocol on Substances that Deplete the Ozone Layer, 1987, as adjusted and amended on 29 June 1990,

Noting the Ministerial Declaration of the Second World Climate Conference adopted on 7 November 1990,

Conscious of the valuable analytical work being conducted by many States on climate change and of the important contributions of the World Meteorological Organization, the United Nations Environment Programme and other organs, organizations and bodies of the United Nations system, as well as other international and intergovernmental bodies, to the exchange of results of scientific research and the coordination of research,

Recognizing that steps required to understand and address climate change will be environmentally, socially and economically most effective if they are based on relevant scientific, technical and economic considerations and continually re-evaluated in the light of new findings in these areas,

Recognizing that various actions to address climate change can be justified economically in their own right and can also help in solving other environmental problems,

Recognizing also the need for developed countries to take immediate action in a flexible manner on the basis of clear priorities, as a first step towards comprehensive response strategies at the global, national and, where agreed, regional levels that take into account all greenhouse gases, with due consideration of their relative contributions to the enhancement of the greenhouse effect,

Recognizing further that low-lying and other small island countries, countries with low-lying coastal, arid and semi-arid areas or areas liable to floods, drought and desertification, and developing countries with fragile mountainous ecosystems are particularly vulnerable to the adverse effects of climate change,

Recognizing the special difficulties of those countries, especially developing countries, whose economies are particularly dependent on fossil fuel production, use and exportation, as a consequence of action taken on limiting greenhouse gas emissions,

Affirming that responses to climate change should be coordinated with social and economic development in an integrated manner with a view to avoiding adverse impacts on the latter, taking into full account the legitimate priority needs of developing countries for the achievement of sustained economic growth and the eradication of poverty,

Recognizing that all countries, especially developing countries, need access to resources required to achieve sustainable social and economic development and that, in order for developing countries to progress towards that goal, their energy consumption will need to grow taking into account the possibilities for achieving greater energy efficiency and for controlling greenhouse gas emissions in general, including through the application of new technologies on terms which make such an application economically and socially beneficial,

Determined to protect the climate system for present and future generations,

Have agreed as follows:

ARTICLE 1
DEFINITIONS

For the purposes of this Convention:

1. "Adverse effects of climate change" means changes in the physical environment or biota resulting from climate change which have significant deleterious effects on the composition, resilience or productivity of natural and managed ecosystems or on the operation of socio-economic systems or on human health and welfare.

2. "Climate change" means a change of climate which is attributed directly or indirectly to human activity that alters the composition of the global atmosphere and which is in addition to natural climate variability observed over comparable time periods.

3. "Climate system" means the totality of the atmosphere, hydrosphere, biosphere and geosphere and their interactions.

4. "Emissions" means the release of greenhouse gases and/or their precursors into the atmosphere over a specified area and period of time.

5. "Greenhouse gases" means those gaseous constituents of the atmosphere, both natural and anthropogenic, that absorb and re-emit infrared radiation.

6. "Regional economic integration organization" means an organization constituted by sovereign States of a given region which has competence in

respect of matters governed by this Convention or its protocols and has been duly authorized, in accordance with its internal procedures, to sign, ratify, accept, approve or accede to the instruments concerned.

7. "Reservoir" means a component or components of the climate system where a greenhouse gas or a precursor of a greenhouse gas is stored.

8. "Sink" means any process, activity or mechanism which removes a greenhouse gas, an aerosol or a precursor of a greenhouse gas from the atmosphere.

9. "Source" means any process or activity which releases a greenhouse gas, an aerosol or a precursor of a greenhouse gas into the atmosphere.

ARTICLE 2
OBJECTIVE

The ultimate objective of this Convention and any related legal instruments that the Conference of the Parties may adopt is to achieve, in accordance with the relevant provisions of the Convention, stabilization of greenhouse gas concentrations in the atmosphere at a level that would prevent dangerous anthropogenic interference with the climate system. Such a level should be achieved within a time-frame sufficient to allow ecosystems to adapt naturally to climate change, to ensure that food production is not threatened and to enable economic development to proceed in a sustainable manner.

ARTICLE 3
PRINCIPLES

In their actions to achieve the objective of the Convention and to implement its provisions, the Parties shall be guided, *inter alia,* by the following:

1. The Parties should protect the climate system for the benefit of present and future generations of humankind, on the basis of equity and in accordance with their common but differentiated responsibilities and respective capabilities. Accordingly, the developed country Parties should take the lead in combating climate change and the adverse effects thereof.

2. The specific needs and special circumstances of developing country Parties, especially those that are particularly vulnerable to the adverse effects of climate change, and of those Parties, especially developing country Parties, that would have to bear a disproportionate or abnormal burden under the Convention, should be given full consideration.

3. The Parties should take precautionary measures to anticipate, prevent or minimize the causes of climate change and mitigate its adverse effects. Where there are threats of serious or irreversible damage, lack of full scientific certainty should not be used as a reason for postponing such

measures, taking into account that policies and measures to deal with climate change should be cost-effective so as to ensure global benefits at the lowest possible cost. To achieve this, such policies and measures should take into account different socio-economic contexts, be comprehensive, cover all relevant sources, sinks and reservoirs of greenhouse gases and adaptation, and comprise all economic sectors. Efforts to address climate change may be carried out cooperatively by interested Parties.

4. The Parties have a right to, and should, promote sustainable development. Policies and measures to protect the climate system against human-induced change should be appropriate for the specific conditions of each Party and should be integrated with national development programmes, taking into account that economic development is essential for adopting measures to address climate change.

5. The Parties should cooperate to promote a supportive and open international economic system that would lead to sustainable economic growth and development in all Parties, particularly developing country Parties, thus enabling them better to address the problems of climate change. Measures taken to combat climate change, including unilateral ones, should not constitute a means of arbitrary or unjustifiable discrimination or a disguised restriction on international trade.

ARTICLE 4
COMMITMENTS

1. All Parties, taking into account their common but differentiated responsibilities and their specific national and regional development priorities, objectives and circumstances, shall:

(a) Develop, periodically update, publish and make available to the Conference of the Parties, in accordance with Article 12, national inventories of anthropogenic emissions by sources and removals by sinks of all greenhouse gases not controlled by the Montreal Protocol, using comparable methodologies to be agreed upon by the Conference of the Parties;

(b) Formulate, implement, publish and regularly update national and, where appropriate, regional programmes containing measures to mitigate climate change by addressing anthropogenic emissions by sources and removals by sinks of all greenhouse gases not controlled by the Montreal Protocol, and measures to facilitate adequate adaptation to climate change;

(c) Promote and cooperate in the development, application and diffusion, including transfer, of technologies, practices and processes that control, reduce or prevent anthropogenic emissions of greenhouse gases not controlled by the Montreal Protocol in all relevant sectors, including the energy, transport, industry, agriculture, forestry and waste management sectors;

(d) Promote sustainable management, and promote and cooperate in the conservation and enhancement, as appropriate, of sinks and reservoirs of all greenhouse gases not controlled by the Montreal Protocol, including biomass, forests and oceans as well as other terrestrial, coastal and marine ecosystems;

(e) Cooperate in preparing for adaptation to the impacts of climate change; develop and elaborate appropriate and integrated plans for coastal zone management, water resources and agriculture, and for the protection and rehabilitation of areas, particularly in Africa, affected by drought and desertification, as well as floods;

(f) Take climate change considerations into account, to the extent feasible, in their relevant social, economic and environmental policies and actions, and employ appropriate methods, for example impact assessments, formulated and determined nationally, with a view to minimizing adverse effects on the economy, on public health and on the quality of the environment, of projects or measures undertaken by them to mitigate or adapt to climate change;

(g) Promote and cooperate in scientific, technological, technical, socio-economic and other research, systematic observation and development of data archives related to the climate system and intended to further the understanding and to reduce or eliminate the remaining uncertainties regarding the causes, effects, magnitude and timing of climate change and the economic and social consequences of various response strategies;

(h) Promote and cooperate in the full, open and prompt exchange of relevant scientific, technological, technical, socio-economic and legal information related to the climate system and climate change, and to the economic and social consequences of various response strategies;

(i) Promote and cooperate in education, training and public awareness related to climate change and encourage the widest participation in this process, including that of non-governmental organizations; and

(j) Communicate to the Conference of the Parties information related to implementation, in accordance with Article 12.

2. The developed country Parties and other Parties included in annex I commit themselves specifically as provided for in the following:

(a) Each of these Parties shall adopt national policies and take corresponding measures on the mitigation of climate change, by limiting its anthropogenic emissions of greenhouse gases and protecting and enhancing its greenhouse gas sinks and reservoirs. These policies and measures will demonstrate that developed countries are taking the lead in modifying longer-term trends in anthropogenic emissions consistent with the objective of the Convention, recognizing that the return by the end of the present decade to earlier levels of anthropogenic emissions of carbon dioxide and other greenhouse gases not controlled by the Montreal Protocol would contribute to such modification, and taking into account the differences in these Parties' starting points and approaches, economic structures and resource bases, the need to maintain strong and sustainable economic growth, available technologies and other individual circumstances, as well as the need for equitable and appropriate contributions by each of these Parties to the global effort regarding that objective. These Parties may implement such policies and measures jointly with other Parties and may assist other Parties in contributing to the achievement of the objective of the Convention and, in particular, that of this subparagraph;

(b) In order to promote progress to this end, each of these Parties shall communicate, within six months of the entry into force of the Convention for it and periodically thereafter, and in accordance with Article 12, detailed information on its policies and measures referred to in subparagraph (a) above, as well as on its resulting projected anthropogenic emissions by sources and removals by sinks of greenhouse gases not controlled by the Montreal Protocol for the period referred to in subparagraph (a), with the aim of returning individually or jointly to their 1990 levels these anthropogenic emissions of carbon dioxide and other greenhouse gases not controlled by the Montreal Protocol. This information will be reviewed by the Conference of the Parties, at its first session and periodically thereafter, in accordance with Article 7;

(c) Calculations of emissions by sources and removals by sinks of greenhouse gases for the purposes of subparagraph (b) above should take into account the best available scientific knowledge, including the effective capacity of sinks and the respective contributions of such gases to climate change. The Conference of the Parties shall consider and agree on methodologies for these calculations at its first session and review them regularly thereafter;

(d) The Conference of the Parties shall, at its first session, review the adequacy of subparagraphs (a) and (b) above. Such review shall be carried out in the light of the best available scientific information and assessment on climate change and its impacts, as well as relevant technical, social and economic information. Based on this review, the Conference of the Parties shall take appropriate action, which may include the adoption of amendments to the commitments in subparagraphs (a) and (b) above. The Conference of the Parties, at its first session, shall also take decisions regarding criteria for joint implementation as indicated in subparagraph (a) above. A second review of subparagraphs (a) and (b) shall take place not later than 31 December 1998, and thereafter at regular intervals determined by the Conference of the Parties, until the objective of the Convention is met;

(e) Each of these Parties shall:

(i) coordinate as appropriate with other such Parties, relevant economic and administrative instruments developed to achieve the objective of the Convention; and

(ii) identify and periodically review its own policies and practices which encourage activities that lead to greater levels of anthropogenic emissions of greenhouse gases not controlled by the Montreal Protocol than would otherwise occur;

(f) The Conference of the Parties shall review, not later than 31 December 1998, available information with a view to taking decisions regarding such amendments to the lists in annexes I and II as may be appropriate, with the approval of the Party concerned;

(g) Any Party not included in annex I may, in its instrument of ratification, acceptance, approval or accession, or at any time thereafter, notify the Depositary that it intends to be bound by subparagraphs (a) and (b) above. The Depositary shall inform the other signatories and Parties of any such notification.

3. The developed country Parties and other developed Parties included in annex II shall provide new and additional financial resources to meet the agreed full costs incurred by developing country Parties in complying with their obligations under Article 12, paragraph 1. They shall also provide such financial resources, including for the transfer of technology, needed by the developing country Parties to meet the agreed full incremental costs of implementing measures that are covered by paragraph 1 of this Article and that are agreed between a developing country Party and the international entity or entities referred to in Article 11, in accordance with that Article. The implementation of these commitments shall take into account the need for adequacy and predictability in the flow of funds and the importance of appropriate burden sharing among the developed country Parties.

4. The developed country Parties and other developed Parties included in annex II shall also assist the developing country Parties that are particularly vulnerable to the adverse effects of climate change in meeting costs of adaptation to those adverse effects.

5. The developed country Parties and other developed Parties included in annex II shall take all practicable steps to promote, facilitate and finance, as appropriate, the transfer of, or access to, environmentally sound technologies and know-how to other Parties, particularly developing country Parties, to enable them to implement the provisions of the Convention. In this process, the developed country Parties shall support the development and enhancement of endogenous capacities and technologies of developing country Parties. Other Parties and organizations in a position to do so may also assist in facilitating the transfer of such technologies.

6.　In the implementation of their commitments under paragraph 2 above, a certain degree of flexibility shall be allowed by the Conference of the Parties to the Parties included in annex I undergoing the process of transition to a market economy, in order to enhance the ability of these Parties to address climate change, including with regard to the historical level of anthropogenic emissions of greenhouse gases not controlled by the Montreal Protocol chosen as a reference.

7.　The extent to which developing country Parties will effectively implement their commitments under the Convention will depend on the effective implementation by developed country Parties of their commitments under the Convention related to financial resources and transfer of technology and will take fully into account that economic and social development and poverty eradication are the first and overriding priorities of the developing country Parties.

8.　In the implementation of the commitments in this Article, the Parties shall give full consideration to what actions are necessary under the Convention, including actions related to funding, insurance and the transfer of technology, to meet the specific needs and concerns of developing country Parties arising from the adverse effects of climate change and/or the impact of the implementation of response measures, especially on:

(a) Small island countries;

(b) Countries with low-lying coastal areas;

(c) Countries with arid and semi-arid areas, forested areas and areas liable to forest decay;

(d) Countries with areas prone to natural disasters;

(e) Countries with areas liable to drought and desertification;

(f) Countries with areas of high urban atmospheric pollution;

(g) Countries with areas with fragile ecosystems, including mountainous ecosystems;

(h) Countries whose economies are highly dependent on income generated from the production, processing and export, and/or on consumption of fossil fuels and associated energy-intensive products; and

(i) Land-locked and transit countries.

Further, the Conference of the Parties may take actions, as appropriate, with respect to this paragraph.

9.　The Parties shall take full account of the specific needs and special situations of the least developed countries in their actions with regard to funding and transfer of technology.

10. The Parties shall, in accordance with Article 10, take into consideration in the implementation of the commitments of the Convention the situation of Parties, particularly developing country Parties, with economies that are vulnerable to the adverse effects of the implementation of measures to respond to climate change. This applies notably to Parties with economies that are highly dependent on income generated from the production, processing and export, and/or consumption of fossil fuels and associated energy-intensive products and/or the use of fossil fuels for which such Parties have serious difficulties in switching to alternatives.

ARTICLE 5
RESEARCH AND SYSTEMATIC OBSERVATION

In carrying out their commitments under Article 4, paragraph 1(g), the Parties shall:

(a) Support and further develop, as appropriate, international and intergovernmental programmes and networks or organizations aimed at defining, conducting, assessing and financing research, data collection and systematic observation, taking into account the need to minimize duplication of effort;

(b) Support international and intergovernmental efforts to strengthen systematic observation and national scientific and technical research capacities and capabilities, particularly in developing countries, and to promote access to, and the exchange of, data and analyses thereof obtained from areas beyond national jurisdiction; and

(c) Take into account the particular concerns and needs of developing countries and cooperate in improving their endogenous capacities and capabilities to participate in the efforts referred to in subparagraphs (a) and (b) above.

ARTICLE 6
EDUCATION, TRAINING AND PUBLIC AWARENESS

In carrying out their commitments under Article 4, paragraph 1(i), the Parties shall:

(a) Promote and facilitate at the national and, as appropriate, subregional and regional levels, and in accordance with national laws and regulations, and within their respective capacities:

(i) the development and implementation of educational and public awareness programmes on climate change and its effects;

(ii) public access to information on climate change and its effects;

(iii) public participation in addressing climate change and its effects and developing adequate responses; and

(iv) training of scientific, technical and managerial personnel.

(b) Cooperate in and promote, at the international level, and, where appropriate, using existing bodies:

(i) the development and exchange of educational and public awareness material on climate change and its effects; and

(ii) the development and implementation of education and training programmes, including the strengthening of national institutions and the exchange or secondment of personnel to train experts in this field, in particular for developing countries.

ARTICLE 7
CONFERENCE OF THE PARTIES

1.　A Conference of the Parties is hereby established.

2.　The Conference of the Parties, as the supreme body of this Convention, shall keep under regular review the implementation of the Convention and any related legal instruments that the Conference of the Parties may adopt, and shall make, within its mandate, the decisions necessary to promote the effective implementation of the Convention.　To this end, it shall:

(a) Periodically examine the obligations of the Parties and the institutional arrangements under the Convention, in the light of the objective of the Convention, the experience gained in its implementation and the evolution of scientific and technological knowledge;

(b) Promote and facilitate the exchange of information on measures adopted by the Parties to address climate change and its effects, taking into account the differing circumstances, responsibilities and capabilities of the Parties and their respective commitments under the Convention;

(c) Facilitate, at the request of two or more Parties, the coordination of measures adopted by them to address climate change and its effects, taking into account the differing circumstances, responsibilities and capabilities of the Parties and their respective commitments under the Convention;

(d) Promote and guide, in accordance with the objective and provisions of the Convention, the development and periodic refinement of comparable methodologies, to be agreed on by the Conference of the Parties, *inter alia,* for preparing inventories of greenhouse gas emissions by sources and removals by sinks, and for evaluating the effectiveness of measures to limit the emissions and enhance the removals of these gases;

(e) Assess, on the basis of all information made available to it in accordance with the provisions of the Convention, the implementation of the Convention by the Parties, the overall effects of the measures taken pursuant to the Convention, in particular environmental, economic and social effects as well as their cumulative impacts and the extent to which progress towards the objective of the Convention is being achieved;

(f) Consider and adopt regular reports on the implementation of the Convention and ensure their publication;

(g) Make recommendations on any matters necessary for the implementation of the Convention;

(h) Seek to mobilize financial resources in accordance with Article 4, paragraphs 3, 4 and 5, and Article 11;

(i) Establish such subsidiary bodies as are deemed necessary for the implementation of the Convention;

(j) Review reports submitted by its subsidiary bodies and provide guidance to them;

(k) Agree upon and adopt, by consensus, rules of procedure and financial rules for itself and for any subsidiary bodies;

(l) Seek and utilize, where appropriate, the services and cooperation of, and information provided by, competent international organizations and intergovernmental and non-governmental bodies; and

(m) Exercise such other functions as are required for the achievement of the objective of the Convention as well as all other functions assigned to it under the Convention.

3. The Conference of the Parties shall, at its first session, adopt its own rules of procedure as well as those of the subsidiary bodies established by the Convention, which shall include decision-making procedures for matters not already covered by decision-making procedures stipulated in the Convention. Such procedures may include specified majorities required for the adoption of particular decisions.

4. The first session of the Conference of the Parties shall be convened by the interim secretariat referred to in Article 21 and shall take place not later than one year after the date of entry into force of the Convention. Thereafter, ordinary sessions of the Conference of the Parties shall be held every year unless otherwise decided by the Conference of the Parties.

5. Extraordinary sessions of the Conference of the Parties shall be held at such other times as may be deemed necessary by the Conference, or at the written request of any Party, provided that, within six months of the request being communicated to the Parties by the secretariat, it is supported by at least one-third of the Parties.

6. The United Nations, its specialized agencies and the International Atomic Energy Agency, as well as any State member thereof or observers thereto not Party to the Convention, may be represented at sessions of the Conference of the Parties as observers. Any body or agency, whether national or international, governmental or non-governmental, which is qualified in matters covered by the Convention, and which has informed the secretariat of its wish to be represented at a session of the Conference of the Parties as an observer, may be so admitted unless at least one-third of the Parties present object. The admission and participation of observers shall be subject to the rules of procedure adopted by the Conference of the Parties.

ARTICLE 8
SECRETARIAT

1. A secretariat is hereby established.

2. The functions of the secretariat shall be:

(a) To make arrangements for sessions of the Conference of the Parties and its subsidiary bodies established under the Convention and to provide them with services as required;

(b) To compile and transmit reports submitted to it;

(c) To facilitate assistance to the Parties, particularly developing country Parties, on request, in the compilation and communication of information required in accordance with the provisions of the Convention;

(d) To prepare reports on its activities and present them to the Conference of the Parties;

(e) To ensure the necessary coordination with the secretariats of other relevant international bodies;

(f) To enter, under the overall guidance of the Conference of the Parties, into such administrative and contractual arrangements as may be required for the effective discharge of its functions; and

(g) To perform the other secretariat functions specified in the Convention and in any of its protocols and such other functions as may be determined by the Conference of the Parties.

3. The Conference of the Parties, at its first session, shall designate a permanent secretariat and make arrangements for its functioning.

ARTICLE 9
SUBSIDIARY BODY FOR SCIENTIFIC AND TECHNOLOGICAL ADVICE

1. A subsidiary body for scientific and technological advice is hereby established to provide the Conference of the Parties and, as appropriate, its other subsidiary bodies with timely information and advice on scientific and technological matters relating to the Convention. This body shall be open to participation by all Parties and shall be multidisciplinary. It shall comprise government representatives competent in the relevant field of expertise. It shall report regularly to the Conference of the Parties on all aspects of its work.

2. Under the guidance of the Conference of the Parties, and drawing upon existing competent international bodies, this body shall:

(a) Provide assessments of the state of scientific knowledge relating to climate change and its effects;

(b) Prepare scientific assessments on the effects of measures taken in the implementation of the Convention;

(c) Identify innovative, efficient and state-of-the-art technologies and know-how and advise on the ways and means of promoting development and/or transferring such technologies;

(d) Provide advice on scientific programmes, international cooperation in research and development related to climate change, as well as on ways and means of supporting endogenous capacity-building in developing countries; and

(e) Respond to scientific, technological and methodological questions that the Conference of the Parties and its subsidiary bodies may put to the body.

3. The functions and terms of reference of this body may be further elaborated by the Conference of the Parties.

ARTICLE 10
SUBSIDIARY BODY FOR IMPLEMENTATION

1. A subsidiary body for implementation is hereby established to assist the Conference of the Parties in the assessment and review of the effective implementation of the Convention. This body shall be open to participation by all Parties and comprise government representatives who are experts on matters related to climate change. It shall report regularly to the Conference of the Parties on all aspects of its work.

2. Under the guidance of the Conference of the Parties, this body shall:

(a) Consider the information communicated in accordance with Article 12, paragraph 1, to assess the overall aggregated effect of the steps taken by the Parties in the light of the latest scientific assessments concerning climate change;

(b) Consider the information communicated in accordance with Article 12, paragraph 2, in order to assist the Conference of the Parties in carrying out the reviews required by Article 4, paragraph 2(d); and

(c) Assist the Conference of the Parties, as appropriate, in the preparation and implementation of its decisions.

ARTICLE 11
FINANCIAL MECHANISM

1. A mechanism for the provision of financial resources on a grant or concessional basis, including for the transfer of technology, is hereby defined. It shall function under the guidance of and be accountable to the Conference of the Parties, which shall decide on its policies, programme priorities and eligibility criteria related to this Convention. Its operation shall be entrusted to one or more existing international entities.

2. The financial mechanism shall have an equitable and balanced representation of all Parties within a transparent system of governance.

3. The Conference of the Parties and the entity or entities entrusted with the operation of the financial mechanism shall agree upon arrangements to give effect to the above paragraphs, which shall include the following:

(a) Modalities to ensure that the funded projects to address climate change are in conformity with the policies, programme priorities and eligibility criteria established by the Conference of the Parties;

(b) Modalities by which a particular funding decision may be reconsidered in light of these policies, programme priorities and eligibility criteria;

(c) Provision by the entity or entities of regular reports to the Conference of the Parties on its funding operations, which is consistent with the requirement for accountability set out in paragraph 1 above; and

(d) Determination in a predictable and identifiable manner of the amount of funding necessary and available for the implementation of this Convention and the conditions under which that amount shall be periodically reviewed.

4. The Conference of the Parties shall make arrangements to implement the above-mentioned provisions at its first session, reviewing and taking into account the interim arrangements referred to in Article 21, paragraph 3, and shall decide whether these interim arrangements shall be maintained. Within four years thereafter, the Conference of the Parties shall review the financial mechanism and take appropriate measures.

5. The developed country Parties may also provide and developing country Parties avail themselves of, financial resources related to the implementation of the Convention through bilateral, regional and other multilateral channels.

ARTICLE 12
COMMUNICATION OF INFORMATION
RELATED TO IMPLEMENTATION

1. In accordance with Article 4, paragraph 1, each Party shall communicate to the Conference of the Parties, through the secretariat, the following elements of information:

(a) A national inventory of anthropogenic emissions by sources and removals by sinks of all greenhouse gases not controlled by the Montreal Protocol, to the extent its capacities permit, using comparable methodologies to be promoted and agreed upon by the Conference of the Parties;

(b) A general description of steps taken or envisaged by the Party to implement the Convention; and

(c) Any other information that the Party considers relevant to the achievement of the objective of the Convention and suitable for inclusion in its communication, including, if feasible, material relevant for calculations of global emission trends.

2.   Each developed country Party and each other Party included in annex I shall incorporate in its communication the following elements of information:

(a) A detailed description of the policies and measures that it has adopted to implement its commitment under Article 4, paragraphs 2(a) and 2(b); and

(b) A specific estimate of the effects that the policies and measures referred to in subparagraph (a) immediately above will have on anthropogenic emissions by its sources and removals by its sinks of greenhouse gases during the period referred to in Article 4, paragraph 2(a).

3.   In addition, each developed country Party and each other developed Party included in annex II shall incorporate details of measures taken in accordance with Article 4, paragraphs 3, 4 and 5.

4.   Developing country Parties may, on a voluntary basis, propose projects for financing, including specific technologies, materials, equipment, techniques or practices that would be needed to implement such projects, along with, if possible, an estimate of all incremental costs, of the reductions of emissions and increments of removals of greenhouse gases, as well as an estimate of the consequent benefits.

5.   Each developed country Party and each other Party included in annex I shall make its initial communication within six months of the entry into force of the Convention for that Party. Each Party not so listed shall make its initial communication within three years of the entry into force of the Convention for that Party, or of the availability of financial resources in accordance with Article 4, paragraph 3. Parties that are least developed countries may make their initial communication at their discretion. The frequency of subsequent communications by all Parties shall be determined by the Conference of the Parties, taking into account the differentiated timetable set by this paragraph.

6.   Information communicated by Parties under this Article shall be transmitted by the secretariat as soon as possible to the Conference of the Parties and to any subsidiary bodies concerned. If necessary, the procedures for the communication of information may be further considered by the Conference of the Parties.

7.   From its first session, the Conference of the Parties shall arrange for the provision to developing country Parties of technical and financial support, on request, in compiling and communicating information under this Article, as well as in identifying the technical and financial needs associated with

proposed projects and response measures under Article 4. Such support may be provided by other Parties, by competent international organizations and by the secretariat, as appropriate.

8. Any group of Parties may, subject to guidelines adopted by the Conference of the Parties, and to prior notification to the Conference of the Parties, make a joint communication in fulfilment of their obligations under this Article, provided that such a communication includes information on the fulfilment by each of these Parties of its individual obligations under the Convention.

9. Information received by the secretariat that is designated by a Party as confidential, in accordance with criteria to be established by the Conference of the Parties, shall be aggregated by the secretariat to protect its confidentiality before being made available to any of the bodies involved in the communication and review of information.

10. Subject to paragraph 9 above, and without prejudice to the ability of any Party to make public its communication at any time, the secretariat shall make communications by Parties under this Article publicly available at the time they are submitted to the Conference of the Parties.

ARTICLE 13
RESOLUTION OF QUESTIONS REGARDING IMPLEMENTATION

The Conference of the Parties shall, at its first session, consider the establishment of a multilateral consultative process, available to Parties on their request, for the resolution of questions regarding the implementation of the Convention.

ARTICLE 14
SETTLEMENT OF DISPUTES

1. In the event of a dispute between any two or more Parties concerning the interpretation or application of the Convention, the Parties concerned shall seek a settlement of the dispute through negotiation or any other peaceful means of their own choice.

2. When ratifying, accepting, approving or acceding to the Convention, or at any time thereafter, a Party which is not a regional economic integration organization may declare in a written instrument submitted to the Depositary that, in respect of any dispute concerning the interpretation or application of the Convention, it recognizes as compulsory *ipso facto* and without special agreement, in relation to any Party accepting the same obligation:

(a) Submission of the dispute to the International Court of Justice, and/or

(b) Arbitration in accordance with procedures to be adopted by the Conference of the Parties as soon as practicable, in an annex on arbitration.

A Party which is a regional economic integration organization may make a declaration with like effect in relation to arbitration in accordance with the procedures referred to in subparagraph (b) above.

3. A declaration made under paragraph 2 above shall remain in force until it expires in accordance with its terms or until three months after written notice of its revocation has been deposited with the Depositary.

4. A new declaration, a notice of revocation or the expiry of a declaration shall not in any way affect proceedings pending before the International Court of Justice or the arbitral tribunal, unless the parties to the dispute otherwise agree.

5. Subject to the operation of paragraph 2 above, if after twelve months following notification by one Party to another that a dispute exists between them, the Parties concerned have not been able to settle their dispute through the means mentioned in paragraph 1 above, the dispute shall be submitted, at the request of any of the parties to the dispute, to conciliation.

6. A conciliation commission shall be created upon the request of one of the parties to the dispute. The commission shall be composed of an equal number of members appointed by each party concerned and a chairman chosen jointly by the members appointed by each party. The commission shall render a recommendatory award, which the parties shall consider in good faith.

7. Additional procedures relating to conciliation shall be adopted by the Conference of the Parties, as soon as practicable, in an annex on conciliation.

8. The provisions of this Article shall apply to any related legal instrument which the Conference of the Parties may adopt, unless the instrument provides otherwise.

ARTICLE 15
AMENDMENTS TO THE CONVENTION

1. Any Party may propose amendments to the Convention.

2. Amendments to the Convention shall be adopted at an ordinary session of the Conference of the Parties. The text of any proposed amendment to the Convention shall be communicated to the Parties by the secretariat at least six months before the meeting at which it is proposed for adoption. The secretariat shall also communicate proposed amendments to the signatories to the Convention and, for information, to the Depositary.

3. The Parties shall make every effort to reach agreement on any proposed amendment to the Convention by consensus. If all efforts at consensus have been exhausted, and no agreement reached, the amendment shall as a last resort be adopted by a three-fourths majority vote of the Parties present and voting at the meeting. The adopted amendment shall be communicated by the secretariat to the Depositary, who shall circulate it to all Parties for their acceptance.

4. Instruments of acceptance in respect of an amendment shall be deposited with the Depositary. An amendment adopted in accordance with paragraph 3 above shall enter into force for those Parties having accepted it on the ninetieth day after the date of receipt by the Depositary of an instrument of acceptance by at least three-fourths of the Parties to the Convention.

5. The amendment shall enter into force for any other Party on the ninetieth day after the date on which that Party deposits with the Depositary its instrument of acceptance of the said amendment.

6. For the purposes of this Article, "Parties present and voting" means Parties present and casting an affirmative or negative vote.

ARTICLE 16
ADOPTION AND AMENDMENT OF ANNEXES
TO THE CONVENTION

1. Annexes to the Convention shall form an integral part thereof and, unless otherwise expressly provided, a reference to the Convention constitutes at the same time a reference to any annexes thereto. Without prejudice to the provisions of Article 14, paragraphs 2(b) and 7, such annexes shall be restricted to lists, forms and any other material of a descriptive nature that is of a scientific, technical, procedural or administrative character.

2. Annexes to the Convention shall be proposed and adopted in accordance with the procedure set forth in Article 15, paragraphs 2, 3, and 4.

3. An annex that has been adopted in accordance with paragraph 2 above shall enter into force for all Parties to the Convention six months after the date of the communication by the Depositary to such Parties of the adoption of the annex, except for those Parties that have notified the Depositary, in writing, within that period of their non-acceptance of the annex. The annex shall enter into force for Parties which withdraw their notification of non-acceptance on the ninetieth day after the date on which withdrawal of such notification has been received by the Depositary.

4. The proposal, adoption and entry into force of amendments to annexes to the Convention shall be subject to the same procedure as that for the proposal, adoption and entry into force of annexes to the Convention in accordance with paragraphs 2 and 3 above.

5. If the adoption of an annex or an amendment to an annex involves an amendment to the Convention, that annex or amendment to an annex shall not enter into force until such time as the amendment to the Convention enters into force.

ARTICLE 17
PROTOCOLS

1. The Conference of the Parties may, at any ordinary session, adopt protocols to the Convention.

2.　The text of any proposed protocol shall be communicated to the Parties by the secretariat at least six months before such a session.

3.　The requirements for the entry into force of any protocol shall be established by that instrument.

4.　Only Parties to the Convention may be Parties to a protocol.

5.　Decisions under any protocol shall be taken only by the Parties to the protocol concerned.

ARTICLE 18
RIGHT TO VOTE

1.　Each Party to the Convention shall have one vote, except as provided for in paragraph 2 below.

2.　Regional economic integration organizations, in matters within their competence, shall exercise their right to vote with a number of votes equal to the number of their member States that are Parties to the Convention.　Such an organization shall not exercise its right to vote if any of its member States exercises its right, and vice versa.

ARTICLE 19
DEPOSITARY

The Secretary–General of the United Nations shall be the Depositary of the Convention and of protocols adopted in accordance with Article 17.

ARTICLE 20
SIGNATURE

This Convention shall be open for signature by States Members of the United Nations or of any of its specialized agencies or that are Parties to the Statute of the International Court of Justice and by regional economic integration organizations at Rio de Janeiro, during the United Nations Conference on Environment and Development, and thereafter at United Nations Headquarters in New York from 20 June 1992 to 19 June 1993.

ARTICLE 21
INTERIM ARRANGEMENTS

1.　The secretariat functions referred to in Article 8 will be carried out on an interim basis by the secretariat established by the General Assembly of the United Nations in its resolution 45/212 of 21 December 1990, until the completion of the first session of the Conference of the Parties.

2.　The head of the interim secretariat referred to in paragraph 1 above will cooperate closely with the Intergovernmental Panel on Climate Change to ensure that the Panel can respond to the need for objective scientific and technical advice.　Other relevant scientific bodies could also be consulted.

3.　The Global Environment Facility of the United Nations Development Programme, the United Nations Environment Programme and the International Bank for Reconstruction and Development shall be the international entity entrusted with the operation of the financial mechanism referred to in Article 11 on an interim basis. In this connection, the Global Environment Facility should be appropriately restructured and its membership made universal to enable it to fulfil the requirements of Article 11.

ARTICLE 22
RATIFICATION, ACCEPTANCE, APPROVAL OR ACCESSION

1. The Convention shall be subject to ratification, acceptance, approval or accession by States and by regional economic integration organizations. It shall be open for accession from the day after the date on which the Convention is closed for signature. Instruments of ratification, acceptance, approval or accession shall be deposited with the Depositary.

2. Any regional economic integration organization which becomes a Party to the Convention without any of its member States being a Party shall be bound by all the obligations under the Convention. In the case of such organizations, one or more of whose member States is a Party to the Convention, the organization and its member States shall decide on their respective responsibilities for the performance of their obligations under the Convention. In such cases, the organization and the member States shall not be entitled to exercise rights under the Convention concurrently.

3. In their instruments of ratification, acceptance, approval or accession, regional economic integration organizations shall declare the extent of their competence with respect to the matters governed by the Convention. These organizations shall also inform the Depositary, who shall in turn inform the Parties, of any substantial modification in the extent of their competence.

ARTICLE 23
ENTRY INTO FORCE

1. The Convention shall enter into force on the ninetieth day after the date of deposit of the fiftieth instrument of ratification, acceptance, approval or accession.

2. For each State or regional economic integration organization that ratifies, accepts or approves the Convention or accedes thereto after the deposit of the fiftieth instrument of ratification, acceptance, approval or accession, the Convention shall enter into force on the ninetieth day after the date of deposit by such State or regional economic integration organization of its instrument of ratification, acceptance, approval or accession.

3. For the purposes of paragraphs 1 and 2 above, any instrument deposited by a regional economic integration organization shall not be counted as additional to those deposited by States members of the organization.

ARTICLE 24
RESERVATIONS

No reservations may be made to the Convention.

ARTICLE 25
WITHDRAWAL

1.　At any time after three years from the date on which the Convention has entered into force for a Party, that Party may withdraw from the Convention by giving written notification to the Depositary.

2.　Any such withdrawal shall take effect upon expiry of one year from the date of receipt by the Depositary of the notification of withdrawal, or on such later date as may be specified in the notification of withdrawal.

3.　Any Party that withdraws from the Convention shall be considered as also having withdrawn from any protocol to which it is a Party.

ARTICLE 26
AUTHENTIC TEXTS

The original of this Convention, of which the Arabic, Chinese, English, French, Russian and Spanish texts are equally authentic, shall be deposited with the Secretary–General of the United Nations.

附錄十：倫敦海拋公約

CONVENTION ON THE PREVENTION OF MARINE POLLUTION BY DUMPING OF WASTES AND OTHER MATTER (WITH ANNEXES AND AS AMENDED TO 1989 BUT WITHOUT ADDENDUM). Concluded at Washington, 29 December 1972. Entered into force, 30 August 1975. 1046 U.N.T.S. 120, 26 U.S.T. 2403, T.I.A.S. No. 8165, 11 I.L.M. 1294 (1973)

The Contracting Parties to this Convention,

Recognizing that the marine environment and the living organisms which it supports are of vital importance to humanity, and all people have an interest in assuring that it is so managed that its quality and resources are not impaired;

Recognizing that the capacity of the sea to assimilate wastes and render them harmless, and its ability to regenerate natural resources is not unlimited;

Recognizing that States have, in accordance with the Charter of the United Nations and the principles of international law, the sovereign right to exploit their own resources pursuant to their own environmental policies, and the responsibility to ensure that activities within their jurisdiction or control do not cause damage to the environment of other States or of areas beyond the limits of national jurisdiction;

Recognizing resolution 2749 (XXV) of the General Assembly of the United Nations on the principles governing the sea-bed and the ocean floor and the subsoil thereof, beyond the limits of national jurisdiction;

Noting that marine pollution originates in many sources, such as dumping and discharges through the atmosphere, rivers, estuaries, outfalls and pipelines, and that it is important that States use the best practicable means to prevent such pollution and develop products and processes which will reduce the amount of harmful wastes to be disposed of;

Being convinced that international action to control the pollution of the sea by dumping can and must be taken without delay but that this action should not preclude discussion of measures to control other sources of marine pollution as soon as possible; and

Wishing to improve protection of the marine environment by encouraging States with a common interest in particular geographical areas to enter into appropriate agreements supplementary to this Convention;

Have agreed as follows:

Article I. Contracting Parties shall individually and collectively promote the effective control of all sources of pollution of the marine environment, and pledge themselves especially to take all practicable steps to prevent the pollution of the sea by the dumping of waste and other matter that is liable to create hazards to human health, to harm living resources and marine life, to damage amenities or to interfere with other legitimate uses of the sea.

Article II. Contracting Parties shall, as provided for in the following Articles, take effective measures individually, according to their scientific, technical and economic capabilities, and collectively, to prevent marine pollution caused by dumping and shall harmonize their policies in this regard.

Article III. For the purposes of this Convention:

1. (*a*) "Dumping" means:

　　(i) any deliberate disposal at sea of wastes or other matter from vessels, aircraft, platforms or other man-made structures at sea;

　　(ii) any deliberate disposal at sea of vessels, aircraft, platforms or other man-made structures at sea.

(*b*) "Dumping" does not include:

　　(i) the disposal at sea of wastes or other matter incidental to, or derived from the normal operations of vessels, aircraft, platforms or other man-made structures at sea and their equipment, other than wastes or other matter transported by or to vessels, aircraft, platforms or other man-made structures at sea, operating for the purpose of disposal of such matter or derived from the treatment of such wastes or other matter on such vessels, aircraft, platforms or structures;

　　(ii) placement of matter for a purpose other than the mere disposal thereof, provided that such placement is not contrary to the aims of this Convention.

(*c*) The disposal of wastes or other matter directly arising from, or related to the exploration, exploitation and associated off-shore processing of sea-bed mineral resources will not be covered by the provisions of this Convention.

2. "Vessels and aircraft" means waterborne or airborne craft of any type whatsoever. This expression includes air-cushioned craft and floating craft, whether self-propelled or not.

3. "Sea" means all marine waters other than the internal waters of States.

4. "Wastes or other matter" means material and substance of any kind, form or description.

5. "Special permit" means permission granted specifically on application in advance and in accordance with Annex II and Annex III.

6. "General permit" means permission granted in advance and in accordance with Annex III.

7. The "Organisation" means the Organisation designated by the Contracting Parties in accordance with Article XIV(2).

Article IV. 1. In accordance with the provisions of this Convention, Contracting Parties shall prohibit the dumping of any wastes or other matter in whatever form or condition except as otherwise specified below:

(*a*) the dumping of wastes or other matter listed in Annex I is prohibited;

(*b*) the dumping of wastes or other matter listed in Annex II requires a prior special permit;

(*c*) the dumping of all other wastes or matter requires a prior general permit.

2. Any permit shall be issued only after careful consideration of all the factors set forth in Annex III, including prior studies of the characteristics of the dumping site, as set forth in Sections B and C of that Annex.

3. No provision of this Convention is to be interpreted as preventing a Contracting Party from prohibiting, insofar as that Party is concerned, the dumping of wastes or other matter not mentioned in Annex I. That Party shall notify such measures to the Organisation.

Article V. 1. The provisions of Article IV shall not apply when it is necessary to secure the safety of human life or of vessels, aircraft, platforms or other man-made structures at sea in cases of *force majeure* caused by stress of weather, or in any case which constitutes a danger to human life or a real threat to vessels, aircraft, platforms or other man-made structures at sea, if dumping appears to be the only way of averting the threat and if there is every probability that the damage consequent upon such dumping will be less than would otherwise occur. Such dumping shall be so conducted as to minimise the likelihood of damage to human or marine life and shall be reported forthwith to the Organisation.

2. A Contracting Party may issue a special permit as an exception to Article IV(1)(*a*), in emergencies, posing unacceptable risk relating to human health and admitting no other feasible solution. Before doing so the Party shall consult any other country or countries that are likely to be affected and the Organisation which, after consulting other Parties, and international organisations as appropriate, shall, in accordance with Article XIV promptly recommend to the Party the most appropriate procedures to adopt. The Party shall follow these recommendations to the maximum extent feasible consistent with the time within which action must be taken and with the general obligation to avoid damage to the marine environment and shall inform the Organisation of the action it takes. The Parties pledge themselves to assist one another in such situations.

3. Any Contracting Party may waive its rights under paragraph (2) at the time of, or subsequent to ratification of, or accession to this Convention.

Article VI. 1. Each Contracting Party shall designate an appropriate authority or authorities to:

(*a*) issue special permits which shall be required prior to, and for, the dumping of matter listed in Annex II and in the circumstances provided for in Article V(2);

(*b*) issue general permits which shall be required prior to, and for, the dumping of all other matter;

(*c*) keep records of the nature and quantities of all matter permitted to be dumped and the location, time and method of dumping;

(*d*) monitor individually, or in collaboration with other Parties and competent international organisations, the condition of the seas for the purposes of this Convention.

2. The appropriate authority or authorities of a Contracting Party shall issue prior special or general permits in accordance with paragraph (1) in respect of matter intended for dumping:

(*a*) loaded in its territory;

(*b*) loaded by a vessel or aircraft registered in its territory or flying its flag, when the loading occurs in the territory of a State not party to this Convention.

3. In issuing permits under sub-paragraphs (1)(*a*) and (*b*) above, the appropriate authority or authorities shall comply with Annex III, together with such additional criteria, measures and requirements as they may consider relevant.

4. Each Contracting Party, directly or through a Secretariat established under a regional agreement, shall report to the Organisation, and where appropriate to other Parties, the information specified in sub-paragraphs (*c*) and (*d*) of paragraph (1) above, and the criteria, measures and requirements it adopts in accordance with paragraph (3) above. The procedure to be followed and the nature of such reports shall be agreed by the Parties in consultation.

Article VII. 1. Each Contracting Party shall apply the measures required to implement the present Convention to all:

(*a*) vessels and aircraft registered in its territory or flying its flag;

(*b*) vessels and aircraft loading in its territory or territorial seas matter which is to be dumped;

(*c*) vessels and aircraft and fixed or floating platforms under its jurisdiction believed to be engaged in dumping.

2. Each Party shall take in its territory appropriate measures to prevent and punish conduct in contravention of the provisions of this Convention.

3. The Parties agree to co-operate in the development of procedures for the effective application of this Convention particularly on the high seas,

including procedures for the reporting of vessels and aircraft observed dumping in contravention of the Convention.

　4.　This Convention shall not apply to those vessels and aircraft entitled to sovereign immunity under international law.　However, each Party shall ensure by the adoption of appropriate measures that such vessels and aircraft owned or operated by it act in a manner consistent with the object and purpose of this Convention, and shall inform the Organisation accordingly.

　5.　Nothing in this convention shall affect the right of each Party to adopt other measures, in accordance with the principles of international law, to prevent dumping at sea.

Article VIII.　In order to further the objectives of this Convention, the Contracting Parties with common interests to protect in the marine environment in a given geographical area shall endeavour, taking into account characteristic regional features, to enter into regional agreements consistent with this Convention for the prevention of pollution, especially by dumping. The Contracting Parties to the present Convention shall endeavour to act consistently with the objectives and provisions of such regional agreements, which shall be notified to them by the Organisation.　Contracting Parties shall seek to co-operate with the Parties to regional agreements in order to develop harmonized procedures to be followed by Contracting Parties to the different conventions concerned.　Special attention shall be given to co-operation in the field of monitoring and scientific research.

Article IX.　The Contracting Parties shall promote, through collaboration within the Organisation and other international bodies, support for those Parties which request it for:

　(*a*) the training of scientific and technical personnel;

　(*b*) the supply of necessary equipment and facilities for research and monitoring;

　(*c*) the disposal and treatment of waste and other measures to prevent or mitigate pollution caused by dumping;

preferably within the countries concerned, so furthering the aims and purposes of this Convention.

Article X.　In accordance with the principles of international law regarding State responsibility for damage to the environment of other States or to any other area of the environment, caused by dumping of wastes and other matter of all kinds, the Contracting Parties undertake to develop procedures for the assessment of liability and the settlement of disputes regarding dumping.

Article XI.　The Contracting Parties shall at their first consultative meeting consider procedures for the settlement of disputes concerning the interpretation and application of this Convention.

Article XII. The Contracting Parties pledge themselves to promote, within the competent specialised agencies and other international bodies, measures to protect the marine environment against pollution caused by:

(*a*) hydrocarbons, including oil, and their wastes;

(*b*) other noxious or hazardous matter transported by vessels for purposes other than dumping;

(*c*) wastes generated in the course of operation of vessels, aircraft, platforms and other man-made structures at sea;

(*d*) radio-active pollutants from all sources, including vessels;

(*e*) agents of chemical and biological warfare;

(*f*) wastes or other matter directly arising from, or related to the exploration, exploitation and associated off-shore processing of sea-bed mineral resources.

The Parties will also promote, within the appropriate international organisation, the codification of signals to be used by vessels engaged in dumping.

Article XIII. Nothing in this Convention shall prejudice the codification and development of the law of the sea by the United Nations Conference on the Law of the Sea convened pursuant to Resolution 2750 C(XXV) of the General Assembly of the United Nations nor the present or future claims and legal views of any State concerning the law of the sea and the nature and extent of coastal and flag State jurisdiction. The Contracting Parties agree to consult at a meeting to be convened by the Organisation after the Law of the Sea Conference, and in any case not later than 1976, with a view to defining the nature and extent of the right and the responsibility of a coastal State to apply the Convention in a zone adjacent to its coast.

Article XIV. 1. The Government of the United Kingdom of Great Britain and Northern Ireland as a depositary shall call a meeting of the Contracting Parties not later than three months after the entry into force of this Convention to decide on organisational matters.

2. The Contracting Parties shall designate a competent Organisation existing at the time of that meeting to be responsible for Secretariat duties in relation to this Convention. Any Party to this Convention not being a member of this Organisation shall make an appropriate contribution to the expenses incurred by the Organisation in performing these duties.

3. The Secretariat duties of the Organisation shall include:

(*a*) the convening of consultative meetings of the Contracting Parties not less frequently than once every two years and of special meetings of the Parties at any time on the request of two thirds of the Parties;

(*b*) preparing and assisting, in consultation with the Contracting Parties and appropriate International Organisations, in the development and implementation of procedures referred to in sub-paragraph (4)(*e*) of this Article;

(c) considering enquiries by, and information from the Contracting Parties, consulting with them and with the appropriate International Organisations, and providing recommendations to the Parties on questions related to, but not specifically covered by the Convention;

(d) conveying to the Parties concerned all notifications received by the Organisation in accordance with Articles IV(3), V(1) and (2), VI(4), XV, XX and XXI.

Prior to the designation of the Organisation these functions shall, as necessary, be performed by the depositary, who for this purpose shall be the Government of the United Kingdom of Great Britain and Northern Ireland.

4. Consultative or special meetings of the Contracting Parties shall keep under continuing review the implementation of this Convention and may, *inter alia:*

(a) review and adopt amendments to this Convention and its Annexes in accordance with Article XV;

(b) invite the appropriate scientific body or bodies to collaborate with and to advise the Parties or the Organisation on any scientific or technical aspect relevant to this Convention, including particularly the content of the Annexes;

(c) receive and consider reports made pursuant to Article VI(4);

(d) promote co-operation with and between regional organisations concerned with the prevention of marine pollution;

(e) develop or adopt, in consultation with appropriate International Organisations, procedures referred to in Article V(2), including basic criteria for determining exceptional and emergency situations, and procedures for consultative advice and the safe disposal of matter in such circumstances, including the designation of appropriate dumping areas, and recommend accordingly;

(f) consider any additional action that may be required.

5. The Contracting Parties at their first consultative meeting shall establish rules of procedure as necessary.

Article XV. 1. (a) At meetings of the Contracting Parties called in accordance with Article XIV amendments to this Convention may be adopted by a two-thirds majority of those present. An amendment shall enter into force for the Parties which have accepted it on the sixtieth day after two thirds of the Parties shall have deposited an instrument of acceptance of the amendment with the Organisation. Thereafter the amendment shall enter into force for any other Party 30 days after that Party deposits its instrument of acceptance of the amendment.

(b) The Organisation shall inform all Contracting Parties of any request made for a special meeting under Article XIV and of any amendments adopted at meetings of the Parties and of the date on which each such amendment enters into force for each Party.

2. Amendments to the Annexes will be based on scientific or technical considerations. Amendments to the Annexes approved by a two-thirds majority of those present at a meeting called in accordance with Article XIV shall enter into force for each Contracting Party immediately on notification of its acceptance to the Organisation and 100 days after approval by the meeting for all other Parties except for those which before the end of the 100 days make a declaration that they are not able to accept the amendment at that time. Parties should endeavour to signify their acceptance of an amendment to the Organisation as soon as possible after approval at a meeting. A Party may at any time substitute an acceptance for a previous declaration of objection and the amendment previously objected to shall thereupon enter into force for that Party.

3. An acceptance or declaration of objection under this Article shall be made by the deposit of an instrument with the Organisation. The Organisation shall notify all Contracting Parties of the receipt of such instruments.

4. Prior to the designation of the Organisation, the Secretarial functions herein attributed to it shall be performed temporarily by the Government of the United Kingdom of Great Britain and Northern Ireland, as one of the depositaries of this Convention.

Article XVI. This Convention shall be open for signature by any State at London, Mexico City, Moscow and Washington from 29 December 1972 until 31 December 1973.

Article XVII. This Convention shall be subject to ratification. The instruments of ratification shall be deposited with the Governments of Mexico, the Union of Soviet Socialist Republics, the United Kingdom of Great Britain and Northern Ireland, and the United States of America.

Article XVIII. After 31 December 1973, this Convention shall be open for accession by any State. The instruments of accession shall be deposited with the Governments of Mexico, the Union of Soviet Socialist Republics, the United Kingdom of Great Britain and Northern Ireland, and the United States of America.

Article XIX. 1. This Convention shall enter into force on the thirtieth day following the date of deposit of the fifteenth instrument of ratification or accession.

2. For each Contracting Party ratifying or acceding to the Convention after the deposit of the fifteenth instrument of ratification or accession, the Convention shall enter into force on the thirtieth day after deposit by such Party of its instrument of ratification or accession.

Article XX. The depositaries shall inform Contracting Parties:

(a) of signatures to this Convention and of the deposit of instruments of ratification, accession or withdrawal, in accordance with Articles XVI, XVII, XVIII and XXI, and (*b*) of the date on which this Convention will enter into force, in accordance with Article XIX.

Article XXI. Any Contracting Party may withdraw from this Convention by giving six months' notice in writing to a depositary, which shall promptly inform all Parties of such notice.

Article XXII. The original of this Convention of which the English, French, Russian and Spanish texts are equally authentic, shall be deposited with the Governments of Mexico, the Union of Soviet Socialist Republics, the United Kingdom of Great Britain and Northern Ireland and the United States of America who shall send certified copies thereof to all States.

ANNEX I

1. Organohalogen compounds.

2. Mercury and mercury compounds.

3. Cadmium and cadmium compounds.

4. Persistent plastics and other persistent synthetic materials, for example, netting and ropes, which may float or may remain in suspension in the sea in such a manner as to interfere materially with fishing, navigation or other legitimate uses of the sea.

5. Crude oil and its wastes, refined petroleum products, petroleum distillate residues, and any mixtures containing any of these, taken on board for the purpose of dumping.

6. High-level radio-active wastes or other high-level radio-active matter, defined on public health, biological or other grounds, by the competent international body in this field, at present the International Atomic Energy Agency, as unsuitable for dumping at sea.

7. Materials in whatever form (e.g. solids, liquids, semi-liquids, gases or in a living state) produced for biological and chemical warfare.

8. The preceding paragraphs of this Annex do not apply to substances which are rapidly rendered harmless by physical, chemical or biological processes in the sea provided they do not:

(i) make edible marine organisms unpalatable, or

(ii) endanger human health or that of domestic animals.

The consultative procedure provided for under Article XIV should be followed by a Party if there is doubt about the harmlessness of the substances.

9. This Annex does not apply to wastes or other materials (e.g. sewage sludges and dredged spoils) containing the matter referred to in paragraphs 1–5 above as trace contaminants. Such wastes shall be subject to the provisions of Annexes II and III as appropriate.

10.　Paragraphs 1 and 5 of this annex do not apply to the disposal of wastes or other matter referred to in these paragraphs by means of incineration at sea.　Incineration of such wastes or other matter at sea requires a prior special permit.　In the issue of special permits for incineration, the Contracting Parties shall apply the regulations for the control of incineration of wastes and other matter at sea set forth in the addendum to this annex (which shall constitute an integral part of this annex) and take full account of the technical guidelines on the control of incineration of wastes and other matter at sea adopted by the Contracting Parties in consultation.

ANNEX II

The following substances and materials requiring special care are listed for the purposes of Article VI(1)(a).

A.　Wastes containing significant amounts of the matters listed below:

arsenic　)
lead　　)
copper　) and their compounds
zinc　　)

organosilicon compounds
cyanides
fluorides
pesticides and their by-products not covered in Annex I.

B.　In the issue of permits for the dumping of large quantities of acids and alkalis, consideration shall be given to the possible presence in such wastes of the substances listed in paragraph A and to the following additional substances:

beryllium　)
chromium　)
nickel　　) and their compounds
vanadium　)

C.　Containers, scrap metal and other bulky wastes liable to sink to the sea bottom which may present a serious obstacle to fishing or navigation.

D.　Radio-active wastes or other radio-active matter not included in Annex I.　In the issue of permits for the dumping of this matter, the Contracting Parties should take full account of the recommendations of the competent international body in this field, at present the International Atomic Energy Agency.

E.　In the issue of special permits for the incineration of substances and materials listed in this annex, the Contracting Parties shall apply the regulations for the control of incineration of wastes and other matter at sea set forth in the addendum to annex I and take full account of the technical guidelines on the control of incineration of wastes and other matter at sea adopted by the Contracting Parties in consultation, to the extent specified in these regulations and guidelines.

F.　Substances which, though of a non-toxic nature, may become harmful due to the quantities in which they are dumped, or which are liable to seriously reduce amenities.

ANNEX III

Provisions to be considered in establishing criteria governing the issue of permits for the dumping of matter at sea, taking into account Article IV(2), include:

A.　CHARACTERISTICS AND COMPOSITION OF THE MATTER

1.　Total amount and average composition of matter dumped (e.g. per year).

2.　Form, e.g. solid, sludge, liquid, or gaseous.

3.　Properties: physical (e.g. solubility and density), chemical and bio-chemical (e.g. oxygen demand, nutrients) and biological (e.g. presence of viruses, bacteria, yeasts, parasites).

4.　Toxicity.

5.　Persistence: physical, chemical and biological.

6.　Accumulation and biotransformation in biological materials or sediments.

7.　Susceptibility to physical, chemical and biochemical changes and interaction in the aquatic environment with other dissolved organic and inorganic materials.

8.　Probability of production of taints or other changes reducing market-ability of resources (fish, shellfish, etc.).

B.　CHARACTERISTICS OF DUMPING SITE AND METHOD OF DEPOSIT

1.　Location (e.g. co-ordinates of the dumping area, depth and distance from the coast), location in relation to other areas (e.g. amenity areas, spawning, nursery and fishing areas and exploitable resources).

2.　Rate of disposal per specific period (e.g. quantity per day, per week, per month).

3.　Methods of packaging and containment, if any.

4.　Initial dilution achieved by proposed method of release.

5.　Dispersal characteristics (e.g. effects of currents, tides and wind on horizontal transport and vertical mixing).

6. Water characteristics (e.g. temperature, pH, salinity, stratification, oxygen indices of pollution—dissolved oxygen (DO), chemical oxygen demand (COD), biochemical oxygen demand (BOD)—nitrogen present in organic and mineral form including ammonia, suspended matter, other nutrients and productivity).

7. Bottom characteristics (e.g. topography, geochemical and geological characteristics and biological productivity).

8. Existence and effects of other dumpings which have been made in the dumping area (e.g. heavy metal background reading and organic carbon content).

9. In issuing a permit for dumping, Contracting Parties should consider whether an adequate scientific basis exists for assessing the consequences of such dumping, as outlined in this Annex, taking into account seasonal variations.

C. GENERAL CONSIDERATIONS AND CONDITIONS

1. Possible effects on amenities (e.g. presence of floating or stranded material, turbidity, objectionable odour, discolouration and foaming).

2. Possible effects on marine life, fish and shellfish culture, fish stocks and fisheries, seaweed harvesting and culture.

3. Possible effects on other uses of the sea (e.g. impairment of water quality for industrial use, underwater corrosion of structures, interference with ship operations from floating materials, interference with fishing or navigation through deposit of waste or solid objects on the sea floor and protection of areas of special importance for scientific or conservation purposes).

4. The practical availability of alternative land-based methods of treatment, disposal or elimination, or of treatment to render the matter less harmful for dumping at sea.

附錄十一：防止船舶污染國際公約

**INTERNATIONAL CONVENTION FOR THE PREVENTION OF POLLU-
TION FROM SHIPS (MARPOL) (WITH ANNEXES I, II, & V AND AS
AMENDED BUT WITHOUT APPENDICES).[1] Concluded at London,
2 November 1973. IMCO Doc. MP/CONF/WP.35 (1973), 12 I.L.M.
1319 (1973)**

ARTICLE 1
General Obligations under the Convention

(1) The Parties to the Convention undertake to give effect to the provisions of the present Convention and those Annexes thereto by which they are bound, in order to prevent the pollution of the marine environment by the discharge of harmful substances or effluents containing such substances in contravention of the Convention.

(2) Unless expressly provided otherwise, a reference to the present Convention constitutes at the same time a reference to its Protocols and to the Annexes.

ARTICLE 2
Definitions

For the purposes of the present Convention, unless expressly provided otherwise:

(1) "Regulations" means the Regulations contained in the Annexes to the present Convention.

(2) "Harmful substance" means any substance which, if introduced into the sea, is liable to create hazards to human health, to harm living resources and marine life, to damage amenities or to interfere with other legitimate uses of the sea, and includes any substance subject to control by the present Convention.

(3)(a) "Discharge", in relation to harmful substances or effluents containing such substances, means any release howsoever caused from a ship and includes any escape, disposal, spilling, leaking, pumping, emitting or emptying;

(b) "Discharge" does not include:

(i) dumping within the meaning of the Convention on the Prevention of Marine Pollution by Dumping of Wastes and Other Matter, done at London on 13 November 1972; or

(ii) release of harmful substances directly arising from the exploration, exploitation and associated off-shore processing of sea-bed mineral resources; or

(iii) release of harmful substances for purposes of legitimate scientific research into pollution abatement or control.

(4) "Ship" means a vessel of any type whatsoever operating in the marine environment and includes hydrofoil boats, air-cushion vehicles, submersibles, floating craft and fixed or floating platforms.

(5) "Administration" means the Government of the State under whose authority the ship is operating. With respect to a ship entitled to fly a flag of any State, the Administration is the Government of that State. With respect to fixed or floating platforms engaged in exploration and exploitation of the sea-bed and subsoil thereof adjacent to the coast over which the coastal State exercises sovereign rights for the purposes of exploration and exploitation of their natural resources, the Administration is the Government of the coastal State concerned.

(6) "Incident" means an event involving the actual or probable discharge into the sea of a harmful substance, or effluents containing such a substance.

(7) "Organization" means the Inter-Governmental Maritime Consultative Organization.

ARTICLE 3
Application

(1) The present Convention shall apply to:

(a) ships entitled to fly the flag of a Party to the Convention; and

(b) ships not entitled to fly the flag of a Party but which operate under the authority of a Party.

(2) Nothing in the present Article shall be construed as derogating from or extending the sovereign rights of the Parties under international law over the sea-bed and subsoil thereof adjacent to their coasts for the purposes of exploration and exploitation of their natural resources.

(3) The present Convention shall not apply to any warship, naval auxiliary or other ship owned or operated by a State and used, for the time being, only on government non-commercial service. However, each Party shall ensure by the adoption of appropriate measures not impairing the operations or operational capabilities of such ships owned or operated by it, that such ships act in a manner consistent, so far as is reasonable and practicable, with the present Convention.

ARTICLE 4
Violation

(1) Any violation of the requirements of the present Convention shall be prohibited and sanctions shall be established therefor under the law of the Administration of the ship concerned wherever the violation occurs. If the Administration is informed of such a violation and is satisfied that sufficient evidence is available to enable proceedings to be brought in respect of the alleged violation, it shall cause such proceedings to be taken as soon as possible, in accordance with its law.

(2) Any violation of the requirements of the present Convention within the jurisdiction of any Party to the Convention shall be prohibited and sanctions shall be established therefor under the law of that Party. Whenever such a violation occurs, that Party shall either:

(a) cause proceedings to be taken in accordance with its law; or

(b) furnish to the Administration of the ship such information and evidence as may be in its possession that a violation has occurred.

(3) Where information or evidence with respect to any violation of the present Convention by a ship is furnished to the Administration of that ship, the Administration shall promptly inform the Party which has furnished the information or evidence, and the Organization, of the action taken.

(4) The penalties specified under the law of a Party pursuant to the present Article shall be adequate in severity to discourage violations of the present Convention and shall be equally severe irrespective of where the violations occur.

ARTICLE 5
Certificates and Special Rules on Inspection of Ships

(1) Subject to the provisions of paragraph (2) of the present Article a certificate issued under the authority of a Party to the Convention in accordance with the provisions of the Regulations shall be accepted by the other Parties and regarded for all purposes covered by the present Convention as having the same validity as a certificate issued by them.

(2) A ship required to hold a certificate in accordance with the provisions of the Regulations is subject, while in the ports or off-shore terminals under the jurisdiction of a Party, to inspection by officers duly authorized by that Party. Any such inspection shall be limited to verifying that there is on board a valid certificate, unless there are clear grounds for believing that the condition of the ship or its equipment does not correspond substantially with the particulars of that certificate. In that case, or if the ship does not carry a valid certificate, the Party carrying out the inspection shall take such steps as will ensure that the ship shall not sail until it can proceed to sea without presenting an unreasonable threat of harm to the marine environment. That Party may, however, grant such a ship permission to leave the port or off-shore terminal for the purpose of proceeding to the nearest appropriate repair yard available.

(3) If a Party denies a foreign ship entry to the ports or off-shore terminals under its jurisdiction or takes any action against such a ship for the reason that the ship does not comply with the provisions of the present Convention, the Party shall immediately inform the consul or diplomatic representative of the Party whose flag the ship is entitled to fly, or if this is not possible, the Administration of the ship concerned. Before denying entry or taking such action the Party may request consultation with the Administration of the ship concerned. Information shall also be given to the Administration when a ship does not carry a valid certificate in accordance with the provisions of the Regulations.

(4) With respect to the ships of non-Parties to the Convention, Parties shall apply the requirements of the present Convention as may be necessary to ensure that no more favorable treatment is given to such ships.

ARTICLE 6
Detection of Violations and Enforcement of the Convention

(1) Parties to the Convention shall co-operate in the detection of violations and the enforcement of the provisions of the present Convention, using all appropriate and practicable measures of detection and environmental monitoring, adequate procedures for reporting and accumulation of evidence.

(2) A ship to which the present Convention applies may, in any port or off-shore terminal of a Party, be subject to inspection by officers appointed or authorized by that Party for the purpose of verifying whether the ship has discharged any harmful substances in violation of the provisions of the Regulations. If an inspection indicates a violation of the Convention, a report shall be forwarded to the Administration for any appropriate action.

(3) Any Party shall furnish to the Administration evidence, if any, that the ship has discharged harmful substances or effluents containing such substances in violation of the provisions of the Regulations. If it is practicable to do so, the competent authority of the former Party shall notify the Master of the ship of the alleged violation.

(4) Upon receiving such evidence, the Administration so informed shall investigate the matter, and may request the other party to furnish further or better evidence of the alleged contravention. If the Administration is satisfied that sufficient evidence is available to enable proceedings to be brought in respect of the alleged violation, it shall cause such proceedings to be taken in accordance with its law as soon as possible. The Administration shall promptly inform the Party which has reported the alleged violation, as well as the Organization, of the action taken.

(5) A Party may also inspect a ship to which the present Convention applies when it enters the ports or off-shore terminals under its jurisdiction, if a request for an investigation is received from any Party together with sufficient evidence that the ship has discharged harmful substances or effluents containing such substances in any place. The report of such investigation shall be sent to the Party requesting it and to the Administration so that the appropriate action may be taken under the present Convention.

ARTICLE 7
Undue Delay to Ships

(1) All possible efforts shall be made to avoid a ship being unduly detained or delayed under Articles 4, 5 or 6 of the present Convention.

(2) When a ship is unduly detained or delayed under Articles 4, 5 or 6 of the present Convention, it shall be entitled to compensation for any loss or damage suffered.

ARTICLE 8

Reports on Incidents Involving Harmful Substances

(1) A report of an incident shall be made without delay to the fullest extent possible in accordance with the provisions of Protocol I to the present Convention.

(2) Each Party to the Convention shall:

(a) make all arrangements necessary for an appropriate officer or agency to receive and process all reports on incidents; and

(b) notify the Organization with complete details of such arrangements for circulation to other Parties and Member States of the Organization.

(3) Whenever a Party receives a report under the provisions of the present Article, that Party shall relay the report without delay to:

(a) the Administration of the ship involved; and

(b) any other State which may be affected.

(4) Each Party to the Convention undertakes to issue instructions to its maritime inspection vessels and aircraft and to other appropriate services, to report to its authorities any incident referred to in Protocol I to the present Convention. That Party shall, if it considers it appropriate, report accordingly to the Organization and to any other party concerned.

ARTICLE 9

Other Treaties and Interpretation

(1) Upon its entry into force, the present Convention supersedes the International Convention for the Prevention of Pollution of the Sea by Oil, 1954, as amended, as between Parties to that Convention.

(2) Nothing in the present Convention shall prejudice the codification and development of the law of the sea by the United Nations Conference on the Law of the Sea convened pursuant to Resolution 2750 C(XXV) of the General Assembly of the United Nations nor the present or future claims and legal views of any State concerning the law of the sea and the nature and extent of coastal and flag State jurisdiction.

(3) The term "jurisdiction" in the present Convention shall be construed in the light of international law in force at the time of application or interpretation of the present Convention.

ARTICLE 10

Settlement of Disputes

Any dispute between two or more Parties to the Convention concerning the interpretation or application of the present Convention shall, if settlement by negotiation between the Parties involved has not been possible, and if these Parties do not otherwise agree, be submitted upon request of any of them to arbitration as set out in Protocol II to the present Convention.

ARTICLE 11

Communication of Information

(1) The Parties to the Convention undertake to communicate to the Organization:

(a) the text of laws, orders, decrees and regulations and other instruments which have been promulgated on the various matters within the scope of the present Convention;

(b) a list of non-governmental agencies which are authorized to act on their behalf in matters relating to the design, construction and equipment of ships carrying harmful substances in accordance with the provisions of the Regulations;

(c) a sufficient number of specimens of their certificates issued under the provisions of the Regulations;

(d) a list of reception facilities including their location, capacity and available facilities and other characteristics;

(e) official reports or summaries of official reports in so far as they show the results of the application of the present Convention; and

(f) an annual statistical report, in a form standardized by the Organization, of penalties actually imposed for infringement of the present Convention.

(2) The Organization shall notify Parties of the receipt of any communications under the present Article and circulate to all Parties any information communicated to it under sub-paragraphs (1)(b) to (f) of the present Article.

ARTICLE 12

Casualties to Ships

(1) Each Administration undertakes to conduct an investigation of any casualty occurring to any of its ships subject to the provisions of the Regulations if such casualty has produced a major deleterious effect upon the marine environment.

(2) Each Party to the Convention undertakes to supply the Organization with information concerning the findings of such investigation, when it judges that such information may assist in determining what changes in the present Convention might be desirable.

ARTICLE 13

Signature, Ratification, Acceptance, Approval and Accession

(1) The present Convention shall remain open for signature at the Headquarters of the Organization from 15 January 1974 until 31 December 1974 and shall thereafter remain open for accession. States may become Parties to the present Convention by:

(a) signature without reservation as to ratification, acceptance or approval; or

(b) signature subject to ratification, acceptance or approval, followed by ratification, acceptance or approval; or

(c) accession.

(2) Ratification, acceptance, approval or accession shall be effected by the deposit of an instrument to that effect with the Secretary–General of the Organization.

(3) The Secretary–General of the Organization shall inform all States which have signed the present Convention or acceded to it of any signature or of the deposit of any new instrument of ratification, acceptance, approval or accession and the date of its deposit.

ARTICLE 14
Optional Annexes

(1) A State may at the time of signing, ratifying, accepting, approving or acceding to the present Convention declare that it does not accept any one or all of Annexes III, IV and V (hereinafter referred to as "Optional Annexes") of the present Convention. Subject to the above, Parties to the Convention shall be bound by any Annex in its entirety.

(2) A State which has declared that it is not bound by an Optional Annex may at any time accept such Annex by depositing with the Organization an instrument of the kind referred to in Article 13(2).

(3) A State which makes a declaration under paragraph (1) of the present Article in respect of an Optional Annex and which has not subsequently accepted that Annex in accordance with paragraph (2) of the present Article shall not be under any obligation nor entitled to claim any privileges under the present Convention in respect of matters related to such Annex and all references to Parties in the present Convention shall not include that State in so far as matters related to such Annex are concerned.

(4) The Organization shall inform the States which have signed or acceded to the present Convention of any declaration under the present Article as well as the receipt of any instrument deposited in accordance with the provisions of paragraph (2) of the present Article.

ARTICLE 15
Entry into Force

(1) The present Convention shall enter into force twelve months after the date on which not less than 15 States, the combined merchant fleets of which constitute not less than fifty per cent of the gross tonnage of the world's merchant shipping, have become parties to it in accordance with Article 13.

(2) An Optional Annex shall enter into force twelve months after the date on which the conditions stipulated in paragraph (1) of the present Article have been satisfied in relation to that Annex.

(3) The Organization shall inform the States which have signed the present Convention or acceded to it of the date on which it enters into force and of the date on which an Optional Annex enters into force in accordance with paragraph (2) of the present Article.

(4) For States which have deposited an instrument of ratification, acceptance, approval or accession in respect of the present Convention or any Optional Annex after the requirements for entry into force thereof have been met but prior to the date of entry into force, the ratification, acceptance, approval or accession shall take effect on the date of entry into force of the Convention or such Annex or three months after the date of deposit of the instrument whichever is the later date.

(5) For States which have deposited an instrument of ratification, acceptance, approval or accession after the date on which the Convention or an Optional Annex entered into force, the Convention or the Optional Annex shall become effective three months after the date of deposit of the instrument.

(6) After the date on which all the conditions required under Article 16 to bring an amendment to the present Convention or an Optional Annex into force have been fulfilled, any instrument of ratification, acceptance, approval or accession deposited shall apply to the Convention or Annex as amended.

ARTICLE 16
Amendments

(1) The present Convention may be amended by any of the procedures specified in the following paragraphs.

(2) Amendments after consideration by the Organization:

(a) any amendment proposed by a Party to the Convention shall be submitted to the Organization and circulated by its Secretary–General to all Members of the Organization and all Parties at least six months prior to its consideration;

(b) any amendment proposed and circulated as above shall be submitted to an appropriate body by the Organization for consideration;

(c) Parties to the Convention, whether or not Members of the Organization, shall be entitled to participate in the proceedings of the appropriate body;

(d) amendments shall be adopted by a two-thirds majority of only the Parties to the Convention present and voting;

(e) if adopted in accordance with sub-paragraph (d) above, amendments shall be communicated by the Secretary–General of the Organization to all the Parties to the Convention for acceptance;

(f) an amendment shall be deemed to have been accepted in the following circumstances:

(i) an amendment to an Article of the Convention shall be deemed to have been accepted on the date on which it is accepted by two-thirds of the Parties, the combined merchant fleets of which constitute not less than fifty per cent of the gross tonnage of the world's merchant fleet;

(ii) an amendment to an Annex to the Convention shall be deemed to have been accepted in accordance with the procedure specified in sub-paragraph (f)(iii) unless the appropriate body, at the time of its adoption, determines that the amendment shall be deemed to have been accepted on the date on which it is accepted by two-thirds of the Parties, the combined merchant fleets of which constitute not less than fifty per cent of the gross tonnage of the world's merchant fleet. Nevertheless, at any time before the entry into force of an amendment to an Annex to the Convention, a Party may notify the Secretary–General of the Organization that its express approval will be necessary before the amendment enters into force for it. The latter shall bring such notification and the date of its receipt to the notice of Parties;

(iii) an amendment to an Appendix to an Annex to the Convention shall be deemed to have been accepted at the end of a period to be determined by the appropriate body at the time of its adoption, which period shall be not less than ten months, unless within that period an objection is communicated to the Organization by not less than one-third of the Parties or by the Parties the combined merchant fleets of which constitute not less than fifty per cent of the gross tonnage of the world's merchant fleet whichever condition is fulfilled;

(iv) an amendment to Protocol I to the Convention shall be subject to the same procedures as for the amendments to the Annexes to the Convention, as provided for in sub-paragraphs (f)(ii) or (f)(iii) above;

(v) an amendment to Protocol II to the Convention shall be subject to the same procedures as for the amendments to an Article of the Convention, as provided for in sub-paragraph (f)(i) above;

(g) the amendment shall enter into force under the following conditions:

(i) in the case of an amendment to an Article of the Convention, to Protocol II, or to Protocol I or to an Annex to the Convention not under the procedure specified in sub-paragraph (f)(iii), the amendment accepted in conformity with the foregoing provisions shall enter into force six months after the date of its acceptance with respect to the Parties which have declared that they have accepted it;

(ii) in the case of an amendment to Protocol I, to an Appendix to an Annex or to an Annex to the Convention under the procedure specified in sub-paragraph (f)(iii), the amendment deemed to have been accepted in accordance with the foregoing conditions shall enter into force six months after its acceptance for all the Parties with the exception of those which, before that date, have made a declaration that they do not accept it or a declaration under subparagraph (f)(ii), that their express approval is necessary.

(3) Amendment by a Conference:

(a) Upon the request of a Party, concurred in by at least one-third of the Parties, the Organization shall convene a Conference of Parties to the Convention to consider amendments to the present Convention.

(b) Every amendment adopted by such a Conference by a two-thirds majority of those present and voting of the Parties shall be communicated by the Secretary-General of the Organization to all Contracting Parties for their acceptance.

(c) Unless the Conference decides otherwise, the amendment shall be deemed to have been accepted and to have entered into force in accordance with the procedures specified for that purpose in paragraph (2)(f) and (g) above.

(4)(a) In the case of an amendment to an Optional Annex, a reference in the present Article to a "Party to the Convention" shall be deemed to mean a reference to a Party bound by that Annex.

(b) Any Party which has declined to accept an amendment to an Annex shall be treated as a non-Party only for the purpose of application of that amendment.

(5) The adoption and entry into force of a new Annex shall be subject to the same procedures as for the adoption and entry into force of an amendment to an Article of the Convention.

(6) Unless expressly provided otherwise, any amendment to the present Convention made under this Article, which relates to the structure of a ship, shall apply only to ships for which the building contract is placed, or in the absence of a building contract, the keel of which is laid, on or after the date on which the amendment comes into force.

(7) Any amendment to a Protocol or to an Annex shall relate to the substance of that Protocol or Annex and shall be consistent with the Articles of the present Convention.

(8) The Secretary-General of the Organization shall inform all Parties of any amendments which enter into force under the present Article, together with the date on which each such amendment enters into force.

(9) Any declaration of acceptance or of objection to an amendment under the present article shall be notified in writing to the Secretary-General of the Organization. The latter shall bring such notification and the date of its receipt to the notice of the Parties to the Convention.

ARTICLE 17
Promotion of Technical Co-operation

The Parties to the Convention shall promote, in consultation with the Organization and other international bodies, with assistance and co-ordination by the Executive Director of the United Nations Environment Programme, support for those Parties which request technical assistance for:

(a) the training of scientific and technical personnel;

(b) the supply of necessary equipment and facilities for reception and monitoring;

(c) the facilitation of other measures and arrangements to prevent or mitigate pollution of the marine environment by ships; and

(d) the encouragement of research;

preferably within the countries concerned, so furthering the aims and purposes of the present Convention.

ARTICLE 18
Denunciation

(1) The present Convention or any Optional Annex may be denounced by any Parties to the Convention at any time after the expiry of five years from the date on which the Convention or such Annex enters into force for that Party.

(2) Denunciation shall be effected by notification in writing to the Secretary-General of the Organization who shall inform all the other Parties of any such notification received and of the date of its receipt as well as the date on which such denunciation takes effect.

(3) A denunciation shall take effect twelve months after receipt of the notification of denunciation by the Secretary-General of the Organization or after the expiry of any other longer period which may be indicated in the notification.

ARTICLE 19
Deposit and Registration

(1) The present Convention shall be deposited with the Secretary–General of the Organization who shall transmit certified true copies thereof to all States which have signed the present Convention or acceded to it.

(2) As soon as the present Convention enters into force, the text shall be transmitted by the Secretary–General of the Organization to the Secretary-General of the United Nations for registration and publication, in accordance with Article 102 of the Charter of the United Nations.

ARTICLE 20
Languages

The present Convention is established in a single copy in the English, French, Russian and Spanish languages, each text being equally authentic. Official translations in the Arabic, German, Italian and Japanese languages shall be prepared and deposited with the signed original.

ANNEX I [2]
OF MARPOL 73/78
INCLUDING PROPOSED AMENDMENTS
REGULATIONS FOR THE PREVENTION OF POLLUTION BY OIL
CHAPTER I—GENERAL
Regulation 1
Definitions

For the purposes of this Annex:

(1) "Oil" means petroleum in any form including crude oil, fuel oil, sludge, oil refuse and refined products (other than petrochemicals which are subject to the provisions of Annex II of the present Convention) and, without limiting the generality of the foregoing, includes the substances listed in Appendix I to this Annex.

(2) "Oily mixture" means a mixture with any oil content.

(3) "Oil fuel" means any oil used as fuel in connexion with the propulsion and auxiliary machinery of the ship in which such oil is carried.

(4) "Oil tanker" means a ship constructed or adapted primarily to carry oil in bulk in its cargo spaces and includes combination carriers and any "chemical tanker" as defined in Annex II of the present Convention when it is carrying a cargo or part cargo of oil in bulk.

(5) "Combination carrier" means a ship designed to carry either oil or solid cargoes in bulk.

(6) "New ship" means a ship:

(a) for which the building contract is placed after 31 December 1975; or

(b) in the absence of a building contract, the keel of which is laid or which is at a similar stage of construction after 30 June 1976; or

(c) the delivery of which is after 31 December 1979; or

(d) which has undergone a major conversion:

    (i) for which the contract is placed after 31 December 1975; or

    (ii) in the absence of a contract, the construction work of which is begun after 30 June 1976; or

    (iii) which is completed after 31 December 1979.

(7) "Existing ship" means a ship which is not a new ship.

(8)(a) "Major conversion" means a conversion of an existing ship:

    (i) which substantially alters the dimensions or carrying capacity of the ship; or

    (ii) which changes the type of the ship; or

    (iii) the intent of which in the opinion of the Administration is substantially to prolong its life; or

    (iv) which otherwise so alters the ship that, if it were a new ship, it would become subject to relevant provisions of the present Convention not applicable to it as an existing ship.

(b) Notwithstanding the provisions of sub-paragraph (a) of this paragraph, conversion of an existing oil tanker of 20,000 tons deadweight and above to meet the requirements of Regulation 13 of this Annex shall not be deemed to constitute a major conversion for the purposes of this Annex.

(9) "Nearest land". The term "from the nearest land" means from the baseline from which the territorial sea of the territory in question is established in accordance with international law, except that, for the purposes of the present Convention "from the nearest land" off the north eastern coast of Australia shall mean from a line drawn from a point on the coast of Australia in

latitude 11°00' South, longitude 142°08' East to a point in latitude 10°35' South,

longitude 141°55' East, thence to a point latitude 10°00' South,

longitude 142°00' East, thence to a point latitude 9°10' South,

longitude 143°52' East, thence to a point latitude 9°00' South,

longitude 144°30' East, thence to a point latitude 13°00' South,

longitude 144°00' East, thence to a point latitude 15°00' South,

longitude 146°00' East, thence to a point latitude 18°00' South,

longitude 147°00' East, thence to a point latitude 21°00' South,

longitude 153°00' East, thence to a point on the coast of Australia in latitude 24°42' South, longitude 153°15' East.

(10) "Special area" means a sea area where for recognized technical reasons in relation to its oceanographical and ecological condition and to the particular character of its traffic the adoption of special mandatory methods for the prevention of sea pollution by oil is required. Special areas shall include those listed in Regulation 10 of this Annex.

(11) "Instantaneous rate of discharge of oil content" means the rate of discharge of oil in litres per hour at any instant divided by the speed of the ship in knots at the same instant.

(12) "Tank" means an enclosed space which is formed by the permanent structure of a ship and which is designed for the carriage of liquid in bulk.

(13) "Wing tank" means any tank adjacent to the side shell plating.

(14) "Centre tank" means any tank inboard of a longitudinal bulkhead.

(15) "Slop tank" means a tank specifically designated for the collection of tank drainings, tank washings and other oily mixtures.

(16) "Clean ballast" means the ballast in a tank which since oil was last carried therein, has been so cleaned that effluent therefrom if it were discharged from a ship which is stationary into clean calm water on a clear day would not produce visible traces of oil on the surface of the water or on adjoining shorelines or cause a sludge or emulsion to be deposited beneath the surface of the water or upon adjoining shorelines. If the ballast is discharged through an oil discharge monitoring and control system approved by the Administration, evidence based on such a system to the effect that the oil content of the effluent did not exceed 15 parts per million shall be determinative that the ballast was clean, notwithstanding the presence of visible traces.

(17) "Segregated ballast" means the ballast water introduced into a tank which is completely separated from the cargo oil and oil fuel system and which is permanently allocated to the carriage of ballast or to the carriage of ballast or cargoes other than oil or noxious substances as variously defined in the Annexes of the present Convention.

(18) "Length" (L) means 96 per cent of the total length on a waterline at 85 per cent of the least moulded depth measured from the top of the keel, or the length from the foreside of the stem to the axis of the rudder stock on that waterline, if that be greater. In ships designed with a rake of keel the waterline on which this length is measured shall be parallel to the designed waterline. The length (L) shall be measured in metres.

(19) "Forward and after perpendiculars" shall be taken at the forward and after ends of the length (L). The forward perpendicular shall coincide with the foreside of the stem on the waterline on which the length is measured.

(20) "Amidships" is at the middle of the length (L).

(21) "Breadth" (B) means the maximum breadth of the ship, measured amidships to the moulded line of the frame in a ship with a metal shell and to the outer surface of the hull in a ship with a shell of any other material. The breadth (B) shall be measured in metres.

(22) "Deadweight" (DW) means the difference in metric tons between the displacement of a ship in water of a specific gravity of 1.025 at the load waterline corresponding to the assigned summer freeboard and the light-weight of the ship.

(23) "Lightweight" means the displacement of a ship in metric tons without cargo, fuel, lubricating oil, ballast water, fresh water and feed water in tanks, consumable stores, and passengers and crew and their effects.

(24) "Permeability" of a space means the ratio of the volume within that space which is assumed to be occupied by water to the total volume of that space.

(25) "Volumes" and "areas" in a ship shall be calculated in all cases to moulded lines.

(26) Notwithstanding the provisions of paragraph (6) of this Regulation, for the purposes of Regulations 13, 13B, 13E and 18(4) of this Annex, "new oil tanker" means an oil tanker:

(a) for which the building contract is placed after 1 June 1979; or

(b) in the absence of a building contract, the keel of which is laid or which is at a similar stage of construction after 1 January 1980; or

(c) the delivery of which is after 1 June 1982; or

(d) which has undergone a major conversion:

(i) for which the contract is placed after 1 June 1979; or

(ii) in the absence of a contract, the construction work of which is begun after 1 January 1980; or

(iii) which is completed after 1 June 1982;

except that, for oil tankers of 70,000 tons deadweight and above, the definition in paragraph (6) of this Regulation shall apply for the purposes of Regulation 13(1) of this Annex.

(27) Notwithstanding the provisions of paragraph (7) of this Regulation, for the purposes of Regulations 13, 13A, 13B, 13C, 13D, 18(5) and 18(6)(c) of this Annex, "existing oil tanker" means an oil tanker which is not a new oil tanker as defined in paragraph (26) of this Regulation.

(28) "Crude oil" means any liquid hydrocarbon mixture occurring naturally in the earth whether or not treated to render it suitable for transportation and includes:

(a) crude oil from which certain distillate fractions may have been removed; and

(b) crude oil to which certain distillate fractions may have been added.

(29) "Crude oil tanker" means an oil tanker engaged in the trade of carrying crude oil.

(30) "Product carrier" means an oil tanker engaged in the trade of carrying oil other than crude oil.

Regulation 2
Application

(1) Unless expressly provided otherwise, the provisions of this Annex shall apply to all ships.

(2) In ships other than oil tankers fitted with cargo spaces which are constructed and utilized to carry oil in bulk of an aggregate capacity of 200 cubic metres or more, the requirements of Regulations 9, 10, 14, 15(1), (2) and (3), 18, 20 and 24(4) of this Annex for oil tankers shall also apply to the construction and operation of those spaces, except that where such aggregate capacity is less than 1,000 cubic metres the requirements of Regulation 15(4) of this Annex may apply in lieu of Regulation 15(1), (2) and (3).

(3) Where a cargo subject to the provisions of Annex II of the present Convention is carried in a cargo space of an oil tanker, the appropriate requirements of Annex II of the present Convention shall also apply.

(4)(a) Any hydrofoil, air-cushion vehicle and other new type of vessel (near-surface craft, submarine craft, etc.) whose constructional features are such as to render the application of any of the provisions of Chapters II and III of this Annex relating to construction and equipment unreasonable or impracticable may be exempted by the Administration from such provisions, provided that the construction and equipment of that ship provides equivalent protection against pollution by oil, having regard to the service for which it is intended.

(b) Particulars of any such exemption granted by the Administration shall be indicated in the Certificate referred to in Regulation 5 of this Annex.

(c) The Administration which allows any such exemption shall, as soon as possible, but not more than ninety days thereafter, communicate to the Organization particulars of same and the reasons, therefor, which the Organization shall circulate to the Parties to the Convention for their information and appropriate action, if any.

Regulation 3
Equivalents

(1) The Administration may allow any fitting, material, appliance or apparatus to be fitted in a ship as an alternative to that required by this Annex if such fitting, material, appliance or apparatus is at least as effective as that required by this Annex. This authority of the Administration shall not extend to substitution of operational methods to effect the control of discharge of oil as equivalent to those design and construction features which are prescribed by Regulations in this Annex.

(2) The Administration which allows a fitting, material, appliance or apparatus, as an alternative to that required by this Annex shall communicate to the Organization for circulation to the Parties to the Convention particulars thereof, for their information and appropriate action, if any.

Regulation 4
Surveys and Inspections

(1) Every oil tanker of 150 tons gross tonnage and above, and every other ship of 400 tons gross tonnage and above shall be subject to the surveys specified below:

(a) An initial survey before the ship is put in service or before the Certificate required under Regulation 5 of this Annex is issued for the first time, which shall include a complete survey of its structure, equipment, systems, fittings, arrangements and material in so far as the ship is covered by this Annex. This survey shall be such as to ensure that the structure, equipment, systems, fittings, arrangements and material fully comply with the applicable requirements of this Annex.

(b) Periodical surveys at intervals specified by the Administration, but not exceeding five years, which shall be such as to ensure that the structure, equipment, systems, fittings, arrangements and material fully comply with the requirements of this Annex.

(c) A minimum of one intermediate survey during the period of validity of the Certificate which shall be such as to ensure that the equipment and associated pump and piping systems, including oil discharge monitoring and control systems, crude oil washing systems, oily-water separating equipment and oil filtering systems, fully comply with the applicable requirements of this Annex and are in good working order. In cases where only one such intermediate survey is carried out in any one Certificate validity period, it shall be held not before six months prior to, nor later than six months after the half-way date of the Certificate's period of validity. Such intermediate surveys shall be endorsed on the Certificate issued under Regulation 5 of this Annex.

(2) The Administration shall establish appropriate measures for ships which are not subject to the provisions of paragraph (1) of this Regulation in order to ensure that the applicable provisions of this Annex are complied with.

(3)(a) Surveys of ships as regards the enforcement of the provisions of this Annex shall be carried out by officers of the Administration. The Administration may, however, entrust the surveys either to surveyors nominated for the purpose or to organizations recognized by it.

(b) The Administration shall institute arrangements for unscheduled inspections to be carried out during the period of validity of the Certificate. Such inspections shall ensure that the ship and its equipment remain in all respects satisfactory for the service for which the ship is intended. These inspections may be carried out by their own inspection services, or by nominated surveyors or by recognized organizations, or by other Parties upon request of the Administration. Where the Administration, under the provisions of paragraph (1) of this Regulation, establishes mandatory annual surveys, the above unscheduled inspections shall not be obligatory.

(c) An Administration nominating surveyors or recognizing organizations to conduct surveys and inspections as set forth in sub-paragraphs (a) and (b) of this paragraph, shall as a minimum empower any nominated surveyor or recognized organization to:

(i) require repairs to a ship; and

(ii) carry out surveys and inspections if requested by the appropriate authorities of a Port State.

The Administration shall notify the Organization of the specific responsibilities and conditions of the authority delegated to the nominated surveyors or recognized organizations, for circulation to Parties to the present Protocol for the information of their officers.

(d) When a nominated surveyor or recognized organization determines that the condition of the ship or its equipment does not correspond substantially with the particulars of the Certificate or is such that the ship is not fit to proceed to sea without presenting an unreasonable threat of harm to the marine environment, such surveyor or organization shall immediately ensure that corrective action is taken and shall in due course notify the Administration. If such corrective action is not taken the Certificate should be withdrawn and the Administration shall be notified immediately; and if the ship is in a port of another Party, the appropriate authorities of the Port State shall also be notified immediately. When an officer of the Administration, a nominated surveyor or recognized organization has notified the appropriate authorities of the Port State, the Government of the Port State concerned shall give such officer, surveyor or organization any necessary assistance to carry out their obligations under this Regulation. When applicable, the Government of the Port State concerned shall take such steps as will ensure that the ship shall not sail until it can proceed to sea or leave the port for the purpose of proceeding to the nearest appropriate repair yard available without presenting an unreasonable threat of harm to the marine environment.

(e) In every case, the Administration concerned shall fully guarantee the completeness and efficiency of the survey and inspection and shall undertake to ensure the necessary arrangements to satisfy this obligation.

(4)(a) The condition of the ship and its equipment shall be maintained to conform with the provisions of the present Convention to ensure that the ship in all respects will remain fit to proceed to sea without presenting an unreasonable threat of harm to the marine environment.

(b) After any survey of the ship under paragraph (1) of this Regulation has been completed, no change shall be made in the structure, equipment, systems, fittings, arrangements or material covered by the survey, without the sanction of the Administration, except the direct replacement of such equipment and fittings.

(c) Whenever an accident occurs to a ship or a defect is discovered which substantially affects the integrity of the ship or the efficiency or completeness of its equipment covered by this Annex the master or owner of the ship shall report at the earliest opportunity to the Administration, the recognized organization or the nominated surveyor responsible for issuing the relevant Certificate, who shall cause investigations to be initiated to determine whether a survey as required by paragraph (1) of this Regulation is necessary. If the ship is in a port of another Party, the master or owner shall also report immediately to the appropriate authorities of the Port State and the nominated surveyor or recognized organization shall ascertain that such report has been made.

Regulation 5
Issue of Certificate

(1) An International Oil Pollution Prevention Certificate shall be issued, after survey in accordance with the provisions of Regulation 4 of this Annex, to any oil tanker of 150 tons gross tonnage and above and any other ships of 400 tons gross tonnage and above which are engaged in voyages to ports or off-shore terminals under the jurisdiction of other Parties to the Convention. In the case of existing ships this requirement shall apply twelve months after the date of entry into force of the present Convention.

(2) Such Certificate shall be issued either by the Administration or by any persons or organization duly authorized by it. In every case the Administration assumes full responsibility for the Certificate.

Regulation 6
Issue of a Certificate by another Government

(1) The Government of a Party to the Convention may, at the request of the Administration, cause a ship to be surveyed and, if satisfied that the provisions of this Annex are complied with, shall issue or authorize the issue of an International Oil Pollution Prevention Certificate to the ship in accordance with this Annex.

(2) A copy of the Certificate and a copy of the survey report shall be transmitted as soon as possible to the requesting Administration.

(3) A Certificate so issued shall contain a statement to the effect that it has been issued at the request of the Administration and it shall have the same force and receive the same recognition as the Certificate issued under Regulation 5 of this Annex.

(4) No International Oil Pollution Prevention Certificate shall be issued to a ship which is entitled to fly the flag of a State which is not a Party.

Regulation 7
Form of Certificate

The International Oil Pollution Prevention Certificate shall be drawn up in an official language of the issuing country in the form corresponding to the model given in Appendix II to this Annex. If the language used is neither English nor French, the text shall include a translation into one of these languages.

Regulation 8
Duration of Certificate

(1) An International Oil Pollution Prevention Certificate shall be issued for a period specified by the Administration, which shall not exceed five years from the date of issue, provided that in the case of an oil tanker operating with dedicated clean ballast tanks for a limited period specified in Regulation 13(9) of this Annex, the period of validity of the Certificate shall not exceed such specified period.

(2) A Certificate shall cease to be valid if significant alterations have taken place in the construction, equipment, systems, fittings, arrangements or material required without the sanction of the Administration, except the direct replacement of such equipment or fittings, or if intermediate surveys as specified by the Administration under Regulation 4(1)(c) of this Annex are not carried out.

(3) A Certificate issued to a ship shall also cease to be valid upon transfer of the ship to the flag of another State. A new Certificate shall only be issued when the Government issuing the new Certificate is fully satisfied that the ship is in full compliance with the requirements of Regulation 4(4)(a) and (b) of this Annex. In the case of a transfer between Parties, if requested within three months after the transfer has taken place, the Government of the Party whose flag the ship was formerly entitled to fly shall transmit as soon as possible to the Administration a copy of the Certificate carried by the ship before the transfer and, if available, a copy of the relevant survey report.

CHAPTER II—REQUIREMENTS FOR CONTROL OF OPERATIONAL POLLUTION
Regulation 9
Control of Discharge of Oil

(1) Subject to the provisions of Regulations 10 and 11 of this Annex and paragraph (2) of this Regulation, any discharge into the sea of oil or oily mixtures from ships to which this Annex applies shall be prohibited except when all the following conditions are satisfied:

(a) for an oil tanker, except as provided for in sub-paragraph (b) of this paragraph:

(i) the tanker is not within a special area;

(ii) the tanker is more than 50 nautical miles from the nearest land;

(iii) the tanker is proceeding en route;

(iv) the instantaneous rate of discharge of oil content does not exceed 60 litres per nautical mile;

(v) the total quantity of oil discharged into the sea does not exceed for existing tankers 1/15,000 of the total quantity of the particular cargo of which the residue formed a part, and for new tankers 1/30,000 of the total quantity of the particular cargo of which the residue formed a part; and

(vi) the tanker has in operation an oil discharge monitoring and control system and a slop tank arrangement as required by Regulation 15 of this Annex.

(b) from a ship of 400 tons gross tonnage and above other than an oil tanker and from machinery space bilges excluding cargo pump room bilges of an oil tanker unless mixed with oil cargo residue:

(i) the ship is not within a special area;

(ii) the ship is more than 12 nautical miles from the nearest land;

(iii) the ship is proceeding en route;

(iv) the oil content of the effluent is less than 100 parts per million; and

(v) the ship has in operation an oil discharge monitoring and control system, oily-water separating equipment, oil filtering equipment or other installation as required by Regulation 16 of this Annex.

(2) In the case of a ship of less than 400 tons gross tonnage other than an oil tanker whilst outside the special area, the Administration shall ensure that it is equipped as far as practicable and reasonable with installations to ensure the storage of oil residues on board and their discharge to reception facilities or into the sea in compliance with the requirements of paragraph (1)(b) of this Regulation.

(3) Whenever visible traces of oil are observed on or below the surface of the water in the immediate vicinity of a ship or its wake, Governments of Parties to the Convention should, to the extent they are reasonably able to do so, promptly investigate the facts bearing on the issue of whether there has been a violation of the provisions of this Regulation or Regulation 10 of this Annex. The investigation should include, in particular, the wind and sea conditions, the track and speed of the ship, other possible sources of the visible traces in the vicinity, and any relevant oil discharge records.

(4) The provisions of paragraph (1) of this Regulation shall not apply to the discharge of clean or segregated ballast or unprocessed oily mixtures which without dilution have an oil content not exceeding 15 parts per million and which do not originate from cargo pump-room bilges and are not mixed

with oil cargo residues. The provisions of sub-paragraph (1)(b) of this Regulation shall not apply to the discharge of the processed oily mixture, provided that all of the following conditions are satisfied:

(a) the oily mixture does not originate from cargo pump-room bilges;

(b) the oily mixture is not mixed with oil cargo residues;

(c) the oil content of the effluent without dilution does not exceed 15 parts per million; and

(d) the ship has in operation oil filtering equipment complying with Regulation 16(7) of this Annex.

(5) No discharge into the sea shall contain chemicals or other substances in quantities or concentrations which are hazardous to the marine environment or chemicals or other substances introduced for the purpose of circumventing the conditions of discharge specified in this Regulation.

(6) The oil residues which cannot be discharged into the sea in compliance with paragraphs (1), (2) and (4) of this Regulation shall be retained on board or discharged to reception facilities.

Regulation 10
Methods for the Prevention of Oil Pollution from Ships while operating in Special Areas

(1) For the purposes of this Annex the special areas are the Mediterranean Sea area, the Baltic Sea area, the Black Sea area, the Red Sea area and the "Gulfs area" which are defined as follows:

(a) The Mediterranean Sea area means the Mediterranean Sea proper including the gulfs and seas therein with the boundary between the Mediterranean and the Black Sea constituted by the 41°N parallel and bounded to the west by the Straits of Gibraltar at the meridian of 5°36'W.

(b) The Baltic Sea area means the Baltic Sea proper with the Gulf of Bothnia, the Gulf of Finland and the entrance to the Baltic Sea bounded by the parallel of the Skaw in the Skagerrak at 57°44.8'N.

(c) The Black Sea area means the Black Sea proper with the boundary between the Mediterranean and the Black Sea constituted by the parallel 41°N.

(d) The Red Sea area means the Red Sea proper including the Gulfs of Suez and Aqaba bounded at the south by the rhumb line between Ras si Ane (12°8.5'N, 43°19.6'E) and Husn Murad (12°40.4'N, 43°30.2'E).

(e) The Gulfs area means the sea area located north west of the rhumb line between Ras al Hadd (22°30'N, 59°48'E) and Ras Al Fasteh (25°04'N, 61°25'E).

(2) Subject to the provisions of Regulation 11 of this Annex:

(a) Any discharge into the sea of oil or oily mixture from any oil tanker and any ship of 400 tons gross tonnage and above other than an oil tanker shall be prohibited while in a special area;

(b) any discharge into the sea of oil or oily mixture from a ship of less than 400 tons gross tonnage, other than an oil tanker, shall be prohibited while in a special area, except when the oil content of the effluent without dilution does not exceed 15 parts per million or alternatively when all of the following conditions are satisfied:

(i) the ship is proceeding en route;

(ii) the oil content of the effluent is less than 100 parts per million; and

(iii) the discharge is made as far as practicable from the land, but in no case less than 12 nautical miles from the nearest land.

(3)(a) The provisions of paragraph (2) of this Regulation shall not apply to the discharge of clean or segregated ballast.

(b) The provisions of sub-paragraph (2)(a) of this Regulation shall not apply to the discharge of processed bilge water from machinery spaces, provided that all of the following conditions are satisfied:

(i) the bilge water does not originate from cargo pump room bilges;

(ii) the bilge water is not mixed with oil cargo residues;

(iii) the ship is proceeding en route;

(iv) the oil content of the effluent without dilution does not exceed 15 parts per million;

(v) the ship has in operation oil filtering equipment complying with Regulation 16(7) of this Annex; and

(vi) the filtering system is equipped with a stopping device which will ensure that the discharge is automatically stopped when the oil content of the effluent exceeds 15 parts per million.

(4)(a) No discharge into the sea shall contain chemicals or other substances in quantities or concentrations which are hazardous to the marine environment or chemicals or other substances introduced for the purpose of circumventing the conditions of discharge specified in this Regulation.

(b) The oil residues which cannot be discharged into the sea in compliance with paragraph (2) or (3) of this Regulation shall be retained on board or discharged to reception facilities.

(5) Nothing in this Regulation shall prohibit a ship on a voyage only part of which is in a special area from discharging outside the special area in accordance with Regulation 9 of this Annex.

(6) Whenever visible traces of oil are observed on or below the surface of the water in the immediate vicinity of a ship or its wake, the Governments of

Parties to the Convention should, to the extent they are reasonably able to do so, promptly investigate the facts bearing on the issue of whether there has been a violation of the provisions of this Regulation or Regulation 9 of this Annex. The investigation should include, in particular, the wind and sea conditions, the track and speed of the ship, other possible sources of the visible traces in the vicinity, and any relevant oil discharge records.

(7) Reception facilities within special areas:

(a) Mediterranean Sea, Black Sea and Baltic Sea areas:

(i) The Government of each Party to the Convention, the coastline of which borders on any given special area undertakes to ensure that not later than 1 January 1977 all oil loading terminals and repair ports within the special area are provided with facilities adequate for the reception and treatment of all the dirty ballast and tank washing water from oil tankers. In addition all ports within the special area shall be provided with adequate reception facilities for other residues and oily mixtures from all ships. Such facilities shall have adequate capacity to meet the needs of the ships using them without causing undue delay.

(ii) The Government of each Party having under its jurisdiction entrances to seawater courses with low depth contour which might require a reduction of draught by the discharge of ballast undertakes to ensure the provision of the facilities referred to in sub-paragraph (a)(i) of this paragraph but with the proviso that ships required to discharge slops or dirty ballast could be subject to some delay.

(iii) During the period between the entry into force of the present Convention (if earlier than 1 January 1977) and 1 January 1977 ships while navigating in the special areas shall comply with the requirements of Regulation 9 of this Annex. However, the Governments of Parties the coastlines of which border any of the special areas under this sub-paragraph may establish a date earlier than 1 January 1977, but after the date of entry into force of the present Convention, from which the requirements of this Regulation in respect of the special areas in question shall take effect:

(1) if all the reception facilities required have been provided by the date so established; and

(2) provided that the Parties concerned notify the Organization of the date so established at least six months in advance, for circulation to other Parties.

(iv) After 1 January 1977, or the date established in accordance with sub-paragraph (a)(iii) of this paragraph if earlier, each Party shall notify the Organization for transmission to the Contracting Governments concerned of all cases where the facilities are alleged to be inadequate.

(b) Red Sea area and Gulfs area:

(i) The Government of each Party the coastline of which borders on the special areas undertakes to ensure that as soon as possible all oil loading terminals and repair ports within these special areas are provided with facilities adequate for the reception and treatment of all the dirty ballast and tank washing water from tankers. In addition all ports within the special area shall be provided with adequate reception facilities for other residues and oily mixtures from all ships. Such facilities shall have adequate capacity to meet the needs of the ships using them without causing undue delay.

(ii) The Government of each Party having under its jurisdiction entrances to seawater courses with low depth contour which might require a reduction of draught by the discharge of ballast shall undertake to ensure the provision of the facilities referred to in sub-paragraph (b)(i) of this paragraph but with the proviso that ships required to discharge slops or dirty ballast could be subject to some delay.

(iii) Each Party concerned shall notify the Organization of the measures taken pursuant to provisions of sub-paragraph (b)(i) and (ii) of this paragraph. Upon receipt of sufficient notifications the Organization shall establish a date from which the requirements of this Regulation in respect of the area in question shall take effect. The Organization shall notify all Parties of the date so established no less than twelve months in advance of that date.

(iv) During the period between the entry into force of the present Convention and the date so established, ships while navigating in the special area shall comply with the requirements of Regulation 9 of this Annex.

(v) After such date oil tankers loading in ports in these special areas where such facilities are not yet available shall also fully comply with the requirements of this Regulation. However, oil tankers entering these special areas for the purpose of loading shall make every effort to enter the area with only clean ballast on board.

(vi) After the date on which the requirements for the special area in question take effect, each Party shall notify the Organization for transmission to the Parties concerned of all cases where the facilities are alleged to be inadequate.

(vii) At least the reception facilities as prescribed in Regulation 12 of this Annex shall be provided by 1 January 1977 or one year after the date of entry into force of the present Convention, whichever occurs later.

Regulation 11

Exceptions

Regulations 9 and 10 of this Annex shall not apply to:

(a) the discharge into the sea of oil or oily mixture necessary for the purpose of securing the safety of a ship or saving life at sea; or

(b) the discharge into the sea of oil or oily mixture resulting from damage to a ship or its equipment:

(i) provided that all reasonable precautions have been taken after the occurrence of the damage or discovery of the discharge for the purpose of preventing or minimizing the discharge; and

(ii) except if the owner or the Master acted either with intent to cause damage, or recklessly and with knowledge that damage would probably result; or

(c) the discharge into the sea of substances containing oil, approved by the Administration, when being used for the purpose of combating specific pollution incidents in order to minimize the damage from pollution. Any such discharge shall be subject to the approval of any Government in whose jurisdiction it is contemplated the discharge will occur.

Regulation 12

Reception Facilities

(1) Subject to the provisions of Regulation 10 of this Annex, the Government of each Party undertakes to ensure the provision at oil loading terminals, repair ports, and in other ports in which ships have oily residues to discharge, of facilities for the reception of such residues and oily mixtures as remain from oil tankers and other ships adequate to meet the needs of the ships using them without causing undue delay to ships.

(2) Reception facilities in accordance with paragraph (1) of this Regulation shall be provided in:

(a) all ports and terminals in which crude oil is loaded into oil tankers where such tankers have immediately prior to arrival completed a ballast voyage of not more than 72 hours or not more than 1,200 nautical miles;

(b) all ports and terminals in which oil other than crude oil in bulk is loaded at an average quantity of more than 1,000 metric tons per day;

(c) all ports having ship repair yards or tank cleaning facilities;

(d) all ports and terminals which handle ships provided with the sludge tank(s) required by Regulation 17 of this Annex;

(e) all ports in respect of oily bilge waters and other residues, which cannot be discharged in accordance with Regulation 9 of this Annex; and

(f) all loading ports for bulk cargoes in respect of oil residues from combination carriers which cannot be discharged in accordance with Regulation 9 of this Annex.

(3) The capacity for the reception facilities shall be as follows:

(a) Crude oil loading terminals shall have sufficient reception facilities to receive oil and oily mixtures which cannot be discharged in accordance with the provisions of Regulation 9(1)(a) of this Annex from all oil tankers on voyages as described in paragraph (2)(a) of this Regulation.

(b) Loading ports and terminals referred to in paragraph (2)(b) of this Regulation shall have sufficient reception facilities to receive oil and oily mixtures which cannot be discharged in accordance with the provisions of Regulation 9(1)(a) of this Annex from oil tankers which load oil other than crude oil in bulk.

(c) All ports having ship repair yards or tank cleaning facilities shall have sufficient reception facilities to receive all residues and oily mixtures which remain on board for disposal from ships prior to entering such yards or facilities.

(d) All facilities provided in ports and terminals under paragraph (2)(d) of this Regulation shall be sufficient to receive all residues retained according to Regulation 17 of this Annex from all ships that may reasonably be expected to call at such ports and terminals.

(e) All facilities provided in ports and terminals under this Regulation shall be sufficient to receive only bilge waters and other residues which cannot be discharged in accordance with Regulation 9 of this Annex.

(f) The facilities provided in loading ports for bulk cargoes shall take into account the special problems of combination carriers as appropriate.

(4) The reception facilities prescribed in paragraphs (2) and (3) of this Regulation shall be made available no later than one year from the date of entry into force of the present Convention or by 1 January 1977, whichever occurs later.

(5) Each Party shall notify the Organization for transmission to the Parties concerned of all cases where the facilities provided under this Regulation are alleged to be inadequate.

Regulation 13
*Segregated Ballast Tanks, Dedicated Clean Ballast
Tanks and Crude Oil Washing*

Subject to the provisions of Regulations 13C and 13D of this Annex, oil tankers shall comply with the requirements of this Regulation.

New oil tankers of 20,000 tons deadweight and above

(1) Every new crude oil tanker of 20,000 tons deadweight and above and every new product carrier of 30,000 tons deadweight and above shall be provided with segregated ballast tanks and shall comply with paragraphs (2), (3) and (4), or paragraph (5) as appropriate, of this Regulation.

(2) The capacity of the segregated ballast tanks shall be so determined that the ship may operate safely on ballast voyages without recourse to the use of cargo tanks for water ballast except as provided for in paragraph (3) or (4) of this Regulation. In all cases, however, the capacity of segregated ballast tanks shall be at least such that, in any ballast condition at any part of the voyage, including the conditions consisting of lightweight plus segregated ballast only, the ship's draughts and trim can meet each of the following requirements:

(a) the moulded draught amidships (dm) in metres (without taking into account any ship's deformation) shall not be less than:

$$dm = 2.0 + 0.02L;$$

(b) the draughts at the forward and after perpendiculars shall correspond to those determined by the draught amidships (dm) as specified in subparagraph (a) of this paragraph, in association with the trim by the stern of not greater than 0.015L; and

(c) in any case the draught at the after perpendicular shall not be less than that which is necessary to obtain full immersion of the propeller(s).

(3) In no case shall ballast water be carried in cargo tanks, except:

(a) on those rare voyages when weather conditions are so severe that, in the opinion of the master, it is necessary to carry additional ballast water in cargo tanks for the safety of the ship;

(b) in exceptional cases where the particular character of the operation of an oil tanker renders it necessary to carry ballast water in excess of the quantity required under paragraph (2) of this Regulation, provided that such operation of the oil tanker falls under the category of exceptional cases as established by the Organization.

Such additional ballast water shall be processed and discharged in compliance with Regulation 9 of this Annex and in accordance with the requirements of Regulation 15 of this Annex and an entry shall be made in the Oil Record Book referred to in Regulation 20 of this Annex.

(4) In the case of new crude oil tankers, the additional ballast permitted in paragraph (3) of this Regulation shall be carried in cargo tanks only if such tanks have been crude oil washed in accordance with Regulation 13B of this Annex before departure from an oil unloading port or terminal.

(5) Notwithstanding the provisions of paragraph (2) of this Regulation, the segregated ballast conditions for oil tankers less than 150 metres in length shall be to the satisfaction of the Administration.

(6) Every new crude oil tanker of 20,000 tons deadweight and above shall be fitted with a cargo tank cleaning system using crude oil washing. The Administration shall undertake to ensure that the system fully complies with the requirements of Regulation 13B of this Annex within one year after the tanker was first engaged in the trade of carrying crude oil or by the end of the third voyage carrying crude oil suitable for crude oil washing, whichever occurs later. Unless such oil tanker carries crude oil which is not suitable for crude oil washing, the oil tanker shall operate the system in accordance with the requirements of that Regulation.

Existing crude oil tankers of 40,000 tons deadweight and above

(7) Subject to the provisions of paragraphs (8) and (9) of this Regulation every existing crude oil tanker of 40,000 tons deadweight and above shall be provided with segregated ballast tanks and shall comply with the requirements of paragraphs (2) and (3) of this Regulation from the date of entry into force of the present Convention.

(8) Existing crude oil tankers referred to in paragraph (7) of this Regulation may, in lieu of being provided with segregated ballast tanks, operate with a cargo tank cleaning procedure using crude oil washing in accordance with Regulation 13B of this Annex unless the crude oil tanker is intended to carry crude oil which is not suitable for crude oil washing.

(9) Existing crude oil tankers referred to in paragraph (7) or (8) of this Regulation may, in lieu of being provided with segregated ballast tanks or operating with a cargo tank cleaning procedure using crude oil washing, operate with dedicated clean ballast tanks in accordance with the provisions of Regulation 13A of this Annex for the following period:

(a) for crude oil tankers of 70,000 tons deadweight and above, until two years after the date of entry into force of the present Convention; and

(b) for crude oil tankers of 40,000 tons deadweight and above but below 70,000 tons deadweight, until four years after the date of entry into force of the present Convention.

Existing product carriers of 40,000 tons deadweight and above

(10) From the date of entry into force of the present Convention, every existing product carrier of 40,000 tons deadweight and above shall be provided with segregated ballast tanks and shall comply with the requirements of paragraphs (2) and (3) of this Regulation, or, alternatively, operate with dedicated clean ballast tanks in accordance with the provisions of Regulation 13A of this Annex.

An oil tanker qualified as a segregated ballast oil tanker

(11) Any oil tanker which is not required to be provided with segregated ballast tanks in accordance with paragraph (1), (7) or (10) of this Regulation

may, however, be qualified as a segregated ballast tanker, provided that it complies with the requirements of paragraphs (2) and (3), or paragraph (5) as appropriate, of this Regulation.

Regulation 13A
Requirements for Oil Tankers with Dedicated Clean Ballast Tanks

(1) An oil tanker operating with dedicated clean ballast tanks in accordance with the provisions of Regulation 13(9) or (10) of this Annex, shall have adequate tank capacity, dedicated solely to the carriage of clean ballast as defined in Regulation 1(16) of this Annex, to meet the requirements of Regulation 13(2) and (3) of this Annex.

(2) The arrangements and operational procedures for dedicated clean ballast tanks shall comply with the requirements established by the Administration. Such requirements shall contain at least all the provisions of the Specifications for Oil Tankers with Dedicated Clean Ballast Tanks adopted by the International Conference on Tanker Safety and Pollution Prevention, 1978, in Resolution 14 and as may be revised by the Organization.

(3) An oil tanker operating with dedicated clean ballast tanks shall be equipped with an oil content meter, approved by the Administration on the basis of specifications recommended by the Organization, to enable supervision of the oil content in ballast water being discharged. The oil content meter shall be installed no later than at the first scheduled shipyard visit of the tanker following the entry into force of the present Convention. Until such time as the oil content meter is installed, it shall immediately before discharge of ballast be established by examination of the ballast water from dedicated tanks that no contamination with oil has taken place.

(4) Every oil tanker operating with dedicated clean ballast tanks shall be provided with a Dedicated Clean Ballast Tank Operation Manual detailing the system and specifying operational procedures. Such a Manual shall be to the satisfaction of the Administration and shall contain all the information set out in the Specifications referred to in paragraph (2) of this Regulation. If an alteration affecting the dedicated clean ballast tank system is made, the Operation Manual shall be revised accordingly.

Regulation 13B
Requirements for Crude Oil Washing

(1) Every crude oil washing system required to be provided in accordance with Regulation 13(6) and (8) of this Annex shall comply with the requirements of this Regulation.

(2) The crude oil washing installation and associated equipment and arrangements shall comply with the requirements established by the Administration. Such requirements shall contain at least all the provisions of the Specifications for the Design, Operation and Control of Crude Oil Washing

Systems adopted by the International Conference on Tanker Safety and Pollution Prevention, 1978, in Resolution 15 and as may be revised by the Organization.

(3) An inert gas system shall be provided in every cargo tank and slop tank in accordance with the appropriate Regulations of Chapter II–2 of the International Convention for the Safety of Life at Sea, 1974, as modified and added to by the Protocol of 1978 Relating to the International Convention for the Safety of Life at Sea, 1974 and as may be further amended.

(4) With respect to the ballasting of cargo tanks, sufficient cargo tanks shall be crude oil washed prior to each ballast voyage in order that, taking into account the tanker's trading pattern and expected weather conditions, ballast water is put only into cargo tanks which have been crude oil washed.

(5) Every oil tanker operating with crude oil washing systems shall be provided with an Operations and Equipment Manual detailing the system and equipment and specifying operational procedures. Such a Manual shall be to the satisfaction of the Administration and shall contain all the information set out in the Specifications referred to in paragraph (2) of this Regulation. If an alteration affecting the crude oil washing system is made, the Operations and Equipment Manual shall be revised accordingly.

Regulation 13C
Existing Tankers Engaged in Specific Trades

(1) Subject to the provisions of paragraph (2) of this Regulation, Regulation 13(7) to (10) of this Annex shall not apply to an existing oil tanker solely engaged in specific trades between:

(a) ports or terminals within a State Party to the present Convention; or

(b) ports or terminals of States Parties to the present Convention, where:

(i) the voyage is entirely within a Special Area as defined in Regulation 10(1) of this Annex; or

(ii) the voyage is entirely within other limits designated by the Organization.

(2) The provisions of paragraph (1) of this Regulation shall only apply when the ports or terminals where cargo is loaded on such voyages are provided with reception facilities adequate for the reception and treatment of all the ballast and tank washing water from oil tankers using them and all the following conditions are complied with:

(a) subject to the exceptions provided for in Regulation 11 of this Annex, all ballast water, including clean ballast water, and tank washing residues are retained on board and transferred to the reception facilities and the appropriate entry in the Oil Record Book referred to in Regulation 20 of this Annex is endorsed by the competent Port State Authority;

(b) agreement has been reached between the Administration and the Governments of the Port States referred to in sub-paragraph (1)(a) or (b) of this Regulation concerning the use of an existing oil tanker for a specific trade;

(c) the adequacy of the reception facilities in accordance with the relevant provisions of this Annex at the ports or terminals referred to above, for the purpose of this Regulation, is approved by the Governments of the States Parties to the present Convention within which such ports or terminals are situated; and

(d) the International Oil Pollution Prevention Certificate is endorsed to the effect that the oil tanker is solely engaged in such specific trade.

Regulation 13D
Existing Oil Tankers Having Special Ballast Arrangements

(1) Where an existing oil tanker is so constructed or operates in such a manner that it complies at all times with the draught and trim requirements set out in Regulation 13(2) of this Annex without recourse to the use of ballast water, it shall be deemed to comply with the segregated ballast tank requirements referred to in Regulation 13(7) of this Annex, provided that all of the following conditions are complied with:

(a) operational procedures and ballast arrangements are approved by the Administration;

(b) agreement is reached between the Administration and the Governments of the Port States Parties to the present Convention concerned when the draught and trim requirements are achieved through an operational procedure; and

(c) the International Oil Pollution Prevention Certificate is endorsed to the effect that the oil tanker is operating with special ballast arrangements.

(2) In no case shall ballast water be carried in oil tanks except on those rare voyages when weather conditions are so severe that, in the opinion of the master, it is necessary to carry additional ballast water in cargo tanks for the safety of the ship. Such additional ballast water shall be processed and discharged in compliance with Regulation 9 of this Annex and in accordance with the requirements of Regulation 15 of this Annex, and entry shall be made in the Oil Record Book referred to in Regulation 20 of this Annex.

(3) An Administration which has endorsed a Certificate in accordance with subparagraph (1)(c) of this Regulation shall communicate to the Organization the particulars thereof for circulation to the Parties to the present Convention.

Regulation 13E
Protective Location of Segregated Ballast Spaces

(1) In every new crude oil tanker of 20,000 tons deadweight and above and every new product carrier of 30,000 tons deadweight and above, the segregated ballast tanks required to provide the capacity to comply with the requirements of Regulation 13 of this Annex which are located within the cargo tank length, shall be arranged in accordance with the requirements of paragraphs (2), (3) and (4) of this Regulation to provide a measure of protection against oil outflow in the event of grounding or collision.

(2) Segregated ballast tanks and spaces other than oil tanks within the cargo tank length (L_t) shall be so arranged as to comply with the following requirement:

$$\Sigma \ PA_c + \Sigma \ PA_s \geq J[L_t \ (B + 2D)]$$

where: PA_c = the side shell area in square metres for each segregated ballast tank or space other than an oil tank based on projected moulded dimensions.

　　　　PA_s = the bottom shell area in square metres for each such tank or space based on projected moulded dimensions.

　　　　L_t　= length in metres between the forward and after extremities of the cargo tanks.

　　　　B　= maximum breadth of the ship in metres as defined in Regulation l(21) of this Annex.

　　　　D　= moulded depth in metres measured vertically from the top of the keel to the top of the freeboard deck beam at side amidships. In ships having rounded gunwales, the moulded depth shall be measured to the point of intersection of the moulded lines of the deck and side shell plating, the lines extending as though the gunwale were of angular design.

　　　　J　= 0.45 for oil tankers of 20,000 tons deadweight, 0.30 for oil tankers of 200,000 tons deadweight and above, subject to the provisions of paragraph (3) of this Regulation.

　　　　　　For intermediate values of deadweight the value of "J" shall be determined by linear interpolation.

Whenever symbols given in this paragraph appear in this Regulation, they have the meaning as defined in this paragraph.

(3) For tankers of 200,000 tons deadweight and above the value of "J" may be reduced as follows:

$$J \text{ reduced} = \left[J - \left(a - \frac{O_c + O_s}{40_A} \right) \right] \text{ or } 0.2 \text{ whichever is greater}$$

where: a　= 0.25 for oil tankers of 200,000 tons deadweight
　　　　a　= 0.40 for oil tankers of 300,000 tons deadweight
　　　　·a　= 0.50 for oil tankers of 420,000 tons deadweight and above,

For intermediate values of deadweight the value of "a" shall be determined by linear interpolation.

O_c = as defined in Regulation 23(1)(a) of this Annex,

O_s = as defined in Regulation 23(1)(b) of this Annex,

O_A = the allowable oil outflow as required by Regulation 24(2) of this Annex,

(4) In the determination of "PA_c" and "PA_s" for segregated ballast tanks and spaces other than oil tanks the following shall apply:

(a) the minimum width of each wing tank or space either of which extends for the full depth of the ship's side or from the deck to the top of the double bottom shall be not less than 2 metres. The width shall be measured inboard from the ship's side at right angles to the centre line. Where a lesser width is provided the wing tank or space shall not be taken into account when calculating the protecting area "PA_c"; and

(b) the minimum vertical depth of each double bottom tank or space shall be B/15 or 2 metres, whichever is the lesser. Where a lesser depth is provided, the bottom tank or space shall not be taken into account when calculating the protecting area "PA_s".

The minimum width and depth of wing tanks and double bottom tanks shall be measured clear of the bilge area and, in the case of minimum width, shall be measured clear of any rounded gunwale area.

Regulation 14

Segregation of Oil and Water Ballast and Carriage of Oil in Forepeak Tanks

(1) Except as provided in paragraph (2) of this Regulation, in new ships of 4,000 tons gross tonnage and above other than oil tankers, and in new oil tankers of 150 tons gross tonnage and above, no ballast water shall be carried in any oil fuel tank.

(2) Where abnormal conditions or the need to carry large quantities of oil fuel render it necessary to carry ballast water which is not a clean ballast in any oil fuel tank, such ballast water shall be discharged to reception facilities or into the sea in compliance with Regulation 9 using the equipment specified in Regulation 16(2) of this Annex, and an entry shall be made in the Oil Record Book to this effect.

(3) All other ships shall comply with the requirements of paragraph (1) of this Regulation as far as reasonable and practicable.

(4) In a ship of 400 tons gross tonnage and above, for which the building contract is placed after 1 January 1982 or, in the absence of a building contract, the keel of which is laid or which is at a similar stage of construction after 1 July 1982, oil shall not be carried in a forepeak tank or a tank forward of the collision bulkhead.

(5) All ships other than those subject to paragraph (4) of this Regulation shall comply with the provisions of that paragraph, as far as is reasonable and practicable.

Regulation 15

Retention of Oil on Board

(1) Subject to the provisions of paragraphs (5) and (6) of this Regulation, oil tankers of 150 tons gross tonnage and above shall be provided with arrangements in accordance with the requirements of paragraphs (2) and (3) of this Regulation, provided that in the case of existing tankers the requirements for oil discharge monitoring and control systems and slop tank arrangements shall apply three years after the date of entry into force of the present Convention.

(2)(a) Adequate means shall be provided for cleaning the cargo tanks and transferring the dirty ballast residue and tank washings from the cargo tanks into a slop tank approved by the Administration. In existing oil tankers, any cargo tank may be designated as a slop tank.

(b) In this system arrangements shall be provided to transfer the oily waste into a slop tank or combination of slop tanks in such a way that any effluent discharged into the sea will be such as to comply with the provisions of Regulation 9 of this Annex.

(c) The arrangements of the slop tank or combination of slop tanks shall have a capacity necessary to retain the slop generated by tank washings, oil residues and dirty ballast residues. The total capacity of the slop tank or tanks shall not be less than 3 per cent of the oil carrying capacity of the ships, except that the Administration may accept:

(i) 2 per cent for such oil tankers where the tank washing arrangements are such that once the slop tank or tanks are charged with washing water, this water is sufficient for tank washing and, where applicable, for providing the driving fluid for eductors, without the introduction of additional water into the system;

(ii) 2 per cent where segregated ballast tanks or dedicated clean ballast tanks are provided in accordance with Regulation 13 of this Annex, or where a cargo tank cleaning system using crude oil washing is fitted in accordance with Regulation 13B of this Annex. This capacity may be further reduced to 1.5 per cent for such oil tankers where the tank washing arrangements are such that once the slop tank or tanks are charged with washing water, this water is sufficient for tank washing and, where applicable, for providing the driving fluid for eductors, without the introduction of additional water into the system;

(iii) 1 per cent for combination carriers where oil cargo is only carried in tanks with smooth walls. This capacity may be further reduced to 0.8 per cent where the tank washing arrangements are such that once the slop tank or tanks are charged with washing water, this water is sufficient for tank washing and, where applicable, for providing the driving fluid for eductors, without the introduction of additional water into the system.

New oil tankers of 70,000 tons deadweight and above shall be provided with at least two slop tanks.

(d) Slop tanks shall be so designed particularly in respect of the position of inlets, outlets, baffles or weirs where fitted, so as to avoid excessive turbulence and entrainment of oil or emulsion with the water.

(3)(a) An oil discharge monitoring and control system approved by the Administration shall be fitted. In considering the design of the oil content meter to be incorporated in the system, the Administration shall have regard to the specification recommended by the Organization. The system shall be fitted with a recording device to provide a continuous record of the discharge in litres per nautical mile and total quantity discharged, or the oil content and rate of discharge. This record shall be identifiable as to time and date and shall be kept for at least three years. The oil discharge monitor and control system shall come into operation when there is any discharge of effluent into the sea and shall be such as will ensure that any discharge of oily mixture is automatically stopped when the instantaneous rate of discharge of oil exceeds that permitted by Regulation 9(1)(a) of this Annex. Any failure of this monitoring and control system shall stop the discharge and be noted in the Oil Record Book. A manually operated alternative method shall be provided and may be used in the event of such failure, but the defective unit shall be made operable before the oil tanker commences its next ballast voyage unless it is proceeding to a repair port. The oil discharge monitoring and control system shall be designed and installed in compliance with the Guidelines and Specifications for Oil Discharge Monitoring and Control Systems for Oil Tankers developed by the Organization. Administrations may accept such specific arrangements as detailed in the Guidelines and Specifications.

(b) Effective oil/water interface detectors approved by the Administration shall be provided for a rapid and accurate determination of the oil/water interface in slop tanks and shall be available for use in other tanks where the separation of oil and water is effected and from which it is intended to discharge effluent direct to the sea.

(c) Instructions as to the operation of the system shall be in accordance with an operational manual approved by the Administration. They shall cover manual as well as automatic operations and shall be intended to ensure that at no time shall oil be discharged except in compliance with the conditions specified in Regulation 9 of this Annex.

(4) The requirements of paragraphs (1), (2) and (3) of this Regulation shall not apply to oil tankers of less than 150 tons gross tonnage, for which the control of discharge of oil under Regulation 9 of this Annex shall be

effected by the retention of oil on board with subsequent discharge of all contaminated washings to reception facilities. The total quantity of oil and water used for washing and returned to a storage tank shall be recorded in the Oil Record Book. This total quantity shall be discharged to reception facilities unless adequate arrangements are made to ensure that any effluent which is allowed to be discharged into the sea is effectively monitored to ensure that the provisions of Regulation 9 of this Annex are complied with.

(5)(a) The Administration may waive the requirements of paragraphs (1), (2) and (3) of this Regulation for any oil tanker which engages exclusively on voyages both of 72 hours or less in duration and within 50 miles from the nearest land, provided that the oil tanker is engaged exclusively in trades between ports or terminals within a State Party to the present Convention. Any such waiver shall be subject to the requirement that the oil tanker shall retain on board all oily mixtures for subsequent discharge to reception facilities and to the determination by the Administration that facilities available to receive such oily mixtures are adequate.

(b) The Administration may waive the requirements of paragraph (3) of this Regulation for oil tankers other than those referred to in subparagraph (a) of this paragraph in cases where:

(i) the tanker is an existing oil tanker of 40,000 tons deadweight or above, as referred to in Regulation 13C(1) of this Annex, engaged in specific trades, and the conditions specified in Regulation 13C(2) are complied with; or

(ii) the tanker is engaged exclusively in one or more of the following categories of voyages:

(1) voyages within special areas; or

(2) voyages within 50 miles from the nearest land outside special areas where the tanker is engaged in:

(aa) trades between ports or terminals of a State Party to the present Convention; or

(bb) restricted voyages as determined by the Administration, and of 72 hours or less in duration;

provided that all of the following conditions are complied with:

(3) all oily mixtures are retained on board for subsequent discharge to reception facilities;

(4) for voyages specified in sub-paragraph (b)(ii)(2) of this paragraph, the Administration has determined that adequate reception facilities are available to receive such oily mixtures in those oil loading ports or terminals the tanker calls at;

(5) the International Oil Pollution Prevention Certificate, when required, is endorsed to the effect that the ship is exclusively engaged in one or more of the categories of voyages specified in sub-paragraphs (b)(ii)(1) and (b)(ii)(2)(bb) of this paragraph; and

(6) the quantity, time and port of the discharge are recorded in the Oil Record Book.

(6) Where in the view of the Organization equipment required by Regulation 9(1)(a)(vi) of this Annex and specified in sub-paragraph (3)(a) of this Regulation is not obtainable for the monitoring of discharge of light refined products (white oils), the Administration may waive compliance with such requirement, provided that discharge shall be permitted only in compliance with procedures established by the Organization which shall satisfy the conditions of Regulation 9(1)(a) of this Annex except the obligation to have an oil discharge monitoring and control system in operation. The Organization shall review the availability of equipment at intervals not exceeding twelve months.

(7) The requirements of paragraphs (1), (2) and (3) of this Regulation shall not apply to oil tankers carrying asphalt or other products subject to the provisions of this Annex, which through their physical properties inhibit effective product/water separation and monitoring, for which the control of discharge under Regulation 9 of this Annex shall be effected by the retention of residues on board with discharge of all contaminated washings to reception facilities.

Regulation 16
*Oil Discharge Monitoring and Control System and Oily–
Water Separating and Oil Filtering Equipment*

(1) Any ship of 400 tons gross tonnage and above but less than 10,000 tons gross tonnage shall be fitted with oily-water separating equipment (100 ppm equipment) complying with paragraph (6) of this Regulation. Any such ship which carries large quantities of oil fuel shall comply with paragraph (2) of this Regulation or paragraph (1) of Regulation 14.

(2) Any ship of 10,000 tons gross tonnage and above shall be fitted either:

(a) with oily-water separating equipment (100 ppm equipment) complying with paragraph (6) of this Regulation and with an oil discharge monitoring and control system complying with paragraph (5) of this Regulation; or

(b) with oil filtering equipment (15 ppm equipment) complying with paragraph (7) of this Regulation.

(3)(a) The Administration may waive the requirements of paragraphs (1) and (2) of this Regulation for any ship engaged exclusively on:

(i) voyages within special areas; or

(ii) voyages within 12 miles of the nearest land outside special areas, provided the ship is in:

(1) trade between ports or terminals within a State Party to the present Convention; or

(2) restricted voyages as determined by the Administration;

provided that all of the following conditions are complied with:

(iii) the ship is fitted with a holding tank having a volume adequate, to the satisfaction of the Administration, for the total retention on board of the oily bilge water;

(iv) all oily bilge water is retained on board for subsequent discharge to reception facilities;

(v) the Administration has determined that adequate reception facilities are available to receive such oily bilge water in a sufficient number of ports or terminals the ship calls at;

(vi) the International Oil Pollution Prevention Certificate, when required, is endorsed to the effect that the ship is exclusively engaged on the voyages specified in sub-paragraph (a)(i) or (a)(ii)(2) of this paragraph; and

(vii) the quantity, time, and port of the discharge are recorded in the Oil Record Book.

(b) The Administration shall ensure that ships of less than 400 tons gross tonnage are equipped, as far as practicable, to retain on board oil or oily mixtures or discharge them in accordance with the requirements of Regulation 9(1)(b) of this Annex.

(4) For existing ships the requirements of paragraphs (1), (2) and (3) of this Regulation shall apply three years after the date of entry into force of the present Convention.

(5) An oil discharge monitoring and control system shall be of a design approved by the Administration. In considering the design of the oil content meter to be incorporated into the system, the Administration shall have regard to the specification recommended by the Organization. The system shall be fitted with a recording device to provide a continuous record of the oil content in parts per million. This record shall be identifiable as to time and date and shall be kept for at least three years. The system shall come into operation when there is any discharge of effluent into the sea and shall be such as will ensure that any discharge of oily mixture is automatically stopped when the oil content of effluent exceeds that permitted by Regulation 9(1)(b) of this Annex. Any failure of the system shall stop the discharge and be noted in the Oil Record Book. The defective unit shall be made operable before the ship commences its next voyage unless it is proceeding to a repair port. Existing ships shall comply with all of the provisions specified above except that the stopping of the discharge may be performed manually.

(6) Oily-water separating equipment referred to in paragraphs (1) and (2)(a) of this Regulation shall be of a design approved by the Administration and shall be such as will ensure that any oily mixture discharged into the sea after passing through the system has an oil content of less than 100 parts per million. In considering the design of such equipment, the Administration shall have regard to the specification recommended by the Organization.

(7) Oil filtering equipment referred to in paragraph (2)(b) of this Regulation shall be of a design approved by the Administration and shall be such as will ensure that any oily mixture discharged into the sea after passing through the system or systems has an oil content not exceeding 15 parts per million. It shall be provided with alarm arrangements to indicate when this level cannot be maintained. In considering the design of such equipment, the Administration shall have regard to the specification recommended by the Organization. In the case of ships less than 10,000 tons gross tonnage, other than those carrying large quantities of oil fuel or those discharging bilge water under Regulation 10(3)(b), which are provided with oil filtering equipment in lieu of oily-water separating equipment, the requirements for the alarm arrangements shall be complied with as far as reasonable and practicable.

Regulation 17
Tanks for Oil Residues (Sludge)

(1) Every ship of 400 tons gross tonnage and above shall be provided with a tank or tanks of adequate capacity, having regard to the type of machinery and length of voyage, to receive the oily residue (sludges) which cannot be dealt with otherwise in accordance with the requirements of this Annex, such as those resulting from the purification of fuel and lubricating oils and oil leakages in the machinery spaces.

(2) In new ships, such tanks shall be designed and constructed so as to facilitate their cleaning and the discharge of residues to reception facilities. Existing ships shall comply with this requirement as far as is reasonable and practicable.

Regulation 18
Pumping, Piping and Discharge Arrangements of Oil Tankers

(1) In every oil tanker, a discharge manifold for connexion to reception facilities for the discharge of dirty ballast water or oil contaminated water shall be located on the open deck on both sides of the ship.

(2) In every oil tanker, pipelines for the discharge to the sea of ballast water or oil-contaminated water from cargo tank areas which may be permitted under Regulation 9 or Regulation 10 of this Annex shall be led to the open deck or to the ship's side above the waterline in the deepest ballast condition. Different piping arrangements to permit operation in the manner permitted in sub-paragraphs (6)(a) to (e) of this Regulation may be accepted.

(3) In new oil tankers means shall be provided for stopping the discharge into the sea of ballast water or oil-contaminated water from cargo tank areas, other than those discharges below the waterline permitted under paragraph (6) of this Regulation, from a position on the upper deck or above located so that the manifold in use referred to in paragraph (1) of this Regulation and the discharge to the sea from the pipelines referred to in paragraph (2) of this Regulation may be visually observed. Means for stopping the discharge need not be provided at the observation position if a positive communication system such as a telephone or radio system is provided between the observation position and the discharge control position.

(4) Every new oil tanker required to be provided with segregated ballast tanks or fitted with a crude oil washing system shall comply with the following requirements:

(a) it shall be equipped with oil piping so designed and installed that oil retention in the lines is minimized; and

(b) means shall be provided to drain all cargo pumps and all oil lines at the completion of cargo discharge, where necessary by connexion to a stripping device. The line and pump drainings shall be capable of being discharged both ashore and to a cargo tank or a slop tank. For discharge ashore a special small diameter line shall be provided and shall be connected outboard of the ship's manifold valves.

(5) Every existing crude oil tanker required to be provided with segregated ballast tanks, or to be fitted with a crude oil washing system, or to operate with dedicated clean ballast tanks, shall comply with the provisions of paragraph (4)(b) of this Regulation.

(6) On every oil tanker the discharge of ballast water or oil contaminated water from cargo tank areas shall take place above the waterline, except as follows:

(a) Segregated ballast and clean ballast may be discharged below the waterline:

(i) in ports or at offshore terminals, or

(ii) at sea by gravity,

provided that the surface of the ballast water has been examined immediately before the discharge to ensure that no contamination with oil has taken place.

(b) Existing oil tankers which, without modification, are not capable of discharging segregated ballast above the waterline may discharge segregated ballast below the waterline at sea, provided that the surface of the ballast water has been examined immediately before the discharge to ensure that no contamination with oil has taken place.

(c) Existing oil tankers operating with dedicated clean ballast tanks, which without modification are not capable of discharging ballast water from dedicated clean ballast tanks above the waterline, may discharge this ballast below the waterline provided that the discharge of the ballast water is supervised in accordance with Regulation 13A(3) of this Annex.

(d) On every oil tanker at sea, dirty ballast water or oil contaminated water from tanks in the cargo area, other than slop tanks, may be discharged by gravity below the waterline, provided that sufficient time has elapsed in order to allow oil/water separation to have taken place and the ballast water has been examined immediately before the discharge with an oil/water interface detector referred to in Regulation 15(3)(b) of this Annex, in order to ensure that the height of the interface is such that the discharge does not involve any increased risk of harm to the marine environment.

(e) On existing oil tankers at sea, dirty ballast water or oil contaminated water from cargo tank areas may be discharged below the waterline, subsequent to or in lieu of the discharge by the method referred to in sub-paragraph (d) of this paragraph, provided that:

(i) a part of the flow of such water is led through permanent piping to a readily accessible location on the upper deck or above where it may be visually observed during the discharge operation; and

(ii) such part flow arrangements comply with the requirements established by the Administration, which shall contain at least all the provisions of the Specifications for the Design, Installation and Operation of a Part Flow System for Control of Overboard Discharges adopted by the Organization.

Regulation 19
Standard Discharge Connection

To enable pipes of reception facilities to be connected with the ship's discharge pipeline for residues from machinery bilges, both lines shall be fitted with a standard discharge connection in accordance with the following table:

STANDARD DIMENSIONS OF FLANGES FOR DISCHARGE CONNECTIONS

Description	Dimension
Outside diameter	215 mm
Inner diameter	According to pipe outside diameter
Bolt circle diameter	183 mm
Slots in flange	6 holes 22 mm in diameter equidistantly placed on a bolt circle of the above diameter, slotted to the flange periphery. The slot width to be 22 mm

Flange thickness	20 mm
Bolts and nuts: quantity, diameter	6, each of 20 mm in diameter and of suitable length

The flange is designed to accept pipes up to a maximum internal diameter of 125 mm and shall be of steel or other equivalent material having a flat face. This flange, together with a gasket of oilproof material, shall be suitable for a service pressure of 6 kg cm^2

Regulation 20
Oil Record Book

(1) Every oil tanker of 150 tons gross tonnage and above and every ship of 400 tons gross tonnage and above other than an oil tanker shall be provided with an Oil Record Book Part I (Machinery Space Operations). Every oil tanker of 150 tons gross tonnage and above shall also be provided with an Oil Record Book Part II (Cargo Ballast Operations). The Oil Record Book(s), whether as a part of the ship's official log book or otherwise, shall be in the Form(s) specified in Appendix III to this Annex.

(2) The Oil Record Book shall be completed on each occasion, on a tank to tank basis if appropriate, whenever any of the following operations take place in the ship:

(a) for machinery space operations (all ships):

(i) ballasting or cleaning of oil fuel tanks;

(ii) discharge of dirty ballast or cleaning water from tanks referred to under (i) of the sub-paragraph;

(iii) disposal of oily residues (sludge);

(iv) discharge overboard or disposal otherwise of bilge water which has accumulated in machinery spaces.

(b) for cargo/ballast operations (oil tankers):

(i) loading of oil cargo;

(ii) internal transfer of oil cargo during voyage;

(iii) unloading of oil cargo;

(iv) ballasting of cargo tanks and dedicated clean ballast tanks;

(v) cleaning of cargo tanks including crude oil washing;

(vi) discharge of ballast except from segregated ballast tanks;

(vii) discharge of water from slop tanks;

(viii) closing of all applicable valves or similar devices after slop tank discharge operations;

(ix) closing of valves necessary for isolation of dedicated clean ballast tanks from cargo and stripping lines after slop tank discharge operations;

(x) disposal of residues.

(3) In the event of such discharge of oil or oily mixture as is referred to in Regulation 11 of this Annex or in the event of accidental or other exceptional discharge of oil not excepted by that Regulation, a statement shall be made in the Oil Record Book of the circumstances of, and the reasons for, the discharge.

(4) Each operation described in paragraph (2) of this Regulation shall be fully recorded without delay in the Oil Record Book so that all the entries in the book appropriate to that operation are completed. Each completed operation shall be signed by the officer or officers in charge of the operations concerned and each completed page shall be signed by the master of the ship. The entries in the Oil Record Book shall be in an official language of the State whose flag the ship is entitled to fly, and, for ships holding an International Oil Pollution Prevention Certificate, in English or French. The entries in an official national language of the State whose flag the ship is entitled to fly shall prevail in case of a dispute or discrepancy.

(5) The Oil Record Book shall be kept in such a place as to be readily available for inspection at all reasonable times and, except in the case of unmanned ships under tow, shall be kept on board the ship. It shall be preserved for a period of three years after the last entry has been made.

(6) The competent authority of the Government of a Party to the Convention may inspect the Oil Record Book on board any ship to which this Annex applies while the ship is in its port or offshore terminals and may make a copy of any entry in that book and may require the Master of the ship to certify that the copy is a true copy of such entry. Any copy so made which has been certified by the Master of the ship as a true copy of an entry in the ship's Oil Record Book shall be made admissible in any judicial proceedings as evidence of the facts stated in the entry. The inspection of an Oil Record Book and the taking of a certified copy by the competent authority under this paragraph shall be performed as expeditiously as possible without causing the ship to be unduly delayed.

(7) For oil tankers of less than 150 tons gross tonnage operating in accordance with Regulation 15(4) of this Annex an appropriate Oil Record Book should be developed by the Administration.

Regulation 21
Special Requirements for Drilling Rigs and other Platforms

Fixed and floating drilling rigs when engaged in the exploration, exploitation and associated offshore processing of sea-bed mineral resources and other platforms shall comply with the requirements of this Annex applicable to ships of 400 tons gross tonnage and above other than oil tankers, except that:

(a) they shall be equipped as far as practicable with the installations required in Regulations 16 and 17 of this Annex:

(b) they shall keep a record of all operations involving oil or oily mixture discharges, in a form approved by the Administration; and

(c) in any special area and subject to the provisions of Regulation 11 of this Annex, the discharge into the sea of oil or oily mixture shall be prohibited except when the oil content of the discharge without dilution does not exceed 15 parts per million.

(d) Outside special areas and more than 12 nautical miles from the nearest land and subject to the provisions of Regulation 11 of this Annex, the discharge from such drilling rigs and platforms when stationary into the sea of oil or oily mixtures shall be prohibited except when the oil content of the discharges without dilution does not exceed 100 parts per million unless there are appropriate national regulations which are more stringent, in which case the appropriate national regulations shall apply.

CHAPTER III—REQUIREMENTS FOR MINIMIZING OIL POLLUTION FROM OIL TANKERS DUE TO SIDE AND BOTTOM DAMAGES

Regulation 22

Damage Assumptions

(1) For the purpose of calculating hypothetical oil outflow from oil tankers, three dimensions of the extent of damage of a parallelepiped on the side and bottom of the ship are assumed as follows. In the case of bottom damages two conditions are set forth to be applied individually to the stated portions of the oil tanker.

(a) *Side damage*

　　(i) Longitudinal extent (l_c): $\frac{1}{3}L^{2/3}$ or 14.5 metres, whichever is less

　　(ii) Transverse extent (t_c): (inboard from the ship's side at right angles to the centreline at the level corresponding to the assigned summer freeboard)　　$\frac{B}{5}$ or 11.5 metres, whichever is less

　　(iii) Vertical extent (v_c): from the base line upwards without limit

(b) *Bottom damage*

	For 0.3L from the forward perpendicular of the ship	Any other part of the ship
(i) Longitudinal extent (l_s):	$\frac{L}{10}$	$\frac{L}{10}$ or 5 metres. whichever is less
(ii) Transverse extent (t_s):	$\frac{B}{6}$ or 10 metres, whichever is less but not less than 5 metres	5 metres

(iii) Vertical extent
from the base $\frac{B}{15}$ or 6 metres, whichever is less
line (v_s):

(2) Wherever the symbols given in this Regulation appear in this Chapter, they have the meaning as defined in this Regulation.

Regulation 23
Hypothetical Outflow of Oil

(1) The hypothetical outflow of oil in the case of side damage (O_c) and bottom damage (O_s) shall be calculated by the following formulae with respect to compartments breached by damage to all conceivable locations along the length of the ship to the extent as defined in Regulation 22 of this Annex.

(a) for side damages:

$$O_c = \Sigma W_i + \Sigma K_i C_i \qquad \text{(I)}$$

(b) for bottom damages:

$$O_s = \tfrac{1}{3}(\Sigma Z_i W_i + \Sigma Z_i C_i) \qquad \text{(II)}$$

where: W_i = volume of a wing tank in cubic metres assumed to be breached by the damage as specified in Regulation 22 of this Annex: W_i for a segregated ballast tank may be taken equal to zero.

C_i = volume of a centre tank in cubic metres assumed to be breached by the damage as specified in Regulation 22 of this Annex: C_i for a segregated ballast tank may be taken equal to zero.

K_i = $1 - \dfrac{b_i}{t_c}$ when b_i is equal to or greater than t_c, K_i shall be taken equal to zero.

Z_i = $1 - \dfrac{h_i}{v_s}$ when h_i is equal to or greater than v_s, Z_i shall be taken equal to zero.

b_i = width of wing tank in metres under consideration measured inboard from the ship's side at right angles to the centreline at the level corresponding to the assigned summer freeboard.

h_i = minimum depth of the double bottom in metres under consideration: where no double bottom is fitted h_i shall be taken equal to zero.

Whenever symbols given in this paragraph appear in this Chapter, they have the meaning as defined in this Regulation.

(2) If a void space or segregated ballast tank of a length less than l_c as defined in Regulation 22 of this Annex is located between wing oil tanks. O_c in formula (I) may be calculated on the basis of volume W_i being the actual volume of one such tank (where they are of equal capacity) or the smaller of the two tanks (if they differ in capacity) adjacent to such space, multiplied by S_i as defined below and taking for all other wing tanks involved in such a collision the value of the actual full volume.

$$S_i = 1 \frac{l_i}{l_c}$$

where l_i = length in metres of void space or segregated ballast tank under consideration.

(3) (a) Credit shall only be given in respect of double bottom tanks which are either empty or carrying clean water when cargo is carried in the tanks above.

(b) Where the double bottom does not extend for the full length and width of the tank involved, the double bottom is considered non-existent and the volume of the tanks above the area of the bottom damage shall be included in formula (II) even if the tank is not considered breached because of the installation of such a partial double bottom.

(c) Suction wells may be neglected in the determination of the value h_i provided such wells are not excessive in area and extend below the tank for a minimum distance and in no case more than half the height of the double bottom. If the depth of such a well exceeds half the height of the double bottom, h_i shall be taken equal to the double bottom height minus the well height.

Piping serving such wells if installed within the double bottom shall be fitted with valves or other closing arrangements located at the point of connexion to the tank served to prevent oil outflow in the event of damage to the piping. Such piping shall be installed as high from the bottom shell as possible. These valves shall be kept closed at sea at any time when the tank contains oil cargo, except that they may be opened only for cargo transfer needed for the purpose of trimming of the ship.

(4) In the case where bottom damage simultaneously involves four centre tanks, the value of O_s may be calculated according to the formula

$$O_s = \tfrac{1}{4}\Sigma Z_i W_i + \Sigma Z_i C_i) \qquad\qquad \text{(III)}$$

(5) An Administration may credit as reducing oil outflow in case of bottom damage, an installed cargo transfer system having an emergency high suction in each cargo oil tank, capable of transferring from a breached tank or tanks to segregated ballast tanks or to available cargo tankage if it can be assured that such tanks will have sufficient ullage. Credit for such a system would be governed by ability to transfer in two hours of operation oil equal to one half of the largest of the breached tanks involved and by availability of equivalent receiving capacity in ballast or cargo tanks. The credit shall be confined to permitting calculcation of O_s according to formula (III). The pipes for such suctions shall be installed at least at a height not less than the vertical extent of the bottom damage v_s. The Administration shall supply the Organization with the information concerning the arrangements accepted by it, for circulation to other Parties to the Convention.

Regulation 24
Limitation of Size and Arrangement of Cargo Tanks

(1) Every new oil tanker shall comply with the provisions of this Regulation. Every existing oil tanker shall be required, within two years after the date of entry into force of the present Convention, to comply with the provisions of this Regulation if such a tanker falls into either of the following categories:

(a) a tanker, the delivery of which is after 1 January 1977; or

(b) a tanker to which both the following conditions apply:

(i) delivery is not later than 1 January 1977; and

(ii) the building contract is placed after 1 January 1974, or in cases where no building contract has previously been placed, the keel is laid or the tanker is at a similar stage of construction after 30 June 1974.

(2) Cargo tanks of oil tankers shall be of such size and arrangements that the hypothetical outflow O_c or O_s calculated in accordance with the provisions of Regulation 23 of this Annex anywhere in the length of the ship does not exceed 30,000 cubic metres or $400 \sqrt[3]{DW}$, whichever is the greater, but subject to a maximum of 40,000 cubic metres.

(3) The volume of any one wing cargo oil tank of an oil tanker shall not exceed seventy-five per cent of the limits of the hypothetical oil outflow referred to in paragraph (2) of this Regulation. The volume of any one centre cargo oil tank shall not exceed 50,000 cubic metres. However, in segregated ballast oil tankers as defined in Regulation 13 of this Annex, the permitted volume of a wing cargo oil tank situated between two segregated ballast tanks, each exceeding l_c in length, may be increased to the maximum limit of hypothetical oil outflow provided that the width of the wing tanks exceeds 1_c.

(4) The length of each cargo tank shall not exceed 10 metres or one of the following values, whichever is the greater:

(a) where no longitudinal bulkhead is provided:

0.1L

(b) where a longitudinal bulkhead is provided at the centreline only:

0.15L

(c) Where two or more longitudinal bulkheads are provided:

(i) for wing tanks:

0.2L

(ii) for centre tanks:

(1) if $\frac{b_i}{B}$ is equal to or greater than ⅕:

0.2L

(2) if $\frac{b_i}{B}$ is less than ⅕:

—where no centreline longitudinal bulkhead is provided:
$$(0.5 \frac{b_i}{B} + 0.1)L$$

—where a centreline longitudinal bulkhead is provided:
$$(0.25 \frac{b_i}{B} + 0.15)L$$

(5) In order not to exceed the volume limits established by paragraphs (2), (3) and (4) of this Regulation and irrespective of the accepted type of cargo transfer system installed, when such system interconnects two or more cargo tanks, valves or other similar closing devices shall be provided for separating the tanks from each other. These valves or devices shall be closed when the tanker is at sea.

(6) Lines of piping which run through cargo tanks in a position less than t_c from the ship's side or less than v_c from the ship's bottom shall be fitted with valves or similar closing devices at the point at which they open into any cargo tank. These valves shall be kept closed at sea at any time when the tanks contain cargo oil, except that they may be opened only for cargo transfer needed for the purpose of trimming of the ship.

Regulation 25
Subdivision and Stability

(1) Every new oil tanker shall comply with the subdivision and damage stability criteria as specified in paragraph (3) of this Regulation, after the assumed side or bottom damage as specified in paragraph (2) of this Regulation, for any operating draught reflecting actual partial or full load conditions consistent with trim and strength of the ship as well as specific gravities of the cargo. Such damage shall be applied to all conceivable locations along the length of the ship as follows:

(a) in tankers of more than 225 metres in length, anywhere in the ship's length;

(b) in tankers of more than 150 metres, but not exceeding 225 metres in length, anywhere in the ship's length except involving either after or forward bulkhead bounding the machinery space located aft. The machinery space shall be treated as a single floodable compartment;

(c) in tankers not exceeding 150 metres in length, anywhere in the ship's length between adjacent transverse bulkheads with the exception of the machinery space. For tankers of 100 metres or less in length where all requirements of paragraph (3) of this Regulation cannot be fulfilled without materially impairing the operational qualities of the ship. Administrations may allow relaxations from these requirements.

Ballast conditions where the tanker is not carrying oil in cargo tanks excluding any oil residue, shall not be considered.

(2) The following provisions regarding the extent and the character of the assumed damage shall apply:

(a) Side damage

(i) Longitudinal extent ⅓(L^i) or 14.5 metres. whichever is less

(ii) Transverse extent $\frac{B}{5}$ or 11.5 metres, whichever is less

(Inboard from the ship's side at right angles to the centreline at the level of the summer load line)

(iii) Vertical extent From the moulded line of the bottom shell plating at centreline, upwards without limit

(b) Bottom damage	For 0.3L from the forward perpendicular of the ship	Any other part of the ship
(i) Longitudinal extent	⅓(L^{⅔}) or 14.5 metres. whichever is less	⅓(L^{⅔}) or 5 metres. whichever is less
Transverse extent	$\frac{B}{6}$ or 10 metres. whichever is less	$\frac{B}{6}$ or 5 metres. whichever is less
(iii) Vertical extent	$\frac{B}{15}$ or 6 metres. whichever is less, measured from the moulded line of the bottom shell plating at centreline	$\frac{B}{15}$ or 6 metres. whichever is less, measured from the moulded line of the bottom shell plating at centreline

(c) If any damage of a lesser extent than the maximum extent of damage specified in sub-paragraphs (a) and (b) of this paragraph would result in a more severe condition, such damage shall be considered.

(d) Where the damage involving transverse bulkheads is envisaged as specified in sub-paragraphs (1)(a) and (b) of this Regulation, transverse watertight bulkheads shall be spaced at least at a distance equal to the longitudinal extent of assumed damage specified in sub-paragraph (a) of this paragraph in order to be considered effective. Where transverse bulkheads are spaced at a lesser distance, one or more of these bulkheads within such extent of damage shall be assumed as non-existent for the purpose of determining flooded compartments.

(e) Where the damage between adjacent transverse watertight bulkheads is envisaged as specified in sub-paragraph (1)(c) of this Regulation, no main transverse bulkhead or a transverse bulkhead bounding side tanks or double bottom tanks shall be assumed damaged, unless:

      (i) the spacing of the adjacent bulkheads is less than the longitu-dinal extent of assumed damage specified in sub-paragraph (a) of this paragraph: or

     (ii) there is a step or a recess in a transverse bulkhead of more than 3.05 metres in length, located within the extent of penetration of assumed damage. The step formed by the after peak bulkhead and after peak tank top shall not be regarded as a step for the purpose of this Regulation.

    (f) If pipes, ducts or tunnels are situated within the assumed extent of damage, arrangements shall be made so that progressive flooding cannot thereby extend to compartments other than those assumed to be floodable for each case of damage.

(3) Oil tankers shall be regarded as complying with the damage stability criteria if the following requirements are met:

    (a) The final waterline, taking into account sinkage, heel and trim, shall be below the lower edge of any opening through which progressive flooding may take place. Such openings shall include air pipes and those which are closed by means of weathertight doors or hatch covers and may exclude those openings closed by means of watertight manhole covers and flush scuttles, small watertight cargo tank hatch covers which maintain the high integrity of the deck, remotely operated watertight sliding doors, and side scuttles of the non-opening type.

    (b) In the final stage of flooding, the angle of heel due to unsymme-trical flooding shall not exceed 25 degrees, provided that this angle may be increased up to 30 degrees if no deck edge immersion occurs.

    (c) The stability in the final stage of flooding shall be investigated and may be regarded as sufficient if the righting lever curve has at least a range of 20 degrees beyond the position of equilibrium in association with a maximum residual righting lever of at least 0.1 metre within the 20 degrees range; the area under the curve within this range shall not be less than 0.0175 metre radians. Unprotected openings shall not be immersed within this range unless the space concerned is assumed to be flooded. Within this range, the immersion of any of the openings listed in sub-paragraph (a) of this paragraph and other openings capable of being closed weathertight may be permitted.

    (d) The Administration shall be satisfied that the stability is suffi-cient during intermediate stages of flooding.

    (e) Equalization arrangements requiring mechanical aids such as valves or cross-levelling pipes, if fitted, shall not be considered for the purpose of reducing an angle of heel or attaining the minimum range of residual stability to meet the requirements of sub-paragraphs (a), (b) and (c) of this paragraph and sufficient residual stability shall be maintained during all stages where equalization is used. Spaces which are linked by ducts of a large cross-sectional area may be considered to be common.

(4) The requirements of paragraph (1) of this Regulation shall be confirmed by calculations which take into consideration the design characteristics of the ship, the arrangements, configuration and contents of the damaged compartments; and the distribution, specific gravities and the free surface effect of liquids. The calculations shall be based on the following:

(a) Account shall be taken of any empty or partially filled tank, the specific gravity of cargoes carried, as well as any outflow of liquids from damaged compartments.

(b) The permeabilities assumed for spaces flooded as a result of damage shall be as follows:

Spaces	Permeabilities
Appropriated to stores	0.60
Occupied by accommodation	0.95
Occupied by machinery	0.85
Voids	0.95
Intended for consumable liquids	0 to 0.95
Intended for other liquids	0 to 0.95

(c) The buoyancy of any superstructure directly above the side damage shall be disregarded. The unflooded parts of superstructures beyond the extent of damage, however, may be taken into consideration provided that they are separated from the damaged space by watertight bulkheads and the requirements of sub-paragraph (3)(a) of this Regulation in respect of these intact spaces are complied with. Hinged watertight doors may be acceptable in watertight bulkheads in the superstructure.

(d) The free surface effect shall be calculated at an angle of heel of 5 degrees for each individual compartment. The Administration may require or allow the free surface corrections to be calculated at an angle of heel greater than 5 degrees for partially filled tanks.

(c) In calculating the effect of free surfaces of consumable liquids it shall be assumed that, for each type of liquid at least one transverse pair or a single centreline tank has a free surface and the tank or combination of tanks to be taken into account shall be those where the effect of free surfaces is the greatest.

(5) The Master of every new oil tanker and the person in charge of a new nonself-propelled oil tanker to which this Annex applies shall be supplied in an approved form with:

(a) information relative to loading and distribution of cargo necessary to ensure compliance with the provisions of this Regulation; and

(b) data on the ability of the ship to comply with damage stability criteria as determined by this Regulation, including the effect of relaxations that may have been allowed under sub-paragraph (1)(c) of this Regulation.

Appendix I
LIST OF OILS

Asphalt solutions
Blending Stocks
Roofers Flux
Straight Run Residue

Oils
Clarified
Crude Oil
Mixtures containing crude oil
Diesel Oil
Fuel Oil No. 4
Fuel Oil No. 5
Fuel Oil No. 6
Residual Fuel Oil
Road Oil
Transformer Oil
Aromatic Oil (excluding vegetable oil)
Lubricating Oils and Blending Stocks
Mineral Oil
Motor Oil
Penetrating Oil
Spindle Oil
Turbine Oil

Distillates
Straight Run
Flashed Feed Stocks

Gas Oil
Cracked

Gasoline Blending Stocks
Alkylates—fuel
Reformates
Polymer—fuel

Gasolines
Casinghead (natural)
Automotive
Aviation
Straight Run
Fuel Oil No. 1 (Kerosene)
Fuel Oil No. 1–D
Fuel Oil No. 2
Fuel Oil No. 2–D

Jet Fuels
JP–1 (Kerosene)
JP–3
JP–4
JP–5 (Kerosene, Heavy)
Turbo Fuel
Kerosene
Mineral Spirit

Naphtha
Solvent
Petroleum
Heartcut Distillate Oil

ANNEX II
REGULATIONS FOR THE CONTROL OF POLLUTION BY NOXIOUS LIQUID SUBSTANCES IN BULK
Regulation 1
Definitions

For the purposes of this Annex:

(1) "Chemical tanker" means a ship constructed or adapted primarily to carry a cargo of noxious liquid substances in bulk and includes an "oil tanker" as defined in Annex I of the present Convention when carrying a cargo or part cargo of noxious liquid substances in bulk.

(2) "Clean ballast" means ballast carried in a tank which, since it was last used to carry a cargo containing a substance in Category A, B, C or D has been thoroughly cleaned and the residues resulting therefrom have been discharged and the tank emptied in accordance with the appropriate requirements of this Annex.

(3) "Segregated ballast" means ballast water introduced into a tank permanently allocated to the carriage of ballast or to the carriage of ballast or cargoes other than oil or noxious liquid substances as variously defined in the Annexes of the present Convention, and which is completely separated from the cargo and oil fuel system.

(4) "Nearest land" is as defined in Regulation 1(9) of Annex I of the present Convention.

(5) "Liquid substances" are those having a vapour pressure not exceeding 2.8 kp/cm^2 at a temperature of 37.8°C.

(6) "Noxious liquid substance" means any substance designated in Appendix II to this Annex or provisionally assessed under the provisions of Regulation 3(4) as falling into Category A, B, C or D.

(7) "Special area" means a sea area where for recognized technical reasons in relation to its oceanographic and ecological condition and to its peculiar transportation traffic the adoption of special mandatory methods for the prevention of sea pollution by noxious liquid substances is required.

Special areas shall be:

(a) The Baltic Sea Area, and

(b) The Black Sea Area.

(8) "Baltic Sea Area" is as defined in Regulation 10(1)(b) of Annex I of the present Convention.

(9) "Black Sea Area" is as defined in Regulation 10(1)(c) of Annex I of the present Convention.

(10) "International Bulk Chemical Code" means the International Code for the Construction and Equipment of Ships Carrying Dangerous Chemicals in Bulk adopted by the Marine Environment Protection Committee of the Organization by resolution MEPC 19(22), as may be amended by the Organization, provided that such amendments are adopted and brought into force in accordance with the provisions of Article 16 of the present Convention concerning amendment procedures applicable to an Appendix to an Annex.

(11) "Bulk Chemical Code" means the Code for the Construction and Equipment of Ships Carrying Dangerous Chemicals in Bulk adopted by the Marine Environment Protection Committee of the Organization by resolution MEPC 20(22), as may be amended by the Organization, provided that such amendments are adopted and brought into force in accordance with the provisions of Article 16 of the present Convention concerning amendment procedures applicable to an Appendix to an Annex.

(12) "Ship constructed" means a ship the keel of which is laid or which is at a similar stage of construction. A ship converted to a chemical tanker, irrespective of the date of construction, shall be treated as a chemical tanker constructed on the date on which such conversion commenced. This conver-

sion provision shall not apply to the modification of a ship which complies with all of the following conditions:

(a) the ship is constructed before 1 July 1986; and

(b) the ship is certified under the Bulk Chemical Code to carry only those products identified by the Code as substances with pollution hazards only.

(13) "Similar stage of construction" means the stage at which:

(a) construction identifiable with a specific ship begins; and

(b) assembly of that ship has commenced comprising at least 50 tons or one per cent of the estimated mass of all structural material, whichever is less.

Regulation 2
Application

(1) Unless expressly provided otherwise the provisions of this Annex shall apply to all ships carrying noxious liquid substances in bulk.

(2) Where a cargo subject to the provisions of Annex I of the present Convention is carried in a cargo space of a chemical tanker, the appropriate requirements of Annex I of the present Convention shall also apply.

(3) Regulation 13 of this Annex shall apply only to ships carrying substances which are categorized for discharge control purposes in Category A, B or C.

(4) For ships constructed before 1 July 1986, the provisions of Regulation 5 of this Annex in respect of the requirement to discharge below the waterline and maximum concentration in the wake astern of the ship shall apply as from 1 January 1988.

(5) The Administration may allow any fitting, material, appliance or apparatus to be fitted in a ship as an alternative to that required by this Annex if such fitting, material, appliance or apparatus is at least as effective as that required by this Annex. This authority of the Administration shall not extend to the substitution of operational methods to effect the control of discharge of noxious liquid substances as equivalent to those design and construction features which are prescribed by Regulations in this Annex.

(6) The Administration which allows a fitting, material, appliance or apparatus as alternative to that required by this Annex, under paragraph (5) of this Regulation, shall communicate to the Organization for circulation to the Parties to the Convention, particulars thereof, for their information and appropriate action, if any.

Regulation 3
Categorization and Listing of Noxious Liquid Substances

(1) For the purpose of the Regulations of this Annex, noxious liquid substances shall be divided into four categories as follows:

(a) Category A—Noxious liquid substances which if discharged into the sea from tank cleaning or deballasting operations would present a major hazard to either marine resources or human health or cause serious harm to amenities or other legitimate uses of the sea and therefore justify the application of stringent anti-pollution measures.

(b) Category B—Noxious liquid substances which if discharged into the sea from tank cleaning or deballasting operations would present a hazard to either marine resources or human health or cause harm to amenities or other legitimate uses of the sea and therefore justify the application of special anti-pollution measures.

(c) Category C—Noxious liquid substances which if discharged into the sea from tank cleaning or deballasting operations would present a minor hazard to either marine resources or human health or cause minor harm to amenities or other legitimate uses of the sea and therefore require special operational conditions.

(d) Category D—Noxious liquid substances which if discharged into the sea from tank cleaning or deballasting operations would present a recognizable hazard to either marine resources or human health or cause minimal harm to amenities or other legitimate uses of the sea and therefore require some attention in operational conditions.

(2) Guidelines for use in the categorization of noxious liquid substances are given in Appendix I to this Annex.

(3) The list of noxious substances carried in bulk and presently categorized which are subject to the provisions of this Annex is set out in Appendix II to this Annex.

(4) Where it is proposed to carry a liquid substance in bulk which has not been categorized under paragraph (1) of this Regulation or evaluated as referred to in Regulation 4(1) of this Annex, the Governments of Parties to the Convention involved in the proposed operation shall establish and agree on a provisional assessment for the proposed operation on the basis of the guidelines referred to in paragraph (2) of this Regulation. Until full agreement between the Governments involved has been reached, the substance shall be carried under the most severe conditions proposed. As soon as possible, but not later than ninety days after its first carriage, the Administration concerned shall notify the Organization and provide details of the substance and the provisional assessment for prompt circulation to all Parties for their information and consideration. The Government of each Party shall have a period of ninety days in which to forward its comments to the Organization, with a view to the assessment of the substance.

Regulation 4
Other Liquid Substances

(1) The substances listed in Appendix III to this Annex have been evaluated and found to fall outside the Categories A, B, C and D, as defined in Regulation 3(1) of this Annex because they are presently considered to present no harm to human health, marine resources, amenities or other legitimate uses of the sea, when discharged into the sea from tank cleaning or deballasting operations.

(2) The discharge of bilge or ballast water or other residues or mixtures containing only substances listed in Appendix III to this Annex shall not be subject to any requirement of this Annex.

(3) The discharge into the sea of clean ballast or segregated ballast shall not be subject to any requirement of this Annex.

Regulation 5
Discharge of Noxious Liquid Substances

Categories A, B and C Substances outside Special Areas and Category D Substances in all Areas

Subject to the provisions of Regulation 6 of this Annex,

(1) The discharge into the sea of substances in Category A as defined in Regulation 3(1)(a) of this Annex or of those provisionally assessed as such, or ballast water, tank washings, or other residues or mixtures containing such substances shall be prohibited. If tanks containing such substances or mixtures are to be washed, the resulting residues shall be discharged to a reception facility until the concentration of the substance in the effluent to such facility is at or below the residual concentration prescribed for that substance in column III of Appendix II to this Annex and until the tank is empty. Any water subsequently added to the tank may be discharged into the sea when all the following conditions are satisfied:

(a) the ship is proceeding en route at a speed of at least 7 knots in the case of self-propelled ships or at least 4 knots in the case of ships which are not self-propelled;

(b) the discharge is made below the waterline, taking into account the location of the seawater intakes; and

(c) the discharge is made at a distance of not less than 12 nautical miles from the nearest land and in a depth of water of not less than 25 metres.

(2) The discharge into the sea of substances in Category B as defined in Regulation 3(1)(b) of this Annex or of those provisionally assessed as such, or ballast water, tank washings, or other residues or mixtures containing such substances shall be prohibited except when all the following conditions are satisfied:

(a) the ship is proceeding en route at a speed of at least 7 knots in the case of self-propelled ships or at least 4 knots in the case of ships which are not self-propelled;

(b) the procedures and arrangements for discharge are approved by the Administration. Such procedures and arrangements shall be based upon standards developed by the Organization and shall ensure that the concentration and rate of discharge of the effluent is such that the concentration of the substance in the wake astern of the ship does not exceed 1 part per million;

(c) the maximum quantity of cargo discharged from each tank and its associated piping system does not exceed the maximum quantity approved in accordance with the procedures referred to in sub-paragraph (b) of this paragraph, which shall in no case exceed the greater of 1 cubic metre or 1/3,000 of the tank capacity in cubic metres;

(d) the discharge is made below the waterline, taking into account the location of the seawater intakes; and

(e) the discharge is made at a distance of not less than 12 nautical miles from the nearest land and in a depth of water of not less than 25 metres.

(3) The discharge into the sea of substances in Category C as defined in Regulation 3(1)(c) of this Annex or of those provisionally assessed as such, or ballast water, tank washings, or other residues or mixtures containing such substances shall be prohibited except when all the following conditions are satisfied:

(a) the ship is proceeding en route at a speed of at least 7 knots in the case of self-propelled ships or at least 4 knots in the case of ships which are not self-propelled;

(b) the procedures and arrangements for discharge are approved by the Administration. Such procedures and arrangements shall be based upon standards developed by the Organization and shall ensure that the concentration and rate of discharge of the effluent is such that the concentration of the substance in the wake astern of the ship does not exceed 10 parts per million;

(c) the maximum quantity of cargo discharged from each tank and its associated piping system does not exceed the maximum quantity approved in accordance with the procedures referred to in sub-paragraph (b) of this paragraph, which shall in no case exceed the greater of 3 cubic metres or 1/1,000 of the tank capacity in cubic metres;

(d) the discharge is made below the waterline, taking into account the location of the seawater intakes; and

(e) the discharge is made at a distance of not less than 12 nautical miles from the nearest land and in a depth of water of not less than 25 metres.

(4) The discharge into the sea of substances in Category D as defined in Regulation 3(1)(d) of this Annex, or of those provisionally assessed as such, or ballast water, tank washings, or other residues or mixtures containing such substances shall be prohibited except when all the following conditions are satisfied:

（a）the ship is proceeding en route at a speed of at least 7 knots in the case of self-propelled ships or at least 4 knots in the case of ships which are not self-propelled;

（b）such mixtures are of a concentration not greater than one part of the substance in ten parts of water; and

（c）the discharge is made at a distance of not less than 12 nautical miles from the nearest land.

(5) Ventilation procedures approved by the Administration may be used to remove cargo residues from a tank. Such procedures shall be based upon standards developed by the Organization. Any water subsequently introduced into the tank shall be regarded as clean and shall not be subject to paragraph (1), (2), (3) or (4) of this Regulation.

(6) The discharge into the sea of substances which have not been categorized, provisionally assessed, or evaluated as referred to in Regulation 4(1) of this Annex, or of ballast water, tank washings, or other residues or mixtures containing such substances shall be prohibited.

Categories A, B and C Substances within Special Areas

Subject to the provisions of Regulation 6 of this Annex,

(7) The discharge into the sea of substances in Category A as defined in Regulation 3(1)(a) of this Annex or of those provisionally assessed as such, or ballast water, tank washings, or other residues or mixtures containing such substances shall be prohibited. If tanks containing such substances or mixtures are to be washed the resulting residues shall be discharged to a reception facility which the States bordering the special area shall provide in accordance with Regulation 7 of this Annex, until the concentration of the substance in the effluent to such facility is at or below the residual concentration prescribed for that substance in column IV of Appendix II to this Annex and until the tank is empty. Any water subsequently added to the tank may be discharged into the sea when all the following conditions are satisfied:

（a）the ship is proceeding en route at a speed of at least 7 knots in the case of self-propelled ships or at least 4 knots in the case of ships which are not self-propelled;

（b）the discharge is made below the waterline, taking into account the location of the seawater intakes; and

（c）the discharge is made at a distance of not less than 12 nautical miles from the nearest land and in a depth of water of not less than 25 metres.

(8) The discharge into the sea of substances in Category B as defined in Regulation 3(1)(b) of this Annex or of those provisionally assessed as such, or ballast water, tank washings, or other residues or mixtures containing such substances shall be prohibited except when all the following conditions are satisfied:

(a) the tank has been prewashed in accordance with the procedure approved by the Administration and based on standards developed by the Organization and the resulting tank washings have been discharged to a reception facility;

(b) the ship is proceeding en route at a speed of at least 7 knots in the case of self-propelled ships or at least 4 knots in the case of ships which are not self-propelled;

(c) the procedures and arrangements for discharge and washings are approved by the Administration. Such procedures and arrangements shall be based upon standards developed by the Organization and shall ensure that the concentration and rate of discharge of the effluent is such that the concentration of the substance in the wake astern of the ship does not exceed 1 part per million;

(d) the discharge is made below the waterline, taking into account the location of the seawater intakes; and

(e) the discharge is made at a distance of not less than 12 nautical miles from the nearest land and in a depth of water of not less than 25 metres.

(9) The discharge into the sea of substances in Category C as defined in Regulation 3(1)(c) of this Annex or of those provisionally assessed as such, or ballast water, tank washings, or other residues or mixtures containing such substances shall be prohibited except when all the following conditions are satisfied:

(a) the ship is proceeding en route at a speed of at least 7 knots in the case of self-propelled ships or at least 4 knots in the case of ships which are not self-propelled;

(b) the procedures and arrangements for discharge are approved by the Administration. Such procedures and arrangements shall be based upon standards developed by the Organization and shall ensure that the concentration and rate of discharge of the effluent is such that the concentration of the substance in the wake astern of the ship does not exceed 1 part per million;

(c) the maximum quantity of cargo discharged from each tank and its associated piping system does not exceed the maximum quantity approved in accordance with the procedures referred to in sub-paragraph (b) of this paragraph which shall in no case exceed the greater of 1 cubic metre or 1/3,000 of the tank capacity in cubic metres;

(d) the discharge is made below the waterline, taking into account the location of the seawater intakes; and

(e) the discharge is made at a distance of not less than 12 nautical miles from the nearest land and in a depth of water of not less than 25 metres.

(10) Ventilation procedures approved by the Administration may be used to remove cargo residues from a tank. Such procedures shall be based upon standards developed by the Organization. Any water subsequently introduced into the tank shall be regarded as clean and shall not be subject to paragraph (7), (8) or (9) of this Regulation.

(11) The discharge into the sea of substances which have not been categorized, provisionally assessed or evaluated as referred to in Regulation 4(1) of this Annex, or of ballast water, tank washings, or other residues or mixtures containing such substances shall be prohibited.

(12) Nothing in this Regulation shall prohibit a ship from retaining on board the residues from a Category B or C cargo and discharging such residues into the sea outside a special area in accordance with paragraph (2) or (3) of this Regulation, respectively.

(13)(a) The Governments of Parties to the Convention, the coastlines of which border on any given special area, shall collectively agree and establish a date by which time the requirement of Regulation 7(1) of this Annex will be fulfilled and from which the requirements of paragraphs (7), (8), (9) and (10) of this Regulation in respect of that area shall take effect and notify the Organization of the date so established at least six months in advance of that date. The Organization shall then promptly notify all Parties of that date.

(b) If the date of entry into force of the present Convention is earlier than the date established in accordance with sub-paragraph (a) of this paragraph, the requirements of paragraphs (1), (2) and (3) of this Regulation shall apply during the interim period.

Regulation 5A
Pumping, Piping and Unloading Arrangements

(1) Every ship constructed on or after 1 July 1986 shall be provided with pumping and piping arrangements to ensure, through testing under favourable pumping conditions, that each tank designated for the carriage of a Category B substance does not retain a quantity of residue in excess of 0.1 cubic metres in the tank's associated piping and in the immediate vicinity of that tank's suction point.

(2)(a) Subject to the provisions of sub-paragraph (b) of this paragraph, every ship constructed before 1 July 1986 shall be provided with pumping and piping arrangements to ensure, through testing under favourable pumping conditions, that each tank designated for the carriage of a Category B substance does not retain a quantity of residue in excess of 0.3 cubic metres in the tank's associated piping and in the immediate vicinity of that tank's suction point.

(b) Until 2 October 1994 ships referred to in sub-paragraph (a) of this paragraph if not in compliance with the requirements of that sub-paragraph shall, as a minimum, be provided with pumping and piping arrangements to ensure, through testing under favourable pumping conditions and surface residue assessment, that each tank designated for the carriage of a Category B substance does not retain a quantity of residue in excess of 1 cubic metre or 1/3,000 of the tank capacity in cubic metres, whichever is greater, in that tank and the associated piping.

(3) Every ship constructed on or after 1 July 1986 shall be provided with pumping and piping arrangements to ensure, through testing under favourable pumping conditions, that each tank designated for the carriage of a Category C substance does not retain a quantity of residue in excess of 0.3 cubic metres in the tank's associated piping and in the immediate vicinity of that tank's suction point.

(4)(a) Subject to the provisions of sub-paragraph (b) of this paragraph, every ship constructed before 1 July 1986 shall be provided with pumping and piping arrangements to ensure, through testing under favourable pumping conditions, that each tank designated for the carriage of a Category C substance does not retain a quantity of residue in excess of 0.9 cubic metres in the tank's associated piping and in the immediate vicinity of that tank's suction point.

(b) Until 2 October 1994 the ships referred to in sub-paragraph (a) of this paragraph if not in compliance with the requirements of that sub-paragraph shall, as a minimum, be provided with pumping and piping arrangements to ensure, through testing under favourable pumping conditions and surface residue assessment, that each tank designated for the carriage of a Category C substance does not retain a quantity of residue in excess of 3 cubic metres or 1/1,000 of the tank capacity in cubic metres, whichever is greater, in that tank and the associated piping.

(5) Pumping conditions referred to in paragraphs (1), (2), (3) and (4) of this Regulation shall be approved by the Administration and based on standards developed by the Organization. Pumping efficiency tests referred to in paragraphs (1), (2), (3) and (4) of this Regulation shall use water as the test medium and shall be approved by the Administration and based on standards developed by the Organization. The residues on cargo tank surfaces, referred to in paragraphs (2)(b) and (4)(b) of this Regulation shall be determined based on standards developed by the Organization.

(6)(a) Subject to the provision of sub-paragraph (b) of this paragraph, the provisions of paragraphs (2) and (4) of this Regulation need not apply to a ship constructed before 1 July 1986 which is engaged in restricted voyages as determined by the Administration between:

　　　　(i) ports or terminals within a State Party to the present Convention; or

(ii) ports or terminals of States Parties to the present Convention.

(b) The provisions of sub-paragraph (a) of this paragraph shall only apply to a ship constructed before 1 July 1986 if:

(i) each time a tank containing Category B or C substances or mixtures is to be washed or ballasted, the tank is washed in accordance with a pre-wash procedure approved by the Administration and based on Standards developed by the Organization and the tank washings are discharged to a reception facility;

(ii) subsequent washings or ballast water are discharged to a reception facility or at sea in accordance with other provisions of this Annex;

(iii) the adequacy of the reception facilities at the ports or terminals referred to above, for the purpose of this paragraph, is approved by the Governments of the States Parties to the present Convention within which such ports or terminals are situated;

(iv) in the case of ships engaged in voyages to ports or terminals under the jurisdiction of other States Parties to the present Convention, the Administration communicates to the Organization, for circulation to the Parties to the Convention, particulars of the exemption, for their information and appropriate action, if any; and

(v) the Certificate required under this Annex is endorsed to the effect that the ship is solely engaged in such restricted voyages.

(7) For a ship whose constructional and operational features are such that ballasting of cargo tanks is not required and cargo tank washing is only required for repair or dry-docking, the Administration may allow exemption from the provisions of paragraphs (1), (2), (3) and (4) of this Regulation, provided that all the following conditions are complied with:

(a) the design, construction and equipment of the ship are approved by the Administration, having regard to the service for which it is intended;

(b) any effluent from tank washings which may be carried out before a repair or dry-docking is discharged to a reception facility, the adequacy of which is ascertained by the Administration;

(c) the Certificate required under this Annex indicates:

(i) that each cargo tank is certified for the carriage of only one named substance; and

(ii) the particulars of the exemption;

(d) the ship carries a suitable operational manual approved by the Administration; and

(e) in the case of ships engaged in voyages to ports or terminals under the jurisdiction of other States Parties to the present Convention, the Administration communicates to the Organization, for circulation to the Parties to the Convention, particulars of the exemption, for their information and appropriate action, if any.

Regulation 6
Exceptions

Regulation 5 of this Annex shall not apply to:

(a) the discharge into the sea of noxious liquid substances or mixtures containing such substances necessary for the purpose of securing the safety of a ship or saving life at sea; or

(b) the discharge into the sea of noxious liquid substances or mixtures containing such substances resulting from damage to a ship or its equipment:

(i) provided that all reasonable precautions have been taken after the occurrence of the damage or discovery of the discharge for the purpose of preventing or minimizing the discharge; and

(ii) except if the owner or the Master acted either with intent to cause damage, or recklessly and with knowledge that damage would probably result; or

(c) the discharge into the sea of noxious liquid substances or mixtures containing such substances, approved by the Administration, when being used for the purpose of combating specific pollution incidents in order to minimize the damage from pollution. Any such discharge shall be subject to the approval of any Government in whose jurisdiction it is contemplated the discharge will occur.

Regulation 7
Reception Facilities and Cargo Unloading Terminal Arrangements

(1) The Government of each Party to the Convention undertakes to ensure the provision of reception facilities according to the needs of ships using its ports, terminals or repair ports as follows:

(a) cargo loading and unloading ports and terminals shall have facilities adequate for reception without undue delay to ships of such residues and mixtures containing noxious liquid substances as would remain for disposal from ships carrying them as a consequence of the application of this Annex; and

(b) ship repair ports undertaking repairs to chemical tankers shall have facilities adequate for the reception of residues and mixtures containing noxious liquid substances.

(2) The Government of each Party shall determine the types of facilities provided for the purpose of paragraph (1) of this Regulation at each cargo loading and unloading port, terminal and ship repair port in its territories and notify the Organization thereof.

(3) The Government of each Party to the Convention shall undertake to ensure that cargo unloading terminals shall provide arrangements to facilitate stripping of cargo tanks of ships unloading noxious liquid substances at these terminals. Cargo hoses and piping systems of the terminal, containing noxious liquid substances received from ships unloading these substances at the terminal, shall not be drained back to the ship.

(4) Each Party shall notify the Organization, for transmission to the Parties concerned, of any case where facilities required under paragraph (1) or arrangements required under paragraph (3) of this Regulation are alleged to be inadequate.

Regulation 8
Measures of Control

(1)(a) The Government of each Party to the Convention shall appoint or authorize surveyors for the purpose of implementing this Regulation. The surveyors shall execute control in accordance with control procedures developed by the Organization.

(b) The Master of a ship carrying noxious liquid substances in bulk shall ensure that the provisions of Regulation 5 and this Regulation have been complied with and that the Cargo Record Book is completed in accordance with Regulation 9 of this Annex whenever operations as referred to in that Regulation take place.

(c) An exemption referred to in paragraph (2)(b), (5)(b), (6)(c) or (7)(c) of this Regulation may only be granted by the Government of the receiving Party to a ship engaged in voyages to ports or terminals under the jurisdiction of other States Parties to the present Convention. When such an exemption has been granted, the appropriate entry made in the Cargo Record Book shall be endorsed by the surveyor referred to in sub-paragraph (a) of this paragraph.

Category A substances in all areas

(2) With respect to Category A substances the following provisions shall apply in all areas:

(a) A tank which has been unloaded shall, subject to the provisions of sub-paragraph (b) of this paragraph, be washed in accordance with the requirements of paragraph (3) or (4) of this Regulation before the ship leaves the port of unloading.

(b) At the request of the ship's master, the Government of the receiving Party may exempt the ship from the requirements referred to in sub-paragraph (a) of this paragraph, where it is satisfied that:

(i) the tank unloaded is to be reloaded with the same substance or another substance compatible with the previous one and that the tank will not be washed or ballasted prior to loading; or

(ii) the tank unloaded is neither washed nor ballasted at sea and the provisions of paragraph (3) or (4) of this Regulation are complied with at another port provided that it has been confirmed in writing that a reception facility at that port is available and is adequate for such a purpose; or

(iii) the cargo residues will be removed by a ventilation procedure approved by the Administration and based on standards developed by the Organization.

(3) If the tank is to be washed in accordance with sub-paragraph (2)(a) of this Regulation, the effluent from the tank washing operation shall be discharged to a reception facility at least until the concentration of the substance in the discharge, as indicated by analyses of samples of the effluent taken by the surveyor, has fallen to the residual concentration specified for that substance in Appendix II to this Annex. When the required residual concentration has been achieved, remaining tank washings shall continue to be discharged to the reception facility until the tank is empty. Appropriate entries of these operations shall be made in the Cargo Record Book and endorsed by the surveyor referred to under paragraph (1)(a) of this Regulation.

(4) Where the Government of the receiving party is satisfied that it is impracticable to measure the concentration of the substance in the effluent without causing undue delay to the ship, that Party may accept an alternative procedure as being equivalent to paragraph (3) of this Regulation provided that:

(a) The tank is prewashed in accordance with a procedure approved by the Administration and based on standards developed by the Organization; and

(b) The surveyor referred to under paragraph (1)(a) certifies in the Cargo Record Book that:

(i) the tank, its pump and piping systems have been emptied; and

(ii) the prewash has been carried out in accordance with the prewash procedure approved by the Administration for that tank and that substance; and

(iii) the tank washings resulting from such prewash have been discharged to a reception facility and the tank is empty.

Category B and C substances outside Special Areas

(5) With respect to Category B and C substances, the following provisions shall apply outside Special Areas:

(a) A tank which has been unloaded shall, subject to the provisions of sub-paragraph (b) of this paragraph, be prewashed before the ship leaves the port of unloading, whenever:

(i) the substance unloaded is identified in the standards developed by the Organization as resulting in a residue quantity exceeding the maximum quantity which may be discharged into the sea under Regulation 5(2) or (3) of this Annex in case of Category B or C substances respectively; or

(ii) the unloading is not carried out in accordance with the pumping conditions for the tank approved by the Administration and based on standards developed by the Organization as referred to under Regulation 5A(5) of this Annex, unless alternative measures are taken to the satisfaction of the surveyor referred to in paragraph (1)(a) of this Regulation, to remove the cargo residues from the ship to quantities specified in Regulation 5A of this Annex as applicable.

The prewash procedure used shall be approved by the Administration and based on standards developed by the Organization and the resulting tank washings shall be discharged to a reception facility at the port of unloading.

(b) At the request of the ship's Master, the Government of the receiving party may exempt the ship from the requirements of sub-paragraph (a) of this paragraph, where it is satisfied that:

(i) the tank unloaded is to be reloaded with the same substance or another substance compatible with the previous one and that the tank will not be washed nor ballasted prior to loading; or

(ii) the tank unloaded is neither washed nor ballasted at sea and the tank is prewashed in accordance with a procedure approved by the Administration and based on standards developed by the Organization and resulting tank washings are discharged to a reception facility at another port, provided that it has been confirmed in writing that a reception facility at that port is available and adequate for such a purpose; or

(iii) the cargo residues will be removed by a ventilation procedure approved by the Administration and based on standards developed by the Organization.

Category B substances within Special Areas

(6) With respect to Category B substances, the following provisions shall apply within Special Areas:

(a) A tank which has been unloaded shall, subject to the provisions of sub-paragraphs (b) and (c), be prewashed before the ship leaves the port of unloading. The prewash procedure used shall be approved by the Administration and based on standards developed by the Organization and the resulting tank washings shall be discharged to a reception facility at the port of unloading.

(b) The requirements of sub-paragraph (a) of this paragraph do not apply when all the following conditions are satisfied:

(i) the Category B substance unloaded is identified in the standards developed by the Organization as resulting in a residue quantity not exceeding the maximum quantity which may be discharged into the sea outside Special Areas under Regulation 5(2) of this Annex, and the residues are retained on board for subsequent discharge into the sea outside the Special Area in compliance with Regulation 5(2) of this Annex; and

(ii) the unloading is carried out in accordance with the pumping conditions for the tank approved by the Administration and based on standards developed by the Organization as referred to under Regulation 5A(5) of this Annex, or failing to comply with the approved pumping conditions, alternative measures are taken to the satisfaction of the surveyor referred to in paragraph (1)(a) of this Regulation, to remove the cargo residues from the ship to quantities specified in Regulation 5A of this Annex as applicable.

(c) At the request of the ship's master, the Government of the receiving party may exempt the ship from the requirements of sub-paragraph (a) of this paragraph, where it is satisfied:

(i) that the tank unloaded is to be reloaded with the same substance or another substance compatible with the previous one and that the tank will not be washed or ballasted prior to loading; or

(ii) that the tank unloaded is neither washed nor ballasted at sea and the tank is prewashed in accordance with a procedure approved by the Administration and based on standards developed by the Organization and resulting tank washings are discharged to a reception facility at another port, provided that it has been confirmed in writing that a reception facility at that port is available and adequate for such a purpose; or

(iii) that the cargo residues will be removed by a ventilation procedure approved by the Administration and based on standards developed by the Organization.

Category C substances within Special Areas

(7) With respect to Category C substances, the following provisions shall apply within Special Areas:

(a) A tank which has been unloaded shall, subject to the provisions of sub-paragraphs (b) and (c) of this paragraph, be prewashed before the ship leaves the port of unloading, whenever:

(i) the Category C substance unloaded is identified in the standards developed by the Organization as resulting in a residue quantity exceeding the maximum quantity which may be discharged into the sea under Regulation 5(9) of this Annex; or

(ii) the unloading is not carried out in accordance with the pumping conditions for the tank approved by the Administration and based on standards developed by the Organization as referred to under Regulation 5A(5) of this Annex, unless alternative measures are taken to the satisfaction of the surveyor referred to in paragraph (1)(a) of this Regulation, to remove the cargo residues from the ship to quantities specified in Regulation 5A of this Annex as applicable.

The prewash procedure used shall be approved by the Administration and based on standards developed by the Organization and the resulting tank washings shall be discharged to a reception facility at the port of unloading.

(b) The requirements of sub-paragraph (a) of this paragraph do not apply when all the following conditions are satisfied:

(i) the Category C substance unloaded is identified in the standards developed by the Organization as resulting in a residue quantity not exceeding the maximum quantity which may be discharged into the sea outside Special Areas under Regulation 5(3) of this Annex, and the residues are retained on board for subsequent discharge into the sea outside the Special Area in compliance with Regulation 5(3) of this Annex; and

(ii) the unloading is carried out in accordance with the pumping conditions for the tank approved by the Administration and based on standards developed by the Organization as referred to under Regulation 5A(5) of this Annex, or failing to comply with the approved pumping conditions, alternative measures are taken to the satisfaction of the surveyor referred to in paragraph (1)(a) of this Regulation, to remove the cargo residues from the ship to quantities specified in Regulation 5A of this Annex as applicable.

(c) At the request of the ship's master, the Government of the receiving party may exempt the ship from the requirements of sub-paragraph (a) of this paragraph, where it is satisfied:

(i) that the tank unloaded is to be reloaded with the same substance or another substance compatible with the previous one and that the tank will not be washed or ballasted prior to loading; or

(ii) that the tank unloaded is neither washed nor ballasted at sea and the tank is prewashed in accordance with a procedure approved by the Administration and based on standards developed by the Organization and resulting tank washings are discharged to a reception facility at another port, provided that it has been confirmed in writing that a reception facility at that port is available and adequate for such a purpose; or

(iii) that the cargo residues will be removed by a ventilation procedure approved by the Administration and based on standards developed by the Organization.

Category D substances in all areas

(8) With respect to Category D substances, a tank which has been unloaded shall either be washed and the resulting tank washings shall be discharged to a reception facility, or the remaining residues in the tank shall be diluted and discharged into the sea in accordance with Regulation 5(4) of this Annex.

Discharge from a slop tank

(9) Any residues retained on board in a slop tank, including those from cargo pump room bilges, which contain a Category A substance, or within a special area either a Category A or a Category B substance, shall be discharged to a reception facility in accordance with the provisions of Regulation 5(1), (7) or (8) of this Annex, whichever is applicable.

Regulation 9

Cargo Record Book

(1) Every ship to which this Annex applies shall be provided with a Cargo Record Book, whether as part of the ship's official log book or otherwise, in the form specified in Appendix IV to this Annex.

(2) The Cargo Record Book shall be completed, on a tank-to-tank basis, whenever any of the following operations with respect to a noxious liquid substance take place in the ship:

(i) loading of cargo;

(ii) internal transfer of cargo;

(iii) unloading of cargo;

(iv) cleaning of cargo tanks;

(v) ballasting of cargo tanks;

(vi) discharge of ballast from cargo tanks;

(vii) disposal of residues to reception facilities;

(viii) discharge into the sea or removal by ventilation of residues in accordance with Regulation 5 of this Annex.

(3) In the event of any discharge of the kind referred to in Article 8 of the present Convention and Regulation 6 of this Annex of any noxious liquid substance or mixture containing such substance, whether intentional or accidental, an entry shall be made in the Cargo Record Book stating the circumstances of, and the reason for, the discharge.

(4) When a surveyor appointed or authorized by the Government of the Party to the Convention to supervise any operations under this Annex has inspected a ship, then that surveyor shall make an appropriate entry in the Cargo Record Book.

(5) Each operation referred to in paragraphs (2) and (3) of this Regulation shall be fully recorded without delay in the Cargo Record Book so that all the entries in the Book appropriate to that operation are completed. Each entry shall be signed by the officer or officers in charge of the operation concerned and each page shall be signed by the Master of the ship. The entries in the Cargo Record Book shall be in an official language of the State whose flag the ship is entitled to fly, and, for ships holding an International Pollution Prevention Certificate for the Carriage of Noxious Liquid Substances in Bulk or a Certificate referred to in Regulation 12A of this Annex in English or French. The entries in an official national language of the State whose flag the ship is entitled to fly shall prevail in case of a dispute or discrepancy.

(6) The Cargo Record Book shall be kept in such a place as to be readily available for inspection and, except in the case of unmanned ships under tow, shall be kept on board the ship. It shall be retained for a period of three years after the last entry has been made.

(7) The competent authority of the Government of a Party may inspect the Cargo Record Book on board any ship to which this Annex applies while the ship is in its port, and may make a copy of any entry in that book and may require the Master of the ship to certify that the copy is a true copy of such entry. Any copy so made which has been certified by the Master of the ship as a true copy of an entry in the ship's Cargo Record Book shall be made admissible in any judicial proceedings as evidence of the facts stated in the entry. The inspection of a Cargo Record Book and the taking of a certified copy by the competent authority under this paragraph shall be performed as expeditiously as possible without causing the ship to be unduly delayed.

Regulation 10
Surveys

(1) Ships carrying noxious liquid substances in bulk shall be subject to the surveys specified below:

(a) An initial survey before the ship is put in service or before the Certificate required under Regulation 11 of this Annex is issued for the first time, and which shall include a complete survey of its structure, equipment, systems, fittings, arrangements and material in so far as the ship is covered by this Annex. This survey shall be such as to ensure that the structure, equipment, systems, fittings, arrangements and material fully comply with the applicable requirements of this Annex.

(b) Periodical surveys at intervals specified by the Administration, but not exceeding five years, and which shall be such as to ensure that the structure, equipment, systems, fittings, arrangements and material fully comply with the requirements of this Annex.

(c) A minimum of one intermediate survey during the period of validity of the Certificate and which shall be such as to ensure that the equipment and associated pump and piping systems fully comply with the applicable requirements of this Annex and are in good working order. In cases where only one such intermediate survey is carried out in any one Certificate validity period, it shall be held not before six months prior to, nor later than six months after the half-way date of the Certificate's period of validity. Such intermediate surveys shall be endorsed on the Certificate issued under Regulation 11 of this Annex.

(d) An annual survey within 3 months before or after the day and the month of the date of issue of the Certificate and which shall include a general examination to ensure that the structure, fittings, arrangements and materials remain in all respects satisfactory for the service for which the ship is intended. Such annual surveys shall be endorsed on the Certificate issued under Regulation 11 of this Annex.

(2)(a) Surveys of ships as regards the enforcement of the provisions of this Annex shall be carried out by officers of the Administration. The Administration may, however, entrust the surveys either to surveyors nominated for the purpose or to organizations recognized by it.

(b) An Administration nominating surveyors or recognizing organizations to conduct surveys and inspections as set forth in sub-paragraph (a) of this paragraph, shall as a minimum empower any nominated surveyor or recognized organization to:

(i) require repairs to a ship; and

(ii) carry out surveys and inspections if requested by the appropriate authorities of a port State.

The Administration shall notify the Organization of the specific responsibilities and conditions of the authority delegated to the nominated surveyors or recognized organizations, for circulation to Parties to the present Convention for the information of their officers.

(c) When a nominated surveyor or recognized organization determines that the condition of the ship or its equipment does not correspond substantially with the particulars of the Certificate,. or is such that the ship is not fit to proceed to sea without presenting an unreasonable threat of harm to the marine environment, such surveyor or organization shall immediately ensure that corrective action is taken and shall in due course notify the Administration. If such corrective action is not taken the Certificate should be withdrawn and the Administration shall be notified immediately; and if the ship is in a port of another Party, the appropriate authorities of the port State shall also be notified immediately. When an officer of the Administration, a nominated surveyor or recognized organization has notified the appropriate authorities of the port State, the Government of the port State concerned shall give such officer, surveyor, or organization any necessary assistance to carry out their obligations under this Regulation. When applicable, the Government of the port State concerned shall take such steps as will ensure that the ship shall not sail until it can proceed to sea or leave the port for the purpose of proceeding to the nearest appropriate repair yard available without presenting an unreasonable threat of harm to the marine environment.

(d) In every case, the Administration concerned shall fully guarantee the completeness and efficiency of the survey and inspection and shall undertake to ensure the necessary arrangements to satisfy this obligation.

(3)(a) The condition of the ship and its equipment shall be maintained to conform with the provisions of the present Convention to ensure that the ship in all respects will remain fit to proceed to sea without presenting an unreasonable threat of harm to the marine environment.

(b) After any survey of the ship under paragraph (1) of this Regulation has been completed, no change shall be made in the structure, equipment, systems, fittings, arrangements or material covered by the survey, without the sanction of the Administration, except the direct replacement of such equipment and fittings.

(c) Whenever an accident occurs to a ship or a defect is discovered which substantially affects the integrity of the ship or the efficiency or completeness of its equipment covered by this Annex, the master or owner of the ship shall report at the earliest opportunity to the Administration, the recognized organization or the nominated surveyor responsible for issuing the relevant Certificate, who shall cause investigations to be initiated to determine whether a survey as required by paragraph (1) of this Regulation is necessary. If the ship is in a port of another Party, the master or owner shall also report immediately to the appropriate authorities of the port State and the nominated surveyor or recognized organization shall ascertain that such report has been made.

Regulation 11
Issue of Certificate

(1) An International Pollution Prevention Certificate for the Carriage of Noxious Liquid Substances in Bulk shall be issued, after survey in accordance with the provisions of Regulation 10 of this Annex, to any ship carrying noxious liquid substances in bulk and which is engaged in voyages to ports or terminals under the jurisdiction of other Parties to the Convention.

(2) Such Certificate shall be issued either by the Administration or by any person or organization duly authorized by it. In every case, the Administration assumes full responsibility for the Certificate.

(3)(a) The Government of a Party to the Convention may, at the request of the Administration, cause a ship to be surveyed and, if satisfied that the provisions of this Annex are complied with, shall issue or authorize the issue of an International Pollution Prevention Certificate for the Carriage of Noxious Liquid Substances in Bulk to the ship in accordance with this Annex.

(b) A copy of the Certificate and a copy of the survey report shall be transmitted as soon as possible to the requesting Administration.

(c) A Certificate so issued shall contain a statement to the effect that it has been issued at the request of the Administration and it shall have the same force and receive the same recognition as the Certificate issued under paragraph (1) of this Regulation.

(d) No International Pollution Prevention Certificate for the Carriage of Noxious Liquid Substances in Bulk shall be issued to a ship which is entitled to fly the flag of a State which is not a Party.

(4) The International Pollution Prevention Certificate for the Carriage of Noxious Liquid Substances in Bulk shall be drawn up in an official language of the issuing country in the form corresponding to the model given in Appendix V to this Annex. If the language used is neither English nor French, the text shall include a translation into one of these languages.

Regulation 12
Duration of Certificate

(1) An International Pollution Prevention Certificate for the Carriage of Noxious Liquid Substances in Bulk shall be issued for a period specified by the Administration, which shall not exceed five years from the date of issue.

(2) A Certificate shall cease to be valid if significant alterations have taken place in the construction, equipment, systems, fittings, arrangements or material required without the sanction of the Administration, except the direct replacement of such equipment or fittings, or if intermediate or annual surveys as specified by the Administration under Regulation 10(1)(c) or (d) of this Annex are not carried out.

(3) A Certificate issued to a ship shall also cease to be valid upon transfer of the ship to the flag of another State. A new Certificate shall be issued only when the Government issuing the new Certificate is fully satisfied that the ship is in full compliance with the requirements of Regulation 10(3)(a) and (b) of this Annex. In the case of a transfer between Parties, if requested within three months after the transfer has taken place, the Government of the Party whose flag the ship was formerly entitled to fly shall transmit as soon as possible to the Administration a copy of the Certificate carried by the ship before the transfer and, if available, a copy of the relevant survey report.

Regulation 12A

Survey and Certification of Chemical Tankers

Notwithstanding the provisions of Regulations 10, 11 and 12 of this Annex, chemical tankers which have been surveyed and certified by States Parties to the present Convention in accordance with the provisions of the International Bulk Chemical Code or the Bulk Chemical Code, as applicable, shall be deemed to have complied with the provisions of the said Regulations, and the Certificate issued under that Code shall have the same force and receive the same recognition as the Certificate issued under Regulation 11 of this Annex.

Regulation 13

Requirements for Minimizing Accidental Pollution

(1) The design, construction, equipment and operation of ships carrying noxious liquid substances of Category A, B or C in bulk, shall be such as to minimize the uncontrolled discharge into the sea of such substances.

(2) Chemical tankers constructed on or after 1 July 1986 shall comply with the requirements of the International Bulk Chemical Code.

(3) Chemical tankers constructed before 1 July 1986 shall comply with the following requirements:

(a) The following chemical tankers shall comply with the requirements of the Bulk Chemical Code as applicable to ships referred to in 1.7.2 of that Code:

(i) ships for which the building contract is placed on or after 2 November 1973 and which are engaged on voyages to ports or terminals under the jurisdiction of other States Parties to the Convention; and

(ii) ships constructed on or after 1 July 1983 which are engaged solely on voyages between ports or terminals within the State the flag of which the ship is entitled to fly;

(b) The following chemical tankers shall comply with the requirements of the Bulk Chemical Code as applicable to ships referred to in 1.7.3 of that Code:

(i) ships for which the building contract is placed before 2 November 1973 and which are engaged on voyages to ports or terminals under the jurisdiction of other States Parties to the Convention; and

(ii) ships constructed before 1 July 1983 which are engaged on voyages between ports or terminals within the State the flag of which the ship is entitled to fly, except that for ships of less than 1,600 tons gross tonnage compliance with the Code in respect of construction and equipment shall take effect not later than 1 July 1994.

(4) In respect of ships other than chemical tankers carrying noxious liquid substances of Category A, B or C in bulk, the Administration shall establish appropriate measures based on the Guidelines developed by the Organization in order to ensure that the provisions of paragraph (1) of this Regulation are complied with.

Regulation 14
Carriage and Discharge of Oil-like Substances

Notwithstanding the provisions of other Regulations of this Annex, noxious liquid substances designated in Appendix II of this Annex as falling under Category C or D and identified by the Organization as oil-like substances under the criteria developed by the Organization, may be carried on an oil tanker as defined in Annex I of the Convention and discharged in accordance with the provisions of Annex I of the present Convention, provided that all of the following conditions are complied with:

(a) the ship complies with the provisions of Annex I of the present Convention as applicable to product carriers as defined in that Annex;

(b) the ship carries an International Oil Pollution Prevention Certificate and its Supplement B and the Certificate is endorsed to indicate that the ship may carry oil-like substances in conformity with this Regulation and the endorsement includes a list of oil-like substances the ship is allowed to carry;

(c) in the case of Category C substances the ship complies with the ship type 3 damage stability requirements of:

(i) the International Bulk Chemical Code in the case of a ship constructed on or after 1 July 1986; or

(ii) the Bulk Chemical Code, as applicable under Regulation 13 of this Annex, in the case of a ship constructed before 1 July 1986; and

(d) the oil content meter in the oil discharge monitoring and control system of the ship is approved by the Administration for use in monitoring the oil-like substances to be carried.

ANNEX V
REGULATIONS FOR THE PREVENTION OF POLLUTION
BY GARBAGE FROM SHIPS
Regulation 1
Definitions

For the purposes of this Annex:

(1) "Garbage" means all kinds of victual, domestic and operational waste excluding fresh fish and parts thereof, generated during the normal operation of the ship and liable to be disposed of continuously or periodically except those substances which are defined or listed in other Annexes to the present Convention.

(2) "Nearest land". The term "from the nearest land" means from the baseline from which the territorial sea of the territory in question is established in accordance with international law except that, for the purposes of the present Convention "from the nearest land" off the north eastern coast of Australia shall mean from a line drawn from a point on the coast of Australia in latitude 11° South, longitude 142°08′ East to a point in latitude 10°35′ South,

longitude 141°55′ East, thence to a point latitude 10°00′ South,

longitude 142°00′ East, thence to a point latitude 9°10′ South,

longitude 143°52′ East, thence to a point latitude 9°00′ South,

longitude 144°30′ East, thence to a point latitude 13°00′ South,

longitude 144°00′ East, thence to a point latitude 15°00′ South,

longitude 146°00′ East, thence to a point latitude 18°00′ South,

longitude 147°00′ East, thence to a point latitude 21°00′ South,

longitude 153°00′ East, thence to a point on the coast of Australia in latitude 24°42′ South, longitude 153°15′ East.

(3) "Special area" means a sea area where for recognized technical reasons in relation to its oceanographical and ecological condition and to the particular character of its traffic the adoption of special mandatory methods for the prevention of sea pollution by garbage is required. Special areas shall include those listed in Regulation 5 of this Annex.

Regulation 2
Application

The provisions of this Annex shall apply to all ships.

Regulation 3
Disposal of Garbage Outside Special Areas

(1) Subject to the provisions of Regulations 4, 5 and 6 of this Annex:

(a) the disposal into the sea of all plastics, including but not limited to synthetic ropes, synthetic fishing nets and plastic garbage bags is prohibited;

(b) the disposal into the sea of the following garbage shall be made as far as practicable from the nearest land but in any case is prohibited if the distance from the nearest land is less than:

(i) 25 nautical miles for dunnage, lining and packing materials which will float;

(ii) 12 nautical miles for food wastes and all other garbage including paper products, rags, glass, metal, bottles, crockery and similar refuse;

(c) disposal into the sea of garbage specified in sub-paragraph (b)(ii) of this Regulation may be permitted when it is passed through a comminuter or grinder and made as far as practicable from the nearest land but in any case is prohibited if the distance from the nearest land is less than 3 nautical miles. Such comminuted or ground garbage shall be capable of passing through a screen with openings no greater than 25 millimetres.

(2) When the garbage is mixed with other discharges having different disposal or discharge requirements the more severe requirements shall apply.

Regulation 4
Disposals from Drilling Rigs

(1) Fixed or floating platforms engaged in the exploration, exploitation and associated offshore processing of sea-bed mineral resources, and all other ships when alongside such platforms or within 500 metres of such platforms, are forbidden to dispose of any materials regulated by this Annex, except as permitted by paragraph (2) of this Regulation.

(2) The disposal into the sea of food wastes when passed through a comminuter or grinder from such fixed or floating drilling rigs located more than 12 nautical miles from land and all other ships when positioned as above. Such comminuted or ground food wastes shall be capable of passing through a screen with openings no greater than 25 millimetres.

Regulation 5
Disposal of Garbage within Special Areas

(1) For the purpose of this Annex the special areas are the Mediterranean Sea area, the Baltic Sea area, the Black Sea area, the Red Sea area and the "Gulfs area" which are defined as follows:

(a) The Mediterranean Sea area means the Mediterranean Sea proper including the gulfs and seas therein with the boundary between the Mediterranean and the Black Sea constituted by the 41°N parallel and bounded to the west by the Straits of Gibraltar at the meridian of 5°36′W.

(b) The Baltic Sea area means the Baltic Sea proper with the Gulf of Bothnia and the Gulf of Finland and the entrance to the Baltic Sea bounded by the parallel of the Skaw in the Skagerrak at 57°44.8′N.

(c) The Black Sea area means the Black Sea proper with the boundary between the Mediterranean and the Black Sea constituted by the parallel 41°N.

(d) The Red Sea area means the Red Sea proper including the Gulfs of Suez and Aqaba bounded at the south by the rhumb line between Ras si Ane (12°8.5′N, 43°19.6′E) and Husn Murad (12°40.4′N, 43°30.2′E).

(e) The "Gulfs area" means the sea area located north west of the rhumb line between Ras al Hadd (22°30′N, 59°48′E) and Ras al Fasteh (25°04′N, 61°25′E).

(2) Subject to the provisions of Regulation 6 of this Annex:

(a) disposal into the sea of the following is prohibited:

(i) all plastics, including but not limited to synthetic ropes, synthetic fishing nets and plastic garbage bags;

(ii) all other garbage, including paper products, rags, glass, metal, bottles, crockery, dunnage, lining and packing materials;

(b) disposal into the sea of food wastes shall be made as far as practicable from land, but in any case not less than 12 nautical miles from the nearest land.

(3) When the garbage is mixed with other discharges having different disposal or discharge requirements the more severe requirements shall apply.

(4) Reception facilities within special areas.

(a) The Government of each party to the Convention, the coast line of which borders a special area undertakes to ensure that as soon as possible in all ports within a special area, adequate reception facilities are provided in accordance with Regulation 7 of this Annex, taking into account the special needs of ships operating in these areas.

(b) The Government of each party concerned shall notify the Organization of the measures taken pursuant to sub-paragraph (a) of this Regulation. Upon receipt of sufficient notifications the Organization shall establish a date from which the requirements of this Regulation in respect of the area in question shall take effect. The Organization shall notify all parties of the date so established no less than twelve months in advance of that date.

(c) After date so established, ships calling also at ports in these special areas where such facilities are not yet available, shall fully comply with the requirements of this Regulation.

Regulation 6
Exception

Regulations 3, 4 and 5 of this Annex shall not apply to:

(a) the disposal of garbage from a ship necessary for the purpose of securing the safety of a ship, the health of its personnel, or saving life at sea;

(b) the escape of garbage resulting from damage to a ship or its equipment provided all reasonable precautions have been taken before and after the occurrence of the damage, for the purpose of preventing or minimizing the escape;

(c) the accidental loss of synthetic fishing nets or synthetic material incidental to the repair of such nets, provided that all reasonable precautions have been taken to prevent such loss.

Regulation 7

Reception Facilities

(1) The Government of each party to the Convention undertakes to ensure the provisions of facilities at ports and terminals for the reception of garbage, without causing undue delay to ships, and according to the needs of the ships using them.

(2) The Government of each party shall notify the Organization for transmission to the parties concerned of all cases where the facilities provided under this Regulation are alleged to be inadequate.

附録十二：生物多樣性公約

CONVENTION ON BIOLOGICAL DIVERSITY (WITH ANNEXES). Concluded at Rio de Janeiro, 5 June 1992. Entered into force, 29 December 1993. 31 I.L.M. 818 (1992)

Preamble

The Contracting Parties,

Conscious of the intrinsic value of biological diversity and of the ecological, genetic, social, economic, scientific, educational, cultural, recreational and aesthetic values of biological diversity and its components,

Conscious also of the importance of biological diversity for evolution and for maintaining life sustaining systems of the biosphere,

Affirming that the conservation of biological diversity is a common concern of humankind,

Reaffirming that States have sovereign rights over their own biological resources,

Reaffirming also that States are responsible for conserving their biological diversity and for using their biological resources in a sustainable manner,

Concerned that biological diversity is being significantly reduced by certain human activities,

Aware of the general lack of information and knowledge regarding biological diversity and of the urgent need to develop scientific, technical and institutional capacities to provide the basic understanding upon which to plan and implement appropriate measures,

Noting that it is vital to anticipate, prevent and attack the causes of significant reduction or loss of biological diversity at source,

Noting also that where there is a threat of significant reduction or loss of biological diversity, lack of full scientific certainty should not be used as a reason for postponing measures to avoid or minimize such a threat,

Noting further that the fundamental requirement for the conservation of biological diversity is the *in-situ* conservation of ecosystems and natural habitats and the maintenance and recovery of viable populations of species in their natural surroundings,

Noting further that *ex-situ* measures, preferably in the country of origin, also have an important role to play,

Recognizing the close and traditional dependence of many indigenous and local communities embodying traditional lifestyles on biological resources, and the desirability of sharing equitably benefits arising from the use of traditional knowledge, innovations and practices relevant to the conservation of biological diversity and the sustainable use of its components,

Recognizing also the vital role that women play in the conservation and sustainable use of biological diversity and affirming the need for the full participation of women at all levels of policy-making and implementation for biological diversity conservation,

Stressing the importance of, and the need to promote, international, regional and global cooperation among States and intergovernmental organizations and the non-governmental sector for the conservation of biological diversity and the sustainable use of its components,

Acknowledging that the provision of new and additional financial resources and appropriate access to relevant technologies can be expected to make a substantial difference in the world's ability to address the loss of biological diversity,

Acknowledging further that special provision is required to meet the needs of developing countries, including the provision of new and additional financial resources and appropriate access to relevant technologies,

Noting in this regard the special conditions of the least developed countries and small island States,

Acknowledging that substantial investments are required to conserve biological diversity and that there is the expectation of a broad range of environmental, economic and social benefits from those investments,

Recognizing that economic and social development and poverty eradication are the first and overriding priorities of developing countries,

Aware that conservation and sustainable use of biological diversity is of critical importance for meeting the food, health and other needs of the growing world population, for which purpose access to and sharing of both genetic resources and technologies are essential,

Noting that, ultimately, the conservation and sustainable use of biological diversity will strengthen friendly relations among States and contribute to peace for humankind,

Desiring to enhance and complement existing international arrangements for the conservation of biological diversity and sustainable use of its components, and

Determined to conserve and sustainably use biological diversity for the benefit of present and future generations.

Have agreed as follows:

Article 1. Objectives

The objectives of this Convention, to be pursued in accordance with its relevant provisions, are the conservation of biological diversity, the sustainable use of its components and the fair and equitable sharing of the benefits arising out of the utilization of genetic resources, including by appropriate access to genetic resources and by appropriate transfer of relevant technologies, taking into account all rights over those resources and to technologies, and by appropriate funding.

Article 2.　Use of Terms

For the purposes of this Convention:

"Biological diversity" means the variability among living organisms from all sources including, *inter alia,* terrestrial, marine and other aquatic ecosystems and the ecological complexes of which they are part; this includes diversity within species, between species and of ecosystems.

"Biological resources" includes genetic resources, organisms or parts thereof, populations, or any other biotic component of ecosystems with actual or potential use or value for humanity.

"Biotechnology" means any technological application that uses biological systems, living organisms, or derivatives thereof, to make or modify products or processes for specific use.

"Country of origin of genetic resources" means the country which possesses those genetic resources in *in-situ* conditions.

"Country providing genetic resources" means the country supplying genetic resources collected from *in-situ* sources, including populations of both wild and domesticated species, or taken from *ex-situ* sources, which may or may not have originated in that country.

"Domesticated or cultivated species" means species in which the evolutionary process has been influenced by humans to meet their needs.

"Ecosystem" means a dynamic complex of plant, animal and micro-organism communities and their non-living environment interacting as a functional unit.

"Ex-situ conservation" means the conservation of components of biological diversity outside their natural habitats.

"Genetic material" means any material of plant, animal, microbial or other origin containing functional units of heredity.

"Genetic resources" means genetic material of actual or potential value.

"Habitat" means the place or type of site where an organism or population naturally occurs.

"In-situ conditions" means conditions where genetic resources exist within ecosystems and natural habitats, and, in the case of domesticated or cultivated species, in the surroundings where they have developed their distinctive properties.

"In-situ conservation" means the conservation of ecosystems and natural habitats and the maintenance and recovery of viable populations of species in their natural surroundings and, in the case of domesticated or cultivated species, in the surroundings where they have developed their distinctive properties.

"Protected area" means a geographically defined area which is designated or regulated and managed to achieve specific conservation objectives.

"Regional economic integration organization" means an organization constituted by sovereign States of a given region, to which its member States have transferred competence in respect of matters governed by this Convention and which has been duly authorized, in accordance with its internal procedures, to sign, ratify, accept, approve or accede to it.

"Sustainable use" means the use of components of biological diversity in a way and at a rate that does not lead to the long-term decline of biological diversity, thereby maintaining its potential to meet the needs and aspirations of present and future generations.

"Technology" includes biotechnology.

Article 3. Principle

States have, in accordance with the Charter of the United Nations and the principles of international law, the sovereign right to exploit their own resources pursuant to their own environmental policies, and the responsibility to ensure that activities within their jurisdiction or control do not cause damage to the environment of other States or of areas beyond the limits of national jurisdiction.

Article 4. Jurisdictional Scope

Subject to the rights of other States, and except as otherwise expressly provided in this Convention, the provisions of this Convention apply, in relation to each Contracting Party:

(a) In the case of components of biological diversity, in areas within the limits of its national jurisdiction; and

(b) In the case of processes and activities, regardless of where their effects occur, carried out under its jurisdiction or control, within the area of its national jurisdiction or beyond the limits of national jurisdiction.

Article 5. Cooperation

Each Contracting Party shall, as far as possible and as appropriate, cooperate with other Contracting Parties, directly or, where appropriate, through competent international organizations, in respect of areas beyond national jurisdiction and on other matters of mutual interest, for the conservation and sustainable use of biological diversity.

Article 6. General Measures for Conservation and Sustainable Use

Each Contracting Party shall, in accordance with its particular conditions and capabilities:

(a) Develop national strategies, plans or programmes for the conservation and sustainable use of biological diversity or adapt for this purpose existing strategies, plans or programmes which shall reflect, inter alia, the measures set out in this Convention relevant to the Contracting Party concerned; and

(b) Integrate, as far as possible and as appropriate, the conservation and sustainable use of biological diversity into relevant sectoral or cross-sectoral plans, programmes and policies.

Article 7. *Identification and Monitoring*

Each Contracting Party shall, as far as possible and as appropriate, in particular for the purposes of Articles 8 to 10:

(a) Identify components of biological diversity important for its conservation and sustainable use having regard to the indicative list of categories set down in Annex I;

(b) Monitor, through sampling and other techniques, the components of biological diversity identified pursuant to subparagraph (a) above, paying particular attention to those requiring urgent conservation measures and those which offer the greatest potential for sustainable use;

(c) Identify processes and categories of activities which have or are likely to have significant adverse impacts on the conservation and sustainable use of biological diversity, and monitor their effects through sampling and other techniques; and

(d) Maintain and organize, by any mechanism data, derived from identification and monitoring activities pursuant to subparagraphs (a), (b) and (c) above.

Article 8. *In-situ Conservation*

Each Contracting Party shall, as far as possible and as appropriate:

(a) Establish a system of protected areas or areas where special measures need to be taken to conserve biological diversity;

(b) Develop, where necessary, guidelines for the selection, establishment and management of protected areas or areas where special measures need to be taken to conserve biological diversity;

(c) Regulate or manage biological resources important for the conservation of biological diversity whether within or outside protected areas, with a view to ensuring their conservation and sustainable use;

(d) Promote the protection of ecosystems, natural habitats and the maintenance of viable populations of species in natural surroundings;

(e) Promote environmentally sound and sustainable development in areas adjacent to protected areas with a view to furthering protection of these areas;

(f) Rehabilitate and restore degraded ecosystems and promote the recovery of threatened species, *inter alia,* through the development and implementation of plans or other management strategies;

(g) Establish or maintain means to regulate, manage or control the risks associated with the use and release of living modified organisms resulting from biotechnology which are likely to have adverse environmental impacts that could affect the conservation and sustainable use of biological diversity, taking also into account the risks to human health;

(h) Prevent the introduction of, control or eradicate those alien species which threaten ecosystems, habitats or species;

(i) Endeavour to provide the conditions needed for compatibility between present uses and the conservation of biological diversity and the sustainable use of its components;

(j) Subject to its national legislation, respect, preserve and maintain knowledge, innovations and practices of indigenous and local communities embodying traditional lifestyles relevant for the conservation and sustainable use of biological diversity and promote their wider application with the approval and involvement of the holders of such knowledge, innovations and practices and encourage the equitable sharing of the benefits arising from the utilization of such knowledge, innovations and practices;

(k) Develop or maintain necessary legislation and/or other regulatory provisions for the protection of threatened species and populations;

(l) Where a significant adverse effect on biological diversity has been determined pursuant to Article 7, regulate or manage the relevant processes and categories of activities; and

(m) Cooperate in providing financial and other support for *in-situ* conservation outlined in subparagraphs (a) to (l) above, particularly to developing countries.

Article 9. Ex-situ Conservation

Each Contracting Party shall, as far as possible and as appropriate, and predominantly for the purpose of complementing *in-situ* measures:

(a) Adopt measures for the *ex-situ* conservation of components of biological diversity, preferably in the country of origin of such components;

(b) Establish and maintain facilities for *ex-situ* conservation of and research on plants, animals and micro-organisms, preferably in the country of origin of genetic resources;

(c) Adopt measures for the recovery and rehabilitation of threatened species and for their reintroduction into their natural habitats under appropriate conditions;

(d) Regulate and manage collection of biological resources from natural habitats for *ex-situ* conservation purposes so as not to threaten ecosystems and *in-situ* populations of species, except where special tempo-rary *ex-situ* measures are required under subparagraph (c) above; and

　(e)　Cooperate in providing financial and other support for *ex-situ* conservation outlined in subparagraphs (a) to (d) above and in the establishment and maintenance of *ex-situ* conservation facilities in devel-oping countries.

Article 10.　Sustainable Use of Components of Biological Diversity

Each Contracting Party shall, as far as possible and as appropriate:

　(a)　Integrate consideration of the conservation and sustainable use of biological resources into national decision-making;

　(b)　Adopt measures relating to the use of biological resources to avoid or minimize adverse impacts on biological diversity;

　(c)　Protect and encourage customary use of biological resources in accordance with traditional cultural practices that are compatible with conservation or sustainable use requirements;

　(d)　Support local populations to develop and implement remedial action in degraded areas where biological diversity has been reduced; and

　(e)　Encourage cooperation between its governmental authorities and its private sector in developing methods for sustainable use of biological resources.

Article 11.　Incentive Measures

Each Contracting Party shall, as far as possible and as appropriate, adopt economically and socially sound measures that act as incentives for the conservation and sustainable use of components of biological diversity.

Article 12.　Research and Training

The Contracting Parties, taking into account the special needs of develop-ing countries, shall:

　(a)　Establish and maintain programmes for scientific and technical education and training in measures for the identification, conservation and sustainable use of biological diversity and its components and provide support for such education and training for the specific needs of develop-ing countries;

　(b)　Promote and encourage research which contributes to the con-servation and sustainable use of biological diversity, particularly in devel-oping countries, *inter alia,* in accordance with decisions of the Conference of the Parties taken in consequence of recommendations of the Subsidiary Body on Scientific, Technical and Technological Advice; and

　(c)　In keeping with the provisions of Articles 16, 18 and 20, promote and cooperate in the use of scientific advances in biological diversity research in developing methods for conservation and sustainable use of biological resources.

Article 13.　Public Education and Awareness

The Contracting Parties shall:

(a)　Promote and encourage understanding of the importance of, and the measures required for, the conservation of biological diversity, as well as its propagation through media, and the inclusion of these topics in educational programmes; and

(b)　Cooperate, as appropriate, with other States and international organizations in developing educational and public awareness programmes, with respect to conservation and sustainable use of biological diversity.

Article 14.　Impact Assessment and Minimizing Adverse Impacts

1.　Each Contracting Party, as far as possible and as appropriate, shall:

(a)　Introduce appropriate procedures requiring environmental impact assessment of its proposed projects that are likely to have significant adverse effects on biological diversity with a view to avoiding or minimizing such effects and, where appropriate, allow for public participation in such procedures;

(b)　Introduce appropriate arrangements to ensure that the environmental consequences of its programmes and policies that are likely to have significant adverse impacts on biological diversity are duly taken into account;

(c)　Promote, on the basis of reciprocity, notification, exchange of information and consultation on activities under their jurisdiction or control which are likely to significantly affect adversely the biological diversity of other States or areas beyond the limits of national jurisdiction, by encouraging the conclusion of bilateral, regional or multilateral arrangements, as appropriate;

(d)　In the case of imminent or grave danger or damage, originating under its jurisdiction or control, to biological diversity within the area under jurisdiction of other States or in areas beyond the limits of national jurisdiction, notify immediately the potentially affected States of such danger or damage, as well as initiate action to prevent or minimize such danger or damage; and

(e)　Promote national arrangements for emergency responses to activities or events, whether caused naturally or otherwise, which present a grave and imminent danger to biological diversity and encourage international cooperation to supplement such national efforts and, where appropriate and agreed by the States or regional economic integration organizations concerned, to establish joint contingency plans.

2.　The Conference of the Parties shall examine, on the basis of studies to be carried out, the issue of liability and redress, including restoration and compensation, for damage to biological diversity, except where such liability is a purely internal matter.

Article 15.　Access to Genetic Resources

1.　Recognizing the sovereign rights of States over their natural resources, the authority to determine access to genetic resources rests with the national governments and is subject to national legislation.

2.　Each Contracting Party shall endeavour to create conditions to facilitate access to genetic resources for environmentally sound uses by other Contracting Parties and not to impose restrictions that run counter to the objectives of this Convention.

3.　For the purpose of this Convention, the genetic resources being provided by a Contracting Party, as referred to in this Article and Articles 16 and 19, are only those that are provided by Contracting Parties that are countries of origin of such resources or by the Parties that have acquired the genetic resources in accordance with this Convention.

4.　Access, where granted, shall be on mutually agreed terms and subject to the provisions of this Article.

5.　Access to genetic resources shall be subject to prior informed consent of the Contracting Party providing such resources, unless otherwise determined by that Party.

6.　Each Contracting Party shall endeavour to develop and carry out scientific research based on genetic resources provided by other Contracting Parties with the full participation of, and where possible in, such Contracting Parties.

7.　Each Contracting Party shall take legislative, administrative or policy measures, as appropriate, and in accordance with Articles 16 and 19 and, where necessary, through the financial mechanism established by Articles 20 and 21 with the aim of sharing in a fair and equitable way the results of research and development and the benefits arising from the commercial and other utilization of genetic resources with the Contracting Party providing such resources.　Such sharing shall be upon mutually agreed terms.

Article 16.　Access to and Transfer of Technology

1.　Each Contracting Party, recognizing that technology includes biotechnology, and that both access to and transfer of technology among Contracting Parties are essential elements for the attainment of the objectives of this Convention, undertakes subject to the provisions of this Article to provide and/or facilitate access for and transfer to other Contracting Parties of technologies that are relevant to the conservation and sustainable use of biological diversity or make use of genetic resources and do not cause significant damage to the environment.

2.　Access to and transfer of technology referred to in paragraph 1 above to developing countries shall be provided and/or facilitated under fair and most favourable terms, including on concessional and preferential terms where mutually agreed, and, where necessary, in accordance with the financial mechanism established by Articles 20 and 21. In the case of technology subject to patents and other intellectual property rights, such access and transfer shall be provided on terms which recognize and are consistent with the adequate and effective protection of intellectual property rights. The application of this paragraph shall be consistent with paragraphs 3, 4 and 5 below.

3. Each Contracting Party shall take legislative, administrative or policy measures, as appropriate, with the aim that Contracting Parties, in particular those that are developing countries, which provide genetic resources are provided access to and transfer of technology which makes use of those resources, on mutually agreed terms, including technology protected by patents and other intellectual property rights, where necessary, through the provisions of Articles 20 and 21 and in accordance with international law and consistent with paragraphs 4 and 5 below.

4. Each Contracting Party shall take legislative, administrative or policy measures, as appropriate, with the aim that the private sector facilitates access to, joint development and transfer of technology referred to in paragraph 1 above for the benefit of both governmental institutions and the private sector of developing countries and in this regard shall abide by the obligations included in paragraphs 1, 2 and 3 above.

5. The Contracting Parties, recognizing that patents and other intellectual property rights may have an influence on the implementation of this Convention, shall cooperate in this regard subject to national legislation and international law in order to ensure that such rights are supportive of and do not run counter to its objectives.

Article 17. Exchange of Information

1. The Contracting Parties shall facilitate the exchange of information, from all publicly available sources, relevant to the conservation and sustainable use of biological diversity, taking into account the special needs of developing countries.

2. Such exchange of information shall include exchange of results of technical, scientific and socio-economic research, as well as information on training and surveying programmes, specialized knowledge, indigenous and traditional knowledge as such and in combination with the technologies referred to in Article 16, paragraph 1. It shall also, where feasible, include repatriation of information.

Article 18. Technical and Scientific Cooperation

1. The Contracting Parties shall promote international technical and scientific cooperation in the field of conservation and sustainable use of biological diversity, where necessary, through the appropriate international and national institutions.

2.　Each Contracting Party shall promote technical and scientific cooperation with other Contracting Parties, in particular developing countries, in implementing this Convention, inter alia, through the development and implementation of national policies.　In promoting such cooperation, special attention should be given to the development and strengthening of national capabilities, by means of human resources development and institution building.

3.　The Conference of the Parties, at its first meeting, shall determine how to establish a clearing-house mechanism to promote and facilitate technical and scientific cooperation.

4.　The Contracting Parties shall, in accordance with national legislation and policies, encourage and develop methods of cooperation for the development and use of technologies, including indigenous and traditional technologies, in pursuance of the objectives of this Convention.　For this purpose, the Contracting Parties shall also promote cooperation in the training of personnel and exchange of experts.

5.　The Contracting Parties shall, subject to mutual agreement, promote the establishment of joint research programmes and joint ventures for the development of technologies relevant to the objectives of this Convention.

Article 19.　Handling of Biotechnology and Distribution of its Benefits

1.　Each Contracting Party shall take legislative, administrative or policy measures, as appropriate, to provide for the effective participation in biotechnological research activities by those Contracting Parties, especially developing countries, which provide the genetic resources for such research, and where feasible in such Contracting Parties.

2.　Each Contracting Party shall take all practicable measures to promote and advance priority access on a fair and equitable basis by Contracting Parties, especially developing countries, to the results and benefits arising from biotechnologies based upon genetic resources provided by those Contracting Parties.　Such access shall be on mutually agreed terms.

3.　The Parties shall consider the need for and modalities of a protocol setting out appropriate procedures, including, in particular, advance informed agreement, in the field of the safe transfer, handling and use of any living modified organism resulting from biotechnology that may have adverse effect on the conservation and sustainable use of biological diversity.

4.　Each Contracting Party shall, directly or by requiring any natural or legal person under its jurisdiction providing the organisms referred to in paragraph 3 above, provide any available information about the use and safety regulations required by that Contracting Party in handling such organisms, as well as any available information on the potential adverse impact of the specific organisms concerned to the Contracting Party into which those organisms are to be introduced.

Article 20.　Financial Resources

1.　Each Contracting Party undertakes to provide, in accordance with its capabilities, financial support and incentives in respect of those national activities which are intended to achieve the objectives of this Convention, in accordance with its national plans, priorities and programmes.

2.　The developed country Parties shall provide new and additional financial resources to enable developing country Parties to meet the agreed full incremental costs to them of implementing measures which fulfil the obligations of this Convention and to benefit from its provisions and which costs are agreed between a developing country Party and the institutional structure referred to in Article 21, in accordance with policy, strategy, programme priorities and eligibility criteria and an indicative list of incremental costs established by the Conference of the Parties.　Other Parties, including countries undergoing the process of transition to a market economy, may voluntarily assume the obligations of the developed country Parties.　For the purpose of this Article, the Conference of the Parties, shall at its first meeting establish a list of developed country Parties and other Parties which voluntarily assume the obligations of the developed country Parties.　The Conference of the Parties shall periodically review and if necessary amend the list. Contributions from other countries and sources on a voluntary basis would also be encouraged.　The implementation of these commitments shall take into account the need for adequacy, predictability and timely flow of funds and the importance of burden-sharing among the contributing Parties included in the list.

3.　The developed country Parties may also provide, and developing country Parties avail themselves of, financial resources related to the implementation of this Convention through bilateral, regional and other multilateral channels.

4.　The extent to which developing country Parties will effectively implement their commitments under this Convention will depend on the effective implementation by developed country Parties of their commitments under this Convention related to financial resources and transfer of technology and will take fully into account the fact that economic and social development and eradication of poverty are the first and overriding priorities of the developing country Parties.

5.　The Parties shall take full account of the specific needs and special situation of least developed countries in their actions with regard to funding and transfer of technology.

6.　The Contracting Parties shall also take into consideration the special conditions resulting from the dependence on, distribution and location of, biological diversity within developing country Parties, in particular small island States.

7.　Consideration shall also be given to the special situation of developing countries, including those that are most environmentally vulnerable, such as those with arid and semi-arid zones, coastal and mountainous areas.

Article 21.　Financial Mechanism

1.　There shall be a mechanism for the provision of financial resources to developing country Parties for purposes of this Convention on a grant or concessional basis the essential elements of which are described in this Article.　The mechanism shall function under the authority and guidance of, and be accountable to, the Conference of the Parties for purposes of this Convention.　The operations of the mechanism shall be carried out by such institutional structure as may be decided upon by the Conference of the Parties at its first meeting.　For purposes of this Convention, the Conference of the Parties shall determine the policy, strategy, programme priorities and eligibility criteria relating to the access to and utilization of such resources. The contributions shall be such as to take into account the need for predictability, adequacy and timely flow of funds referred to in Article 20 in accordance with the amount of resources needed to be decided periodically by the Conference of the Parties and the importance of burden-sharing among the contributing Parties included in the list referred to in Article 20, paragraph 2.　Voluntary contributions may also be made by the developed country Parties and by other countries and sources.　The mechanism shall operate within a democratic and transparent system of governance.

2.　Pursuant to the objectives of this Convention, the Conference of the Parties shall at its first meeting determine the policy, strategy and programme priorities, as well as detailed criteria and guidelines for eligibility for access to and utilization of the financial resources including monitoring and evaluation on a regular basis of such utilization.　The Conference of the Parties shall decide on the arrangements to give effect to paragraph 1 above after consultation with the institutional structure entrusted with the operation of the financial mechanism.

3.　The Conference of the Parties shall review the effectiveness of the mechanism established under this Article, including the criteria and guidelines referred to in paragraph 2 above, not less than two years after the entry into force of this Convention and thereafter on a regular basis.　Based on such review, it shall take appropriate action to improve the effectiveness of the mechanism if necessary.

4.　The Contracting Parties shall consider strengthening existing financial institutions to provide financial resources for the conservation and sustainable use of biological diversity.

Article 22.　Relationship with Other International Conventions

1.　The provisions of this Convention shall not affect the rights and obligations of any Contracting Party deriving from any existing international agreement, except where the exercise of those rights and obligations would cause a serious damage or threat to biological diversity.

2. Contracting Parties shall implement this Convention with respect to the marine environment consistently with the rights and obligations of States under the law of the sea.

Article 23. Conference of the Parties

1. A Conference of the Parties is hereby established. The first meeting of the Conference of the Parties shall be convened by the Executive Director of the United Nations Environment Programme not later than one year after the entry into force of this Convention. Thereafter, ordinary meetings of the Conference of the Parties shall be held at regular intervals to be determined by the Conference at its first meeting.

2. Extraordinary meetings of the Conference of the Parties shall be held at such other times as may be deemed necessary by the Conference, or at the written request of any Party, provided that, within six months of the request being communicated to them by the Secretariat, it is supported by at least one third of the Parties.

3. The Conference of the Parties shall by consensus agree upon and adopt rules of procedure for itself and for any subsidiary body it may establish, as well as financial rules governing the funding of the Secretariat. At each ordinary meeting, it shall adopt a budget for the financial period until the next ordinary meeting.

4. The Conference of the Parties shall keep under review the implementation of this Convention, and, for this purpose, shall:

(a) Establish the form and the intervals for transmitting the information to be submitted in accordance with Article 26 and consider such information as well as reports submitted by any subsidiary body;

(b) Review scientific, technical and technological advice on biological diversity provided in accordance with Article 25;

(c) Consider and adopt, as required, protocols in accordance with Article 28;

(d) Consider and adopt, as required, in accordance with Articles 29 and 30, amendments to this Convention and its annexes;

(e) Consider amendments to any protocol, as well as to any annexes thereto, and, if so decided, recommend their adoption to the Parties to the protocol concerned;

(f) Consider and adopt, as required, in accordance with Article 30, additional annexes to this Convention;

(g) Establish such subsidiary bodies, particularly to provide scientific and technical advice, as are deemed necessary for the implementation of this Convention;

(h) Contact, through the Secretariat, the executive bodies of conventions dealing with matters covered by this Convention with a view to establishing appropriate forms of cooperation with them; and

(i) Consider and undertake any additional action that may be required for the achievement of the purposes of this Convention in the light of experience gained in its operation.

5. The United Nations, its specialized agencies and the International Atomic Energy Agency, as well as any State not Party to this Convention, may be represented as observers at meetings of the Conference of the Parties. Any other body or agency, whether governmental or nongovernmental, qualified in fields relating to conservation and sustainable use of biological diversity, which has informed the Secretariat of its wish to be represented as an observer at a meeting of the Conference of the Parties, may be admitted unless at least one third of the Parties present object. The admission and participation of observers shall be subject to the rules of procedure adopted by the Conference of the Parties.

Article 24. Secretariat

1. A secretariat is hereby established. Its functions shall be:

(a) To arrange for and service meetings of the Conference of the Parties provided for in Article 23;

(b) To perform the functions assigned to it by any protocol;

(c) To prepare reports on the execution of its functions under this Convention and present them to the Conference of the Parties;

(d) To coordinate with other relevant international bodies and, in particular to enter into such administrative and contractual arrangements as may be required for the effective discharge of its functions; and

(e) To perform such other functions as may be determined by the Conference of the Parties.

2. At its first ordinary meeting, the Conference of the Parties shall designate the secretariat from amongst those existing competent international organizations which have signified their willingness to carry out the secretariat functions under this Convention.

Article 25. Subsidiary Body on Scientific, Technical and Technological Advice

1. A subsidiary body for the provision of scientific, technical and technological advice is hereby established to provide the Conference of the Parties and, as appropriate, its other subsidiary bodies with timely advice relating to the implementation of this Convention. This body shall be open to participation by all Parties and shall be multidisciplinary. It shall comprise government representatives competent in the relevant field of expertise. It shall report regularly to the Conference of the Parties on all aspects of its work.

2. Under the authority of and in accordance with guidelines laid down by the Conference of the Parties, and upon its request, this body shall:

(a) Provide scientific and technical assessments of the status of biological diversity;

(b) Prepare scientific and technical assessments of the effects of types of measures taken in accordance with the provisions of this Convention;

(c) Identify innovative, efficient and state-of-the-art technologies and know-how relating to the conservation and sustainable use of biological diversity and advise on the ways and means of promoting development and/or transferring such technologies;

(d) Provide advice on scientific programmes and international cooperation in research and development related to conservation and sustainable use of biological diversity; and

(e) Respond to scientific, technical, technological and methodological questions that the Conference of the Parties and its subsidiary bodies may put to the body.

3. The functions, terms of reference, organization and operation of this body may be further elaborated by the Conference of the Parties.

Article 26.　Reports

Each Contracting Party shall, at intervals to be determined by the Conference of the Parties, present to the Conference of the Parties, reports on measures which it has taken for the implementation of the provisions of this Convention and their effectiveness in meeting the objectives of this Convention.

Article 27.　Settlement of Disputes

1. In the event of a dispute between Contracting Parties concerning the interpretation or application of this Convention, the parties concerned shall seek solution by negotiation.

2. If the parties concerned cannot reach agreement by negotiation, they may jointly seek the good offices of, or request mediation by, a third party.

3. When ratifying, accepting, approving or acceding to this Convention, or at any time thereafter, a State or regional economic integration organization may declare in writing to the Depositary that for a dispute not resolved in accordance with paragraph 1 or paragraph 2 above, it accepts one or both of the following means of dispute settlement as compulsory:

(a) Arbitration in accordance with the procedure laid down in Part 1 of Annex II;

(b) Submission of the dispute to the International Court of Justice.

4. If the parties to the dispute have not, in accordance with paragraph 3 above, accepted the same or any procedure, the dispute shall be submitted to conciliation in accordance with Part 2 of Annex II unless the parties otherwise agree.

5. The provisions of this Article shall apply with respect to any protocol except as otherwise provided in the protocol concerned.

Article 28. Adoption of Protocols

1. The Contracting Parties shall cooperate in the formulation and adoption of protocols to this Convention.

2. Protocols shall be adopted at a meeting of the Conference of the Parties.

3. The text of any proposed protocol shall be communicated to the Contracting Parties by the Secretariat at least six months before such a meeting.

Article 29. Amendment of the Convention or Protocols

1. Amendments to this Convention may be proposed by any Contracting Party. Amendments to any protocol may be proposed by any Party to that protocol.

2. Amendments to this Convention shall be adopted at a meeting of the Conference of the Parties. Amendments to any protocol shall be adopted at a meeting of the Parties to the Protocol in question. The text of any proposed amendment to this Convention or to any protocol, except as may otherwise be provided in such protocol, shall be communicated to the Parties to the instrument in question by the Secretariat at least six months before the meeting at which it is proposed for adoption. The Secretariat shall also communicate proposed amendments to the signatories to this Convention for information.

3. The Parties shall make every effort to reach agreement on any proposed amendment to this Convention or to any protocol by consensus. If all efforts at consensus have been exhausted, and no agreement reached, the amendment shall as a last resort be adopted by a two-thirds majority vote of the Parties to the instrument in question present and voting at the meeting, and shall be submitted by the Depositary to all Parties for ratification, acceptance or approval.

4. Ratification, acceptance or approval of amendments shall be notified to the Depositary in writing. Amendments adopted in accordance with paragraph 3 above shall enter into force among Parties having accepted them on the ninetieth day after the deposit of instruments of ratification, acceptance or approval by at least two thirds of the Contracting Parties to this Convention or of the Parties to the protocol concerned, except as may otherwise be provided in such protocol. Thereafter the amendments shall enter into force for any other Party on the ninetieth day after that Party deposits its instrument of ratification, acceptance or approval of the amendments.

5. For the purposes of this Article, "Parties present and voting" means Parties present and casting an affirmative or negative vote.

Article 30. Adoption and Amendment of Annexes

1. The annexes to this Convention or to any protocol shall form an integral part of the Convention or of such protocol, as the case may be, and, unless expressly provided otherwise, a reference to this Convention or its protocols constitutes at the same time a reference to any annexes thereto. Such annexes shall be restricted to procedural, scientific, technical and administrative matters.

2. Except as may be otherwise provided in any protocol with respect to its annexes, the following procedure shall apply to the proposal, adoption and entry into force of additional annexes to this Convention or of annexes to any protocol:

(a) Annexes to this Convention or to any protocol shall be proposed and adopted according to the procedure laid down in Article 29;

(b) Any Party that is unable to approve an additional annex to this Convention or an annex to any protocol to which it is Party shall so notify the Depositary, in writing, within one year from the date of the communication of the adoption by the Depositary. The Depositary shall without delay notify all Parties of any such notification received. A Party may at any time withdraw a previous declaration of objection and the annexes shall thereupon enter into force for that Party subject to subparagraph (c) below;

(c) On the expiry of one year from the date of the communication of the adoption by the Depositary, the annex shall enter into force for all Parties to this Convention or to any protocol concerned which have not submitted a notification in accordance with the provisions of subparagraph (b) above.

3. The proposal, adoption and entry into force of amendments to annexes to this Convention or to any protocol shall be subject to the same procedure as for the proposal, adoption and entry into force of annexes to the Convention or annexes to any protocol.

4. If an additional annex or an amendment to an annex is related to an amendment to this Convention or to any protocol, the additional annex or amendment shall not enter into force until such time as the amendment to the Convention or to the protocol concerned enters into force.

Article 31. Right to Vote

1. Except as provided for in paragraph 2 below, each Contracting Party to this Convention or to any protocol shall have one vote.

2. Regional economic integration organizations, in matters within their competence, shall exercise their right to vote with a number of votes equal to the number of their member States which are Contracting Parties to this Convention or the relevant protocol. Such organizations shall not exercise their right to vote if their member States exercise theirs, and vice versa.

Article 32.　Relationship between this Convention and Its Protocols

1.　A State or a regional economic integration organization may not become a Party to a protocol unless it is, or becomes at the same time, a Contracting Party to this Convention.

2.　Decisions under any protocol shall be taken only by the Parties to the protocol concerned.　Any Contracting Party that has not ratified, accepted or approved a protocol may participate as an observer in any meeting of the parties to that protocol.

Article 33.　Signature

This Convention shall be open for signature at Rio de Janeiro by all States and any regional economic integration organization from 5 June 1992 until 14 June 1992, and at the United Nations Headquarters in New York from 15 June 1992 to 4 June 1993.

Article 34.　Ratification, Acceptance or Approval

1.　This Convention and any protocol shall be subject to ratification, acceptance or approval by States and by regional economic integration organizations.　Instruments of ratification, acceptance or approval shall be deposited with the Depositary.

2.　Any organization referred to in paragraph 1 above which becomes a Contracting Party to this Convention or any protocol without any of its member States being a Contracting Party shall be bound by all the obligations under the Convention or the protocol, as the case may be.　In the case of such organizations, one or more of whose member States is a Contracting Party to this Convention or relevant protocol, the organization and its member States shall decide on their respective responsibilities for the performance of their obligations under the Convention or protocol, as the case may be.　In such cases, the organization and the member States shall not be entitled to exercise rights under the Convention or relevant protocol concurrently.

3.　In their instruments of ratification, acceptance or approval, the organizations referred to in paragraph 1 above shall declare the extent of their competence with respect to the matters governed by the Convention or the relevant protocol.　These organizations shall also inform the Depositary of any relevant modification in the extent of their competence.

Article 35.　Accession

1.　This Convention and any protocol shall be open for accession by States and by regional economic integration organizations from the date on which the Convention or the protocol concerned is closed for signature.　The instruments of accession shall be deposited with the Depositary.

2.　In their instruments of accession, the organizations referred to in paragraph 1 above shall declare the extent of their competence with respect to the matters governed by the Convention or the relevant protocol.　These organizations shall also inform the Depositary of any relevant modification in the extent of their competence.

3. The provisions of Article 34, paragraph 2, shall apply to regional economic integration organizations which accede to this Convention or any protocol.

Article 36. Entry Into Force

1. This Convention shall enter into force on the ninetieth day after the date of deposit of the thirtieth instrument of ratification, acceptance, approval or accession.

2. Any protocol shall enter into force on the ninetieth day after the date of deposit of the number of instruments of ratification, acceptance, approval or accession, specified in that protocol, has been deposited.

3. For each Contracting Party which ratifies, accepts or approves this Convention or accedes thereto after the deposit of the thirtieth instrument of ratification, acceptance, approval or accession, it shall enter into force on the ninetieth day after the date of deposit by such Contracting Party of its instrument of ratification, acceptance, approval or accession.

4. Any protocol, except as otherwise provided in such protocol, shall enter into force for a Contracting Party that ratifies, accepts or approves that protocol or accedes thereto after its entry into force pursuant to paragraph 2 above, on the ninetieth day after the date on which that Contracting Party deposits its instrument of ratification, acceptance, approval or accession, or on the date on which this Convention enters into force for that Contracting Party, whichever shall be the later.

5. For the purposes of paragraphs 1 and 2 above, any instrument deposited by a regional economic integration organization shall not be counted as additional to those deposited by member States of such organization.

Article 37. Reservations

No reservations may be made to this Convention.

Article 38. Withdrawals

1. At any time after two years from the date on which this Convention has entered into force for a Contracting Party, that Contracting Party may withdraw from the Convention by giving written notification to the Depositary.

2. Any such withdrawal shall take place upon expiry of one year after the date of its receipt by the Depositary, or on such later date as may be specified in the notification of the withdrawal.

3. Any Contracting Party which withdraws from this Convention shall be considered as also having withdrawn from any protocol to which it is party.

Article 39.　Financial Interim Arrangements

Provided that it has been fully restructured in accordance with the requirements of Article 21, the Global Environment Facility of the United Nations Development Programme, the United Nations Environment Programme and the International Bank for Reconstruction and Development shall be the institutional structure referred to in Article 21 on an interim basis, for the period between the entry into force of this Convention and the first meeting of the Conference of the Parties or until the Conference of the Parties decides which institutional structure will be designated in accordance with Article 21.

Article 40.　Secretariat Interim Arrangements

The secretariat to be provided by the Executive Director of the United Nations Environment Programme shall be the secretariat referred to in Article 24, paragraph 2, on an interim basis for the period between the entry into force of this Convention and the first meeting of the Conference of the Parties.

Article 41.　Depositary

The Secretary–General of the United Nations shall assume the functions of Depositary of this Convention and any protocols.

Article 42.　Authentic Texts

The original of this Convention, of which the Arabic, Chinese, English, French, Russian and Spanish texts are equally authentic, shall be deposited with the Secretary–General of the United Nations.

Annex I
IDENTIFICATION AND MONITORING

1.　Ecosystems and habitats: containing high diversity, large numbers of endemic or threatened species, or wilderness; required by migratory species; of social, economic, cultural or scientific importance; or, which are representative, unique or associated with key evolutionary or other biological processes;

2.　Species and communities which are: threatened; wild relatives of domesticated or cultivated species; of medicinal, agricultural or other economic value; or social, scientific or cultural importance; or importance for research into the conservation and sustainable use of biological diversity, such as indicator species; and

3.　Described genomes and genes of social, scientific or economic importance.

Annex II
Part 1
ARBITRATION
Article 1

The claimant party shall notify the Secretariat that the parties are referring a dispute to arbitration pursuant to Article 27. The notification shall state the subject-matter of arbitration and include, in particular, the articles of the Convention or the protocol, the interpretation or application of which are at issue. If the parties do not agree on the subject matter of the dispute before the President of the tribunal is designated, the arbitral tribunal shall determine the subject matter. The Secretariat shall forward the information thus received to all Contracting Parties to this Convention or to the protocol concerned.

Article 2

1. In disputes between two parties, the arbitral tribunal shall consist of three members. Each of the parties to the dispute shall appoint an arbitrator and the two arbitrators so appointed shall designate by common agreement the third arbitrator who shall be the President of the tribunal. The latter shall not be a national of one of the parties to the dispute, nor have his or her usual place of residence in the territory of one of these parties, nor be employed by any of them, nor have dealt with the case in any other capacity.

2. In disputes between more than two parties, parties in the same interest shall appoint one arbitrator jointly by agreement.

3. Any vacancy shall be filled in the manner prescribed for the initial appointment.

Article 3

1. If the President of the arbitral tribunal has not been designated within two months of the appointment of the second arbitrator, the Secretary–General of the United Nations shall, at the request of a party, designate the President within a further two-month period.

2. If one of the parties to the dispute does not appoint an arbitrator within two months of receipt of the request, the other party may inform the Secretary–General who shall make the designation within a further two-month period.

Article 4

The arbitral tribunal shall render its decisions in accordance with the provisions of this Convention, any protocols concerned, and international law.

Article 5

Unless the parties to the dispute otherwise agree, the arbitral tribunal shall determine its own rules of procedure.

Article 6

The arbitral tribunal may, at the request of one of the parties, recommend essential interim measures of protection.

Article 7

The parties to the dispute shall facilitate the work of the arbitral tribunal and, in particular, using all means at their disposal, shall:

(a) Provide it with all relevant documents, information and facilities; and

(b) Enable it, when necessary, to call witnesses or experts and receive their evidence.

Article 8

The parties and the arbitrators are under an obligation to protect the confidentiality of any information they receive in confidence during the proceedings of the arbitral tribunal.

Article 9

Unless the arbitral tribunal determines otherwise because of the particular circumstances of the case, the costs of the tribunal shall be borne by the parties to the dispute in equal shares. The tribunal shall keep a record of all its costs, and shall furnish a final statement thereof to the parties.

Article 10

Any Contracting Party that has an interest of a legal nature in the subject-matter of the dispute which may be affected by the decision in the case, may intervene in the proceedings with the consent of the tribunal.

Article 11

The tribunal may hear and determine counterclaims arising directly out of the subject-matter of the dispute.

Article 12

Decisions both on procedure and substance of the arbitral tribunal shall be taken by a majority vote of its members.

Article 13

If one of the parties to the dispute does not appear before the arbitral tribunal or fails to defend its case, the other party may request the tribunal to continue the proceedings and to make its award. Absence of a party or a failure of a party to defend its case shall not constitute a bar to the proceedings. Before rendering its final decision, the arbitral tribunal must satisfy itself that the claim is well founded in fact and law.

Article 14

The tribunal shall render its final decision within five months of the date on which it is fully constituted unless it finds it necessary to extend the time-limit for a period which should not exceed five more months.

Article 15

The final decision of the arbitral tribunal shall be confined to the subject-matter of the dispute and shall state the reasons on which it is based. It shall contain the names of the members who have participated and the date of the final decision. Any member of the tribunal may attach a separate or dissenting opinion to the final decision.

Article 16

The award shall be binding on the parties to the dispute. It shall be without appeal unless the parties to the dispute have agreed in advance to an appellate procedure.

Article 17

Any controversy which may arise between the parties to the dispute as regards the interpretation or manner of implementation of the final decision may be submitted by either party for decision to the arbitral tribunal which rendered it.

Part 2
CONCILIATION
Article 1

A conciliation commission shall be created upon the request of one of the parties to the dispute. The commission shall, unless the parties otherwise agree, be composed of five members, two appointed by each Party concerned and a President chosen jointly by those members.

Article 2

In disputes between more than two parties, parties in the same interest shall appoint their members of the commission jointly by agreement. Where two or more parties have separate interests or there is a disagreement as to whether they are of the same interest, they shall appoint their members separately.

Article 3

If any appointments by the parties are not made within two months of the date of the request to create a conciliation commission, the Secretary-General of the United Nations shall, if asked to do so by the party that made the request, make those appointments within a further two-month period.

Article 4

If a President of the conciliation commission has not been chosen within two months of the last of the members of the commission being appointed, the Secretary-General of the United Nations shall, if asked to do so by a party, designate a President within a further two-month period.

Article 5

The conciliation commission shall take its decisions by majority vote of its members. It shall, unless the parties to the dispute otherwise agree, determine its own procedure. It shall render a proposal for resolution of the dispute, which the parties shall consider in good faith.

Article 6

A disagreement as to whether the conciliation commission has competence shall be decided by the commission.

國家圖書館出版品預行編目資料

國際環境法專論／吳嘉生著. －－初版. －－
臺北市：五南, 2012.11
　面；　公分
ISBN 978-957-11-6913-2（平裝）
1.國際法　2.環境保護
579.948　　　　　　　　　101023030

1V33

國際環境法專論

作　　者 ― 吳嘉生（70.1）

發 行 人 ― 楊榮川

總 編 輯 ― 王翠華

主　　編 ― 劉靜芬

責任編輯 ― 游雅淳

封面設計 ― 童安安

出 版 者 ― 五南圖書出版股份有限公司

地　　址：106台北市大安區和平東路二段339號4樓

電　　話：(02)2705-5066　　傳　　真：(02)2706-6100

網　　址：http://www.wunan.com.tw

電子郵件：wunan@wunan.com.tw

劃撥帳號：01068953

戶　　名：五南圖書出版股份有限公司

台中市駐區辦公室/台中市中區中山路6號

電　　話：(04)2223-0891　　傳　　真：(04)2223-3549

高雄市駐區辦公室/高雄市新興區中山一路290號

電　　話：(07)2358-702　　傳　　真：(07)2350-236

法律顧問　元貞聯合法律事務所　張澤平律師

出版日期　2012年11月初版一刷

定　　價　新臺幣500元